Richard Pococke, Daniel William Kemp

Tours in Scotland 1747, 1750, 1760

Richard Pococke, Daniel William Kemp

Tours in Scotland 1747, 1750, 1760

ISBN/EAN: 9783337323899

Printed in Europe, USA, Canada, Australia, Japan

Cover: Foto ©Andreas Hilbeck / pixelio.de

More available books at **www.hansebooks.com**

Scottish History Society.

THE EXECUTIVE.

President.
THE EARL OF ROSEBERY, LL.D.

Chairman of Council.
DAVID MASSON, LL.D., Professor of English Literature, Edinburgh University.

Council.
GEORGE BURNETT, LL.D., Lyon-King-of-Arms.
J. T. CLARK, Keeper of the Advocates' Library.
THOMAS DICKSON, LL.D., Curator of the Historical Department, Register House.
Right Rev. JOHN DOWDEN, D.D., Bishop of Edinburgh.
J. KIRKPATRICK, LL.B., Professor of History, Edinburgh University.
ÆNEAS J. G. MACKAY, LL.D., Sheriff of Fife.
Sir ARTHUR MITCHELL, K.C.B., M.D., LL.D.
G. W. T. OMOND, Advocate.
JOHN RUSSELL, Esq.
W. F. SKENE, D.C.L., LL.D., Historiographer-Royal for Scotland.
Rev. MALCOLM C. TAYLOR, D.D., Professor of Divinity and Church History, Edinburgh University.
J. MAITLAND THOMSON, Advocate.

Corresponding Members of the Council.
OSMUND AIRY, Esq., Birmingham; Very Rev. J. CUNNINGHAM, D.D., Principal of St. Mary's College, St. Andrews; Professor GEORGE GRUB, LL.D., Aberdeen; Rev. A. W. C. HALLEN, Alloa; Rev. W. D. MACRAY, Oxford; DAVID M. MAIN, Esq., Doune; Professor A. F. MITCHELL, D.D., St. Andrews; Professor W. ROBERTSON SMITH, Cambridge; Rev. Dr. SPROTT, North Berwick; Professor J. VEITCH, LL.D., Glasgow.

Hon. Treasurer.
J. J. REID, B.A., Advocate, Queen's Remembrancer.

Hon. Secretary.
T. G. LAW, Librarian, Signet Library.

RULES.

1. The object of the Society is the discovery and printing, under selected editorship, of unpublished documents illustrative of the civil, religious, and social history of Scotland.

2. The number of Members of the Society shall be limited to 400.

3. The affairs of the Society shall be managed by a Council consisting of a Chairman, Treasurer, Secretary, and twelve elected Members, five to make a quorum. Three of the twelve elected members shall retire annually by ballot, but they shall be eligible for re-election.

4. The Annual Subscription to the Society shall be One Guinea. The publications of the Society shall not be delivered to any Member whose Subscription is in arrear, and no Member shall be permitted to receive more than one copy of the Society's publications.

5. The Society shall undertake the issue of its own publications, i.e. without the intervention of a publisher or any other paid agent.

6. The Society will issue yearly two octavo volumes of about 320 pages each.

7. An Annual General Meeting of the Society shall be held on the last Tuesday in October.

8. Two stated Meetings of the Council shall be held each year, one on the last Tuesday of May, the other on the Tuesday preceding the day upon which the Annual General Meeting shall be held. The Secretary, on the request of three Members of the Council, shall call a special meeting of the Council.

9. Editors shall receive 20 copies of each volume they edit for the Society.

10. The Annual Balance-Sheet, Rules, and List of Members shall be printed.

11. No alteration shall be made in these Rules except at a General Meeting of the Society. A fortnight's notice of any alteration to be proposed shall be given to the Members of the Council.

PUBLICATIONS.

Works already Issued, 1887.

1. BISHOP POCOCKE'S TOURS IN SCOTLAND, 1747-1760. Edited by D. W. KEMP.

2. DIARY OF CUNNINGHAM OF CRAIGENDS, 1673-1680. Edited by the Rev. JAMES DODDS, D.D.

Works in Preparation.

PANURGI PHILO-CABALLI SCOTI GRAMEIDOS LIBRI SEX. THE GRAMIAD: An heroic poem descriptive of the Campaign of Viscount Dundee in 1689, by JAMES PHILIP of Almericclose. Edited with Notes by the Rev. CANON MURDOCH.

THE REGISTER OF THE KIRK SESSION OF ST. ANDREWS. Part I. 1559-1582. Edited by D. HAY FLEMING.

DIARY OF THE REV. JOHN MILL, Minister of Dunrossness, in Shetland, 1742-1805. Edited by GILBERT GOUDIE, F.S.A. Scot.

A NARRATIVE OF MR. JAMES NIMMO, A COVENANTER, 1654-1708. Edited by W. G. SCOTT MONCRIEFF, Advocate.

PUBLICATIONS

OF THE

SCOTTISH HISTORY SOCIETY

VOLUME I.

POCOCKE'S TOURS

OCTOBER 1887

FROM A PHOTOGRAPH OF A PAINTING

THE RIGHT REV. RICHARD POCOCKE, D.D.
LORD BISHOP OF MEATH

TOURS IN SCOTLAND

1747, 1750, 1760

BY

RICHARD POCOCKE

BISHOP OF MEATH

FROM THE ORIGINAL MS. AND DRAWINGS IN
THE BRITISH MUSEUM

Edited with a Biographical Sketch of the Author by
DANIEL WILLIAM KEMP

EDINBURGH
Printed at the University Press by T. and A. Constable,
for the Scottish History Society
1887

PREFATORY NOTE.

When the Scottish History Society was formed last year I was preparing for the press an inedited account of Bishop Pococke's tour in Sutherland, from a manuscript which I found in the Library of the British Museum.

The Council of the Society, recognising in Dr. Pococke's journal of his travels in Scotland an interesting contribution to our knowledge of the country during the eighteenth century, agreed to publish all the Scottish portion of the MS. under the auspices of the Society, and invited me to act as editor. I felt some misgivings in undertaking a work covering so wide a field of Scottish topography, to which I could only devote leisure hours at the close of a busy day. But my labours have been greatly facilitated by the assistance of a number of gentlemen who have kindly verified for me local questions, and supplied notes. To these I tender my best thanks. Their number must be my apology for not recording individually their many and valuable services.

The text of the MS., in its orthography and diction, has been carefully adhered to; and the drawings, notwithstanding their frequent disregard of perspective and proportion, have been faithfully, if roughly, reproduced.

D. WILLIAM KEMP.

Trinity,
Edinburgh, *October* 1887.

CONTENTS.

PREFATORY NOTE, ... v-vi

LIST OF ILLUSTRATIONS. . . xxvii-xxix

BIOGRAPHICAL SKETCH—

Richard Pococke born in Southampton, 1704—His father's death, 1710—He removes to the parsonage of his grandfather, the Rev. Isaac Milles, by whom he is educated, and where he resides until Mr. Milles's death in 1720—Enters Corpus Christi College in 1722—Ordained Precentor of Lismore 1725—Receives Degrees of M.A. and LL.B. in 1731, and of LL.D. 1733—Travels on Continent with Dean Milles from 1733 to 1736—Travels in Egypt and the East, 1737 to 1742—Publishes first volume, *A Description of the East : Observations on Egypt*, 1743—Visits Midland Counties of England—Made Precentor of Waterford, 1744—Publishes second volume, *Observations on Palestine or the Holy Land, Syria, Mesopotamia, Cyprus, and Candia*, 1745—Appointed Domestic Chaplain to Lord-Lieutenant of Ireland—Opinions of Gibbon, Pinkerton, Dibdin, Jablonski, Stevenson, Mant on his writings—Prices of his volumes at auction sales—Reprints and references published in German, French, and English—Richard Cumberland's opinion of him disproved—Receives patent as Archdeacon of Dublin, 1745—Letters to Dr. Stukeley —Letters from Da Costa—First visit to Scotland, 1747—Second visit, 1750—Publishes *Inscriptionum Antiquarum Graec.*, 1752—Letter to Dr. Ducarel— Preferred to the Bishopric of Ossory—Promotes

CONTENTS

PAGES

restoration of St. Canice's Cathedral, Kilkenny—His inscription commemorative of the restoration—Replaces stained glass in Cathedral window—Presents a rich communion-table cover, and a painting of a 'Glory'—Replaces old monuments, and collects inscriptions—Communicates *An Account of some Antiquities found in Ireland* to the London Society of Antiquaries, 1757—Visits Scotland for the third time, journeying from Portpatrick to the Orkneys—Receives the Freedom of Aberdeen, Glasgow, Perth, Lanark, Forres, Nairn, and Dornoch—Letter to the Duke of Athole—Offers Fifty Guineas for Queen Anne's bed, in Dunfermline—Preaches on behalf of the Magdalen House Charity, London, 1761—Preaches on behalf of Protestant Schools' Society, Dublin, 1762—Kilkenny floods, 1760—Inquiries as to second sight—Retires to his Chaplain's parsonage for literary labours—Encourages the Rev. M. Archdall in the preparation of his *Monasticon*—Founds a weaving-school, subsequently known as 'The Pococke College'—His portraits—Travels in England, 1764—Preferred to the Bishopric of Meath, 1765—Dies same year—Interred in Bishop Montgomery's tomb, Ardbraccan—Illiterate inscription on tomb—Letter from Bishop of Carlisle to Dr. Ducarel—Elaborate monumental inscription in St. Canice's—Monument in Chamounix, Switzerland—His first will—Codicil, or later will—His MSS. bequeathed to the British Museum—Books, coins, fossils, etc., sold by auction —Letter from Mr. Walker to Mr. Gough—Evidences that Thomas Pennant, the traveller, was familiar with Dr. Pococke's writings relating to Scotland,   xxxi-lxix

LETTER I.

Richmond—Preaches for Mr. Blackbourne—Mr. York's improvements — Mr. Robinson at Holy Island—Dines at Berwick—A sliving Scot—Laird of Ayton

CONTENTS.

—Old Cambus—Dunbar—Dines at Beltonford—
Prestonpans—Edinburgh—Dr. Grant, Episcopal
Minister—Preaches—Inchkeith and Inchcolm—
Musselburgh and Dalkeith—Advocates' Library—
Holyrood and Castle—Roslin Chapel—Hawthornden
—Baron Clerk—Lord Provost Drummond—College
Library—Visits Lord and Lady Hopetoun—Description of breakfast—Stirling Castle—Glasgow Cathedral—Receives Freedom of Glasgow—Dines with
Professors—Kilmarnock—Sells his horse—Castle
Kennedy—Lord Stair's improvements—Portpatrick
—Sails to Donaghadee—Reaches Dublin.   1-5

LETTER II.

Birrens—Roman inscription—Camp of Burnswork—Ecclefechan—Hoddam Castle—Dumfries—St. Michael's
Church—Bridge over Nith—Tobacco trade—Lincluden Abbey—Holywood Abbey—New Abbey—
Markland—Drumlanrig Castle—Tibber's Castle—
Roman road.   6-10

LETTER III.

Portpatrick—Shipping horses—Packet boat—Herring-fishing, deal boats—Castle Kennedy—Glenluce
Abbey—Sir Thomas Hay—Sir William Maxwell—
Whithorn Priory—Leucopibia—Candida Casa—The
Priory Font—St. Peter's Cross—Isle of Whithorn—
Wigtown Church—Galloway cattle, .   11-19

LETTER IV.

Newton-Stewart—Garlais Castle—The Cairnsmuirs—
Cardonness Castle—Kirkcudbright—Dundrennan
Abbey—Munches—Mr. John Maxwell—Wild cats—
Kirkgunzeon—New Abbey—Dumfries—Caerlaverock
Castle—Comlongon, .   19-31

CONTENTS.

LETTER V.

Ruthwell Church—Ruthwell Cross—Walker's Monument —Hoddam Castle—Fragment of sculpture; winged figure—Roman camp—Repentance Tower, and legend —Annan—Robert Bruce's Castle—Inscription (Robert de Brvs, etc.)—Clochmaben Stone, . . . 32-35

LETTER VI.

Gretna Green Church—River Esk—Guide necessary— Dangerous crossing—Penrith—Carts with wooden wheels and axles, 36

LETTER VII.

Ecclefechan — Middlebie — Castlemilk — Double boat— Lockerbie—Lochmaben—Roman works—Tower of Lochwood, . . 37-38

LETTER VIII.

Moffat— Old Spa—Bishop Whiteford's daughter—Hartfell Spa—John Williamson—Copper mines—Marquis of Annandale's tub—Source of Annan, Clyde, and Tweed — Leadhills — Miners' houses — Lead and Copper — Smelting hearths—Susannah Mine—Piglead to Leith for shipment to Holland—Mr. Archibald Stirling of Garden—Larch trees, . 39-42

LETTER IX.

Glengonar river gold—Carmichael—Lanark—St. Kentigern's Church—Monastery—Carstairs—Roman work —Antiquities found—Falls of Clyde—Bonnington— Made Burgess of Lanark—Cadzow Castle—Hamilton Palace—Hamilton Church—Bothwell Church, 43-48

CONTENTS.

LETTER X.

Glasgow—Streets—Merchants' houses—Markets—The Green—Cathedral—Episcopal Chapel (St. Andrew's)—Preaches and confirms—Approves of strict Sabbath observance—Exports, imports, and manufactures—University—Roman inscription,   49-53

LETTER XI.

Govan—King's Inch—Paisley—Monastery—Tradition of King Robert II.'s birth—Abbey Church—Monuments—The last Abbot—Lord Claud Hamilton—Beith—Kilwinning Abbey—Irvine—Extensive trade—Monastery—Seagate Castle—Earl of Eglinton—Kilmarnock—Thatched houses—Carpet manufacture—Fast day—Water of Ayr stones—Dean Castle—Cathcart,   53-60

LETTER XII.

Old Kilpatrick—New Kilpatrick—Roman wall—St. Patrick—Dunglass Castle—Dumbarton—Early settlement—The Castle—Church (St. Patrick's)—Levenside—Bonhill—Loch Lomond—The islands—Castle of Luss—Rossdhu—Luss Church—Tarbet—Inscription on rock—Inveruglass—Tumulus—Eilean Vhou—Laird of Macfarlane—Inversnaid—Loch Slowie—Tyndrum—Lead mines,   60-64

LETTER XIII.

New Tarbet—Loch Long—Inscription on seat—Glencroe—Cairndow—Inveraray—The Castle—The Cross—Mr. Cumin's curious clock—St. Catherine's Stone,   64-67

LETTER XIV.

Inverary Park—Roe deer—Loch Awe—Kilchurn Castle—Ardchonal Castle—The Ferry—Ben Cruachan—

Loch Etive—Ardchattan—Mr. Campbell's house—
Old Church— Beregonium—Dun Macsniachan—Loch-
nell House—Sir Duncan Campbell—Kerrera—Oban
—Scarba—Coryvreckan—Colonsay Abbey—Easdale
slate quarries—Hermit's garden, Lochnell—*Bos
Primigenius* bones from Lismore—Service tree,   67-72

LETTER XV.

Horses sent to Fort William—Dunstaffnage—Reputed
antiquity—Antique ivory chessman—Old Church—
Echo from rocks—Dunolly Castle—Oban custom-
house—Mull—Small horses; never shod, value £4—
Magnetic rock—Druid Temple, Rossal—Rev. Neil
Macleod—Bunessan—Ferry Port—Basaltic rocks,   72-77

LETTER XVI.

Iona—Mr. Campbell, Bailiff of Tiree—St. Columba—Bene-
dictine Monastery—Jurisdiction—The Cathedral—
The Altar—Monuments: Macfingone's; Macdonald's;
Maclennan's; Maclean's—The Maelpatrick Stone—
Reilig Ourain—Clach an Diesart—Nunnery—Prior-
ess's tomb — Burial-place — Angels' Hill — Horse
races: ancient customs—Port na Churaich—Pebbles
—Population of Iona—Population of Tyree—Two-
handed sword and helmet—Manners and hospitality
of the Islanders—Customs at burials—Second-sight—
Rev. John Macpherson's Latin poems—Population of
Mull—Charnel-root for whisky-drinkers,   .   .   78-89

LETTER XVII.

Lismore—Whales—St. Moluag—The Church—Tirefoor
Broch Population of the Island—Airds—Abundance of Spinage—Leg and thigh bones of the *Bos
Primigenius*—Norwegian oval bowl-shaped brooch
from Isle of Lingay—Western Islands—St. Kilda,   .   90-94

CONTENTS.

LETTER XVIII.

White Cairn, Port na Crois—Picts' houses—Tigh na Stalcaire, the hunting lodge of James IV.—Letershuna, formerly belonging to the Stewarts of Appin—High stone at Duror—Factor shot for evicting tenants—Hill resembling Mount Tabor—Massacre of Glencoe—Glenfinnan, where the Pretender first set up his Standard, 1745—Fort-William fortress—Lochaber—Story of Macbeth, 95-98

LETTER XIX.

Inverlochy Castle—Ben Nevis—Achnacarry, site of Lochiel's house—Invergarry Castle—Stone circle—Copper mines—Fort Augustus—Loch Ness 'Highland Galley'—Sail down Loch Ness with Governor Trapaud—Glen Moriston—Linen-weaving school—Fall of Foyers—General's hut—Castle Urquhart—Driven to Inverness—Druid Temple—Stone circles, 99-102

LETTER XX.

Inverness—Salted Salmon Trade—Dominican Monastery—The Castle—Cromwell's Fort—Fort George, designed by Colonel Skinner—Stone circles—Culloden House—Battle of Culloden—Position of Highland army—The graves of the soldiers, . 103-108

LETTER XXI.

Beauly—Dingwall—The Church—The Earl of Cromarty's Obelisk—Strathpeffer—Castle Leod—Foulis—Culcairn—Coal in the mountains—Burial urn and spearhead—Capercaillie, . . 108-110

CONTENTS.

LETTER XXII.

Pict's House—Stone circle—Shell-beds—Dunalishaig-Strathkyle—Rosehall House—Cassley Falls—Dun Achness—Shells found on summit of Scurr na Lapaich—MacLeod of Assynt's betrayal of Montrose.   111-115

LETTER XXIII.

Rosehall—Durcha Broch—Loch Shin—Sea-gulls' nests—Highland cabin—Highland manners and hospitality—Making Fran from Whey—Severe winter, 1738—Numerous swans—Black-throated Diver—Gentlewoman followed by maid—Brochs common—Minister of Lairg, Mr. Mackay—Entertained with cake and wine—Earl of Sutherland's forest, Clibree—Drinking health in Whey—Gaelic names for red deer—Minced Collop of Venison—No rats,   115-120

LETTER XXIV.

Loch Meadie—Mudale to Strathmore—A thousand red deer in Lord Reay's forest—Proposed roads—Dun-Dornadilla, outside and inside views—Loch Erriboll—Farout Head,   120-124

LETTER XXV.

Durness—Seath fishing—Hart killed by an eagle—Islands Rona and Soulisgeir—Seals and Solan Geese—Adders killed and eaten by goats—The Cave of Smoo—Hardiness of the inhabitants—Hospitality and politeness—Pension to Lord Reay,   124-128

LETTER XXVI.

Inverhope—Large salmon weir—The Moine—Bay of Tongue—Story of the capture of the French Sloop 'Hazard'—House of Tongue, the Master of

CONTENTS.

Reay's residence—Dun Varrich—Ben Loaghal—
Entertained by Captain Mackay—Soft sands of
Farr Bay—Farr Church and Ancient Cross—Tin
ore—Dines with the Rev. George Munro of Farr—
Captain Mackay of Strathy—Lord Sutherland's
Highlanders — Bighouse — Ancient sepulchre —
Pict's house, . 129-133

LETTER XXVII.

Mr. Innes, Sandside—Pict's house, Giesse—Entertained
by Mr. Murray of Pennyland—Crosses to Orkney
from Thurso—Hoy Walls—Story of eagle and child
—Pict's house—Dwarfiestone—Circular Chapel at
Orphir—Imports and exports at Stromness—Small
pigs—Shearing and marking sheep—The Snow
Bird, the Chack, etc., 133-140

LETTER XXVIII.

Stennis—Large and smaller Stone Circles—The Stone
of Odin—Stennis Church—Stennis Loch—Linen-
weaving and bleaching. 140-144

LETTER XXIX.

Kirkwall—Population—Seath, etc., fisheries—St. Magnus' Cathedral and Palace—The Earl of Orkney's
Arms and Inscription, 1593—Church offertory
lates—Cathedral bells—Kirkwall Castle—Cromwell's Fort—Barrows—Old Castle on Westray—
Offered the Freedom of Kirkwall, . 145-150

LETTER XXX.

Græmeshall, Mr. Graham's—Captain Moodie, Melsetter—Story of Commodore Moodie—Population
of Orkney and Shetland—Shell-fish, large quantities—Fair Isle—Shetland—Iceland—Faroe Islands, 151-155

b

LETTER XXXI.

Sails to Ratter, Caithness—Sir James Sinclair—John o'-Groat's House—Stroma and Swona Islands—Pict's house, . 155-158

LETTER XXXII.

Murkle, Earl of Caithness—Sir Patrick Dunbar—Storage of corn—Thatching houses—Ackergill Tower—The ruins of Castles Girnigoe and Sinclair—Wick Church—Lybster—Castle of Dunbeath, . 158-163

LETTER XXXIII.

The Ord—Berriedale—Navidale—Helmsdale—Minister of Loth, Mr. MacCulloch—Picts' Houses, Uagbeg and Uagmore—Fossils in limestone—Caves in sea-cliff—Dunrobin Castle—Fishers—Picts' Castles—Ancient sea margins—Dornoch—Earl's Cross—The Cathedral—The Palace—Receives the freedom of the Burgh—Cyder Hall—Skibo Castle—Mr. Mackay, M.P.—Invercarron, . 163-169

LETTER XXXIV.

Tain—Offered Freedom of Burgh—St. Duthus' Church—Abbey of Fearn—Abbot's monument—Church roof fell in, 1742—Story of Minister's escape—Mr. MacLeod of Geanies—Mr. MacLeod of Cadboll—Large Collection of Coins—Remarkable earthen pyramid—Monument at Shandwick—Shell bed near Ankerville—Cromarty House, Tarbet—Balnagown Castle—Resemblance of Cromarty headland to Mount Olivet. 169-176

CONTENTS.

LETTER XXXV.

Castle Craig—Sir Harry Munro of Foulis—Katharine Mackenzie, aged 118—Allt graunda; the ugly burn—Pea and bean bread—Beauly Priory—Monument to Lord Lovat in Kirkhill Church—The Fraser Sanskrit, etc., MSS.—Fortrose Church, . 176-181

LETTER XXXVI.

Mr. Rose of Kilravock—Cawdor Castle—Tradition regarding hawthorn tree—Receives Freedom of Nairn—Darnaway Castle—Oak chair in hall—Receives Freedom of Forres—Forres Pillar—Abbey of Kinloss—Burghead—Spynie Cathedral and Palace, 181-187

LETTER XXXVII.

Elgin—Population—Manufactures—The Cathedral—Monasteries—Chapels—Thunderton House—Pluscardine—Birnie Church, . 188-191

LETTER XXXVIII.

Urquhart Church—Innes House—Soldiers crossing the Spey in flood—Fochabers—Salmon fishery—Duke of Gordon's tenants—Cullen—Beacon hills—Mounts at Urquhart for calling hawks—Stone circles—Earl of Findlater's pictures—Portsoy—Scotch serpentine—Banff—Manufactures and fishery—Population—Lord Deskford's house—Earl of Fife—Convent—Sea-caves—Forglen, 191-196

LETTER XXXIX.

Turriff—Episcopal Chapel—New Deer—Abbey of Deer—Pitfour—Peterhead—The harbour—The Spa—Trade and manufactures—Fisheries—Slain's Castle—The Bullers of Buchan—Cave with stalactites—Red jasper—Petrified egg, . . . 196-198

CONTENTS.

LETTER XL.

Ellon—Udny Castle—Old Meldrum—Stocking-making—Kintore—Kemnay, the seat of the Burnetts—Monymusk—Sir Archibald Grant's improvements—Bennochie—Cairn William—Tap o' Noth vitrified fort—Cairngorm crystals—Monymusk Church—Aberdeen—City burnt—St. Nicholas' Church—Other Churches—The Trades' Hall—Convent and Monastery—The Cross—Royal Charters—Manufactures—Five Guinea Stockings—St. Machar's Cathedral—Emblazoned ceiling, names and inscriptions—Epitaphs on Monuments to Bishop Lychtoun, Bishop Dunbar, etc.—Fine carved pulpit—King's College—The library—Pictures—Marischal College—Library—Keith's Coins—Lists of Professors—Roman inscription—Story of boat accident—Supping with civic authorities—Receives Freedom of the city—Preaches in two Churches, .   199-210

LETTER XLI.

Aberdeen—Druid temple—Stonehaven—Population—Cowie—Manufactures—Dunnottar Castle—Inscription—Bervie—Manufactures—Fishery—Montrose—Church and Chapels—Gold fibula found in urn—Whale fishery, etc.—Granaries—Manufactures—Usan—Curious pebbles,   211-214

LETTER XLII.

Brechin—Lord Panmure's Castle—Cathedral—The Round Tower—Chapels—Town-house and cross—Scivewright's MSS.—Caterthun—Caristoun—Aberlemno crosses—Priory of Restenet—Forfar—Glamis Castle—Glamis Cross,   .   214-219

CONTENTS.

LETTER XLIII.

Hynde Castle—Arbroath—Manufactures—Osnaburghs—Aberbrothock Abbey—Broughty Castle—Dundee—Harbour—Town-house—Parish church—Other churches—Trade—Extraordinary windmill,   219-224

LETTER XLIV.

Fowlis Church—Coupar Angus—Inchtuthil—Murthly—Dunkeld—The Cathedral—Duke of Athole's house—The kitchen garden—Cascades—The Hermitage—Birnam Hill—Ancient spearhead—Larch wainscoting,   224-228

LETTER XLV.

Pass of Killiecrankie—Druid Temples—The Tilt—Blair Castle—The gardens—Tapestry and carvings—Bureau of broom-wood, . . .   229-232

LETTER XLVI.

Garth Castle—Bridge over River Tay—Inscriptions on Bridge—Kenmore—Taymouth Castle—Druid temple—Priory on Isle of Loch Tay—Glen Lyon—Fortingall—An ancient Vase—Roman fort—Struan—Loch Tay and its fish,   233-238

LETTER XLVII.

Menzies Castle—Glenalmond—Drummond Castle—Camp of Ardoch—Sir William Stirling—Burial urn containing burnt skull—Lead pipe found in camp, . .   238-241

LETTER XLVIII.

Tullibardine Church—Aged soldier—Muthill—Kilcardine Castle—Roman camp—Lawers—Ochtertyre, Sir Patrick Murray's, . .   242-244

CONTENTS.

LETTER XLIX.

Camp of Strageth—Innerpeffary—Maderty Church—Inchaffray Abbey—Land cultivation—Methven Church—Portrait of the Admirable Crichton—Battle of Luncarty—Valour of the Hays—Dunsinane. . 245-248

LETTER L.

Dupplin House—The paintings—Elcho Nunnery—Perth—Castle Gable—The Parish Church, St. John's—Monasteries and Nunneries—Town-house—Trade, value of exports—Summary of principal writs and charters—Receives the Freedom of the city—St. Johnston's ribbon—Combat on the North Inch—Royal palaces—Tradition concerning origin of Abernethy Tower, . 249-257

LETTER LI.

Scone Abbey, Coronation Chair and Stone—Historic paintings—Tapestry—Queen Mary's bed—Lord Stormont's tomb—Kinnoull—Carse of Gowrie—Errol—Megginch Castle—Rotation of crops—Abernethy Church—The Round Tower—The Reverend A. Moncrieff—Secession Church students, 257-262

LETTER LII.

Mugdrum Cross—Macduff's Cross—Newburgh—Burning of three witches—Lindores Abbey—Large holly tree killed by frost—Wallace's den—Ballanbreich Castle—Balmerino Abbey—Cupar—Population—Cross—Convent—Dairsie Church and Tower. . 262-266

CONTENTS.

LETTER LIII.

St. Andrews—Broad streets—Legend regarding relics of St. Andrews—St Regulus' Church—Cathedral — Priory — Castle — Parish Church — Archbishop Sharp's monument — Monasteries — Convent — University—Library—Population—Kirkhaugh,   266-273

LETTER LIV.

St. Andrews—Secale plant—Boar Hills—Crail—Church —Bone lace manufacture—Pilgrimage of women to cell; Isle of May—Pittenweem—Church— Whale fishery—Carpet manufacture—St. Monance Church—Elie—Garnets—Sir John Anstruther's house—Pictures, books, and coins—Pict's house, .   273-276

LETTER LV.

Balgonie Castle—Druid temple, Lundin House—Leven harbour—Earl of Rothes—Leslie house—Falkland Palace—Kinross—Lochleven Castle,   .   .   276-279

LETTER LVI.

Lochleven Priory—Lochore—Roman camp—Lochgelly — Abbotshall — Dysart — Large colliery pumping engine, ...   279-281

LETTER LVII.

Kirkcaldy — Population — Manufactures — Inverteil quarry—Fossils—Kinghorn—Ferry to Edinburgh— Petrified moss—Burntisland—Church—Harbour— Aberdour—Castle—Church—Fordel Glen—Dalgety Church—Donibristle House—Paintings and tapestry — Inverkeithing harbour — Queensferry — Lead-mine — Dunfermline — Palace — Abbey — St. Margaret's Shrine—Tombs of Scottish Kings—Queen Anne's bedstead — Offers fifty guineas for it — Churches—Manufactures—Population,   281-287

LETTER LVIII.

Torryburn—Culross Church—Bruce family monumental tomb—Tulliallan—Clackmannan—King Robert the Bruce's sword and helmet—Sauchie—Schaw Park House—Seat of Lord Alva—Alloa Tower and grounds—Abbey Craig, . . . 288-290

LETTER LIX.

Dunblane—The Cathedral—Bishop Leighton's library—Manufactures—Seceders—Kippenross—Large sycamore—Battle of Sheriffmuir—Strathallan, . 291-293

LETTER LX.

Keir; Mr. Stirling's—Shell-bed—Cambuskenneth Abbey—Stirling—Castle—Monastery—Royal Chapel—Palace—Brass cannon—St. Ninian—Bannockburn—Falkirk Fair—Droves of cattle—Fossils—Carron—Arthur's Oven—Iron works—Battle of Falkirk—Linlithgow—Palace—Church—Hopetoun House—Library—Pictures—Lawn—Yew hedges—Queensferry—Inchcolm Abbey—Cramond—Roman works—The Catstone—Corstorphine Church, . . 293-299

LETTER LXI.

Edinburgh—High houses—St. Giles's Cathedral—Greyfriars Church—Holyrood Palace—Parish churches—Burgh of Herbergare—Streets—Population—Workhouse—Heriot's Hospital—Infirmary—Hospitals—Holyrood Abbey—Monumental tombs—Arthur's Seat, . . . 299-305

CONTENTS. xxiii

LETTER LXII.

PAGES

Edinburgh Castle—Queen Mary's room—Verse written on wall—Regalia—Great cannon—Deep well—Royal Exchange—New Town—Parliament House—Law Courts—Advocates' Library—Rare mss.—Coins and medals, . 305-308

LETTER LXIII.

Edinburgh—North Loch—Newhaven—Leith harbour—St. Anthony's monastery—South and North Leith parish churches—Population—Restalrig Church—Craigmillar Castle—Sciennes Nunnery, 308-310

LETTER LXIV.

Musselburgh—New Hailes—Sir David Dalrymple's library—Scotch pebbles—Subterranean mill-lade—Battle of Pinkie—Battle of Prestonpans—Dalkeith Palace—Paintings and tapestry, . . . 310-312

LETTER LXV.

Newbattle Abbey—Arniston House and grounds—Large ash-tree—Library—Solemn League and Covenant—Hawthornden—Grotto and cave—Roslin Chapel—Battles near Roslin—Baron Clerk's antiquities—Rullion Green, 312-315

LETTER LXVI.

Lochend quarry—Fossils—Crichton—Castle—Church—Ancient camp—Milton—Fossils—Yester House—Paintings by Sir Peter Lely and Vandyck—Old Castle of Yester—The Church, . 315-317

LETTER LXVII.

Haddington—Manufactures—Monastery—Fortifications and sieges—New Mills—The Abbey—Nungate—North Berwick—The Law—Manufactures—Ruins of Nunnery—Tantallon Castle—Bass Rock—Tynninghame, ... 317-320

LETTER LXVIII.

Dunbar—Harbour—Parish Church—Earl of Dunbar's tomb—Castle ruins—Geological formations resembling Giant's Causeway—Fossils—Manufactures—Fishery—Skates' eggs—Town-house—Ancient Militia pikes—Cromwell's victory, . . 320-324

LETTER LXIX.

Broxmouth Park—Fossils—Dunglass Dean—Dunglass House—Coal-pit—Decaying fir roots destructive to other trees, ... 324-326

LETTER LXX.

Coldingham—St. Abb's Head—Nunnery—Tragic story about nuns—Priory—Eyemouth, . . . 326-328

LETTER LXXI.

Coldstream Nunnery—Kelso Abbey—Old castle—Floors Castle—Fine Lawn—Beautiful country, 'The Flower of Scotland'—Duns—Stitchell, Sir Robert Pringle's—Ancient bronze armlet—Two large stones near Mellerstains, . . . 328-332

CONTENTS.

LETTER LXXII.

Mellerstain Grounds—The Baillies' family vault—Latin and English inscriptions on tombs—Spottiswoode — Dryburgh Abbey — Melrose Abbey — Sculptures — Inscriptions — Ancient bridge over Tweed—Druids—Roman camp and coins—Eildon Hills—Skirmish Hill, . . . 332-342

LETTER LXXIII.

Galashiels—Selkirk—Roman camp—Ancrum—Jedburgh—Fine Abbey—Churches—Population—Fine fruit country—Cessford Castle. . . . 342-346

LETTER LXXIV.

Berwick-on-Tweed—Old Castle—Fortifications—Parish Church—Town-house—Kingdom of Northumbria—Norham Castle—Church—Ribby—Knight's belt and hilt of sword—Ford Castle—Flodden Field—The Battle—Tradition of death of James IV.; his penance chain not iron. but silver; was in Lord Marchmont's possession. . 346-351

ITINERARY.

Weekly account of places visited and miles travelled—Ireland, Scotland, and in England—Summary of total number of miles—List of Stages between London and Edinburgh—Distances by East and West Routes, . . . 351-356

INDEX, . 357

NOTES.

Letters III. to V., and VII. to XIII., appeared in *The Glasgow Herald* during November 1884; Letters XXVI., XXVII., and XXXI. to XXXIII. (in whole or in part) appeared in *The Northern Ensign* during July 1886, having been communicated to those newspapers by 'Alpha'—Mr. Thomas Sinclair, M.A., Author of *Humanities*, etc., vide *The Athenæum*, July 31, 1886.

The transcription of the seventy-four letters, etc., from the original MSS., was undertaken by Mr. Adam H. Darlington, London, very much as a matter of personal friendship. The Editor gratefully acknowledges his indebtedness to Mr. Darlington, not only for his careful transcripts, but also for valuable researches into other MSS. only to be seen in the British Museum.

LIST OF ILLUSTRATIONS.

Portrait—The Right Rev. Dr. Richard Pococke, Lord Bishop of Meath,	*Frontispiece*
Roman Inscription—Axsan Conis,	Page 6
Norman Doorway, Whithorn Priory,	16
Chimneypiece in Cardonness Castle—Upper Room,	21
Chimneypiece in Cardonness Castle—The Hall,	21
Abbey of Dundrennan—The North End of the Church,	22
Arch in the Church of Dundrennan Abbey,	23
New Abbey—West Front of the Church,	28
New Abbey—South End of the Church,	29
Illustrations of Gothic Architectural Terms,	31
Sculpture of Winged Figure, one foot on a globe, *bas relievo*—Fragment from Hoddam Castle,	33
Inscription—Robert de Brvs Counte de Carrik et Seityur du Val de Anann Ano 1300,	35
Inscription—God Revenge Mvrder, 1689, G. C.,	37
Plan—Double Boat, like two troughs joined,	37
Ground-plan—Hamilton Parish Church,	48
Plan—Roofing-tiles, Bothwell Church,	48
Roman Inscription—Imp. Caesari. T. Aelio. Hadriano. Antonino. Avg. Pio. P.P. Vexilla. Leg. vi. Vic. P.F. Per. M.P.,	52
Abbey of Paisley—Inside View of the Church,	55
Seagate Castle, Irvine—Doorway,	58
Seagate Castle, Irvine—Window,	59
Dunstaffnage Castle,	73
Ivory Chessman in Dunstaffnage Castle,	75
Back and Side Views of Chessman's Chair,	75
Iona Cathedral,	80

LIST OF ILLUSTRATIONS.

Inscription—The Maelpatrick Stone, Iona,	Page 84
Norwegian Oval Brooch from Lingay Island,	92
Brass Needle from Lingay Island,	92
Tigh-na-Stalcaire on Island Stalker,	96
Castle of Urquhart,	102
Plan of Order of Battle at Culloden, 1746,	106
Ground-plan of Dun-alishaig,	112
Dun-Dornadilla—Elevation,	122
Dun-Dornadilla—Interior,	123
Dwarfie Stone, Hermit's Cell, Orkney,	136
Stone Circle at Stennis—Large Group,	141
Stone Circle at Stennis—Small Group,	143
Kirkwall Cathedral and Bishop's Palace,	146
Kirkwall Cathedral—View of East End,	147
Inscription—P.E.O. Sic fvit est et erit 1593,	148
Ground-plan of a Pict's House,	157
Castle Girnigoe,	161
Castle Sinclair,	162
Roman Inscription—Imp. Caesar T. Aelio Hadriano Antonino Avg. Pio. P.P. Vexillatio 10 Leg. xx. Val. Vic. P. Per Mil. P. III.,	209
Fibula—Gold Ornament,	213
Round Tower at Brechin,	215
Copper Ewer at Taymouth Castle,	237
Round Tower at Abernethy,	261
Tower of Dairsie Church,	265
Roman Inscription—Brigantiaes. Amandvs Arcitectvs Imperii Imp. I.,	314
Skate's Egg,	323
Armlet—An Ancient Bracelet (three views),	331

The inscriptions are not facsimiles of the original objects, but are reproduced as they appear in the MSS., so that Dr. Pococke's doubtful readings may be easily shown, *e.g.* p. 314.

Dr. Pococke's drawings are pen sketches, shaded by brush with Indian ink. The reduced copies for this work were drawn by Mr. George R. Primrose, London. By permission of the Trustees of the British Museum, he was enabled to take tracings from the original drawings, which having reduced in size about one-third, and arranged as line drawings on prepared paper with transfer ink, they were transferred by Mr. Robert Dawson, Zincotyper, Edinburgh, to zinc plates, and mounted to print with the text. The Editor embraces this opportunity of thanking Mr. Primrose for his faithful representations of the Bishop's rough work, and for other services rendered therewith.

' WHAT dost thou now ?   Beside the hearth, no doubt,
　　The map is spread, your eye pursues my route ;
　　You say, " Where is he ? may each place supply
　　　　Kind service, and some heart that loves and cares—
　　　　Some hostess like myself, who prays and fears
　　For some loved being 'neath a foreign sky.

' " Now fast he journeys on.   I'm sure by now
　　That far-off city he has travelled through,
　　That wood, that bridge, scene of some mighty deed ;
　　　　E'en now he may through that lone valley stray,
　　　　Marked by the fatal Cross, that speaks dismay,
　　Where but last year—O, may he safely speed ! " '

　　　　　　　　　　The Journey, by VICTOR HUGO.
　　　　　　　　　　Dean Carrington's Translation, 1885.

BIOGRAPHICAL SKETCH

OF

RICHARD POCOCKE, D.D., LL.D., F.R.S., F.S.A.,

LORD BISHOP SUCCESSIVELY OF OSSORY AND MEATH.

'I have often wished that no Travels or Journey should be published but those undertaken by persons of integrity, and capacity to judge well, and describe faithfully and in good language, the situation, condition, and manners of the countries past through.'—SIR ALEXANDER DICK.[1]

ALTHOUGH an Englishman by birth, and an Irishman by adoption, Bishop Pococke was not without some connection with Scotland—he was the honorary citizen of no fewer than seven Scottish cities and royal boroughs.

As a Scottish burgess, then, it seems not only graceful but appropriate to preface his *Tours Through Scotland*, on their first publication,[2] with as full a memoir of their author as the limited materials at our command will permit of.

Richard Pococke was born in Southampton on 19th November 1704.[3] His father, the Rev. Richard Pococke, LL.B. (who is said to be related to the Oriental scholar, Dr. Edward Pococke, who died in 1691), was Rector of Colmer in Hampshire, and afterwards Headmaster of the King Edward VI. Free Grammar School, and Sequestrator and Minister of All Saints' Church in Southampton. He is described as a man of more worth than wealth, and when, on April 26, 1698, he

---

[1] Dr. Johnson had presented a copy of his *Journey to the Western Islands of Scotland* to Sir A. Dick.—Boswell's *Life of Johnson*.

[2] See Note, p. xxvi.

[3] This date makes Dr. Pococke twenty-one at his ordination, and sixty-one at his death. If, however, his birth took place in 1702, it would synchronise with those events, by making him twenty-three years of age when ordained, and sixty-three years old when he died.

married Miss Milles, only daughter of the Rev. Isaac Milles, 'he received with her a fortune of nearly £1000—a considerable portion in those days,' and a sum more likely to have been the joint gift of her brothers, who had all obtained lucrative church preferments, than to have been saved out of the Rector's limited income. Richard is stated to have received his earlier education at King Edward's School; but that is very doubtful, for when only six years old his father died (1710), and his mother, with her two young children— Richard and Elizabeth—removed to her father's rectory at Highclere, Hampshire. Mrs. Pococke was with much tender sympathy welcomed beneath the parental roof, and as her mother had died two years previously, Mr. Milles gladly committed his domestic concerns to her care.

For ten years Mrs. Pococke enjoyed the happy society of her father, and was unremitting in her dutiful attentions, especially during the last years of his life, when he required careful nursing, being rendered helpless by his great age and infirmities. On 6th July 1720 he died aged 82. His remains are interred in the chancel of Highclere Church, under the north end of the altar. A black marble slab which covers his grave bears the following inscription:—

'Subtus depositæ sunt reliquiæ venerabilis viri Isaaci Milles, Suffolciensis, A.M. Cantabrigiensis è Coll. Divi Joannis, hujusce ecclesiæ Rectoris. Qui postquam annos triginta septem in erudiendis optimæ spei adolescentibus, et in munere pastorali summâ fide defungendo insumpsisset, senectute ingravescente variisque laboribus fractus, placide tandem in Christo obdormivit die sexto mensis Julii, anno Domini 1720; ætatis 82.

'Ab Elizabethâ uxore, quæ die quarto Januarii anno 1708 ex hac vitâ migravit, cujusque reliquiæ huc juxta sunt, suscepit tres filios: Thomam, primum apud Oxonienses Græcæ linguæ Professorem Regium, deinde apud Hibernos Episcopum Waterfordiensem et Lismorensem; Hieremiam, collegii Balliolensis apud eosdem Oxonienses socium, postea Vicarium de Duloe, in agro Cornubiensi; Isaacum, Ecclesiæ Waterfordiensis Thesaurarium, in Ecclesiâ Lismorensi Præbendarium de Modeligo; et filiam unicam Elizabetham,

Ricardo Pocokio, LL.B., Scholae Southantoniensis Archididascalo peritissimo, nuptam.

'Optimis parentibus hoc marmor poni voluêre liberi eorum supradicti superstites.

'Animis eorum propitietur Deus.
Requiescant in pace.
Eternam requiem det illis Deus.'[1]

On the north wall of the chancel of Highclere Church is another monument, erected by his son the Bishop of Waterford. It is white marble, and bears the following inscription:—

'In memory of the pious and learned Mr. Isaac Milles, born at Cockfield, near St. Edmund's Bury in Suffolk, M.A. of St. John's College in Cambridge, whose body is deposited under a black marble stone not far from this place.

'He was a man of great integrity of life and manners, sober, just, holy, temperate, holding fast the faithful word, as he had been taught, and able, by sound doctrine, both to exhort and to convince gainsayers. He was abundantly charitable to the poor, and liberally hospitable to the rich, and kind and beneficent to all. He was a faithful friend, a tender parent, and a good master. He never spoke evil of any one; but endeavoured, by all means, to promote the interest, both temporal and eternal, of every one, more especially of those committed to his charge. He was always cheerful, and desirous to render others so too. He ordered his whole conversation, so as to make it plainly appear that he had a

[1] 'Beneath are deposited the reliques of that venerable man, Isaac Milles, of Suffolk, A.M. of St. John's College, Cambridge, Rector of this Church, who, after he had employed seven-and-thirty years in the instruction of youth of the highest promise, and in the most faithful discharge of the pastoral office, broken down by the weight of age and the variety of his labours, gently fell asleep in Christ, 6th July, 1720, in the 82d year of his age.

'By Elizabeth, his wife, who departed this life on the 4th January, 1708, and whose reliques are just here deposited, he had three sons: Thomas, first Regius Professor of Greek at Oxford, then Bishop of Waterford and Lismore, in Ireland; Jeremy, Fellow of Balliol Coll. Oxon., afterwards Vicar of Duloe, in Cornwall; Isaac, Treasurer of Waterford Cathedral, Prebendary of Modeligo in Lismore Cathedral; and one daughter, Elizabeth, married to Richard Pococke, LL.B., the learned headmaster of Southampton School.

'Their above-named surviving children have erected this marble to the best of parents. May God be merciful to their souls. May they rest in peace. May God give them eternal rest.'—*Life of the Rev. Isaac Milles*, Lond. 1842, p. 128.

most lively sense of God and his providence on his mind. He was perfectly constant and regular in his private and public devotions. He educated many sons of the nobility and gentry, instilling into their minds, together with good literature, the best principles of religion and morality. He was a constant and faithful, a zealous and learned preacher. He was continually resident, and carefully diligent in the cure of this parish of Highclere, for thirty-nine years, two months, and seven days; when, after having contracted a great feebleness by the labours of his life, he sweetly fell asleep in Christ, without struggle, groan, or sigh, on Wednesday, the 6th day of July, 1720, and of his age the 82d year.

'By Elizabeth Luckin, his wife, he had three sons and one daughter. His eldest son is Bishop of Waterford and Lismore, in the kingdom of Ireland; his second son is Vicar of Duloe, in Cornwall; and his third son is Treasurer of the Cathedral Church of Waterford, and Prebendary of Modeligo in the church of Lismore. His daughter was married to the Reverend Mr. Richard Pococke, minister of All Saints' Church in Southampton, and head master of the free school there.

'"The righteous is ever merciful, and lendeth; and his seed is blessed."—*Psalm* xxxvii. 26.

'T. W. L.[1] *posuit.*'

Associated during his childhood and youth with such a grandfather as is here commemorated, and surrounded by relatives and friends all connected with the Church, it is not surprising that he should have had his mind directed to the clerical profession. Mr. Milles was a sound and accomplished scholar, and, with the view of augmenting his slender income, conducted a school in his Parsonage, which he more than once enlarged. He taught first his own sons the elements of Hebrew and classical literature, and after they and some other pupils had been to Oxford, and there by their successes demonstrated the character of the scholastic training at Highclere, Mr. Milles was never without as many scholars as he could accommodate.

It would therefore be at his grandfather's school that

---

[1] 'T. W. L.,' Thomas Waterford Lismore—The Right Rev. Dr. Thomas Milles, Bishop of Waterford and Lismore.—*Life of Rev. Isaac Milles*, p. 132.

Richard received his earlier education, and that moral and Christian training which influenced his life.

'Mr. Milles[1] looked upon the knowledge of letters, and all intellectual acquirement, as very necessary and valuable, but very subsidiary to the inculcation of religious sentiments, habits of piety, and the practice of truth, virtue, and charity. His mode of establishing authority was far from that of the tyrant, nor was he willing to create personal awe of himself in the minds of the children under his charge. He preferred the gentler methods of reasoning with them, representing the necessity of some things, and the advantage of abstaining from others; or by some good-humoured turn of expression, he would rally them on the folly of a weak, and lead them to the practice of a contrary line of conduct. Always cheerful himself, he naturally conveyed his instructions in a cheerful and even facetious manner, believing the impression thus made to be more lively, and as lasting as that of a graver style. He took care to suppress everything tending to vice, and to encourage everything honest, pure, lovely, and of good report. His example yet more than his precept taught them to be kind, humane, and civil to all, especially to the poor, towards whom he would contrive little opportunities for the exercise of the generosity of his boys. He sought to infuse some of his own charity in all around him, and promoted church collections for charitable objects at home and abroad, e.g. for the Vaudois, the French Protestant refugees, and the captives in Morocco. The parish register of Highclere abounds with accounts of such philanthropic efforts, in which the names of the subscribers occur, notably among whom were the schoolboys and domestics of Mr. Milles. His constant anxiety was to make his boys wise and good, manly and honourable; to abhor everything mean and dirty, and to love whatever was fair and open.'

With such a training Richard Pococke commenced his academical career.

On the death of Mr. Milles, Mrs. Pococke and family appear to have left the Rectory of Highclere, and taken up their residence at Newtown, near Newbury, with which place they maintained a lifelong connection, and where subsequently Bishop Pococke acquired property.

[1] *Life of Rev. Isaac Milles*, p. 67.

From the new home at Newtown, Richard was sent to Oxford, and was entered on 3rd February 1722 as an exhibitioner of Corpus Christi College.

In the year 1725, his uncle, the Bishop of Waterford and Lismore, appointed him to the Precentorship of Lismore, and in 1727 the chapter of Lismore chose him for their proctor to Convocation.

In 1731 he took his degree of Master of Arts and LL.B., and of LL.D. on June 28, 1733, together with Dr. Secker, then Rector of St. James's, and afterwards Archbishop of Canterbury. In 1734 (apparently during his absence on the continent) he was appointed Vicar-General of the Dioceses of Waterford and Lismore.

From 1733 to 1736 Dean Jeremiah Milles, D.D., and Dr. Pococke, his cousin (both nephews of the Bishop of Waterford), travelled in company through France, Switzerland, Italy, Belgium, Holland, Hanover, Prussia, Austria, Greece, etc.

Immediately on their return, Dr. Pococke took a short trip in England, travelling from Holyhead to Oxford, and visiting Old Sarum, Salisbury, Andover, and Stonehenge. From this time he was possessed with a passion for travelling, which earned for him the title of 'Pococke the traveller'; the mantle of his celebrated relative, Dr. Edward Pococke,[1] Oriental scholar and traveller, had evidently fallen on him. He had resolved to visit Egypt and the East, and employed the summer of 1737 in making extensive preparations for a long absence. Armed with passports and letters of introduction, he sailed for Alexandria in the autumn of that year, arriving there on 29th September. The recommendations to the ambassadors, consuls, and important personages were of the greatest value to him; and thus he experienced less difficulty in seeing and examining historical places than his contemporary, Mr. Norden. The two

[1] 'Smith's Latin verses are on Edward Pococke, the great Oriental linguist. He travelled, it is true, but Dr. Richard Pococke, late Bishop of Ossory, who published travels through the East, is usually called the great traveller.'—Boswell's *Life of Johnson*, ed. 1811, vol. iv. p. 58, n. Kearney.

travellers are supposed to have passed each other during the night on the Nile, Dr. Pococke being on his homeward journey.

On his return in 1742 he prepared an account of his travels for the press, and in 1743 Mr. Bowyer printed the first volume, folio, entitled *A Description of the East and of some other Countries: Vol. I.—Observations on Egypt.*

In 1743 he took a month's tour through Leicestershire, Nottinghamshire, Derbyshire, and neighbouring counties, the MSS. of which are in the possession of an Irish gentleman.[1]

The following year he was made Precentor of Waterford. In 1745 he finished the second volume of his travels, under the title of *Observations on Palestine, or the Holy Land, Syria, Mesopotamia, Cyprus, and Candia*, in two parts. This he dedicated to the Earl of Chesterfield, who had just been appointed Lord-Lieutenant of Ireland, and on whom he attended, as one of his Lordship's domestic chaplains.

These volumes attracted for a period of over half a century a considerable amount of attention, and at once gave him a standing amongst the literati of his day.

The works were illustrated by between 170 and 180 sketches: 'but the Doctor was little acquainted with the Art of drawing and the rules of perspective.' Gibbon speaks of the works as characterised by 'superior learning and dignity, but the Author too often confounds what he had seen, and what he had heard.' Pinkerton says, 'The high value of Pococke's travels with respect to antiquities and science is universally acknowledged.' Dibdin remarks that 'these are noble tomes; and the author rises in estimation more and more every day. He is *facile princeps* in his department, Antiquities and Science are the leading features of his work.' Pauli Ernesti Jablonski eulogises the first volume on Egypt thus: 'Profecto quantum attinet ad Aegyptum Sacram, quam aliquando moliebar, video operam istam a praestantissimo Rich. Pocockio, in Descriptione

[1] P. 19.

Aegypti, jam occupatam, mihique profecto non invito, praereptam suisse. Is enim in isthoc argumento, plerumque tam diligenter et feliciter versatus est, ut Spicilegio nonnissi tenui, locum reliquerit.' Stevenson says, 'The merits of this work in pointing out and describing the Antiquities of Egypt and the East are well known.' Mant describes the *Travels* 'as among the foremost of modern European descriptions of those regions, and which, notwithstanding the numerous narratives that have since been published, still continue to rank with the most valuable standard productions of their class.'

If auction sale prices may be taken as indicating their value, it may be mentioned that the 2 vols. brought £21 at the Marquis of Townshend's sale, £16, 10s. at Heaths', £14 at Townby's, and forty years ago for large paper copies £10 was a common price; but these prices are things of the past. What with reprints, and above all the more accurate and scientific works of recent years, Dr. Pococke's great literary undertaking has been superseded; but he himself will ever live as a distinguished pioneer of that class of antiquarian and historical research. The following are some of the references and reprints of his Works:—Dr. Shaw's[1] *Travels, or Observations*, etc. Supplement wherein some objections . . . [by R. P.] are . . . answered. etc., 1746, fol. *Beschreibung des Morgenlanders und einiger anderer Lander.* Englischen ubersetzet durch C. E. von Windheim und von . . . dem Canzler von Motheim; mit einer Vorrede versehen [with illustrations]. 3 Theil Erlangen, 1754-5. 4°. *Voyage de R. Pococke en Orient, dans l'Egypte* . . . traduit de l'Anglois, sur la seconde edition par M. Eydous [et de la Flotte]. Nouvelle edition augmentú. 7 tom. Neuchatel, 1772-73. 12 . *The World Displayed, Travels through Egypt.* Illustrated. Vols. xii. and xiii. 3d. edition, 1774, London. 12². Moore's *New . . . Collection of Voyages*, etc., vol. ii.

---

[1] Dr. Shaw 'complains of his friend Dr. Pococke being so mean as to publickly object to his book without first telling him of it, and says he . . . held the torch for Dr. Pococke in his travels.'

Pinkerton's *General Collection of* . . . *Voyages,* etc. A
Description of the East, vol. x., 1808. 4°. *Travels in Egypt,*
vol xv., 1808. 4°.

Dr. Pococke's great work being now published and out of the
author's hand, he is represented as having had a desire to
dismiss the subject, if we can credit Richard Cumberland's
brief allusion to him in his *Memoirs*: 'That celebrated
Oriental traveller, and author,' he says, ' was a man of mild
manners and primitive simplicity. Having given the world a
full detail of his researches in Egypt, he seemed to hold himself excused from saying any more about them, and observed
in general an obdurate taciturnity. In his carriage and deport-
ment he seemed to have contracted something of the Arab
character, yet there was no austerity in his silence, and though
his air was solemn, his temper was serene.'

This obduracy of character is scarcely borne out by other
evidences; rather we find him frequently making pleasing com-
parisons between places in Britain and Egypt and the Holy
Land. Thus, as we shall see in his *Tours Through Scotland,*
he compared the rocks near Cape Wrath to the granite of
which the statues of Memnon are made;[1] Ben Vheir to Mount
Tabor;[2] the appearance of Dingwall was not unlike Jerusalem,[3]
and a hill near that town resembled Calvary; a cave near
Brora in Sutherland was like those about Bethlehem,[4] and a
mount near Cromarty rose like Olivet[5] over Jerusalem. Bishop
Forbes records that Mr. Sutherland[6] of Wester Caithness had
a lengthy conversation with Dr. Pococke, in which they compared notes of the various places in the East which they had seen.
Indeed he rather appeared to have had a justifiable pride in his
travels and work as an author, for we find him frequently
making presents of the two volumes to distinguished friends,
sometimes ordering them to be elegantly bound.

The Earl of Chesterfield promoted him in 1745 to the

[1] P. 125.   [2] P. 97.   [3] P. 108.   [4] P. 165.   [5] P. 175.   [6] P. 162.

Archdeaconry of Dublin; his patent is dated Jan. 28, he was instituted Jan. 31, and installed at St. Patrick's on Feb. 1st, and at Christ Church on Feb. 3rd.

In the midst of his ecclesiastical duties we find the Archdeacon this year gathering information for a journey to Scotland. He desired pastures new, fresh fields for inquiry, a different direction in which to expend his restless energies. Having visited foreign lands, he evidently thought there were some things worth seeing nearer home. Amongst those from whom he desired suggestions was the celebrated archaeologist, Dr. Stukeley, who most probably had been the recipient of an author's copy of *A Description of the East*, and had returned the compliment by sending Dr. Pococke a copy of *Stonehenge*, which the following letter acknowledges—

To Dr. W. STUKLEY, M.D., F.R.S., F.S.A.

LONDON, *June* 7. 1745. RAWTHMELL'S COFFEE-HOUSE, HENRIETTA-STREET, COVENT GARDEN.

DEAR SIR,—Soon after my return from Ireland, I received the favour of your kind present of "Stonehenge"; which will be a great ornament of my library, and a particular honour, as it comes from the Author; and I do return you my hearty thanks for it.

I am going again to Ireland, in the month of August, having the honour to wait on the Lord Lieutenant as his Domestic Chaplain. If at any time you have any commands in that country, you will do me a particular pleasure if you will honour me with them. As I hope sometimes to come to England, so I have not laid aside my thoughts of a Northern journey; which I shall undertake with greater satisfaction, as I am sure you will favour me with all the hints you can give; and I shall not despise even Scotland, and the Orkney Islands, where I expect to meet with something curious, at least in relation to their customs and manners; and I shall be greatly obliged to you if you will mark anything down for me which you meet with in your reading. Pray my compliments to your lady, and family.—I am, Dear Sir, your most obedient humble servant, RICHARD POCOCKE.

Dr. Pococke's journeys to and from Ireland must have been very frequent; and Cumberland, in the *Memoir* already referred to, gives a sketch of him which is more likely to be correct than his former description was:—

'When we were on our road to Ireland, I saw from the Windows of the inn at Daventry, Cornwall, a cavalcade of horsemen approaching on a gentle trot, headed by an elderly chief in clerical attire, who was followed by five servants, at distances geometrically measured, and most precisely maintained, and who upon entering the inn, proved to be this distinguished prelate, conducting his horde with the phlegmatic patience of a Scheik.'

Archdeacon Pococke, on returning to Dublin, held a visitation at St. Patrick's in 1746, which perhaps is the latest of such visitations on record in Ireland.

This year was an eventful one. The political interest was centred in Scotland, where the last scene in the drama of civil war in great Britain was being enacted. Dr. Pococke doubtless watched the progress of the royal army with the keenest anxiety, and at the same time shrewdly gathered from the military news any item which might prove of interest on his proposed visit to Scotland.

His sympathies were of course with the reigning family; and when fatal Culloden sealed for ever the hopes of the Stuarts, and Bonnie Prince Charlie had fled into exile, we can imagine his reverent satisfaction, judging from his remarks when he subsequently visited the battlefield: 'Thus ended this day of such consequence to the British Dominions, and crowned the Duke with immortal laurels.'[1]

It appears to have been generally known amongst his antiquarian and scientific friends that he was about to make a northern journey, and as he expressed it to Dr. Stukeley, he would not despise even Scotland and the Orkney Islands. His long-wished-for visit was about to be realised, to a country of which he must have heard many a quaint story in his grandfather's barns when a boy—for even the Scotch pedlars

[1] P. 108.

BIOGRAPHICAL SKETCH.

who travelled into England resorted to Highclere parsonage, and had their packs safely lodged there, and themselves in the barns or outhouses, where Mr. Milles would himself take care that they had plenty of clean straw and wholesome refreshment. Having procured a number of letters of introduction, as was his wont, he started on his first northern journey in the autumn of 1747. Reaching Penrith, he writes: 'I laid in the bed the Pretender lay in.' At Carlisle he visited the castle, having as his *open-sesame* 'a letter to the storekeeper of the castle written by the Duke of Montague's order.' During the progress of this journey he wrote to Emanuel Mendez Da Costa, Foreign Secretary to the Royal Society, about fossils. Mr. Da Costa seems to have been a most exact man, keeping scrolls of his letters, from which, after many corrections, the final copy would be written. We are indebted to his scrolls for the following letter. It is interesting not only as showing the respect in which Dr. Pococke was held, but how thoroughly he was able to enlist the interest and assistance of others in his favourite pursuits.

Rev^d Dr. Richard Pococke, Archdeacon of Dublin,
  Ans^d 1st *January* 174⁷⁄₈.

    Adams Court in Broad Street
     Behind the Royal Exchange
      London, 19 *September* 1747.

Sir,—I rec^d the Letter you did me the honour to write me, acquainting me of the desire you had that I should send those Specimens of fossils &c. I purposed for you to Mr. Mathers, to be sent with your footman to Ireland.

As the place you wrote from was not specified in the Letter I could not acquaint you by an answer that your desires were always a pleasure to me: And in consequence thereof, with this I have deliverd Mr. Mathers with 2 parcells cont^g the fossils of wch the annext is a Catalogue, wch I hope you'll rank as a mark of my esteem for the friendship you honour me with.

There are as you'll find 2 spec: of small shells, wch you had formerly desired, and were laid by for you, but could not send you any other sorts, being very poor in duplicates of Shells.

These fossils were are all the present time I have would permit me to send you; but assure yourself S^r the pleasure you do me by your friendship, will always recall you to my mind, to keep by duplicates for you of what may come to my hands: and send them you as opportunitys offer.

I take the liberty S^r to Recommend myself to your thoughts for what duplicates of Natural History you may have to spare, of the Collections you make in the Travels you are on. Scotland is full of curious things, and as they have not been much searched into, doubt not but with the fund of Knowledge & Industry we know you possessd of you will, if I may use the Metaphor, be a Columbus in New discoveries of the fossil World, and other parts of Natural History.

The Western Islands I hear you intend to visit. Mr. Martin & he only has given us an Acc^t of those Islands interspersed wth some particulars of their Natural History; by wch I observe they abound in Curious things of all kinds. Your Philosophical searches there, I do not doubt, will abundantly make us acquainted wth them, of wch at present we only know they exist.

Had my time permitted me I should have boldly (relying on your goodness for Pardon) flung into this letter some N. Bene & Instructions of things I have read of for your examination: but if you permit, & will favour me with your full direction, I shall reserve that for a future letter.

I desire S^r that if you want anything done in this Metropolis wch I can be the Actor of, you^d freely command me by Letter: & should any Obs: offer, wch you'll be so good to participate to me, my greatest thanks will attend them.

I shall close this letter with my Prayers to the Almighty being who preserved you hitherto in your Travels through the Arabian & the deserts of Sin, and other the Eastern Parts of the World, to also preserve you health & pleasure through the bleak Northern parts you are now visiting, that I may again congratulate you on your Return.—I am S^r with all Esteem your Obliged

[EMANUEL M. DA COSTA.]

The gossipy letter to his mother (then about 70) which is the first letter of this volume of *Tours*, forms a striking contrast to all the subsequent ones, which are strictly topographical, scarcely ever unbending to make even a personal allusion. The MS. accounts which appear to have been written concurrently with the letter were probably descriptive, like the others, and are not known to exist; most likely they were incorporated in his 1760 tour when traversing the same ground, and afterwards destroyed. During this holiday trip of a month's duration he first visited Berwick, thence he rode to Edinburgh, and after a short stay in Stirling and Glasgow, travelled by the old coach road to Portpatrick, where he embarked for Ireland.

Pues Occurrences records that 'Last Tuesday [3 Nov. 1747] the Rev. Dr. Pococke, Archdeacon of Dublin, arrived here [Dublin] from Great Britain.' The lateness of the season and the unsettled state of the Highlands probably deterred him from attempting to go further north than Stirling, and Orkney had still to remain *terra incognita*.

The outstanding incidents of this tour are his visits to the Earl of Hopetoun[1] and short stay there, and his being presented with the freedom of Glasgow.[1] On returning to Dublin he loses no time in making a round of calls on the chief ecclesiastics and *élite* of the city—Dr. Cobbe, Archbishop of Dublin; Dr. Stone, The Primate, Archbishop of Armagh; Mr. Speaker Boyle (afterwards Earl of Shannon); Dr. Downes, the Bishop of Fernes; the Lord Mayor, Sir George Ribton; Mrs. Reynell, wife of Dr. Henry Reynell, Precentor of Connor, etc.[2]

In 1750 he made an extensive tour through the Northern Counties of England, and just visited the borderland of Scotland. The letter (also addressed to his mother) descriptive of this visit forms the Second Tour in the present volume.

Every year Dr. Pococke appears to have mapped out a district in England or Ireland for investigation; and whilst his friends were spending their holiday stalking the deer or following the grouse, he was wending his solitary steps amidst

---

[1] P. 3.
[2] Communicated by the Rev. William Reynell, B.D., Dublin; a kinsman of the Precentor of Connor.

ruined abbeys and castles, inquiring into their history—into their glory in the days of other years.

About this time was published Dean Milles and Dr. Pococke's *Inscriptionum Antiquarum Graec. et Latin liber. Accidit numismatum . . . in Aegypto cusorum . . . catalogus* (Inscriptionum Antiquarum liber alter a J. Milles et R. P. . . . exscript [London] 1752, folio).

Among Da Costa's scrolls is an example of one of the letters of recommendation he gave our traveller on the occasion of his visiting Cornwall—

Revd W. Borlase.

Dear Sir,—The Bearer of this is the Rev. Dr. R. Pococke a Gent. well known to the Learned World, & whom I have the honour to recommend to you, as said Gentⁿ is now making a Western Tour [England] I beg you will do me the favour to show him and acquaint him of what is curious in your country. I remain with great esteem and respect Dear Sir your very obliged

[Emanuel M. Da Costa.]

There can be little doubt Dr. Pococke enjoyed a large correspondence with the leading *savans* of his day; very few of his letters, however, have been preserved. The following is particularly interesting as containing the observation from which he has been credited with the architectural discovery of the origin of the Gothic Arch, a statement as unlikely as it is inaccurate. In this letter, and throughout his writings, he, in common with most of the writers of that period, confounds the terms Saxon and Norman. In almost every case it is the latter style that is referred to—the rounded arch, examples of the Saxon style being extremely rare :—

To Dr. Ducarel.

Dublin, *Aug.* 27, 1753.

Dear Sir,—I received the favour of your letter of the 21st with great pleasure, in relation to the Bishop of Clogher's book, and the description of the North-east parts. I fear no person will be found fit for the journey to the Wilderness that would undertake it. If Swinton [The Rev. Dr. John Swinton of Oxford] were not married, he would be a very proper man, as his talent lies that way.

I never heard of the book you mention, and should be very glad to see it. If you could send it to Mr. Ball, at the Duke of Dorset's, with my compliments, and request to him to bring it over, I should be obliged to you; but it must be done immediately, for the Duke sets out on the 2d of September. If you should be too late, and could be informed of Mr. Gustavus Brander, a Swedish merchant, in White Lion-court, beyond the Royal Exchange, Cornhill, whether he sends any thing to me; in case he does, he will convey it to me.

You do not mention what kind of character they are;—the Runick are most to be suspected.

I should have been glad of some hint what kind of buildings the Norman are, and whether you are sure those you mention were built before the Conquest. We know what the Saxon buildings are; but what I want to be informed is, from what part the style of our Gothic buildings came, for the English built many fabrics in France after the Conquest, and these are to be looked on as of the same rank as ours. What puzzles is; the Saxon style continued certainly after the Gothic was brought in, so that we cannot judge of the time by the style of building in that respect. I believe I observed to you that the original of the Gothic arch is two arches intersecting, that is visible at Christ Church in Hampshire. I shall be very glad to see your observations, and am obliged to you for thinking of me. I shall be glad to know what that very learned Antiquary Dr. Lyttelton, Dean of Exeter, thinks on that subject. I shall at all times be glad to hear from you, and am in haste, going out of town for a few days, —With great regard, Sir,

Your most obedient humble servant, RICHARD POCOCKE.

We have already seen a letter to Dr. Stukeley. This learned antiquary, keeping in remembrance the request to note down anything which might be useful on the Northern travels, had sent a book, for which the following is an acknowledgment:—

DUBLIN, *Jan.* 3, 1754.

DEAR SIR,—I received the favour of your letter, and of the book of the Northern History, for which I return you my hearty thanks.

BIOGRAPHICAL SKETCH.

I long to see your account of the Norman Antiquities. The County of Kerry is not yet come out; I will take care and get it for you. Simon has not published any addition to his Irish Coins, nor have I heard of any such intention, but I will ask him. I am sorry to hear Dr. Mead is in so declining a way;—his collection ought to be bought by the publick, and added to Sir Hans Sloane's. There is nothing whatsoever doing here in the literary way. Turning over my papers, I found an inscription taken off from a stone in Mr. Ame's possession. Some of the letters a little resemble your Northern inscriptions. It was brought from Alexandria in Egypt in 1726, and was found buried in the sands there.

With the best wishes of the season, I am, dear Sir, your most obedient humble servant. RICHARD POCOCKE.

In 1756 the Archdeacon received an important preferment. He was appointed to the Bishopric of Ossory, then vacant by the death of Bishop Maurice. His elevation to the episcopate was due to Lord-Lieutenant the Duke of Devonshire, and it was fraught with the happiest consequences to the diocese of Ossory, in which Dr. Pococke's memory is still green. No sooner was he settled in the palace of Kilkenny than his observant and experienced eye saw that the beautiful Cathedral Church of St. Canice would soon, if not renovated, be a pile of ruins similar to hundreds of others he had seen in his travels. An entry in the chapter-books, 11th June 1757, shows that on coming to Kilkenny he immediately began the work of restoration.[1] The thanks of the chapter are awarded to him for a gift of fifty guineas towards the improving and adorning of the inside of the choir. On the 30th of July following, the chapter agreed to give thirty guineas annually until the work was completed. It must be confessed the improvements were not in the best of taste, as they were mostly in Ionic style, whereas the Cathedral is Gothic; but this was rather the fault of the age than of the man, and probably but for him the Cathedral would have been past restoration.

[1] Communicated by the Right Rev. W. Pakenham Walsh, D.D., Lord Bishop of Ossory.

BIOGRAPHICAL SKETCH.

A slab of black Kilkenny marble was placed in the northern transept of the Cathedral at the time of Bishop Pococke's restorations. Amongst the contributions to the Repair Fund of the Cathedral, his name appears on the tablet for one hundred guineas.

In another part of the Cathedral there is a stone on which is cut the following inscription, believed to have been written by this prelate—

HANC[1]
BASILICAM
VETUSTATE
LABESCENTEM
RESTITUERUNT
ORNARUNT
OSSORIENSES
ANNO
MDCCLXIII

The Bishop's curious eye was quick to discover bits of the stained glass that once filled the grand east window lying scattered about, and which had lain unheeded for a century; these he placed in a window over the west door. The original window appeared so precious a work of art that it was coveted by Rinuccini, the Pope's nuncio, who offered Bishop Roth and the chapter £700 for it, as he desired to carry it to Italy, surely a great price in those days (about 1645). The offer was refused, and the window left, but only to be utterly destroyed by the vandalism of Cromwell's soldiers.

He built a colonnade leading from the door of the north transept to the entrance into the palace garden. It was in the Tuscan style, and in the carrying out of more recent and correct improvements was removed, as it concealed this very remarkable door of the Cathedral.

He also presented a rich cover for the communion table—

[1] The people of Ossory restored and adorned this church, falling into decay from old age, A.D. 1763.

purple and gold—and placed over it the painting of a 'glory,' which he brought from Italy. The latter is still preserved in the chapter-room.

The Bishop caused all the old monuments in St. Canice's Cathedral to be repaired and arranged, though not all in their original position, and employed John O'Phelan, 'a learned and ingenious man,' who kept a school in Kilkenny, to copy all the existing inscriptions. This MS. was afterwards printed by Dr. Peter Shee, entitled *Inscriptions on the Tombs in St. Canice's*. It is illustrated by plates, which were drawn by a self-taught Kilkenny artist named Coffey, and etched by William Maxton, a private soldier belonging to a regiment then quartered in Kilkenny. The original MS. was recently in the possession of that learned antiquary, the late Rev. James Graves, A.M., Rector of Inisnaig, diocese of Ossory.

During the three or four years following his settlement in Kilkenny Bishop Pococke found much to occupy his attention in his diocese, with intervals for the study of Irish antiquities and ecclesiastical remains.[1] Thus in 1757 he communicated 'An Account of some Antiquities found in Ireland' to the London Society of Antiquaries, and after his death it was published in the second volume of *The Archæologia*, 1773, together with plates of twelve gold ornaments. In that paper the Bishop alludes to a communication on Irish golden antiquities made in 1747 by Mr. Simon[2] of Dublin. The MS. of the latter paper was found in the archives of the Society, and was communicated to the Royal Irish Academy on Feb. 10, 1862, by Mr. W. R. Wilde, V.P.

All the literature relating to Scotland which he could command had been carefully digested—Bede, *Anglo-Saxon Chronicles*, Camden, Buchanan; Sacheverell's *Isle of Man and Iona*; Dean Munro's and Martin's *Western Isles*; Gordon's *Itinerarium Septentrionale*; De Foe's and Mackay's *Journeys*; Richard of Cirencester's *Itinerary*, etc. He now felt himself fully informed

[1] Communicated by Dr. W. Frazer, Dublin.   [2] P. xlvii.

and equipped for his extensive tour through Scotland, and for realising his long-cherished wish of visiting the Orkneys. He left his palace in Kilkenny on the 12th April, and visited Eirke by the way, where he discharged the last ecclesiastical duty required of him, as recorded in *Pues Occurrences*, Kilkenny, April 14, 1760. 'Sunday last [April 13] Mr. Francis Warden Flood was ordained a Deacon in the Parish Church of Eirke by the Right Rev. the Lord Bishop of Ossory.'

He then went by Dublin *en route* for Donaghadee, where he embarked for Scotland, accompanied by his two servants, a valet and groom. Landing in Portpatrick on 30th April, he started on his six months' tour. Immediately he commenced letter-writing, and seems to have literally written whilst he rode. Having landed on soil sacred with memories of St. Ninian, he went in search of the site of the City of Leucopibia, and Bede's traditional Candida Casa, and appears to have been well satisfied with his investigations.

A few days later he is at work sketching the ruined Abbey of Dundrennan, and has favoured us with a cartoon of himself[1] interrogating a rustic, who with doffed hat is respectfully but earnestly describing what little he knew of the venerable remains.

After visiting the south-western counties, he crossed the border into England, and spent a week revisiting some places he had seen in 1747 and 1750. Returning into Scotland, he travelled on through Clydesdale to Glasgow, finding along his route abundant employment for his pen. Glasgow he had seen in 1747, then a city of about 20,000 inhabitants; but as he proceeded northwards along the western banks of Loch Lomond all was new. Reaching Inveraray he trended still westwards, bent on a pilgrimage to I-Colm-Kill—the sacred Isle of the West.

There is a little circumstance connected with the Bishop's visit to this illustrious island which may not be too trifling to notice.

[1] P. 12.

BIOGRAPHICAL SKETCH.

It will have been observed that the first and second letters addressed to his mother are commenced in somewhat stiff and unfilial terms, 'Honoured Madam,' although the concluding sentence of the first letter, 'Pray give my very kind love to my sister,' shows that he was not devoid of affection. All the letters to his sister up to the one descriptive of Iona commenced 'Dear Madam,' but afterwards invariably 'Dear Sister.' Had his heart been touched, or his affection grown more tender, amidst the ruins of Iona—had he felt impressed by changeful time and a forgotten past? Or had he felt a sense of loneliness, deepening into sadness, and, thinking of his sister, soliloquised—

> 'What dost thou now? Beside the hearth, no doubt,
> The map is spread, your eye pursues my route;
> You say, "Where is he? may each place supply
> Kind service, and some heart that loves and cares?"'

Turning his back on St. Columba's Isle, the Bishop proceeded northwards through the wilds of Lochaber, following the road made by General Wade, and, sailing down Loch Ness, reached Inverness, where he visited the tragic field of Culloden. The battle, having taken place only fourteen years previously, would be fresh in the memories of those from whom he gathered his information respecting it.

Travelling northwards through Easter Ross, he entered Sutherland, and penetrated through the midland wilds and morasses to the famous Broch Dun Dornadilla.

> 'Dun Dhornghil mac Dhuibhe
> Air an taobh ris an ear do 'n t-srath.'

Perhaps the accounts of Iona and Sutherland are the most interesting and valuable of the Bishop's Journals.

Proceeding from Cape Wrath to Thurso along the north coast, he was ready to embark for the Orkneys.

His cotemporary, Bishop Forbes, has preserved a pen-picture of Dr. Pococke which differs from Cumberland's opinion already quoted, and represents him rather as a pleasant, genial, jocular man, able to adapt himself to every circumstance and society —qualities essential to a traveller.

The Doctor had been the guest of Mr. Murray of Pennyland, near Thurso, and 'had dined and ate heartily of fried chicken, and liked it so well that he desired to have a receipt for dressing of it, as there is no such dish in England or Ireland. There was another Dish, which he took to be Enammelet, but it happened to be toasted Ears. "Toasted ears!" said he; "what is that?" "Why," said Mr. Murray, "the Ears of a Calf toasted on Bread." He liked it much. But what surprized him most of all was the fine Wheat-Bread he ate here, of which he said he had not got any since he came into Strathnaver, through which he travelled in his way to Caithness; and he begged to know how they came by it. When they told him it was baked in a Pot, he was amazed, insomuch that it behoved them to assure him it was so, before he could believe it; and he declared he had never ate better all his Life; and so plentifully did he take of it, that Mr. Murray jokingly said, "Stop, my Lord, else your Lordship will raise a Famine in ye Country;" which pleased him so well, that he called to his own Servant, "John, pray, give me t'other cut of that fine Loaf." And, when he came to Wick, he desired his Servant to see if he could have a Loaf baked in a Pot to take along with them. He had two Servants, viz., a Valet and a Groom.'[1]

We are indebted also to Bishop Forbes for the statement that the Doctor was accompanied by two servants.

Thence he sailed to Orkney, the *Ultima Thule* of his long-cherished wishes. Here he found much to occupy his pen and pencil—the Dwarfie Stone, the larger and smaller groups of Standing Stones at Stennis, the Cathedral and the Palace at Kirkwall.

Returning to the mainland, he continued his travels south through the eastern counties, scarcely omitting to visit and describe any one of the many abbeys, ruins, or places of in-

[1] Bp. Forbes's *Journals*, by the Rev. J. B. Craven, p. 200.

BIOGRAPHICAL SKETCH.

terest on his route. At Elgin he was much impressed with its beautiful Cathedral.

'Bishop Pococke was the only Bishop of the Church of England, since the Revolution, that preached and confirmed in Scotland when Episcopacy was there abolished. For in the summer of 1760, this prelate made a journey from Ireland to the north parts of it, viewing everything that was curious, and carrying away with him a variety of fossils, stones, minerals, and other natural curiosities. He preached and confirmed in the English Church in Elgin, and continued to do so in every other of that persuasion which he had occasion to be near, greatly regarded and esteemed by all ranks and degrees of people.'—*The Cambridge Chronicle*, October 5, 1765.

At Aberdeen he was received with every mark of respect, not only by the Episcopal clergy but by the Professors of the two Universities and the civil authorities. His biographer is indebted to the accurately kept Town Council Records for the account of his admission as an Honorary Citizen of Aberdeen.

Aberdoniae Quarto die Mensis Augusti Anno Domini 1760, In praesentia Magistratum.

Quo die Reverendus admodum in Christo Pater Richardus Miseratione Divina, Dominus Episcopus Ossoriensis, Municeps et Frater Guildae praefati Burgi de Aberdeen, In deditissimi amoris et affectus ac Eximae observantiae Tesseram quibus dicti Magistratus illum amplectuntur, Receptus et admissus fuit.

Conformably with the time-honoured custom, the new Freeman would wear the parchment and seal in his hat for one day.

Glasgow, Perth, Lanark, Forres, Nairn, Dornoch, did him the like honour of presenting him with a Burgess Ticket, but failed to record the presentations in their Minutes.

Pennant, the traveller, in 1772 also received the freedom of Glasgow and Perth; but we have it only on his own testimony, the respective cities not having recorded it.

We cannot follow the Bishop in his journeyings so closely as we could wish. On leaving Aberdeen he travelled to

Dundee, thence through the Carse of Gowrie and along the Banks of Tay to bonnie Dunkeld and Blair in Athole, where he spent some days with the Duke of Athole. We have already observed that Bishop Pococke frequently presented copies of his description of the East, *Egypt, the Holy Land, etc.* to gentlemen, as a mark of friendship, and in appreciation of kindnesses shown him. One set of volumes, with an autograph letter, was presented to Cadboll (Roderick M'Leod of the '45), but they were burnt in the destruction of Invergordon Castle. Another set of three volumes[1] was given to Captain Murray (who succeeded his uncle as third Duke of Athole in 1764), and the following letter is pasted in the first volume.

DUBLIN, *Nov.* 19, 1761.

SIR,—I received the honour of your letter. As I experience so many favours from your family; I took the liberty to request one more that you would do me the honour to permit that book to have a place in your library. I beg to present my best respects to the Duke and Dutchess and your Lady.—I am with great regard, Sir, your most obedient humble servant,

(Signed) R. OSSORY.

Pursuing his journey, he visited Perth, thence through Fife to the University City of St. Andrews. He then travelled along the northern shores of the Firth of Forth to Dunfermline. Ever inquiring after the curious, he was informed that at the inn here there was preserved an antique piece of royal furniture of elaborately carved workmanship—the nuptial bedstead of Queen Anne. He was much struck with it, and describes it most carefully; his admiration induced him to offer the landlady, Mrs. Walker, fifty guineas for it. She rejected the offer, and, being a zealous Jacobite, remarked that 'she still retained so great reverence for the two royal personages whose property it was, and who slept in it when they resided here, and to their posterity, all the gold and silver in Ireland was not fit to buy it.' Thus it was saved from eventually coming under the auctioneer's hammer with the Bishop's other

---

[1] Communicated by His Grace the Duke of Athole, p. 227.

curiosities, and is now preserved in Broomhall, having been converted into an ornamental chimney-piece.[1]

Leaving Dunfermline, he visited Dunblane, and travelled thence by Stirling to Edinburgh.

In the capital he found much to interest him, and his pen was not idle. He revisited many of the places he had seen in 1747. Proceeding eastwards, he visited Dunbar.[2] The geological formations there, attracted his attention so much that they formed the subject of a communication to the Royal Society.

Soon he arrived at the borders, where we must bid the traveller-Bishop adieu so far as his Scottish tours are concerned. His other tours may be the subject of another work.

It was now the end of September. He had been travelling incessantly since the middle of April, and yet apparently was not at all fatigued. The whole of October he occupied in journeying to London, where he arrived on the 29th, having travelled, according to an accurately kept itinerary, $3391\frac{1}{4}$ miles. His arrival in the Metropolis was at a time of great political commotion. King George II. had died four days previously, and all was excitement connected with the accession of the young King, George III., to the throne. People were all looking for the unexpected to happen, and those holding offices from the Crown, were personally and greatly interested in the new sovereign. The newspapers of the period had their limited news-space completely taken up with Court proclamations and accounts of the wars then proceeding, so we look in vain for any reference to Bishop Pococke's return from his wanderings, which at any other time might have received a passing notice.

The Bishop appears to have remained in London during the winter, and on the 12th March 1761 we find him preaching before the Governors of the Magdalen House Charity on behalf of that institution. His subject was 'The Happiness of

[1] Communicated by the Right Honourable the Earl of Elgin, p. 286.
[2] P. 322.

Doing Good' from the text, Hebrews xiii. 16, 'But to do good and to communicate forget not; for with such sacrifices God is well pleased.' This sermon was published, together with the account of the Charity (4to). A year later, on 27th June 1762, we find him again preaching in Dublin on behalf of a charity—The Society for Promoting English Protestant Schools in Ireland—text, 1 Thess. ii. 19, 20, 'For what is our hope, or joy, or crown of rejoicing? Are not even ye in the presence of our Lord Jesus Christ at His coming? For ye are our Glory and Joy.'

Bishop Mant, in his brief Memoir of Bishop Pococke (the best extant, though short), remarks, 'Of his mode of discharging his episcopal functions within his charge I find no account. But it is related that on an excursion which he made into Scotland, he visited many episcopal congregations, and preached and confirmed in them all. . . . It is mentioned here in connection with Bishop Pococke's life, for the sake of the inference that the zeal which animated him to such an exercise of his ministry in Scotland; could hardly have failed in prompting him to corresponding exertions in the sphere of his prescribed duty in his diocese. No notice has occurred to me of any theological works by Bishop Pococke, except of two sermons' (those referred to above).

That no other sermons were printed, and that no MS. sermons have been discovered among his literary remains, is not surprising when we recall his grandfather's example and precept, which doubtless would have weight with him—

'The mode of preaching of which Mr. Milles approved, and in which he more or less persevered through life, was rather a premeditation and recollection from only short notes or heads of discourses, than from whole sermons committed to writing. Nothing displeased him more, nor was more heartily despised by him, than a sermon wherein the preacher endeavoured to set forth his own fine thoughts, his gifts and talent, in the art of rhetoric and harangue, or his abstruse and nervous reasonings.'

Mr. Milles, however, had exceptions, for on occasion of his addressing a more educated audience than usual, such as at an assize or visitation, he preached from book.

If Bishop Pococke followed the example of his reverend grandfather, most of his sermons would be extemporaneous.

During the Bishop's absence from Ireland in October 1760, Kilkenny was visited with extraordinary floods. On his return to Ireland, he, with his characteristic acquisitiveness, gathered up all the information he could about them. The late Bishop O'Brien found amongst the Diocesan Records a bundle of MSS. labelled 'Pococke on the Flood,' and thought he had lighted on a treatise relating to the Noachean Deluge by this learned man; but on examination, found to his great disappointment, that they related to the Great Flood of October 1760, which caused such devastation and loss of life in Kilkenny. It is not known where those MSS. now are.[1]

When travelling through Mull he heard of the superstitious belief in second sight, and wrote: 'This is a subject I may consider in another place.' We are not aware that he carried out his intention; but the following letter from the minister of Golspie, shows that he must have been questioning every one at all likely to give him information on the subject. Probably the publication in the meantime of the volume by the pseudonymous author of the *Treatise on Second Sight*, Theophilus Insulanus,[2] deterred him.

To the Author. [*Treatise on Second Sight*, etc.]

Dear Sir,— . . . I am sorry you did not see the Bishop of Ossory in his travels through Scotland: that learned prelate, who has almost made the tour of Europe, Asia and Africa, was particularly fond to inquire into every thing that ascertained and threw light on the Second Sight; and I persuade myself, if you corresponded with him, that he would give a round sum for your

[1] Communicated by the late Rev. James Graves, Inisnaig.
[2] M'Leod of Hamir. *Vide* Article on Second Sight in Chambers's *Encyclopædia*.

lucubrations, and give them to the world in the history of his travels through Scotland, which he is now writing out for the press. He is a famous man in the learned world, and was, on that account sent, at the public's expense, to travel, long before the merit of his discoveries gained him the mitre; and I must acknowledge, I should have much higher joy in seeing you transmitted to posterity, hand in hand with Dr. Pocock, than in the way of publishing by subscription. You may easily correspond with the Bishop of Ossory, by sending your letters to a friend at London, who will see them into the Irish bag, if his Lordship happens not to be at London, where he is generally in the winter, or when he happens not to be immediately engaged in travelling. My friend begs to be remembered most respectfully to you, and you will please make my best compliments acceptable to your Lady, and Miss Mally.—I am, with esteem, dear Sir, your most obedient, and most humble servant, MARTIN MACPHERSON.

GOLSPIE, *February* 15. 1762.

During 1761-62 Bishop Pococke partially edited his Scotch Tours. The letters which had been sent home were now amplified and corrected, and copied by amanuenses into four quarto volumes. He enjoyed withdrawing from his palace at Kilkenny to the retirement of his chaplain's parsonage at Attanagh—the Rev. Mervyn Archdall's—where he framed the narratives of his travels through Ireland and Scotland, and which, Bishop Mant states, 'are said to have been lost.' The following letter from the Bishop of Carlisle, apparently in answer to an inquiry from Dr. Ducarel, confirms this:—

TAYMOUTH, PERTHSHIRE, *Sunday July* 31, 1768.

DEAR SIR,— . . . I am now at Lord Braidalbin's, one of the most improved spots in Great Britain; to-morrow Mr. Pitt and I go to the Duke of Athol's at the Blair. . . .

One quarto volume of Bishop Pococke's MS. Letters, containing his Travels over England, Scotland, and the adjacent Islands, is lost. The rest are in Dean Milles's possession; and there, if any where, occur his remarks on the Isle of Man. . . . —Your very obliged and faithful servant, CHA. CARLISLE.'

[1] Rev. Dr. Charles Lyttelton (afterwards Dean of Exeter, Bishop of Carlisle, and President of the Society of Antiquaries).

At those quiet literary meetings in his chaplain's parsonage, the Bishop and the Rev. Mr. Archdall studied to some purpose the monastic antiquities of Ireland; and, when the latter eventually published them in his *Monasticon*, he gratefully acknowledges his indebtedness to his Bishop thus:—

Dr. Pococke 'frequently noticed the defects of our monastic history, and urged the necessity of its improvement. He pointed out the method here adopted, procured many necessary documents, and had the goodness to encourage the author with solid favours. The work was difficult, and required unremiting perseverance. Authentick vouchers were not easily had, and, when they were, it was no small labour to decipher musty and worm-eaten manuscripts, and ascertain their contents.'

In addition to his episcopal duties, and antiquarian, scientific, and æsthetic pursuits, Bishop Pococke was eminently practical and benevolent. He encouraged Irish manufactures, especially the linen trade, and in furtherance of those objects he established the 'Lintown Factory' about the year 1763. It was situated on an eminence over the River Nore, in the suburbs of Kilkenny. Part of it is still standing, and occupied as a private house, with a good garden and field attached.[1]

Here were boarded very young boys, chiefly foundlings and illegitimate children of Roman Catholics and poor Protestants: they received Protestant religious and secular instruction, and were taught the trade of weaving. Subsequently the school was removed to a place distant about a mile from Kilkenny, and is now known as 'The Pococke College,' and conducted on a new system under the fostering care of the Incorporated Society for Promoting English Protestant Schools in Ireland.

The admission to this College—a very valuable institution—is in recent years by competitive examinations, and it turns out some excellent scholars. It is open to all children between the ages of twelve and sixteen attending parochial schools. They are fed, clothed, and taught for three years free, and

[1] Communicated by Mr. J. G. Robertson, Kilkenny.

may then compete for scholarships in higher schools under the management of the Incorporated Society. In the Board Room of the Society in Dublin is a fine oil painting of Bishop Pococke. The frontispiece[1] of this volume is from a photograph of it. Another portrait is said to have been painted.

'There was an admirable whole length of Dr. Pococke in Turkish dress, by Liotard in the possession of Dean Milles of Exeter, his first cousin.' It is not known where this portrait is now.

The founding of the weaving-school in Lintown led him to execute a will on the 10th July 1763, in which he made provision for its maintenance.

In 1764 the Bishop is again engaged on a lengthy tour through part of England, the account of which forms two volumes of MS.

In 1765 the Bishopric of Meath became vacant, and Dr. Gore, Bishop of Elphin, was appointed; and Dr. Pococke preferred to Elphin. But Dr. Gore, for monetary reasons, declined to take out his patent, so Dr. Pococke was translated directly from Ossory to Meath in July.

Bishop Pococke's life in Meath was measured by months, and yet his intense activity found scope in improving the grounds round the episcopal residence, where he planted cedar and chestnut trees, which still wave their luxuriant foliage at Ardbraccan, living monuments to this industrious man. Tradition says these cedars and some papyrus are the product of seeds brought by him from Syria.

On the 15th September the Bishop was engaged in a parochial visitation of his diocese, and when at Charleville, near Tullamore, suddenly died. Thus, just as he would have wished it, whilst engaged in his primary duties, the silver cord was loosed, the golden bowl was broken, and the spirit returned to God who gave it.

[1] The pen-and-ink sketch of the portrait was kindly executed by Mr. W. Allan Carter, C.E., Edinburgh.

BIOGRAPHICAL SKETCH. lxi

His body was interred in Bishop Montgomery's tomb at Ardbraccan, and on the south side of the monument is inserted a small slab in memory of the great traveller:—

By a strange fatality indeed it has fallen to the lot of a most unlettered muse to record the place where are deposited the remains of this amiable, learned, and charitable prelate, whose thirst after Knowledge prompted him to encounter so many dangers and labours.

>HERE LIES INTERED THE BODY OF
>DOCTER RICHARD POCOCKE
>BISHOP OF MEATH WHO DIED
>september 15th 1765 in
>the 63rd year of his age.

The inscription is cut on a tablet of Ardbraccan stone.

The two mutual friends of the late Bishop of Meath, Dr. Ducarel and the Bishop of Carlisle, exchanged sympathies on the occasion of their bereavement—

To Dr. A. C. DUCAREL, LL.D., F.R.S., & F.S.A.

HAGLEY HALL, *Oct.* 21, 1765.

DEAR SIR,—Though I hope to be in town some time next week and consequently shall see you soon, yet I cannot defer returning you my thanks by letter, for the very kind condolence you express on the great loss I have sustained in the death of my much esteemed old friend Bp. Pococke. Indeed, few things have ever affected me with deeper concern; but it is my duty to submit patiently to the will of God. . . . —Your obliged and faithful humble servant, CHA. CARLISLE.[1]

In the Cathedral of St. Canice, Kilkenny, a more worthy monument, bearing the following inscription, was erected to his memory by his former grateful parishioners—

>Sacred to the memory of Richard Pococke, LL.D:
>Who from the Archdeaconry of Dublin,
>Was promoted to this See [Ossory] MDCCLVI,

---

[1] Rev. Dr. Charles Lyttelton (afterwards Dean of Exeter, Bishop of Carlisle, and President of the Society of Antiquaries).

And translated to that of Meath MDCCLXV,
Where he died, September the 15th in the same year.
He discharged every duty of the Pastoral and Episcopal office
With prudence, vigilance, and fidelity;
Adorning his station
With unshaken integrity of heart and purity of conduct;
Attention to the interests of religion,
He caused several parochial churches to be rebuilt
Within this diocese.
He promoted and liberally contributed to the repairs
And embellishment of this Cathedral Church,
Then unhappily falling into decay.
A zealous encourager of every useful public work,
Especially the linen-manufacture,
He bequeathed a very considerable legacy
To the Governors of the Incorporated Society,
For promoting the united interests of industry
And charity,
Within this Borough of St. Canice.

There is yet another monument to this distinguished traveller, in a situation as romantic as it is unlooked for. There stands close by the famous Mer de Glace, in the picturesque Vale of Chamounix, a huge boulder of granite, left there many long years ago by the action of the glacier. On the side of this grand natural monument there is carved in deep letters:—

RICHARD POCOCKE, 1741.

This has been done by the inhabitants of the valley, who were anxious to commemorate the name of the man who, it may be said, first made it known to the world. Previously, those mountain wilds were sacred to the chamois hunter, and a few Benedictine Monks belonging to a Priory founded in 1090.

On the 19th June 1741, a little band of explorers set out from Geneva, by the valley of the Arve, for their difficult, and, as it was then considered, desperate march. The party con-

sisted of Dr. Pococke as leader; Lord Haddington,[1] his brother
Mr. George Baillie,[1] and Messrs. Chetwynd, Aldworth, Price,
Wyndham, and Stillingfleet. They took with them five domestics, and all were well armed.

After three days of peril and fatigue they arrived in sight
of Chamounix, about fifty miles from Geneva. The following
day they reached Montanvert and descended to the glacier
near the spot where the boulder now bears the name of
" Pococke " deep graven on its front. As they stood upon the
ice they drank to the health of Admiral Vernon (then engaged
in the war connected with the Austrian succession), and success
to the British arms.

An account of the journey appeared in the *Mercure de
Suisse*, and in the next year several Genevese, profiting by the
experience of the Englishmen, visited Chamounix. Others
soon followed, and when Dr. Pococke's and Mr. Wyndham's
account of their visit was published in England, a stream of
travel set in towards the highlands and valleys of Savoy.[2]

The Bishop's will already referred to, and the codicil, or
later will, dated just six months previous to his death, are so
unconventional and interesting that we give them in full.
They also clear up some mistakes his biographers have fallen
into—

WILL[3] of RICHARD POCOCKE Bishop of Meath. 1766.

I Richard Pococke Doctor of Law and Bishop of Ossory do
make my last Will and Testament in manner following. First I
give and bequeath to my dearly beloved Sister Elizabeth Pococke
Spinster of Newtown in Hampshire my house and land in Newtown Hampshire on which she now lives. I do leave all my
manuscripts to the Ratcliffe Library in Oxford. I do make the
Incorporated Society in Dublin for promoting English Protestant

---

[1] See Letter LXXII. p. 332.
[2] From a letter in the *Kilkenny Moderator*, by the Right Rev. the Bishop of
Ossory, 19th Nov. 1886. See note, p. xlvii.
[3] In the Public Record Office of Ireland, Four Courts, Dublin.

Schools in Ireland the Executors of this my last Will and Testament and I do give devise and bequeath to them all my Estate real and personal except as before excepted in trust for the uses following—I do leave to each of my Servants William Belcher and his Wife the sum of Ten pounds and to all the rest of my Men servants living with me in my House at Kilkenny the sum of five pounds each and to all my English Servants the sum of five pounds each over and above the ten pounds & five pounds in case they leave Ireland to settle in England—I do leave the Interest of all my Estate real and personal and all the income of my s^d Estate real and personal to my Sister aforesaid during her natural life, desiring it may be remitted to her quarterly as it comes in. And after the decease of my s^d Sister I do leave my Estate real and personal for the uses following, To found a weaving School at Lintown near Kilkenny in the House I built for weaving, for Papist boys who shall be from twelve to sixteen years old and who have not been at any school before of any publick foundation & particularly in none of the Charter Schools, to be apprentic'd to the Society at fourteen years old for seven years, said boys to be bred to the Protestant religion, I do desire that all my antiquities and everything relating to natural History and all my coins & medals be sent to England to London to be sold by public auction as likewise all my books which will not sell here according to a just value. And I desire that the Rev^d Mr. Mervyn Archdall be requested to pack up my natural curiosities and label them for which I desire that a proper present be made to him tho' he is a signing Witness to this Will. I declare this to be my last Will & Testament all written with mine own hand & desire it may stand good tho it may be deficient in point of law. Signd seald and declard this tenth day of July 1763

Signd seald and declard to be the last Will & Testament in presence of the Testator and of each other—   Richard Ossory   (Seal)

Wm Cockburn—Mervyn Archdall—Nich^s Marten.

In the Name of God Amen, I Doctor Richard Pococke Bishop of Ossory Being in pretty good health and of sound mind & memory but sensible of the uncertainty of human life Do make this my last Will & Testament in manner & form following, And first I do bequeath my Soul through the Merits and Intercession of Christ Jesus and most mercifull Redeemer to be washd

BIOGRAPHICAL SKETCH. lxv

clean & pure by his Most precious blood to be presented without spot to our most mercifull Creator and my body to be privately buried as either my Executors or the next of kin shall direct I do leave to my dear Sister Elizabeth Pococke of Newtown in Hampshire Spinster my house and land in said parish of Newtown. I do leave to my Servants William Belcher & his Wife each of them twenty pounds. And to all my other Servants living with me in my house at the time of my death the sum of five pounds each and to all those who are English and immediately transplant themselves into England five pounds more to each to bear their charges. I do desire that my Chaplain the Rev^d Mr. Mervyn Archdall do pack up carefully my natural collection and direct the packing up all my antiquities all to be sent to London to be sold in proper lotts at public auction for which trouble I do bequeath him the sum of Twenty five pounds And it is my Will that they be sent by long sea to London as my Executors shall direct. I do leave all the rest of my Estate real and personal to the incorporated Society in Dublin for promoting English Protestant Schools in Ireland in trust for the uses following, First that the Interest and rents be paid half yearly to my said Sister Elizabeth Pococke or her order for & during her natural life and then to Elizabeth Milles Spinster of Higham Towers for & during her natural life, excepting that I do leave to said Elizabeth Milles four pounds a year English money during her life, four pounds a year English money to Jane Bingham of Havant Spinster during her life. And then I do leave all my Estate real and personal for founding a School for papist boys from twelve to sixteen years old who shall become protestants and to be bred to linnen weaving and instructed in the principles of the protestant religion s^d boys not to have been at any school before of any public legal foundation, & particularly in none of the Charter Schools, to be apprenticed to the Society after they are fourteen years old for seven years. Desiring that my manufactury house at Lintown Kilkenny if not disposd of by me be applied for that use. And if the Society shall think it better to sell any of my leases I desire the produce may be disposd of in some Government security. And if any other religion shall at any time be established than the present protestant religion I do then leave the whole for such time to St. Patricks Hospital in Dublin for lunatics under the direction of the Archbishop of Dublin for the time being and of the other Governors of said Hospital. To revert to the said Society whenever it shall be re-established for the purposes above mentiond I do leave the said Incorporated Society in Dublin the Executors of this my last Will & Testament I do leave all my manuscripts to the British Musœum in London to the Governors or Trustees thereof.

The above Will written with my own hand on the 24th day of March 1765 I do desire may be lookd on as a Codicil to the other Will signd & seald as far as it differs for it not having here in London convenient witnesses.

These wills were duly proved in the Prerogative Court, and his executors, the Incorporated Society of Dublin, gave at least partial effect to the Testator's wishes.

Bishop Pococke in his first will bequeathed his MSS. to the Radcliffe Library, but in his codicil revoked the bequest in favour of the British Museum, and on the 9th May 1766, the Bishop's Irish collections were duly presented to the Museum by Dean Milles. They are numbered from MS. 4755 to MS. 4802.

Very many volumes of MSS. which ought to have been delivered to the Museum were withheld, and for a couple of generations remained private property; but subsequently some of them, as they were offered for sale, were purchased by the British Museum Library authorities. Thus the four quarto volumes[1] which supplied the text for the present publication, and two volumes of travels in England, were not presented to the Museum, but were bought at the sale of Dean Milles' library at Sotheby's so lately as the 15th April 1843, for £33. The Bishop's rich literary legacy appears to have lain unnoticed for twenty-one years, when the following letter drew some little attention to it:—

To RICHARD GOUGH, Esq. [Enfield].

TREASURY CHAMBERS, *Sept.* 26. 1787.

SIR,— . . . Whenever you happen to visit the British Museum I would recommend it to you to run your eye through the minutes of a Philosophical Society formerly held in Trinity College, Dublin, which Bishop Pococke presented to the Museum. . . .

J. C. WALKER.

[1] Add. MSS. 14,256 to 14,259, Brit. Mus. Dept. of MSS.

Among the MS. treasures the gift of Bishop Pococke, are the 'Minutes and Registers of the Philosophical Society at Dublin, from 1683 to 1687, with a copy of the papers read before them, and Register of the Philosophical Society of Dublin from August 14, 1707, with copies of some of the papers read before them; also several extracts taken out of the records of Bermingham's Tower; an account of the Franciscan abbeys, houses, and friaries in Ireland; and many other curious articles of Irish history. The Philosophical Society was founded on the plan of the Royal Society of London in 1683, by Mr. William Molyneux, the friend and correspondent of Mr. Locke, under the encouragement of Sir William Petty, who was the first President, as Mr. Molyneux was the first Secretary, in which post he was succeeded by Mr. Saint George Ashe, Professor of Mathematics in the University of Dublin. The Society met at first weekly, and their minutes were from time to time communicated to the Royal Society. In the confusion of 1688 they were dispersed, and never resumed their meetings.'

Of the sale of the Bishop's books we have no account, but of his collection of Greek, Roman, and English coins and medals we have a full description. They were sold by auction by Langford & Son, at their house in the Great Piazza, Covent Gardens, London, on the 27th and 28th May 1766. A printed catalogue of this sale is preserved in the Trinity College Library, Dublin, and it has the additional interest of being marked with the prices realised. Two articles may be mentioned:—No. 114. A silver pastoral staff of St. Kerian, the first Bishop of Ossory (no price). No. 115. A curious antique British bracelet, weight 3 oz. 10 dwt. 7 gr. £2, 12s. 6d.

His collection of antiquities and fossils was sold by Messrs. Langford, June 5th and 6th, 1766.[1] Among these was a singular petrified echinus, found in a chalk-pit in Bovingdon parish, in Hertfordshire, which Sir Thomas Fludyer bought

---

[1] I should be glad to be informed where a copy of the printed catalogue of Fossils, etc., may be seen.—D. W. K.

for three guineas; Mr. Seymour offered five guineas for it at his sale, Mr. Foster six guineas, and it was sold for ten guineas.

These sales dispose of the erroneous statement in Cotton's *Fasti Eccles. Hib.* that 'he bequeathed his collection of coins, medals, fossils, etc., to the British Museum.'

There is another error which it may be as well to correct. Bishop Mant speaks with feelings of pride of his connection with Bishop Pococke, through his sister having been 'married to the reverend and very learned Joseph Bingham, author of *The Antiquities of the Christian Church.* We have seen in the wills that Miss Elizabeth Pococke, the Bishop's only sister, is called a spinster—she was never married. Bishop Pococke's father's sister, Dorothea Pococke, however, married the Rev. Joseph Bingham, and it was through a daughter of this marriage that Bishop Mant ought to have claimed descent and connection with the Pococke family.

The wills, especially the later one, are sweetly simple and reverent, affectionate and benevolent. The testator wrote his settlement none too soon—the shadow had already begun to fall, and, realising the momentous responsibilities and obligations of life, he, strong in that faith of which he had been the exponent, committed his spiritual being to his Creator through redemption, and his material being to repose again among the dust.

Having no other ties, he, with true fraternal affection, made his sister his chief legatee, and after she and other beneficiaries had enjoyed during their lifetime the revenues of his estate, they were free for the benevolent uses conceived by him for the education, clothing, and feeding of a number of poor boys—thus the Pococke College eventually arose—through means of which many a boy has had good cause to call the pious Founder blessed.

Bishop Pococke probably appraised his literary legacy to the nation even at a higher value than his material wealth.

It was his own, his life's work—had cost him much time and money, fatigue and hardship—was the product of untold labours and sacrifices. No wonder, then, that he thought the only fitting resting-place for his MSS. was alongside similar literary treasures in our greatest national library—in the hope that one day they might be of value, and we are only now waking up to appreciate the gift.

Scottish literature would have been all the richer had Bishop Pococke's *Tours* been published at the time they were written, and under the editorship of their author.

They would doubtless have been as often quoted as Pennant. That topographist appears both to have known and consulted the Pococke MSS., and probably drank more deeply into them than we are aware.

His general plan, descriptions, and itinerary, closely resemble them. On a blank page of the MS. is a note[1] initialed 'T. P.': most probably Thomas Pennant. In his account of Iona, referring to the Cladh an Diesart, he writes:[2] 'Bishop Pococke *mentions* that he had seen two stones seven feet high,' etc. Where had the Bishop mentioned it? only in his MSS., where Pennant doubtless saw it. Referring to the Angel's Hill in Iona, he writes:[3] 'Bishop Pococke informed me that the natives were accustomed to bring their horses to it.' It was twelve years before this that the Bishop had been to Iona, and he had been dead seven years before Pennant visited the island. Again, referring to those lofty hills above Loch Leven, he wrote:[4] 'My old friend, the late worthy Bishop Pococke, compared the shape of one to Mount Tabor.' It is improbable that Pennant could have remembered scraps of conversation about places he had never seen, and which at the time he perhaps never thought of seeing. The Bishop of Carlisle, in the letter already given, wrote in 1768: 'One quarto volume of Bishop Pococke's MS. letters, containing his travels over England, Scotland, and the adjacent islands, is lost.' May it not have been then in the

[1] P. 68.   [2] P. 85.   [3] P. 86.   [4] P. 97.

possession of Pennant, who was preparing for his first tour through Scotland in 1769 ?

Thus Pococke's *Tours*, although sleeping in manuscript for more than a century, may have been to a considerable extent living in Pennant's pages.

At this time of day the Bishop's *Tours* are more confirmative than informative; still the archæologist and topographist will find much to interest them, especially in the descriptions of the western and northern districts; and the student will here and there get pleasing glimpses of Scottish life and character in the middle of the eighteenth century.

If the work should be tried even by the severe standard so well expressed by the venerable physician, Sir Alexander Dick, to the great lexicographer, Dr. Johnson—that no travels should be published but those undertaken by persons of integrity, and who describe faithfully—we venture to think the verdict would amply justify the present publication; coupled with the regret that its appearance should have been delayed so long. D. W. K.

JOURNEY THROUGH SCOTLAND

IN 1747—FIRST TOUR.

LETTER I.

DUBLIN, *Nov. 5th*, 1747.

HONOURED MADAM,[1]—As I observe some things which will not properly come into my account, so I propose to give you my journal[2] besides the account[3] I send you, and I will begin with Sunday the 27th of Septr., when Mr. Blackbourn at Richmond sent me his canonicals,[4] I went to his house, preached for him and dined with him, Mr. York with us; went to even prayers,—walked over Mr. York's improvements, drank tea there, came home and writ. . . .[5]

I had compliments to Mr. Robinson at Holy Island, who showed me all and dined with me at Berwick. I soon after came into Scotland; and almost the first thing that presented to my view was a Scot lying down with a great club by him and his eyes fixed down—and as I passed by him he gave me such a slive,[6] as a dog that has done some mischief.

---

[1] Dr. Pococke's mother, Mrs. Elizabeth Pococke, addressed to Newtown, near Newbury, Berkshire.

[2] This letter, which Dr. Pococke calls his *Journal*, is more personal and sketchy in style than are the accounts of his journeys.

[3] The MS. of the *account* referred to is not known to exist, and the probability is that the Dr. incorporated it in that of his great journey in 1760.

[4] Dr. Pococke was at the time Archdeacon of Dublin.

[5] The part omitted describes the journey from Richmond by way of Appleby, Penrith, Carlisle, Hexham, Durham, Morpeth, to Berwick.

[6] *Slive;* a local word—to sneak. 'Pegge calls a sliving fellow one who, in our northern dialect, loiters about with a bad intent.'—*Todd's Johnson's Dict.*

At Eding I asked whose house[1] that was? they told me the house of the Laird of Eding; I asked his name, they said, Thomas Feldice. At Old Cambay[2] I asked them if they went to the Kirk? yes, and they had no meeting-house there.

10th [Oct.].—I rid through Dunbar, dined at Beltonford, saw the spot of Prestonpans;—came to Edinburgh—went to lodgings: Dr. Grant an Episcopal minister I had a letter to, came and spent the even with me.

11th.—I went to the Kirk, drank tea, preached[3] for Dr. Grant, he dined with me at 4 and spent the even with me.

12th.—Dr. Grant breakfasted with me, we walked to Leith, —went to the Islands called Inchkeith and Inchcomb.

13.—Rid with Dr. Grant to Mussulboroug, Inverask, and seat of the Duke of Buccleugh at Smyton[4] and Dalkeith; came home and dined, saw the Advocates' Library. Dr. Grant sat a while with me.

14.—I was at Dr. Grant's door—visited Messrs. Hamilton & Balfour—saw the Hospitals and King's palace—dined with Dr. Grant, saw some other Hospitals—went to the Coffee-house, gave a letter there to Mr. Lyon of the Castle—went to the Kirk.

15.—Breakfasted with Mr. Hamilton; rid to St. Catherine's Spring, to Roslin Chapel, where Baron Clerk met me carryed me to Hawthornden and to dine at his house; where the Lord Provost[5] was come home, sup'd with the Lord Provost.

16.—I saw the Abbey Church and the Castle, breakfasted there with Mr. Lyon. Saw the College Library and set out.

---

[1] Probably the mansion-house of Ayton, then the seat of Mr. Fordyce.

[2] Old Cambus, in the parish of Cockburnspath, was then a considerable village, but is now reduced to a few cottages.

[3] On January 25th, 1747, a qualified Episcopal meeting-house was opened in Skinner's Close, Edinburgh, 'by Mr. James Grant, who was assistant to the minister of Inveresk, but went thence to London last summer, and is now a Presbyter of the Church of England.'—*Scots Mag.*, Jan. 1747, p. 47. The Bishop of London licensed Mr. Grant. It was probably in this meeting-house that Archdeacon Pococke preached.

[4] Smeaton, an old jointure house of the Buccleuchs.

[5] George Drummond, seven times elected Lord Provost of Edinburgh. A marble bust of him by Nollekins, also a portrait, long occupied conspicuous places in the old Royal Infirmary, with which he was so honourably associated; they are now in the new one—the former in the entrance hall, and the latter in the board room.

Rid through Cramond seven miles to Lord Hopetown's, to whom I had a letter, he was abroad, to Dr. Dundass, he walked with me in the garden, returning found my friend Mr. Mitchel, member for Aberdeen and secretary under the Marquise of Twidale, with my Lord we dined;—I saw the house and pictures my Lady putting herself in the way, went with me;—she is a most amiable woman, daughter of Lord Finlater, and has charming children. I walked with my Lord in his gardens and grand stables; we drank tea, spent the even in discourse; in seing my Lord's minerals, Cameo's, and Intaglio's; and at supper. I had made a motion to go after dinner, but my Lord desired me to stay till the next morning.

17th.—We breakfasted, they always bring toasted bread, and besides butter, Honey and jelly of Currants and preserved orange peel. My Lady had on the . . . . .[1] of the arms, with open work, and fine lace at the end, which looked very neat. My Lord rid with me two miles. I went to Lithgow, dined at Falkirk, came to Sterling,—Mr. Duncan fellow of St. John's Col. Oxon, and chaplain to Barril's Regiment there.

18th.—I went up to the Castle, Mr. Duncan called on me, I went to his lodging, took a walk; preached to the Soldiers in the Court-house—saw the Castle, dined with Mr. Duncan and the officers—went to prayers—called at Captn. Thorns, we all went to see the rest of the Castle: drank tea at Captn. Thorns. I went home and writ.

19th.—I rid to Buchanan Castle near Lough Louman;[2]— dined, rid towards Dunbarton, lay at Kilmarnock.[3]

20.—Rid to Dunbarton, dined, saw the Castle:—came to Glasgow, Major Rufane spent the even with me: Mr. Professor Simpson[4] of the Mathematicks, called on me, I having a letter for him.

21st.—I saw the Cathedral, the manufactures etc.: Major Rufane joyn'd me, and Mr. Professor Simpson, showed us the College and Library. I was made a freeman[5] of Glasgow, the

---

[1] Blank in the MS. [2] Loch Lomond.
[3] Kilmaronock, on the military road from Stirling to Dunbarton.
[4] Robert Simson, M.D., author of several Mathematical works in Latin.
[5] Mr. J. D. Marwick, LL.D., Town-Clerk of Glasgow, has caused the Council records to be thoroughly searched, but no reference to Dr. Pococke has been found. The Roll of Burgesses by purchase has been most accurately kept, but

Lord Provost presenting me with it; and then putting it in my hat,—I put on my hat;—we drank some healths, and I wore it through the town, to the place where I dined with the Professors. I did some business;—Major Rufane and Mr. Uri,[1] a learned bookseller came and sat a while with me.

22d.—Major Rufane two officers and the Dr. rid with me, saw Bosworth[2] Castle and Duke Hamilton's dog-house and house; dined took leave of them; rid 18 miles to Kilmarnock, where Lady Kilmarnock died lately.[3]

23d.—Rid to Air, dined, sold my 3 guinea horse, for one guinea, he had performed well. I baited at Garvey,[2] lay at Balenfrey.[2]

24.—Rid to Lord Stair's[4] improvements[5] at Castle Kennedy, —went by the rout to Port Patrick.

25.—Sent my things aboard, but being windy would not go, they had a terrible wet passage. Mr. Hamilton, Collector of . . .[6] who was going over, and the controller spent the even with me.

26.—We sailed in 5 hours to Donaghadee, a fine passage but I was very sick:—they go in open Hoys,[7] which have no deck.

---

it would appear not to have been thought worth while to engross the names of all the honorary freemen. It looks as though in those good old times, councils presented the freedom of their burghs to distinguished visitors, less for the honour of building up their Rolls of Fame, than as occasions affording agreeable opportunities for conviviality, speech-making, and drinking of healths. See notes to Lanark, Dunrobin, Forres, and Aberdeen letters.

[1] Robert Urie, a printer and publisher of a number of works, both in classical and general literature; perhaps his finest specimens are his editions of the Greek New Testament and the *Spectator*.

[2] Bothwell.—Girvan [?], and Ballantrae, towns on the old mail-coach road between Glasgow and Portpatrick.

[3] Lady Kilmarnock's recent death would be a subject of conversation at this time. Her late husband, William, fourth Earl of Kilmarnock, had joined the Rebellion chiefly at her instance, and was beheaded 18th August 1746. She did not long survive her sorrows, and died of a broken heart a month previous to Dr. Pococke's visit.

[4] John, second Earl of Stair, died 9th May 1747.

[5] On again visiting Castle Kennedy, thirteen years later, Dr. Pococke was disappointed with the improvements. See p. 12.

[6] Blank in the MS.

[7] A Hoy was a small coasting vessel, usually rigged as a sloop, and generally employed in carrying passengers and luggage.

I took over my excellent mare. Mr. Nevin the Minister came and took me to his house.[1] . . .

29. Rid to Burgh mills—went to Mr. Clenes a clergyman dined with him and he went with me to see that most stupendous work of nature, the Giant's Causeway.[2] . . .[1]

Nov. 4th.—My coach met me, and Dr. Thomas in it at Drumcondra, I came to Dublin;—called at the Bishop of Waterfords door. On Mr. Fletcher, Mrs. Hyde, at Mr. Colemans, and Mrs. Travers door; visited Mr. Bristow—came home, Dr. Barber came to see me. He and Dr. Thomas dined with me. I went out incog. to a gallery to see the new Ball room and company. The Lord Mayor S^r. George Ribton came to see me,—the Alderman knighted by the Ld. Lieutenant.

5.—I visited the Archbishop of Dublin, the Primate, the Speaker, and Mrs. Chinevix,—went to Christ Church where the Bishop of Fernes preached before the House of Lords. I dined with the Lord Mayor a grand Entertainment: visited Mrs Reynell.—Pray my very kind love to my sister, I am, dear Madam, your most Dutiful Son,

RICHARD POCOCKE.

[1] The parts omitted describe the journey from Donaghadee to Drogheda, *via* Belfast, Antrim, Ardmagh, Newry, and Dundalk.

[2] Dr. Pococke communicated 'An Account of the Giant's Causeway in Ireland' to the Royal Society, London. *Philosophical Transactions* 1748, vol. xlv. p. 124; and 'A farther Account' in 1753, vol. xlviii. pt. 1., pp. 226 and 238. See Note about Dunbar, 20th September 1760.

JOURNEY INTO SCOTLAND
IN 1750—SECOND TOUR.

LETTER II.

PENRITH IN CUMBERLAND, *July* 22*d*, 1750.[1]

HONOURED MADAM,[2]—I came into Scotland the 16th of July when I crossed over the river Sarke and came to Greatney Bridge, where we took some refreshments, and rid about six miles to the north to Bernis[3] near Middleby, which was a Roman town, and is thought to be Blatum Bulgium the fossee of the town remains, and on a stone in one of the houses I saw these letters

AXSAN
CONIS.

We went to Midleby where there is a hill which had been fortified by art, and what they call a strength;[4]—we then went on to that famous hill Burnswork,[5] which appears at a distance with a square top like a lake;—we ascended this hill which commands a glorious view of the country round as well as of

---

[1] In that year Dr. Pococke made an extensive tour through the northern counties of England, and visited a few places of interest in the Scottish Border.

[2] This letter is addressed to his mother.

[3] Birrens: 'Several inscriptions have been found here, but most of them broke to pieces; some are entirely built up within the walls of the cottages. I saw one stone with Roman letters upon it, but so defaced, that it was unintelligible.'—*Gordon's Itinerarium*, 1727, p. 18. This fragment of an inscription, CONIS, probably should have been read COH, *i.e.* Cohort. Pennant records the same stone, but spells the first word differently, AXAN CONIS.—*Pen. Scot.*, App. vol. iii. p. 409.

[4] Middleby Fort. See engraving, *Gordon's Itin.*, pl. 2.

[5] Camp of Burnswork. See engraving, *Gordon's Itin.*, pl. 1.

the sea and the western coast of England and of all the country of Annandale, and especially of those lakes which are made by the rivers to the north-west. This hill has two summits and tho' it is high affords very good pasturage;—there is a camp on the north side, and another on the south side on the very foot of the hill;—the people say that to the south was made by King Charles the first his army under Duke Hamilton and they certainly did encamp on it; but there is no doubt but that they are both Roman works; they are about half a mile long from east to west, and a quarter of a mile broad from north to south—that to the south has three entrances to the north with ramparts before them to defend the entrance, there is one entrance to the west. To the other there are three entrances to the south and I could discern a barrow only to the middle one:—they are supposed to be Castra Æstiva of Blatum Bulgium; and some think they are *Castra exploratorum*, and it is probable they were encamped on the north or south-side of the hill according as the weather favoured.

We descended from this beautiful hill and passed through a village called Todory Pill,[1] where I saw the ruins of an old tower or castle, and came to Eacle-Fechon[2] where we took some farther refreshments, and went on towards Dumfries, we crossed the river Anan and passed by Hotham[3] Castle very finely situated over the river, we crossed a ridge of hills and came into Nithsdale and arrived at Dumfries, which is pleasantly situated on the river Nith which winds so as to make a peninsula of the town and the fields to the north of it: the principal street is broad and well built of the red free stone in which this country abounds: there are two churches in the town, one of which if I do not mistake, is for an Episcopal congregation. They have an old building here called the Nework,[4] which as well as I could be informed served formerly as a warehouse.

---

[1] [?] Torbeck Hill, an upland farm, with adjoining village called Waterbeck.
[2] Ecclefechan.
[3] Hoddam Castle, the seat of the Kirkpatrick-Sharpe family. Sir Roger Kirkpatrick made 'siccar' the slaughter of John Comyn, who had been stabbed, not by command, but by the hand of Robert Bruce before he was King.
[4] The New Wark, a strong defensive edifice erected after the ancient Castle of Dumfries had fallen into ruins. No vestiges of it, the castle, or friary, now remain.

There are some litle remains of an old Friary in the town, famous in History for being the place where Cummins (who was suspected by Robert Bruce King of Scotland to have been treacherous towards him, in his conduct with the English) took refuge and was murdered by the King's command, on which the King was excommunicated by the Pope, and the chapel for ever interdicted in which the murder was committed; on which St. Michaels at the east end of town was built for the friary, which has a handsome steeple to it. There is a fine bridge here over the Nith into Galloway, this bridge and a waterfall made by art, to keep up the river for some uses, make a very beautiful prospect from the side of the river, boats come up to the town, and ships of forty tuns within two miles of it, and they have here a great trade in Tobacco;—this town maintained its loyalty in the last rebellion, and severe contributions being raised on them 'twas made up to them by the government. Over the river near the town is a small mount[1] which would not hold at the top above thirty people, it is called the moot, and it is supposed that the heads of the place held their meetings here, and promulged their laws to the people:—there is a very fine prospect from it of the country round, I saw from it Lincluddin,[2] an old nunnery, and near it is a monastery called Holy Rhood;[3] and at some distance from Dumfries what is called New Abby and in their records Abbatia dulcis Cordis. Not far from Dumfries is a chapel called Christo,[4] where S^r.

---

[1] The Moat Brae.

[2] Founded in the reign of Malcolm IV., as a cloister of Black Nuns, by Uchtred, Lord of Galloway, but changed into a College or Provostry in reign of King Robert III. by Archibald the Grim, Earl of Douglas, for alleged scandalous lives of the nuns. Robert Burns composed several poems under the shadow of the ruins of Lincluden Abbey. Vide *Chronicles of Lincluden*, by Wm. M'Dowall, F.S.A. Scot., 1886.

[3] Holywood Abbey, called also Haliwood and Sacrinemoris, on the opposite or left bank of the Cluden from Lincluden, and said to have been founded by the Lady Devorgilla, Foundress of the New Abbey.

[4] Popularly called the Crystal Chapel; on its site stands St. Mary's Church. The Chapel was built by King Robert Bruce in memory of his father-in-law Sir Christopher Seton, the 'Gude Schir Christell,' who was hanged, not beheaded, on the spot, 'Christall's Mount.' The bulk of the ruins were used in forming a rampart wall at the time of the Rebellion in 1715. The last remains were used more recently in making the Kirk style at St. Michael's Church; *vide The Genealogie of the House and Surname of Setoun.*

Christopher Setin is buried, who was beheaded (tho' a Scotchman and no subject), for treason by Edward the First.

At Markland[1] in the shire of Galway, six miles from Dumfries, are chalybeat waters, esteem'd good for the appetite and spirits. Moffit is to the north east and forty miles from Carlisle, is much frequented for its mineral waters.

17.—I set out from Drumlandrig, the seat of the Duke of Queensborough, and came down into that fine vale in which the river Nith runs, gentle risings to the south, higher hills to the north, several country seats with improvements round them, with groves and clumps of fir trees over the whole valley, make it for about five computed miles, or eight measured miles, one of the most beautiful spots I ever beheld. We crossed the foot of the hill which stretches to the river; and going to the south of the Nith, passed by a mount to the left, much like a Danish fort, now planted by the Duke, this is called Tibers[2] Castle, and from the name, they have a notion that it is a Roman work. Drumlandrig is on the road from Glasgow to London, 42 computed miles s.w. from Edingburgh and 12 n.w. from Dumfries. This fine improvement is a very beautiful situation;—there is a gentle ascent to the house of about half-a-mile, which is on a flat on the side of the hill, with a descent from it of 100 feet perpendicular to the rivlet, the hills rising up every way except to the north, are covered with wood and cut into ridings. The house is something in the castle way, with a mixture of Roman Architecture in a bad taste:—they were at first hanging gardens, but the present Duke has turned them all into slopes, except the upper one, which is thirty feet high, and could not be so easily formed into a slope. His Grace has likewise planted this part with forest trees, and made a large piece of water at the bottom by keeping up the rivlet; there

---

[1] Markland Well, in the parish of Lochrutton, Kirkcudbrightshire, province of Galloway. It is a small chalybeate spring, 'an excellent restorer of appetite.' *New Stat. Ac.*

[2] Tibber's Castle: 'A *Roman Castellum*, but afterwards made a place of defence in the wars betwixt the English and Scotch, in the time of Edward I., and part of it re-edified with a stone and lime wall.'—*Gordon's Itin.*, p. 19. A spear-head, arrow-heads, etc., have been found in the ruins. Additional interest attaches to the site from the traditional adventure of Sir William Wallace, in surprising the English garrison, and burning the castle.

are 20 acres in the garden, and 700 under plantations: the prospect to the north is of the valley and hills and high mountains. The old seat and burial place of the family is six miles off at Sanchers,[1] where the present Duke's grandfather, who built this house lived, entertained his company here and rid home at night. The silver and lead mines belonging to the Duke and Lord Hopton are about twelve miles from this place.

I was informed that there are remains of a Roman road from Drumlanrig twelve miles to a loan foot[2] where it meets the road from Netherby, which goes fifty miles by Kirkle,[3] Eagle Fechon,[4] Lauherby,[5] Wamfrey,[6] Lough Cautie[7] and Erechstein.[8]—I am, dear Madam, your most dutiful Son,

RICHARD POCOCKE.

[1] Sanquhar. [2] Elvanfoot. [3] Kirtle.
[4] Ecclefechan. [5] Lockerbie. [6] Wamphray.
[7] Probably the old loch near Beattock Railway Station now drained; part of the ancient lands of the Johnston family, known as the Coitis, Coutis, or Cowtis, hence the name Loch Cautie. The loch lay behind the old Craigielands village, and was used within living memory as a curling-pond in winter; but when the Caledonian Railway was made, the village was removed and the loch filled up. There is on the Craigieland estate, not far distant, a place still designated Cautie Knowe.
[8] Errickstane.

Itinerary in computed and English measured miles, reckoning that 2 computed, make 3 measured miles—

	Computed Miles.	Measured Miles.
Gratney Bridge in Scotland,	6	8
Burnswork Hill,	8	10
Ecclefegan,	5	6
Dunfries,	12	16
Drumlandrig,	12	17
Dumfries,	12	17
Anan,	12	16
Carlisle,	12	15
	79	105

A JOURNEY ROUND SCOTLAND TO THE ORKNEYS

IN 1760—THIRD TOUR.

Letter III.

DUMFRIES, *May the 6th*, 1760.

DEAR MADAM,[1]—On the 30th of April, early in the morning, I arrived at Port Patrick in Scotland, which is a very poor place. Here [Port Patrick] they ship the horses from a rock, and when they land them from Ireland they help them out of the packet-boat into the sea, when they have brought the boat as near as they can to the shore. This place is in the [2]Mull of Galway, which is a peninsula about thirty miles in length and six broad, made by the bay of Loch Raiyen to the north, and the bay of Glenluce to the south. It was part of the country of the Novantæ, and called the Chersonesus of the Novantæ by Ptolemy. I went six miles to Stranraer on the former bay. This was doubtless the ancient Rerigonium of Ptolemy, from which it must have its name, as the bay is called by him Rerigonium. It is a small neat town, with an old castle in it. The inhabitants live chiefly by the Hering fishery, and use boats built of deal, which last five or six years. They manufacture flannel, blankets, and frize for their own

---

[1] Bishop Pococke set out from his palace, Kilkenny, on the 12th April 1760, for his extensive six months' tour through Scotland. He reached Dublin on the 23d April, and Donaghadee on the 29th, where he embarked in the regular packet-boat for Portpatrick, accompanied by his groom and valet. The letters are addressed to his sister Miss Elizabeth Pococke.

[2] Properly the Rhinns of Galloway.

use. The castle here was built by the Kenedys, from whom Lord Stair's famous place, Castle Kenedy, has its name. It is said they were drove out by the Dalrymples, who now enjoy the title of Stair.

The country of the Novantæ comprehends Galloway and the shire of Aire. The former is distinguished into the west part called the shire of Galloway,[1] and to the eastern part from Newton-Stewart, which is called the Stewartry of Galloway.

On the first of May I sett out eastward, and passed near Castle Kennedy, belonging to the late Lord Stair, which I saw in 1747, but it did not answer my expectations.[2] It is on a small lough, and laid out in walks planted on each side with high hedges, and is in a country where nothing is seen from it but hills and mountains covered with heath. We had in view the sandy banks near the bay of Glanluce, and coming near to the end of that bay towards the town of Glanluce, I turned off to the left to the Abbey of Luce, about a mile up the river Luce, which is supposed to be the Abravannus of Ptolemy, and to have had its name from the primitive word *Aber Avon* (the mouth of the river). It rises about twelve computed miles to the north-west. It was an abbey of Cistercians, called Glenluce or Vallis Lucis, founded in 1190 by Rolland,[3] Lord of Galloway, and Constable of Scotland. The Monks were brought from Melross. Lawrence Gordon, son to Alexander, Bishop of Galloway and Archbishop of Athens, was abbot of this place, that is, had the lands after the Reformation, his father having complied with the Reformation, and James VI. in his favour erected Glenluce into a temporal barony. His brother, John Gordon, Dean of Salisbury, succeeded him in it, who gave it to his son-in-law, Sir Robert Gordon.[4] It was afterwards

---

[1] The province of Galloway is divided into Wigtownshire and the Stewartry of Kirkcudbright.

[2] The Lord Stair referred to died in 1747. See p. 4.

[3] Rolland was the son of Uchtred M'Dowall, Lord of Galloway, who built Lincluden Abbey.

[4] Sir Robert Gordon was the second son of Alexander, Earl of Sutherland, and was created Premier Knight Baronet of Scotland. He married Louisa Gordon (then only 15 years and 2 months of age), only child and heiress of John, Dean of Salisbury or Sarum, and Lord of Longormes in France. Sir Robert

united to the see of Galloway. Then Sir James Dalrymple was created Lord Glenluce, and was succeeded by his son Sir John, who was Earl of Stair. There remains very little of the Abbey Church except a Gothic pier[1] of the middle arch. But to the west of it the chapter-house[2] is entire, and is about 24 feet square, built with a fine groined arch, supported by a beautiful slender Gothic pillar in the middle. Opposite to the entrance are some carved ornaments which were probably over the Abbot's seat, and on a scroll under a head that supports the arch is an inscription of one line, which is defaced. The ceiling is adorned with sculpture of roses, and there are two shields,[3] in one is a lyon rampant with a crown, in another the same without a crown, but there is a crown on the coat. Near this are ruins, probably of the Abbot's apartments, as to the north[4] of the church are remains of what we were told was the cloister with the dormitory, and adjoining to that the refectory.

Half-a-mile below this abbey, over the river, is The Park, Sir Thomas Hay's, a castle most beautifully situated on a ridge which is the foot of a hill, having towards the river a steep hanging ground covered with wood, and a more gentle descent southwards to the meadows on the bay adorned with trees. We soon came to Glanluce, a little town pleasantly situated. There we left the road to England, and went a mile in that which leads to Wigtown, and leaving it to the right, we took our way to Whithern, and in about two miles came to the bay of Glanluce, and travelled southwards

was the celebrated historian of the *Earldom of Sutherland*, which was published for the first time in 1813; the MS. is dated Dornogh, 1630. The original MS. is in the charter-room in Dunrobin Castle, but a beautiful transcript 'by Alexander Munro, Master of the Musick School at Tain, Anno Domini 1736,' is preserved in the Advocates' Library, No. 34, 3. 3.

[1] This pier still exists, it is the eastern pier of the south transept arch.

[2] The chapter-house lies to the south of the Church, not to the west, being part of the range of buildings running from the south transept, and forming the eastern side of the cloisters. The Bishop has made here a primary error in the points of the compass, consequently nearly all his bearings in this district are wrong.

[3] These shields carry respectively the lion rampant of Scotland, tressured and surmounted by a crown; and the crowned lion of the province of Galloway.

[4] The cloisters and all the monastic buildings lie to the south of the church, the existing nave wall forming their northern boundary.

near that bay about seven miles. They catch but little fish in this bay except mackrel, and between the rocks, when the tide is out, they find plenty of crabbs and lobsters. Towards the end of the head of land which is to the east of this bay, we turned to eastward, and soon passed by Sir William Maxwell's,[1] a castle with a lough[2] before it, and came to a very pretty village called Glass'ton [Glasserton].

Two miles more brought us to Whithern, finely situated about half-a-mile[3] from the sea. It is without doubt Leucopibia, or rather Leucooikia[4] of Ptolemy, probably from the British name Whithern, a white vessel or house. Here it is said Ninian, in the time of Theodosius the younger, preaching the gospel to the South Picts, built a church, which, Bede observes, was not according to the British fashion. It is said this church was dedicated to St. Martin; and, inquiring about it, they told me there was a church in the isle of Whithern dedicated to him, and they have a tradition that St. Martin came from Tours to this island. Bede says this country was in the hands of the English in his time, and that when Christianity got more ground here, it was erected into an episcopal see under the name of Candida Casa, which name it is said to have had from some white building. I came to this place to examine into the antiquities of it.

[1] Third baronet, now represented by Sir Herbert Eustace Maxwell, Bart. of Monreith, M.P., a gentleman who has done much for the archæology of Galloway, and whose forthcoming work on the place-names and topography of that ancient Province promises to be of the highest interest.

[2] Known as the 'White Loch.' On its banks, a short distance from the castle, is situated Monreith House, now the family seat. The castle, which is still extant, stands on an ancient mote, and was occupied till the close of last century.

[3] At the nearest point, Port-Yerrock, Whithorn is two miles distant from the sea.

[4] 'Near this [Wigtown] Ptolemy places the City Leucopibia, which I know not where to look for; yet, by the place, it should be the Episcopal See of Ninian, which Bede calls Candida Casa, and the English and Scots, in the same sense, Whit-herne. Now Ptolemy might (as he usually did) translate Candida Casa (as the Britons called it) into Leucoikidia, *i.e.* White-houses, for which the transcribers may have obtruded on us, Leucopibia. Furthermore, in this place, Ninia, or Ninian the Brittain, a holy man (who first instructed the Southern Picts in the Christian faith in the reign of Theodosius the younger) resided, and built a church dedicated to St. Martin.'—*Camden,* Edition 1701.

This rendering of the term used by the Greek geographer is quite unwarrantable, and equally so the attempt to identify it with Whithorn. All that is known of Ptolemy's Leucopibia is, that it refers to some place in the country of the Novantes and neighbourhood of Luce Bay.

Going to the church, I saw a Saxon[1] gateway, on one side of which are the episcopal arms, as they said, three chalices, but they seemed to be incense pots, and another coat, quartered, which appeared like a belt. Coming to the present church, on the south side of it is a very old Saxon door-case, a view of which is here given, and in another part a Gothic door of several members.[2] I am in doubt whether this might not be the old church, the cornice being very simple, consisting of a fillet and quarter round, and the quire seems to have been east of it, as they say the church extended that way, and the cloister to the south.[3] There are two arches,[4] part of large rooms remaining a little further to the south, and east of that is what they call the Prior's house. Near the supposed choir is a burial vault for the Priors, the last of whom, they say, was of the name of Flemming,[5] and near this is a large

[1] Here, as elsewhere throughout these letters, the term 'Saxon' is a misnomer, and, as used by Bishop Pococke, merely designates a round arch of any period in contradistinction to a pointed arch. The gateway mentioned still exists, and is known as 'The Pend,' giving access from the main street to the Parish Church, churchyard, manse, etc.

The arch itself, here called 'Saxon,' is modern, not older than 17th century. The pillars at the sides, bearing the arms referred to, are said to have been taken from the Prior's House, and may be of the 15th century. The shield on the right-hand pillar is surmounted by a mitre, and no doubt represents the arms of the Bishop of Galloway when the Priory House was erected. It is quarterly, first and fourth a bend dexter for Vans, second and third the objects referred to by Dr. Pococke, which are neither chalices nor incense pots, but the three covered cups forming the cognizance of the Shaws, quartered owing to marriage of Blaise Vaux of Barnbarroch with Elizabeth, daughter and heiress of Sir John Shaw of Haillie. On the left-hand pillar is a shield charged with a bend dexter diapered, and a pastoral staff behind it in pale, most probably representing the arms of the Prior, who seems also to have been a Vans. It is singular no mention is made of a large panel immediately over the arch with the Scottish Arms as borne before the Union, and forming the most prominent feature of 'The Pend.'

[2] Both of these doorways are still extant, the one of the 12th and the other probably of the 15th century. It was 'the old church,' or at least its nave, and then used as the Parish Church. A good part of the cornice or water tabling referred to still exists.

[3] The cloisters and monastic buildings at Whithorn must have been undoubtedly to the north of the Church.

[4] These arches existed within living memory, and were only demolished in 1822 in clearing the site for the present Parish Church, which is founded throughout on ancient remains.

[5] Malcolm Fleming was prior in 1540, and died 1568.

vault[1] open at one end. For in the time of David the First, Fergus, Lord of Galloway, founded here a priory of Premonstratenses, the members of which composed dean and chapter of the Cathedral. James Betune, Archbishop of St. Andrews [1522] and Chancellor of Scotland, was prior of this place.

Norman Doorway, Whithorn Priory.[2]

A quarter of a mile to the southeast of the town, towards the sea, is what they call the Castle of Bishopstown, which, it is said,

[1] Crypt of the south transept. This has been recently cleared out, and made the starting-point of extensive excavations undertaken at the instance of the Ayr and Galloway Archæological Association. In a forthcoming volume of the Association, Mr. W. Galloway, F.S.A. Scot., purposes to fully illustrate all the buildings, etc., of the Priory.

[2] This doorway is illustrated in *Ecclesiological Notes on Some of the Islands of Scotland*, by T. S. Muir, Edin. 1885, Frontispiece and p. 231.

was the Bishop's house. It seems to have been an oblong square.[1]
They speak of the garden extending towards the sea, and it is
indeed a most delightfull situation. This town consists mostly
of farmers and a few tradesmen and manufacturers in woollen
and linnen for home consumption. There is a square tower in
the middle of the street, which they always keep well whitened.
At the market-house is an old font[2] in shape of a capital, with
sort of reliefs at the top, something like the roses of a capital
of the Corinthian order. This they say always lay there, and
that the papists used to dip their children in it at baptism. It
was probably a font brought from the church. A little way
out of town, towards the isle of Whithern, is a stone like a
boundary, with a cross on it in a wheel. As the name of Peter[3]
is on it, the common people say St. Peter was buried there. It
was probably put up in memory of some like event. In all their
towns they set up dials on a pillar at the old market cross.[4]

Going to the isle, I saw they had been digging for coal, and
had raised a fine sandy yellow clay, but were obstructed by the
water. I could learn no other reason for their sinking for coals,
but that it was in the right line from Whitehaven, I suppose
north-west. I came to the isle, which is a little harbour
formed by a pier, within which they have 18 feet water at high
tydes, and a ship of 300 tuns can come in. They export barley,
and import plank and iron from Gottenburgh in Sweden, and
send it by boats to Wigtown, as the entrance and harbour
there are not good. There is a bridge over to the island, under
which the sea passes at high water. The principal houses are
on the west side of it, and on the Isle near the bridge is a row
of poor houses. This part of the isle is flat, and in high seas
the water seems to have come over and divided it from the

[1] This site is still pointed out, but being under the plough, all traces of the building have disappeared.

[2] There is no doubt that this was the original font pertaining to the 12th century church, and was recently removed from the Town Hall to its former place in the Priory.

[3] 'Hic est locus Petri Apostoli' is the inscription on the stone, according to Dr. Davidson in the *Old Stat. Ac.*, vol. xvi. p. 287, but the more correct reading is 'Loci Ti Petri Apvstoli.' For illustrations see Stuart's *Sc. St. Scot.*, part ii. pl. lxxvii., Muir's *Notes*, p. 233, Anderson's *Scot. in Early Chris. Times*, vol. ii. p. 252.

[4] Removed with the old Town Hall in 1814.

rising ground beyond it, on which there is a small church. The stones [1] have been taken out of the door and windows. There is only one remarkable thing in it, that on the south side of the east window, is a rough stone [2] that projects about eighteen inches, which probably was to set the vessels on for the sacrament. The ground rises higher beyond the church, and the east [3] end of the island has been defended by a fossee, which seemed to be very old, and it is probable that this was the ancient Candida Casa.

On the second of May I set out, and in about two miles passed Powtoun, [4] Lord Galway's seat, and three miles from Wigtown came to the Downs of Wigtown, which are very fine and edged with beautiful small hills. The top of one of them has been fortified. This down, as it is all called, is towards the river a marsh. Here they graze a great number of small oxen, which they send to a fair near Norwich, and they are fattened for six months in Norfolk, Suffolk, and Essex, for the London market. [5] Though small, they are larger than the common Scotch kind. We passed over the river Cree [6] on a large bridge, and soon came up to Wigtown, the capital of Galloway, most delightfully situated on an eminence which commands a view of this river, the bay, the sea, and all the adjacent coasts of Scotland and England. It consists of one broad street which, about the cross and market house, is like a square, and the houses are tolerable, but below it is narrower, with thatched houses on each side. The church is old, but the large Gothic east window is walled up. I could not get any account of a Dominican convent here, founded in 1267 by Dervorgilla, daughter of Alexander, [7] Lord Galloway, and mother of John Bruce [Baliol] King of Scotland. Near three miles from this is a ferry to Ferrytown, and a ford at low water.

---

[1] The only exception is the freestone sill of north window.
[2] This stone is still *in situ*.   [3] South end, not east.
[4] Powton House, a seat of the Earl of Galloway, is 3¼ miles from Whithorn.
[5] 'At the close of the third quarter of last century [*i.e.* 1675] from 20,000 to 30,000 Galloways (black polled cattle) were annually driven from their native pastures, feeding as they went along the old well-worn trails to the Norfolk or Suffolk fairs or markets, where they were bought up and fattened for the London Market.'—*Agricul. Reports Scot.* 1794-95.
[6] Bladenoch River, not the Cree.   [7] Alan, not Alexander.

We had a very pleasant ride, passed by Clary, a pleasant situation, being a ruined house of Lord Galloway's, and came to Newtown-Stewart, situated in a narrow valley, much like the face of Switzerland, adorned with firr groves. Some of the low hills are covered with wood, and there are high mountains to the north.—I am, etc.[1]

Letter IV.

Orton,[2] *May* 10*th*, 1760.

Dear Madam,—Newtown-Stewart is a neat little town, and there is a fine bridge of four arches over the river. On the 3d I went two miles to Garlais Castle in the middle of a wood. It is much destroyed, but there were great buildings about it. This place gives title to Lord Galloway's eldest son. What is called Cromwell's map, or the Quartermaster's, is so imperfect in these parts that I shall not attempt to correct it. I returned to Newtown, and came six miles to Ferrytown,[3] passing by some holes where they had attempted to get lead,[4] but it did not answer. They had the same fortune about three miles above Newtown.[5] Ferrytown is a poor little place on the side of the hill. We turned to the east and came among disagreeable mountains, travelled over a hill to a vale, and over

---

[1] None of the following letters are signed, and it is more than probable the originals were not. (See note 2.) Three of Dr. Pococke's *original* letters, dated 1743, describing places in the midland counties of England, in the possession of Robert Malcomson, Esq., Bennekerry Lodge, Carlow, are all unsigned. From these, and others in the British Museum, it would seem not to have been the Doctor's habit to subscribe merely descriptive accounts.

[2] In the MS. this place is written Corcum instead of Orton in Westmoreland, and is evidently a *lapsus pennæ*, arising from the difficulty of deciphering hastily written place-names in the original letters. Nearly all the volumes of letters relating to Scotland are the work of an amanuensis, and were apparently written under the personal superintendence of Bishop Pococke after his return to Ireland; the originals were then probably destroyed. It seems to have been the Bishop's practice to locate and date the letters immediately before franking them by the mail-coach; thus Orton, if scrawlingly written, might easily have been misread Corcum. See note, p. 32.

[3] The Ferrytown of Cree, Creetown.

[4] Traces of these old mines still exist at Balcraig, a short distance from Newton-Stewart on the Creetown road. At a place a little further on, lead mining was prosecuted latterly with considerable success.

[5] Perhaps the 'Wood of Cree' mine, where traces of old workings still exist.

two more to that pleasant romantic country through which the river Flete[1] runs into the bay, and came to the inn called Gatehouse of Flete. From the highest mountain[2] we passed I saw two other chains of mountains. From the south side of the first I suppose the two or three rivers to the east rise which run southward into the sea, and from the other side the Nyth.[3] From the second chain I suppose the Clyde, the Anan, the Tweed, and the Esk have their rise, as well as the several rivers which fall into the Tweed. I went a mile to see Caerdynas[4] on a little eminence over the Flete, naturally strong. It is a very fine old castle about thirty by forty feet within. The walls are twelve feet thick, and many closets are practic'd in them. There was a dark story under the arch above the ground floor, and four stories over it. The first is a grand room with a Saxon chimneypiece of which there is a drawing on the other side, *B*. Over it were two rooms. In the inner is another chimneypiece in the same style, which see at *A*.

There were two rooms in the other two stories. The coins of the building are very fine. This was the castle of the Maculloghs, and now belongs to the Maxwells, some of that family living near it. There is a little creek at the mouth of the river which opens into the bay, called by Ptolemy Jena.[5]

On the 5th I left the Gatehouse, and going soon to the right, off from the road to Dumfries, came in five miles to a small river called the Tarf, and in another mile to Tungland[6] on the Dee, which is generally thought to be the Deva of Ptolemy, over which we passed on a fine bridge, built out of the abbey, where the Parish church now is, with a Saxon doorcase to it. The abbey is entirely ruined, and great part of it was lately undermined for the sake of the stone. It was an abbey of Præmonstratenses, founded by Fergus, Lord of Galloway, in the twelfth century. Two miles below this is a town and large castle called Kirkcudbright, commonly called Kirkoubry. Here in the harbour, at the mouth of the Dee,

---

[1] Fleet.
[2] The three *mountains* are distinguished in a local distich as—
    'Cairnsmuir o' Fleet, Cairnsmuir o' Dee,
    Cairnsmuir o' Carsphairn, the biggest o' a' the three.'
[3] Nith. [4] Cardonness.
[5] Fleet bay, part of the Roman Iena Æstuarium.   [6] Tongueland.

B.—Chimneypiece in Cardonness Castle.[1]

A.—Chimneypiece in Cardonness Castle.[1]

[1] In MacGibbon and Ross's *Castel. Arch. of Scot.* a view of the 'Interior of Hall' is given, showing the position of both chimneypieces, but the lintel of the lower one (*A*) is gone. *Vide* vol. i. p. 246.

King William embarked his troops when he sailed for Ireland. It is defended against the weather by two or three islands. One of them is called Mary's Island, in which Lord Selkirk

The North End of the Church of the Abbey of Dundrennan.

lives, next heir to the Duke of Douglas, and his grandfather was Duke of Hamilton. Kirkoubry is a stewartry of the shire of Galloway, of which this town is the capital. Here was a monastery of Conventuals, of which Jno. Carpenter was a great engineer, and in the time of David the second, fortified Dunbarton castle. They have a considerable salmon fishery here. At Saint Mary's Island, Fergus, Lord Galloway, founded a priory of Canons Regular in the time of David the First. It was called Prioratus sanctæ Mariæ de Trayl.[1] The prior was a lord of Parliament.

An Arch of the inside of the Church of Dundrennan Abbey.

We came about five miles over the mountains to Dundrennan, a small village in which there are most magnificent remains of a fine abbey. It was founded by Fergus, Lord of Galloway, in 1142, for Cistercians, who were brought from Rieval[2] in

---

[1] From the previous name of the island, Trahil or Trayl.
[2] Rivaulx, N. R. of Yorkshire.

England. King James the Sixth annexed it to the chapel at Stirling. The *Chronicle of Melross* is said to have been writ by an abbot of this place, being a continuation of Bede's History. Alexander,[1] Lord of Galloway, and Constable of Scotland, was buried here in 1233. The Abbey is built of a freestone brought a mile off from Lough Nadir. The church is much in the style of that of Christ Church in Hampshire, the Saxon and Gothic mixed. The west part is entirely destroyed, except that the Gothic arch on each side leading to the Isle remains. The east part is standing. It consists of Saxon windows above. To the south of the altar is a Nich with an arch, and further west are three Gothick niches, as for the priest, and the two persons who assisted at the sacrament. Opposite to this there seem to have been ornaments, which are taken away. They speak of one part which was called the *sanctum sanctorum*, which was probably the choir. The cross isle is very grand on the east side. In both parts are three Gothic arches leading to so many chappels. Over each of the southern arches are two Gothic windows, and over the northern two couplets of Gothic windows, all supported by Saxon pilastres and capitals, some plain, in the general style of the church, others with leaves, but those leaves are mostly plain, and over these is one Saxon window to each of the great arches, which are supported by pillars consisting of twelve semicircular pilastres, as the grand pillars which supported the middle arch,—fallen in, consisted of twenty. I had a drawing taken of the side arches, and of the north end of the church. The plainest part of the church and the least adorned is the west side, in which there are only two or three Saxon windows on each side of the body of the church. The grand gate of entrance to the abbey is opposite to the east end of the church.

From the south end of the church was a covered way to the cloyster, which was large. Part of the inside wall remains, adorned with Gothic arched niches. On the east side of the cloister, and to the south of the church, was the chapter house, with a beautiful Gothic doorcase, and Gothic windows on each side, highly adorned with carved work over each window; and,

---

[1] Alan, not Alexander.

in particular, there is a cross[1] in a circle cut like Constantine's Cross. On the north side is a large arched Nich, and there seem to have been one on each side, and probably the same on the other two sides. To the south of this seems to have been the refectory, and the kitchen near it; and many arched offices to the west of the cloyster. They say Queen Mary came to this abbey, took boat near it, and landed near Workington, when she escaped from the castle of Kinross,[2] and fled from her enemies to England, and never returned more.

I went three miles to Aghakern[3] (the field of the carn), a village so called from a carn near. They found some iron ore about this place, but it did not answer in the smelting. They have also searched for coal at Roscorriel, at a small distance, and propose to carry it on by subscription. This place is near the river Our or Orr,[4] in which they have a bed of oysters, and they catch in the sea cod and Mackrel, but they have no herings in this part, as they probably go to the west of the Isle of Man. They have many mounts in this country, which they call motes, and they imagine the use of them was to hold their moots or meetings on publick bussiness, and that they have their names from this circumstance.

About twelve years agoe they found here, on the estate of Mr. Maxwel[5] of Minches, a bed of cockle-shells about a foot under ground, and four feet deep, extending over three acres of ground, which are most excellent manure. They use

---

[1] A Greek or Byzantine cross, equal armed, and enclosed in a circle,—a favourite type in the south-west counties.

[2] Lochleven Castle, near Kinross.   [3] Auchencairn.   [4] Urr.

[5] Munches was then owned and occupied by Mr. John Maxwell, a distinguished agricultural improver. He wrote an interesting letter when in his 91st year, describing his early recollections of the state of agriculture and social condition of the people in the Stewartry: see *New Stat. Ac.*, Kirkcudbright, vol. iv. p. 206. Mr. Maxwell is also remembered as a friend of Burns; when he attained his 71st birthday the bard presented him with a complimentary address. The wishes expressed in the lines—

'I see thy life is stuff o' prief,
    Scarce quite half worn,'

and—

'That bounteous Heaven
On thee a tack o' seven times seven
    Will yet bestow,'

were almost prophetic, for Mr. Maxwell lived to the age of ninety-four years.

also sea-shells in this country for the same purpose, at the expensive carriage of seven or eight pounds for an acre. They have grouse and the black game on the mountains, and abundance of foxes. They have also a wild cat three times as big as the common cat, as the polecat is less. They are of a yellow red colour, their breasts and sides white. They take fowls and lambs, and brede two at a time. I was assured that they sometimes bring forth in a large bird's nest, to be out of the reach of dogs; and it is said they will attack a man who would attempt to take their young ones, but they often shoot them and take the young. The county pays about £20 a-year to a person who is obliged to come and destroy the foxes when they send to him.

On the 6th I went on through pleasant vales edged with rocky hills and mountains, thinly covered with trees and shrubs, and some small lakes interspersed, and passed by the round castle of Sir Thomas Maxwell, the walls of which, I was told, are twelve feet thick, but they have practiced several closets in them, which make it a convenient house. We passed the Our[1] on a bridge, and came, in two miles, to Caer Gunnian.[2] I observed the little church was old, with a round window in the east end, and a cross in relief over the door. I was told that about two miles from Caerlwork,[3] in the road to Dumfries from the Gatehouse, there are two or three ancient round encampments on hills.

As the new map[4] places Carbantum on the Deva, in the situation of Caer Gunnian, one would be inclined to think that

[1] Urr.   [2] Kirkgunzeon.
[3] This is evidently a slip; should be Kirkgunzeon.
[4] In a note to an Irish letter Dr. Pococke wrote: 'As I shall often refer to the new Itinerary, and Map of Richard of Cirencester, a monk of Westminster, found in Denmark, and lately published by Bertram (which was probably taken out of the library at Westminster), so I shall distinguish them [from Cromwell's map and others] by the names of the New Map and Itinerary.'

Throughout his whole journey Dr. Pococke laboured to identify the places he visited with Richard's map, and doubtless believed he was doing a signal service to historical research. This is not surprising when we remember that Bertram's book had been only published five years, and had been accepted by eminent archæologists, including Dr. Stukely, a correspondent of the bishop's, who most probably urged him to carry the map on his journey through Scotland.

Bertram's *De Situ* is now universally admitted to be a base literary forgery, and we may dismiss it by quoting the trenchant conclusions of Mr. Mayor's

the Orr was the Deva, if the name of Dee did not rather favour the other opinion. We left the road to Dumfries to the right, and came to a lake with an island in it, covered with wood, to which a small kind of eagle resorts that they call a yern, which frequents the rocky mountains near, and preys on hens and lambs.

Four miles brought us, by a very rough road through a valley and over hills covered with stones of grey granite, to what they call commonly the New Abbey, situated under a hill to the north of a very pleasant fruitful country, extending to the sea and to the bay, with small hills in it adorned with wood, and a lake between the foot of the mountains with two islands in it, being under the mountain which is to the west, and it is computed to be the highest in all these parts, it is called Scrufel.[1]

There is a poor village close to the New Abbey, which was founded by Dervorgilla, daughter to Alexander,[2] Lord of Galloway, wife of John Baliol, Lord of Castle Bernard, who died in 1260,[3] and was buried here;[4] and his heart, being embalmed, put in a box of ivory, and enclosed in a vault near the high altar, it was called 'the abbey of sweet heart,'—Abbacia dulcis cordis, or suavi cordium—afterwards changed into the name of New Abbey. Sir Robert Spotieswood, President of the [Court of] Session, and Secretary of State to Charles the

exhaustive analysis of the work. He says: 'If these criticisms are just, Bertram's success is a signal reproach on the historical inquiries of the last 120 years. To say nothing of antiquaries whose canons of evidence are so lax that they cite a supposed monk of 1400 A.D. as authority for events of 1000 B.C., we find a forger alike contemptible as penman, Latinist, historian, geographer, critic, imposing upon members of the Royal and Antiquarian Societies, and of the two ancient universities, of the youthful society—D. C. K., on the writers of Germany, and Denmark, of England and of Scotland (this last bribed by the invention of Vespasiana).'—*Ricardi de Cirencestria Speculum Historiale De Gestis Regum Angliæ*, by John E. B. Mayor, M.A., 1869, vol. ii., clxiv.

[1] Criffel, 1867 feet. [2] Alan, not Alexander. [3] 1269.
[4] John Baliol, Devorgilla's husband, was not buried in New Abbey, but in the neighbourhood of Barnard Castle, his heart having been previously taken out, embalmed, and placed in an ivory casket. When Devorgilla died at an advanced age, her body was interred in New Abbey, and, in obedience to her dying wish, the heart of her husband was placed upon her bosom; 'another affecting illustration,' as it has been said, ' of the strong love which made them one.' Owing to this circumstance the sacred edifice bore afterwards the name of Dulce Cor, or Sweetheart Abbey.

First, was designed Lord of New Abbey, to whom the dissolved abbey was granted. The common people say that she [Dervorgilla] had her husband's heart put into a box of ebony within a box of gold, and deposited it in the church, which is built of red freestone that is dug near. It is a uniform Gothic building, and seems at first to have been designed with single pointed windows, but afterwards to have been changed to the Gothic,

West Front of the Church of the New Abbey.

composed of several arches, with circles on each side to fill up the intermediate spaces. There are four chapels on the east side of the transept. The arch of the grand tower is built on four fine arches, supported by pillars consisting of twenty half round pilastres. These six arches on each side of the body consist of twelve, with plain capitals. A large window seems to have been first designed in the west end, which has been built up, and now there are only two long windows in it. Over these is a fine round window divided into twelve compartments like those of Westminster Abbey, and over this is a triangular window case, the window without being in the shape of the trefoil, both of them emblems of the Trinity, which is very particular. In the top of the south end of the transept is part of a round window, but the gabel end of the chapter house building rises above the middle of it, and takes off so much of the window. A view of both are here seen.

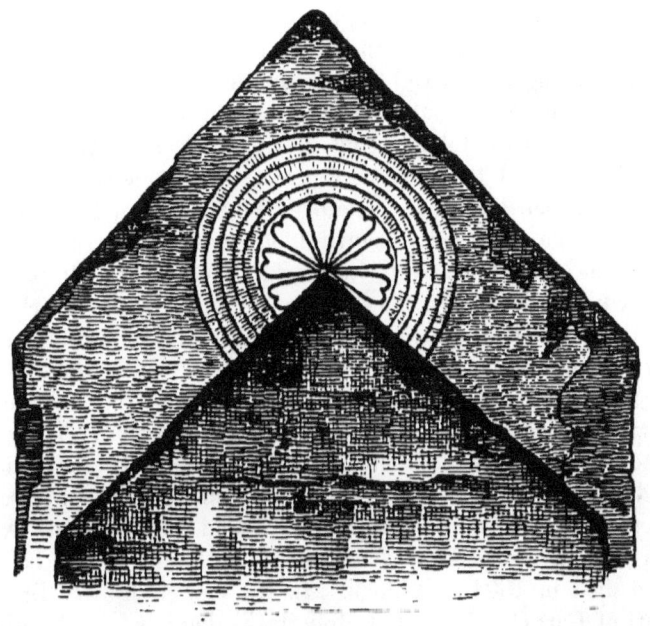

South End of the Church of the New Abbey.

The Isles are destroyed, so that the six arches of the body of the church appear in view. To the south of the cross is the passage, probably to the abbot's lodging, over the chapter house, which consists of two groin arches without a pillar. South of that seems to have been the refectory. West of this was the cloister, and in it, near the refectory, a cistern for water remains entire, with fine semi-circular basons. They talk much of money found in several parts, and the communion plate which was sold for brass, but all this is doubtful. The last abbot of the place was living on some lands adjacent in the memory of some very old people who were lately living. I was informed that this abbey was but just finished before the Reformation. Before I knew this I saw plainly the church had been altered, and most part of the body added to it, for the windows over two of the arches consist of four plain pointed arches. The others have a little arch on each side, and I had reason to think that the whole consisted of windows of a single pointed arch, and could perceive that several of the windows had been made new in the high Gothic taste.

I came six miles near the Nith, the old Novius or Nidius, having a bog to the right, and pleasant hills to the left, to Dumfries in Nythesdale, where I was in 1747.[1] This town carried on a great tobacco trade until the Tobacco Act passed, which destroyed that commerce; and the people being grown rich, and their money not employed in trade, they have lately adorned the town with beautiful buildings of the red hewn freestone, and the streets are most exceedingly well paved. They have a handsome Townhouse, and all is kept very clean, so that it is one of the neatest towns in Great Britain, and very pleasantly situated on the Nith, over which there is a large bridge; and, as the Assizes are held here for all the south part of Scotland, the town is much frequented by lawyers. The shiping lie under Skrefel,[2] eight miles below Dumfries, and come up three miles higher to unload at Glanteyrel.[3] Here was a Friery of Conventuals founded by the same Dervorgilla, in which John Duns Scotus took on him the habit, who died in 1308 at Cologn. In the church Robert Bruce, Earl of Carrick, killed Red Robert Cuming[4] before the high altar in 1305, and James Lindsey and Roger Kilpatrick murdered Sir Robert Cuming in the sacristy, and were excommunicated by [Pope] John the twenty-second in Avignon.

[1] It was in 1750 Dr. Pococke previously visited Dumfries, see p. 7.
[2] Criffel. Burns refers to this mountain at the mouth of the Nith in his address to 'The Dumfries Volunteers'—
'The Nith shall run to Corsincon,
And Criffel sink in Solway.'
[3] Glencaple, an old harbour and village five miles below Dumfries. The Old Quay is still the common name for it.
[4] Red John Comyn of Badenoch, see p. 7.

DUMFRIES, NITHSDALE.

We were now in Clydedale[1] and the country of the Selgovæ. I came on near the other side of the river, and not far from the mouth of it, where Caerlavrock Castle stands, which they say is a fine fabric, and that there are some good carvings in it. It was the habitation of the Maxwells, lords of the country. It is by some thought to be the Carbantorigum of Ptolemy, and was esteemed a strong place in the time of Edward the First. But Uxellum is rather thought by some to be Caerlavrock, and that Carbantorigum was at Bardanna or Kier. Caerlaverock by the new map is about the situation of Uxellum, which must determine it. Corda of Ptolemy is conjectured to have been near Lough Cure at the rise of the Nyth, the Novius about Castle Cumnock or Cummock. We came along by the seaside to Stank, near Comlongon, the seat of Lord Stormont, who is now Ambassador at Warsaw.—I am, etc.

[1] Should be Nithsdale.

In a note to one of his Irish letters Dr. Pococke explains some Gothic architectural terms which he purposed using in the following letters, and gives six illustrations:—

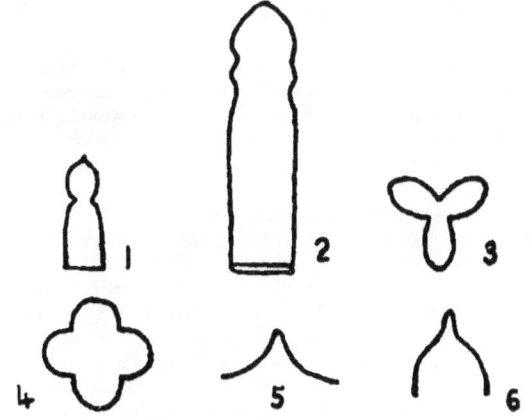

1. The trefle arch, from the trefoil, of which it is an imitation.
2. The double trefle arch.
3. The trefoil window.
4. The round or rounded cross.
5. The cave arch, being flatter, as such natural arches have been seen in caves.
6. The bough arch.

LETTER V.

¹ PENRITH, *May the 9th*,² 1760.

DEAR MADAM,—On the 7th I went to Ruthvel [Ruthwell] Church to see an extraordinary square obelisk, broken in two, which is engraved in Gordon,³ to which I refer for an account of it, on which there seems to have been a cross. It is 12½ ft. long, 1 ft. 10 ins. at bottom, and a foot at top one way, two feet at bottom, and one foot three inches at top another way, and was put in a round base which is in the church. Here, also, is the monument⁴ of Patrick Walker, a nonjuring clergyman who lived at Oxford, and died in Lord Stormont's family, who erected this monument to him. From about this place to the north, as far as to the wall⁵ about seven miles north-east of Brampton, and for about half-a-mile in breadth, is a vein of limestone. Some is blewish, with shells in it, others reddish, with pieces of blew mixed in it, and some with coral in it, both of the large and small kinds. They make kilns with sods where they want to improve, draw the limestone to them, and burn it with furse. They have come into this improvement about a dozen years, which will greatly

---

¹ This letter in the MS. is dated from Perth. Dr. Pococke invariably contracts Penrith—sometimes Pen'th—hence doubtless the error. See note, p. 19.

² Although this letter is dated a day earlier than the preceding one, there is no reason to suppose an error. The order in tour and narrative is correct. Dr. Pococke appears to have slept in Penrith on the night of the 8th, and to have passed through Orton on the 10th (see Itinerary at the end of the Tour). Probably Letter IV. was not finished; hence it was delayed a day. The Bishop generally dated and located the letters the day they were forwarded.

³ Gordon's *Itin.*, pp. 160, 161, and pl. 57, 58; *Pen. Scot. Tours*, 1772, Pt. i. p. 96; *Trans. Soc. Ant. Scot.*, vol. iv. p. 313, by Rev. Henry Duncan, D.D.; *The Ruthwell Cross*, by Prof. Geo. Stephens, F.S.A., 1866; *Scot. in Early Christian Times*, by Jos. Anderson, LL.D., vol. ii. pp. 233-246, 1881; *The Ruthwell Cross*, 1885, by Rev. James M'Farlan, Ruthwell Parish Church.

⁴ A small oval brass plate, inserted into a large flat tombstone. The inscription is very much worn, a part being now illegible. 'Hic conditur quod mortale fuit Reverendi Viri Patricii Walker, Artium Magister. . . . Deinde . . . per spatium viginti trium annorum apud nobilem virum Davidem Vicecomtem Stormont cujus sacris Domesticis praefuit. Commemoratus est. Ob. XXVIII. Mar. MDCCXXVII Eta. LXXIV.'

⁵ Hadrian's Wall, north of Brampton, described by the Rev. C. Bruce in *The Roman Wall*, p. 261, *seq.*; cf. also p. 328.

tend to alter the face of the whole country. There is also great plenty of marle in many parts, especially in the bogs.

I went on three miles to the north-east into Anandale, and came to the fine castle of Hodam[1] on the Anan, from which there is a hanging ground to this river covered with wood, and it is a very beautiful country. I had a view

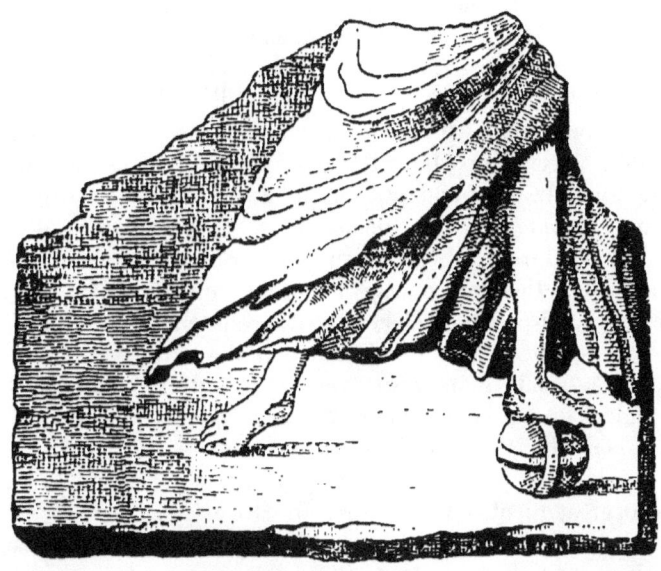

A Fragment at Hoddam Castle.[2]

up the Anan of Melk Castle,[3] very pleasantly situated on a hill in the vale. Here I saw an altar found at the Roman Camp, called The Lawn,[4] at Midleby, which camp I saw in 1747. There is a road from that camp to Carlisle, and also to another, which I saw at a mile distance under

[1] Hoddam Castle.

[2] This sculpture is preserved in the Soc. of Ant. Mus., Edinburgh. In the left corner is the tip of a wing, and although Dr. Pococke calls it 'a fragment of a winged figure' (p. 34), he has not shown the wing in the drawing.

[3] Castlemilk.

[4] This is a curious error. The Roman camp mentioned is situated within and upon the marches of the farm of Land, Middlebie—pronounced in the broad dialect of Annandale, *the Län* (ä being sounded as in Lawn), and has no relation to a well-kept greensward. The Bishop visited this place in 1750, not in 1747. See p. 6.

Burnswork, and it goes on to Moffet. Here is an altar with an inscription on it, which has not been published, and may be seen on the other side.[1] Here is also a relief, which seems to be the drapery of a figure; and there is a fragment of a winged figure in relief, one foot of which is on a globe with a cross on it. It is thought to represent Fortune by a wheel. Here is also a stone exactly in the shape of an egg, found in the same place, 18 lo: and 11 broad, and very smoothly wrought.

The drawing of the former is here inserted. 'From this place I went up to a tower on a hill called Repentance. It was built by a Maxwel who had committed great ravages against Queen Mary, but afterwards became a papist, and built this for a beacon, and put up in Saxon characters over the door—*Repentance*.[2] It commands a very fine view of the country and bay. I went down to the ruined church of Hoddam, where there are some pieces of an imperfect Latin inscription, which is so much defaced that I could make nothing of it.

We ascended the hill and came over the heath three miles to Anan, a small poor town, very pleasantly situated on the hanging ground over the Anan, and commanding a view of the sea. It is thought by some to be the Trimontium of Ptolemy, and here it is placed in the new map. As they have great plenty of a soft red freestone they use it for door frames, and window frames to their thatched cabins, and make arched rustic door frames of it for their barns. But the most beautifull situation is the site of the house of Robert Bruce,

---

[1] The inscription is not in the MS. The Bishop's amanuensis probably left it for him to write, and thus it has been lost.

[2] If this tradition is rather apocryphal, it has the merit of being new. That it was a Maxwell that erected the Tower is borne out by Pennant, who says: 'It was built by a Lord Harries, as a sort of atonement for putting to death some prisoners whom he had made under a promise of quarter.'—Pennant's *Scot.*, vol. ii. p. 106. Another story is, 'A chieftain from the northern side, having made a successful inroad into the English border, was crossing the Solway on his return, laden with booty, when a sudden storm arose. In order to lighten his labouring vessel he threw his prisoners overboard in preference to the cattle he had stolen. The danger past, he was smitten with remorse. In order to make such amends as he could, he built a beacon tower which overlooks the Solway, and to this day is called the Tower of Repentance. Tradition avers that the penitent himself carried all the stones used in its erection to the top of the hill.'—Bruce's *Roman Wall*, p. 278. For plan and view see MacGibbon and Ross's *Castellated Architecture of Scotland*, 1887, vol. ii. p. 60.

grandfather to Robert Bruce, king of Scotland. It is on an eminence which commands a fine view of the river both up and down. It was an oblong square, defended by a deep fossee to the south, and by a double fossee to the north, on which side is the keep. The garden they say extended to the east, and is now a very rich piece of ground. On a stone taken from the old building is the following inscription, which I copied.[1]

```
ROBERT DE BRVS
COVNTE DE CA
RRIK ET SEITYU
RDUVAL DE ANANN
AN O BOO
```

They mention a stone[2] set up in memory of a battle with the English, probably that which was fought near this place in the time of Edward the Sixth. They have a very fine marl near this town. The new map makes the wall to come on to Ituna Estuarium about this place, so that the wall seems to have been carried on both sides; and they say there are marks of a wall which was built from this place to the great wall. They have here a great salmon-fishery. I was told that their flounders are remarkably good.—I am, etc.

[1] This inscription has been variously transcribed. '*Robert de Brus* Counte de *Carrick* et senteur du val de *Annand*, 1300.'—Pennant's *Scot.*, vol. ii. p. 96. 'Robert De Brus Counte De Carrick et Seniour De Val De Annand, 1300. *New Stat. Ac.*, vol. iv. p. 525. Bruce thus designates himself in a letter of date 1304, 'Robert de Bruys Seignour du Val de Anaunt.'—Raimes's *Historical Papers and Letters from Northern Registers*, p. 163.

[2] Probably the Clochmaben. 'On the farm of Old Gretna there is a boulder-stone, 8 or 9 feet in height, and about 20 feet in breadth, called the Clochmaben or Lochmaben Stone, at which the Scottish warriors generally rendezvoused before they entered England by the Roman road at Plomp.'—*Trans. Dumf. and Gal. Antiq. Soc.*, 1865-66, p. 48, Article, 'The Debateable Land,' by T. J. Carlyle.

LETTER VI.

SHAP IN WESTMORELAND, *May* 10*th*, 1760.

DEAR MADAM,—I went on six miles to Gretna Green where there is a very antient small Saxon Church. On the 8th we came over the Sarke into England and crossed the Esk with a guide ; it being dangerous after high tydes, which bring in the sand, and make it very difficult to pass without a guide, and so they send one at all times with strangers. . . .

I passed old Penrith the Voreda of the Itinerary. This is the third time I have seen Penrith. They make use of a covering of their houses very much in this country which is of the red thin freestone. They have also the Workington slate, which are a large green slate. The wheels and Axel trees of their carts turn together, and the wheel consists of three pieces of wood ; a small segment of a circle being cutt out of the two side pieces and a little from the middle piece.

The whole country from Penrith to Carlisle was formerly the forrest of Engelwood.

The Duke of Portland made a present to some of the inhabitants of this place for taking eighty of the Rebels, which they laid out on Branches from the Church, on which there is an historical inscription. . . . [1]

[1] Bishop Pococke crossed the river Sark into England on the 8th May, and made a thirteen-days' tour in the northern counties, visiting the following places : Carlisle, Penrith, Brougham Castle, Lowther Hall, Abbey of Shap, Orton, Pendragon Castle, Wharton Hall, Kirkby Stephen, Winton, Brough, Bowes, Richmond, Easby Abbey, Appleton, Darlington, Staindrop, Raby Castle, Bishop Auckland, Stanhope, Alstonmoor, Haltwhistle, Brampton, Haworth Castle, Lanercost Abbey, Beau Castle, Netherby, Longtown. He re-entered Scotland again, crossing the river Sark on the 20th May, having travelled about 232 miles and written seven letters. *Vide Add.* MSS. 14,256, *British Museum.*

Letter VII.

Moffet in Anandale, May the 20th, 1760.

Dear Madam,—On the 20th I set out to the west, and passed the Sark into Scotland. On the English side of the river is a cross on which is this inscription—

> GOD REVENGE
> MVRDER
> 1689
> G. C

the occasion of which was, a Custom-House officer murdered by some persons running goods who were acquitted. We passed through Gretna Green, and leaving the road we had come into England, in about three miles further we came to Kirk Patrick[1] Church, where there is a rivulet, and in two miles more to Dykehead, on Kirklewater[2] rivulet, and over a pleasant glyn adorned with trees, and in twelve miles from Longtown to a small town Eglefekin,[3] near a rivulet called Mene.[4] Here there is a linnen manufacture which employs the people in spinning. About two miles from the Lawn[5] is the site of Old Middleby, supposed to be Blatum Bulgrium, as the camp above, under Burnswork seems to be the Æstiva Castra Exploratorum, both which I saw in 1747.[6] In two miles I crossed the Anan near the pleasant castle of Melk now destroyed, and a modern house is built on a beautiful mount over the Anan adorned with trees. Here I saw a double kind of a boat, like two troughs joined thus :—

each of which would hold any beast to be ferried over. In two

[1] Kirkpatrick-Fleming.
[2] Kirtle River.
[3] Ecclefechan.
[4] Mein Water.
[5] Lawn, *i.e.* Lān or Land ; see note, p. 33.
[6] It was in 1750 that Dr. Pococke visited Middlebie, p. 6.

miles more I came to Loughkerby[1] on a morass, which probably was a lake. Going from this place, I saw two or three lakes to the southwest. One of them is Loughaban,[2] on which there is a ruined castle[3] on a peninsula. We passed the Anan again, and perceived the Roman road in several places.

About four miles before I came to Moffet I saw a small hill which seemed to have been worked into a regular shape, so as with the river to make a triangle, and there is a single entrance up to it near the angle, which is close to the road. About half a mile further is such another, but square and on the river, and there is an entrance up to it on the west side, near the north-west angle. They are both flat at top, and about thirty feet high, as I conjectured and imagined they might be the Castra Æstiva of some station near. But the common people look on them as entirely natural, and say that nothing is found about them. They are certainly not altogether works of art.

We came in between the mountains, which open and make a wider vale towards the part where the river has run from the north, and begins to run east and west, and forms a pleasant romantick amphitheatre encompassed with high mountains. Moffet is a small town in this vale. It is the estate of the Marquis of Anandale, who is lunatic, and Lord Hopton is the curator, who is setting on foot a manufacture of shalloons and serges here. On the mountain to the south-east is Loughwood, an old castle[4] encompassed with morass,—the seat of Sir Theodore Johnston in the time of James the Sixth, who lived in this place, almost inaccessible, and did what he pleased. It is said that King James in one of his progresses, as he went to administer justice, sent to him, but he refused to come, on which the king went to him, granted him a pardon, and created him Lord Johnston, and his descendent was made Marquis of Anandale.—I am, etc.

[1] Lockerbie. [2] Lochmaben.
[3] King Robert the Bruce's Castle.
[4] The old Castle or Tower of Lochwood.

LETTER VIII.

LEADHILLS IN CLYDESDALE, *May 21st*, 1760.

DEAR MADAM,—On the 21st I went two measured miles to the old well, passing near a British round fort with a keep in it in which they had dug to find treasure. The old Spaw was found above a hundred years agoe by Bishop Whiteford's daughter.[1] It comes out of a rock over a rivulet[2] that runs down the rocks in a deep glyn adorned with wood in a very romantick manner. For this mineral water, strongly impregnated with sulphur, I refer to the treatises[3] writ on the mineral waters of Scotland, and printed at Edinburgh. There are two springs. One comes out of the top of the rock, and is the strongest of sulphur, which settles on the rock. This is carried to Moffet to bathe in, and may be drank. But they commonly drink the other which comes out lower on the other side of the cave, and is softer. It is esteemed particularly good in all scorbutick disorders, both to bathe and drink, and is particularly good for any sores. Dr. ———— has built a long room and conveniencies here for the people to come and drink the waters on the spot.

From this place I crossed the mountains towards the road to Edinburgh, and turning up a rivulet[4] to the north-west, which runns in a romantick glyn, we came at the head of it to the new well called Hartfield Spaw,[5] found out about seven years agoe by Mr. Williamson the Pythagorean, who eats nothing that causes the destruction of an animal, as it is said, occasioned by his compassion for the game he saw dying when he was about eighteen years old, and a great sportsman. This spaw is on the Duke of Queensborough's estate, who has made a carriage road to it. It is an alum water, and good for many

---

[1] Miss Rachel Whiteford, afterwards Mrs. James Johnston, is credited with having discovered this Spa in 1633.

[2] The Well Burn, or Birnock Water; so called from Birnock Clooves, the hill whence it flows.

[3] These two treatises are probably those by Dr. Milligan and Professor Plummer, in the *Edinburgh Medical Essays*, 1747.

[4] Auchencat, or Hartfell Burn.

[5] Hartfell Spa was discovered in 1748. A monument was erected to the memory of John Williamson in 1775; he died 1769.

inward disorders. The well is arched over and locked up, and the water is brought to Moffet.

On the other side of the rivulet, lower down, are copper mines. The ore is in a black slate, and they work in horizontally. They belong to Mr. Grampton,[1] from whom they have their name. On the height over this stream on the heath is an old entrenchment of three sides forming right angles, the precipice being to the south, and there are two entrances on the north side, which is about eighty yards long, the other two sides about forty. Coming to this place from the other well, I saw a Kern made of stones laid round a spot of ground about 20 paces in diameter.[2] We came to the road to Edinburgh and Glasgow 3 miles from Moffet, at the foot of the mountain called Brayfoot Ericstone.[3] To the north of this the Anan rises out of a deep hole between the mountains, called the Marquis of Anandale's Tub.[4] I was assured that there is no lake there. Ascending the hill I saw over the bed of a mountain torrent a British semi-circular fort, with treble fossees in some parts and four fossees in other parts, and four likewise extending to the west of it for about 40 yards, which seem to be designed to defend the pass. We ascended the mountains,[5] which are beautiful in their shape and covered with herbage and heath. In four miles we came to Clyde's Nop, or Nape I suppose, which is a head of a river that I imagine to be the last that runs to the east, and so may be said to be the Nape of Clyde. We soon came to the Clyde which runs from the north out of a vale in which there are two single hills. It forms several little pools, and rises eight miles off from Allanfoot, I suppose to the east, for it is said that Anan, Clyde, and Tweede[6] rise within a mile of each other. Opposite to Allanfoot,[7]

---

[1] The estate of Granton. Probably the proprietor being locally styled by his estate, the polite traveller supplied the 'Mr.'

[2] A doubtful piece of antiquity; more likely to have been a sheep-pen.

[3] Ericstane-brae foot.

[4] The 'Marquis of Annandale's Beef-stand,' or 'The Deil's Beef-Tub.'

[5] The Moffat Hills, also called the Lowther Hills.

[6] Described well in the old lines:—

          'Annan, Tweed, an' Clyde,
          A' rise out o' ae hillside;
          Tweed ran, Annan wan,
          Clyde fell, an' lrak its neck o'er Cora Linn.'

[7] Elvanfoot.

that is, Elwin, the foot of Elwin, the river running straight, as they say like an ell. Opposite to this is a pretty place called Newtown. Here the Clyde is large. We crossed it to Allanfoot, and went four miles by very bad road, mostly northward, by the side of a stream, and over a hill to Leadhills, which is a town of thatched houses of miners, consisting of between three and four hundred houses, and about fifteen hundred souls, situated between low heathy hills. It is reckoned to be in Clydesdale, and is the high road from Wigtown and Dumfries to Edinburgh. The former road joyns the latter near Drumlandrig. It is the estate of Lord Hopton, and about a mile to the south the Duke of Queensborough's estate comes in, who has mines on them. It is all lead, except a small quantity of copper they have lately met with, but it did not hold. They are worked by two or three companies, and some Lord Hopton works himself. Off the company he has a sixth of pure lead.[1] They have not gone deeper than three hundred feet. They do not smelt with a furnace, but in smelt mills on common hearths blown with bellows. They smelt it with coal, turf, and lime—a horse load of coal, twelve stone, two loads of turf, and one load of lime of eight bushels. They use the coal of Douglas eight miles off. But for their houses they burn a lighter coal, that of the Sanchar at the old family castle of the Duke of Queensborough. They bring their lime also from Douglas. As to the ores, those of the different mines are much of the same nature. They say they are more easily worked than the Duke of Queensborough's. Besides the common lead ore, they have what they call a diamond ore in oblong square plates, which shine like glass. Susannah mine, or vein as they call it, in the side of the hill, is a very large rich vein. It has been worked several years, and goes down near perpendicular. They have followed it 360 feet deep. In the mines they meet with the diamond kind in large lumps, the pieces cemented together, and sometimes incrusted over with a brown coat. Sometimes they find other ore incrusted with a mixture of spar and mundik. They have also ore which shoots like crystal in small threads, of a light grey colour and a deeper grey, and they have a white ore which is

---

[1] 'The Earl of Hopetoun receives the sixth bar for rent.'—*Old Stat. Ac.*, vol. iv. p. 512.

rare. They are commonly found in hollow parts of the rock which is close to the vein. They find also a flat spar, not very white, and what they call chrystal pillar, about three-quarters of an inch thick, not formed like chrystal, but in irregular round figures, and not smooth. I have a little piece of the chrystal found in the middle of a rock. They met with a vein of copper which seemed to be rich, but it soon failed, and they have not tried it. The lead is carried to Leith, the port of Edinburgh, and shipped off for Holland, where, it is said, they get out the small quantity of silver that is in it, and use much of it in making white and red lead. They carry a load of five pigs, 500 wt., with a horse and carr for five shillings, being thirty-two miles or two days' journey. The Scotch company have a great part of these mines. A gentleman of learning of the name of Sterling,[1] who has travelled in Italy, and is a man of great politeness, has the care of their affairs. They have a very handsome house, and he has improved the garden in lawn and plantations of trees, so as to hide the thatched cabins below, and to make it very pretty in itself. The larch grows very well here, but no sort of fruit ripens except strawberries, not so much as a gooseberry.[2] Tho' in July and August they have plenty of common garden stuff. They are subject to colic if they work where the air is not perfectly good. The remedy is purgatives and emetics, but sometimes it proves fatal.—I am, etc.

[1] 'Arch. Stirling of Garden, Esq., agent for the Scotch Mine Company, at Leadhil's, a worthy and well-informed gentleman.'—*Old Stat. Ac.*, vol. xxi. p. 97.

[2] 'Every sort of vegetable is with difficulty raised, and seldom comes to perfection.'—*Old Stat. Ac.*, vol. xxi. p. 98. This statement by the Rev. William Peterkin, Minister of Ecclesmachan, written about 1799, confirms Dr. Pococke's observations, and the Doctor's informant would be the Mr. Stirling referred to. A century of soil amelioration seems to have wrought a marvellous change, and the climate may have improved, as appears from the following :—' Leadhills. By successful cultivation on the part of the miners, some 300 acres of land have been reclaimed, which afford potatoes and crops of hay. This green, surrounding the village, forms a pleasant feature to this healthy district. Though 1400 feet above sea-level, the villagers had a grand display of lovely flowers, choice fruits, and vegetables at their flower-show. . . . The quality of the exhibits was very good, the judges making special mention of the pansies and marigolds. The vegetables were slightly inferior to those of last year, but the long and round potatoes were very good. The fruits were above the average, and much notice was taken of the size and quality of the black currants.'—*Hamilton Advertiser*, Sept. 12, 1885. At the show there were ten entries of gooseberries.

LETTER IX.

LANERK, *May 22d*, 1760.

DEAR MADAM,—On the 22d I set out and travelled three miles to Glangoner river in the Edinburgh road, from which another goes up the hills to the north-west to Douglas mill and Douglas town, which is the way to Glasgow. At the latter the Duke of Douglas[1] had a castle, where he resided, that was lately burnt, and he is building a house there. They say gold dust[2] was formerly found in Glangoner river. Another road goes by Crawfordjohn, the shortest way to Lanerk, but over the moors. Soon after we came to the Clyde. This road is joyned by the great Dumfries Road to Glasgow, and the Edinburgh Road a little further crosses the Clyde from this road, and a little further the Glasgow Road goes to the south-west of this road, which is the way we took to Lanerk. We passed through a British fort[3] with a keep on the Clyde, and by Robertstown[4] under a fine hill called Duncavan,[5] and saw a bridge called Cleyden Bridge,[6] over which the road to Edinburgh goes when the water is high. We passed near Littlegill,[6] where there is such another old fort, and came to the limestone quarries in a bottom. The stone is in patches, and they burn it on the spot. There is more about two miles to the south, and at Douglas. We crossed over to another valley under Kentick Hill,[7] which is high, and going over a foot of it,[8] came

---

[1] The Dukedom became extinct in 1761. The estates are now held by the Earl of Home, created Baron Douglas in 1875.

[2] 'Queen Elizabeth . . . sent down a German to gather gold dust in the waters of Elvan and Glengonar.'—*Old Stat. Ac.*, vol. iv. p. 515. Mr. Noble estimates that not less than £500,000 has been extracted from Crawford gold district (*Upward Lanarkshire*, 1864, vol. iii. p. 195 ; see also vol. i. pp. 50 *seq.*). The marriage ring of Sir Edward Colebrooke's lady was made of Glengoner gold.

[3] On farm of Nether Abington. See *Upward Lanarkshire*, vol. i. p. 27 ; also Plate III. fig. 5.

[4] Roberton.   [5] Dungavel Hill, 1675 ft.

[6] Clydes Bridge still stands. Near it is the farm-house of Moat, which was formerly the residence of the Baillies of Littlegill.

[7] Tinto, locally Tintock, 2335 ft.

[8] The pass at Howgate mouth, part of the Tinto range.

to a valley in which there runs a rivulet[1] that passes through Carmichael, the seat of Lord Hindeford,[2] with a church and park adjoyning that extends up the western hill, having Kentic to the east. It is a good house, close to another which I was told was an old castle. It is a pretty thing in itself, in a situation fixed on for the sake of shelter, but within a mile of a most beautiful country on the Clyde, to which we crossed over the hill[3] and then over the Clyde itself to Lanerk, passing by a quarry[4] of good stone with a bed of fine flaggs in it.

Lanerk is a small town prettily situated. This country is charmingly fine in a most peculiar manner, consisting chiefly of high ground over the river, and rising ground in common fields like Hampshire, and seats finely improved. I observed between the little hills small bogs from an acre to three or four acres, which in winter are ponds,[5] and if cleansed for manure might produce great plenty of fish. Lanerk is tolerably well built, though most of the houses are thatched, and the ascent to the upper rooms is mostly on the outside. They have a manufacture of Scotch carpets. This is a royal borough, and belongs to the king. To the south of the town is the castle hill, like a Celtic tumulus towards the river. From it a fossee extends to the north, as will be mentioned below. The site of the castle is turned into a bowling-green.[6] It was a castle of the Kings of Scotland, and they have a tradition that King David passed some time here. A quarter of mile to the east of the town is a ruined church.[7] The east part is entirely down. The body only consists of one row of pillars supporting six arches. Two of the pillars are octagons. It is all Gothick, and the windows consist of one narrow arch. This might be the church[8] of the Monastery of Conventuals founded by Robert Bruce, King of

---

[1] Carmichael Burn, which falls into Clyde at Pretts-mill.
[2] John, third Earl of Hyndford. The earldom became extinct in 1817. The estate is now held by Sir Windham Carmichael Anstruther, Bart.
[3] Carmichael Hill.   [4] Bride's Close Quarry. It now only yields road metal.
[5] One of the bogs is probably now Lanark Loch, the others have disappeared through agricultural improvements.
[6] Still used as a bowling-green.
[7] The church of St. Kentigern in churchyard; the remains are in good preservation.
[8] The monastery founded by Bruce was in the *west* of the town; the site of which was in the yard of the Clydesdale Hotel.

Scotland in 1814. There was an hospital in the town called St. Leonard.

I rid four measured miles to Carstairs,[1] a large village. To the east of the village, near the church, are remains of the ancient town supposed to be Colania. It is near a rivulet, which is to the east of it, and was about a hundred yards broad from east to west, and two hundred long, the parsonage house being very near the north wall. There is a large head from the north wall extending to the east as to keep up the water of the rivulet for the use of the town. They have found pieces of iron, one like a pick-axe, another like a broad knife, and some little thin pieces of lead, a stone trough, a stone like a Console with two ornaments in front like a small pillar and base crowned with a *flower de lis*, and another which appeared like a Gothick ornament of a head, but they said it was taken out of the old town, and as the cap was remarkable, a drawing[2] was taken of it. In the churchyard is a most extraordinary Gothick capital, the bottom of which is put upwards, and serves for a dial, and is 23 inches in diameter, probably the size of the pillar. It is in the bell shape, and is covered with eight pilasters, as probably the pillar was, each consisting of five sides. That in the middle is three inches broad, the other two four. About a mile nearer Lanerk at a village[3] I saw signs of what I took to be large irregular entrenchments.[4]

The town of Lanerk seems anciently to have extended towards the Castle, for there is a deep fossee to the east which seems to be natural, and carries off the water from the town,

---

[1] 'The [Roman] Iter next bends round the remarkable turn here taken by the Clyde, and enters the important Roman Station of Castledykes, or Carstairs. The progress of modern improvement has in a great measure destroyed its ramparts: a small portion is, however, preserved on the side of the avenue at the back of the modern mansion-house. Fortunately it was surveyed by General Roy in 1753, and a plan of it preserved in Plate XXVII. of his great work. From this we learn that it consisted of an area of about 180 yards square, defended by a deep ditch and formidable rampart. The remains of a Roman bath were here discovered, and many articles of their manufacture have been dug up, such as pots, dishes, instruments of war or sacrifice, a nether millstone, and coins, chiefly those of Aurelius, Antoninus, and Trajan.'—*Upward Lanarkshire*, vol. i. p. 16. Castledykes was situated in the vicinity of the church and village of Carstairs. *Ibid.*, vol. ii. p. 447. Lanark is generally understood to be Colonia.

[2] The drawing referred to does not appear to have been preserved.

[3] Ravenstruther. [4] On the farm of Corbiehall.

and on the other side are remains of a rampart, very much like the Roman works, and might run down on the west side of the present hill called the Castle. There is a beautifull glyn behind the Castle, and beyond that, a little to the south, is the Clyde, which to the east, runs between high, beautifull rocks adorned with wood. Above that the river runs on rocks, with several little falls[1] but higher up between hills covered with wood and forms several beautiful ca- 'es. Coming towards Lord President Dundasses[2] estate and house, called Bonnytown, the south side appears in two hills—one like a long tumulus, with a rivulet to the west falling down in several sheets. The other is beautifully covered with wood, on which the house stands, on the south side of the river.[3] As one approaches there seems to be a third hill on the same side of the river, with a summer-house[4] on it, but as you come nearer you are most agreeably surprised in seeing a most extraordinary cataract[5] of the whole river, and to find that this hill is on the north side of it, for here the river runs down the rocks from the south and turns immediately to the west. The high rocks on each side are most beautifully adorned with trees, being altogether the finest cascade I ever saw. It first falls about five feet down, and about fifteen feet wide. It then widens on both sides, and runs down fifty, and for ten feet before the next fall the water forms a froth by the breaking on the rocks, it then falls about twelve feet, and there are two streams divided by the rocks on the west side. After running about fifty feet it falls first about ten feet on a shelf, and then about twenty in a sheet a little broken by the rocks, forms a large basin, and turns to the west. From the summer-house there is a ride on the high cliffs over the river out of which trees grow, and there is a wood to the left of the river, running a little above the fall from east to west, and several small cascades are seen falling down the rocks. At last a most grand broad cataract[6] presents

---

[1] Dundaff Linn.

[2] The Lord President was never laird of Bonnington. This curious error may have arisen from Sir John Carmichael Ross of Bonnington having married the daughter of Dundas of Arniston.

[3] The Corehouse side of the river Clyde.

[4] Built by Sir James Carmichael of Bonnington in 1708.

[5] Corra Linn.   [6] Bonnington Fall.

to view, a little broken by a turn in the rock on the north side. It falls, I believe, for about twenty feet, in a white froth. From this the ride is to the north, and north-east, round the whole improved estate on that side, which is divided into several large fields, mostly by six rows of firr trees, which have a most beautifull effect in the prospect.

When I came home and was at dinner, the Magistrates of the town sent to know when they might wait on me. The two Bailies and the town-clerk came: I had wine ready for them, and then they would entertain me. They told me of their intention to present me with the freedom of the town. The Bailey held up the parchment in his right hand, and swore me to allegiance to the King and to preserve and defend the priviledges of the Borough.[1]

This is the county town of Lanerkshire in which the city of Glasgow is situated, having been anciently a town of considerable trade when Glasgow was not a place of great traffick. This town with Pebles, Selkirk, and Linlithgow, send a Member to Parliament.

I set out, and in three miles forded the Clyde, and came over the high ground, eight miles in the whole, to Chatelherault, originally built by the late Duke of Hamilton's father for a doghouse. It is on an eminence over the river. The building is beautifull, consisting of two large pavilions, with a handsome room in each, and a small pavilion at each end, the building between being at first designed for the dogs. Opposite to it are the remains of the old family castle[2] on the other side of the river, which runs between high cliffs most beautifully covered with wood and extends for some way. In this wood on the other side is a water that forms open petrifications like fine rock work. Near a mile below this, at the end of the town, is Hamilton House, which is an Half H. There are grand appartments in it, as well as a fine gallery above 100 feet long and about 20 broad, and there are many good pictures in the

---

[1] Mr. William Annan, Town Clerk, Lanark, has searched the Burgh records for this presentation without result. The Rolls of Burgesses extant only date from 1776. The gentlemen who waited on the Bishop were probably Bailies Robert Bell and Christopher Bannatyne, and William Wilson, Town Clerk. See note 5, p. 3.

[2] Cadzow Castle.

house.¹ At one end of it is the Parish Church in ruins, which is the burial place of the family.² The late Duke's father built a very handsome church ³ on the hill, in this shape—

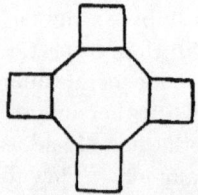

Hamilton is a well-built town, in which they have a linnen manufactory. The Duke built good walls, and has all kind of fruits on them in great perfection.

On the 24th I set out for Glasgow, and in a mile crossed the Clyde on a bridge, and rode through a very fine country, in all eight miles to Glasgow. Two miles from Hamilton we came to Bothwell, where there is a small Gothick church covered with stone about two inches thick in a singular manner.⁴ In each stone is a small segment of a circle, and one is laid over the joints in this manner⁵ in order to keep out the water. It was a collegiate church, founded in 1398 by Archibald Earl of Douglass, for a provost and eight prebendaries.—I am, etc.

¹ The Palace (never called a House) was very much altered and enlarged by the grandfather of the present Duke, who also made one of the finest collections of art in the kingdom. This was dispersed by the present Duke a few years ago by auction in London.

² This church, in ruins, was finally removed at the alterations in the Palace, as it stood close to the buildings, and the same Duke that enlarged the Palace (Duke Alexander) expended an enormous sum in making a new burial-place for the family. He built a huge Mausoleum, in imitation of the Emperor Hadrian's tomb at Rome, on a knoll of ground in the park.

³ Erected in 1732, from a design by Mr. Adams.

⁴ A new church, with tower, has been added to the old one, which is retained as a burial-chapel, forming part of the cruciform structure.

⁵ 'The arched roof is covered with large polished flags of stone, somewhat in the form of pan-tiles.'—*Old Stat. Ac.*, vol. xvi. p. 321.

GLASGOW.

Letter X.

GLASGOW, *May the 25th*, 1760.

DEAR MADAM,—Glasgow is finely situated on the Clyde. The old town is on a hill at some distance from the river, bounded to the east by a rivulet[1] which runs in a rocky glyn. The Cathedral is at the east end. The rest of the hill is formed into gardens to the south, which have a pretty effect, though they have very few fruit trees in them. The new town consists of two streets nearly a measured mile in length, with several other streets crossing at right angles. The town is finely built of hewn stone. Most of the houses are four stories high, and some five. The streets are extremely well paved and in the middle of them is a stone a foot broad, and in some a stone also on each side, on which the people walk, but mostly in the middle. Several merchants have grand houses. They have a fine old townhouse, and a beautifull new townhouse adjoyning to it. There are fine markets opposite one another, which are fronted with hewn stone, with three pediments over three doors, and false windows between them. One is for the flesh of small cattle, in the other there are conveniencies for hanging up beeves. They have also a market for herbs. There is a singular conveniency here, which is a sort of portico built round a court for washing, with a large furnace in each corner. It is in the Green, and is farmed out by the city. Everyone pays for boiling water by the measure, and they lay the cloaths to dry on the Green, which grazes a hundred cattle, at twenty shillings a head. They have six or seven parish churches.

The Cathedral of St. Mungo, alias Kentigern, by whom some say it was founded in 560, and that he was Bishop of Glasgow, others think that he was only the first preacher of Christianity here. Bishop Jocelyn in 1197 is said to have built the present Cathedral, which is a good Gothick fabric, much finer and grander within as to the architecture than without. An inscription at Melross mentions Murdoe, the architect

---

[1] The Molendinar Burn, on whose banks St. Kentigern set up his cell. See Jocelyn's Life.

of that church, as the contriver both of this and Paisley.[1] There is an old church under the east end, probably the remains of the first cathedral. The Gothick arches seem to have been turned on the old Saxon pillars. Bishop James Bethune[2] went abroad on the approach of the Reformation with the archives of the church, which he deposited at Paris in the Scotch College, and at the Carthusians. He was the last Archbishop. Before him Archbishop James Bethune of 1508, being turned out of the Chancellorship (after he had moved in relation to reading of the Scriptures in English that it should be referred to a National Synod) improved his house, and built that fine gateway in the front of it. The whole is encompassed with a high well built wall. The revenues of the Bishoprick chiefly consisting of tythes and duties, which latter, I suppose are chiefries were granted to the College. At the Reformation, in these chiefries, it was valued at £987, 8s. 7d. They have an agent who pays the stipends to the ministers, and I was told they do not make above £1000 a year clear of it. The new Church is on the design of St. Martin's-in-the-Fields, but I was told not above half as big. The freestone is yellow, and it has turned of different colours, which takes off greatly from the beauty of it. They have some churches of Seceders, and a small nonjuring Episcopal congregation. The English Licenced Episcopal congregation have built a very handsome oblong square church near the Green,[3] on the model of the churches in London, for galleries which are not yet built. It cost about £1100. The minister has about £60 a year from the collec-

---

[1] The inscription is on a tablet to the south side of the transept door of the Abbey of Melrose, and has been rendered thus:—

' John Murdo, sum tym callyt was I,	' Of Glasgu, Melros, and Paslay,
And born in Parysse certainly,	Of Nyddsdall, and of Galway:
And had in keping all mason werk	I pray to God and Mary bath,
Of Santandrays, ye hye Kirk	And sweet St. John kep this haly Kirk fra skaith.'

[2] For a detailed inventory of the relics and valuables removed by Archbishop Beaton, or Bethune second, in 1560, see *Registrum Episcopatus Glasguensis*.

[3] St. Andrew's Willow Acre, Low Green Street, the oldest Episcopal Chapel in Scotland. It was built in 1750. The Mason engaged in its construction was excommunicated by the religious body of Anti-Burghers to which he belonged, for the 'sinful and scandalous work of building the Episcopal Meeting House,' an eloquent commentary on the religious tolerance of the times. The Rev. Dr. J. F. S. Gordon, the present Incumbent, has not succeeded in finding any reference to Bishop Pococke's visitation in the books of the Church.

tions. They perform divine service in a most decent and solemn manner, chanting the hymns and singing the psalms extremely well insomuch that I think I never saw divine offices performed with such real edification.[1] The people here and at Paisley keep Sunday with great strictness. They all attend divine service, and are not allowed to walk out on a Sunday in company.[2] They have no holydays and this preserves them perfectly sober and industrious, and if it could be kept to, it is certainly a very good regulation, even in a political point of view. They shut up their shops early in the evening, open late in the morning, and take proper refreshments. There were two monasteries in this town. The Blackfriers was at the church of that name, near the college, which is entirely new built. It was founded by the dean and chapter in 1270. The other of Observantines was founded in 1476 by Bishop John [Laing] and Thomas Forsyth, rector of Glasgow. The learned Friar John Russel[3] was of it, who was burnt in 1539 for an Heretick, and the next year [1559] it was destroyed by the Duke of Chatelherault and the Earle of Argyle.

This City has above all others felt the advantages of the Union, by the West India trade they enjoy, which is very great, especially in Tobacco, Indigoes, and Sugar. The first is a great trade in time of war; as they send the Tobacco by land to the port of the Frith of Forth, almost as far as Hopton, and supply France. They have sugar houses, and make what is called Scotch Indigo, which is compounded with starch as to

---

[1] Dr. Pocock does not record that he preached twice during his short stay in Glasgow. The following appeared in *The Glasgow Journal* of 29th May 1760: 'On Saturday last arrived here the Right Reverend Doctor Richard Pocock, bishop of Ossory, and next day being Whitsunday, performed divine Service in the English chapel, and on Tuesday after a sermon suited to the occasion, confirmed a great number.' A similar paragraph appeared in *The Edinburgh Evening Courant* of 31st May.

[2] This excessive zeal for Sunday observance appears to have been after the Bishop's own heart. The good custom, however, had degenerated into tyranny, being enforced with magisterial authority. There were men appointed called 'compurgators,' who apprehended and publicly prosecuted Sunday desecrators, and even those who were walking for pleasure. This state of matters continued until Mr. Blackburn was taken into custody for walking on the Green; whereupon he raised an action in the Court of Session against the Magistrates for an 'unwarranted exercise of authority,' and obtained a decision against them.

[3] The martyrdom of Jerom Russel took place in 1538.

make a very fine light blue. In order to carry on this trade properly they have gone into a great variety of manufactures, to have sortments of goods to be exported, as all the inkle [1] smallwares, linnens of all kinds, small ironwares, glass bottles, and earthenwares, which latter they make in great perfection. Many considerable estates have been made here, especially by those who have gone to the West Indies, many of whom have returned and purchased in Clydesdale.

The college consists of a principal, a clergyman put in by the Government, and several professors. The six principal live in the Colledge. There are besides these head professors others, one or more in every science, who act for them occasionally. Some students of distinction live with the professors, but the rest abroad. They all wear red gowns, mostly of cloth. They commonly enter very young, and in that case are kept the first year to Humanity. A great number come from Ireland, some of them for the Church and Physick as well as for the Presbyterian assemblies.

This inscription in the Colledge was found lately at Kirkintilloch, six miles from Glasgow, on the Roman wall. There is a crack in the stone [2]—

S IMP. CAESARI. T
AELIO. HADRIANO.
ANTONINO. AVG.
PIO P.P. VEXILLA
LEG. VI. VIC. P F
PER. M P.

[1] Inkle or incle: anciently a kind of crewel or worsted work, but generally known as a sort of narrow fillet or tape made of linen yarn. This trade was begun in Glasgow in 1732 by Alexander Harvey, who had the enterprise to go to Holland, the seat of the inkle smallware trade, and in spite of the secrecy observed, succeeded in purchasing in Haarlem two looms, and engaging an experienced workman.

[2] This tablet is preserved in the Hunterian Museum, Glasgow University. It is illustrated in Stuart's *Caledonia Romano*, Plate x. fig. 5, p. 324, 2d Ed.

There is a narrow bridge, which is rather failing, over the Clyde, so that they propose to build another lower down the country. About Glasgow is a very fine open country, with trees about the houses, hamlets, and villages that have a very fine effect.—I am, etc.

LETTER XI.

Lus, on Lough Loumond, *May* 30*th*, 1760.

DEAR MADAM,—On the 28th I made an excursion to the west of Glasgow, going near the river. We came in two miles to Givan,[1] where there is a square mount. Two miles more brought us to Renfrew, a small town. It was on the Clyde, but the river on a thaw after a great frost, about a hundred years agoe, changed its course, leaving King's Inch Castle,[2] the seat of the ancient Stewards of Scotland, on the south side, which had been formerly on the north. A little stream runs in the old course, and forms an island of about one hundred acres, near half a mile in length.

From this place we crossed two miles north to Paisley, a great manufacturing town for Linnen. It is thought to be the Vanduara of Ptolemy, called in the new map Vandugria. What I saw to the south-east of the Abbey Church on the river Carte appeared most like a Roman work. It is just opposite to the fine water cataract down the rocks, which may fall about eight feet. The Monastery of Paisley was first a priory, and made an abbey of black monks, of the order of Cluny from Wenlock, in England, by Walter, son of Alan, Lord Steward of Scotland, in 1164.[3] It was the burial-place of that family untill they were made Kings of Scotland. Robert the Second, the first of this

---

[1] Govan.
[2] King's Inch, now part of the demesne of Eldersly House.
[3] In the Chartulary of Paisley the monastery is stated to have been founded in 1163 for a Prior and thirteen Cluniac Monks, whom its founder brought from Wenlock Abbey in Shropshire. 'The Order derived its name from the Abbey of Cluni in Burgundy, the first, and always the chief, house of what were termed the reformed Benedictines.'—Pref. to *Chart. Paisley*, p. 3, Maitland Club Pub.

family, his first wife, Elizabeth Muir,[1] famous in history, and Euphemia Ross, his queen, were buried here; and Marjory Bruce, his mother; whose tomb with a couchant statue on it I saw, and what they call an altar near, with a Gothick ornament on it, as if it had been over some statue, but this probably was part of another tomb. There is a tradition that she broke her neck a-hunting, and that a surgeon being near, Robert was taken out of her body. There is a vault in which they are all deposited. It is a chapel, now uncovered and ruinous, to the south of the church. The architecture of the west end of the church is singular, with a sharp pointed arch to the door and a nich on each side in the same taste, like great part of the Cathedral of Glasgow, built about the same time, and without doubt by the same architect[2] as observed before. The inside is also singular, particularly in a sort of large console between the upper windows as if to place statues on. The architecture of the inside is here represented. In the north of the church is an inscription of 1333, of which I could make nothing. They have taken down the isles, and the body wanting that support the arches are failing. The choir is entirely down. On the south side of the transept is the burial-place, if I mistake not of Lord Dundonald. The enclosure of the garden, fourteen acres, is of very fine hewn stone inside and outside, built by Abbot George Schaw. At the north-west corner is an inscription, which was not legible to me, but I was informed it is as follows:—

> They called the Abbot George of Schaw
> About my Abby make this wall,
> A thousand and four hundred years
> And eighty four the date but were,
> Let these pray for his salvation
> That layed this noble foundation.[3]

In another part which I did not see is a statue of the Virgin Mary in a nich. The distich under it is thus printed:—

> Hac ne vade via, nisi dixeris Ave Maria:
> Sit semper sine væ quæ tibi dixit Ave.

---

[1] Elizabeth More or Mure, daughter of Sir Adam More or Mure of Rowallan.
[2] John Murdo, one of the architects of the Churches of St. Andrews, Glasgow, Melrose, etc. See note, p. 50.
[3] A modernised rendering of the quaint inscription.

The Inside of the Church of the Abbey of Paisley.

The last Abbot,[1] Lord Claud Hamilton, third son of James Duke of Chatelheraut, Governour of Scotland, was made abbot at twelve years old, and having forfeited on Queen Mary's side at the battle of Langside in 1568, the abbey was granted to William, Lord Semple, heritable Bailey of Paisley. But Lord Claude being restored to his fortune by James the Sixth, was created Lord Paisley. His son, the Earl of Abercorn, parted with this abbey to William, first Earl of Dundonald, in whose posterity it remains at present. There are two other kirks in this place, and a congregation of Seceders, and they have a large poorhouse. Lord Dundonald is disposing of all the land of the abbey garden for the manufactory, a plan of which design is engraved.

On a hill to the west was an old British fort, which seemed to have been round. There is a pleasant bowling green within it. On a hill a little to the west is another called Hothead Camp, and to the south about half-a-mile is another on a hill called Woodside, each of them about three-quarters of an acre. From this height we saw Lord Rosses, about two miles off called Hawkhead, and to the east Cardonal,[2] Lord Blantyre's. We went on and had in view to the north the river[3] which runs by Kilwining Abbey, and forms beautifull pieces of water before a handsome country seat.

We came in eight miles to Baith, a poor small town of farmers. Going on, in about a mile we passed by a mote,[4] and had in view a long low hill[5] called the Bank Head of the Blair, which at first appeared much as if it had been worked into a Roman fortification at one end.

In about five miles from Baith, we came to Kilwining Abbey, two miles north-west of Irwin. This abbey was founded in 1140 by Hugh Morevile, Constable of Scotland,

---

[1] Lord Claud Hamilton had the abbacy conferred on him by his uncle, John Hamilton, the last Abbot, in 1549. Through his adhering to Queen Mary he was superseded, and *Robert*, Lord Semple, was appointed Commendator. He was afterwards restored, but had to fly into England, and was again restored in 1587, when he was created Lord Paisley, and had the whole monastery property granted to him in fee. In 1606 his son was created Earl of Abercorn, and the property remained in that family till 1652, when part of it was sold to Lord Dundonald.

[2] Cardonald.   [3] The Garnock River.
[4] Hill of Beith.   [5] Caerwinning Hill.

and dedicated to St. Winning. The monks were of the order of St Bernard, called Tyronenses, from Tyro in the diocese of Chartres, where he settled them. They were brought to that place from Kelso Abbey. It is finely situated on a river which falls into the sea at Irwin. The tower is very grand, but what is singular, the entrance was only on the south side of it. The body of the church is entirely destroyed. The quire was not so magnificent, and is turned into a parish church.[1] I observed the members of the architecture are very much in the plain Saxon style, but the arches are Gothic.

I went two miles to Irwin,[2] and having crossed the river, observed a tumulus, and some works that were much like a Roman camp. Irwin is situated between two rivers,[3] and a third falls in very near them. It is a pretty good harbour, and they have a great trade[4] in fishing, and in exporting coal to Ireland called Scotch coal. They make Scotch blew, and have a great manufactory of ropes for shipping. There is something singular in the door and window cases of the castle[5] or old ruined mansion-house of the Earl of Eglington, to whose ancestor the lands of Kilwining Abbey were granted and erected into a Lordship. They are adorned with a kind of twisted pilaster and other members, the ornaments of which are very delicate, drawings of them are here seen. [See pp. 58, 59.]

Here was a Monastery[6] of Carmelites, founded by the Laird of Fullarton in 112 . . . The Church,[6] which now serves for the parish, seems to be very old, with small windows, turned with two arches. I could get no information whether this was the church of the monastery.

I came from this place four miles through a very fine country to Kilmarnock, observing a square mount or mote

---

[1] The tower fell in 1814, and the 'quire' was removed in 1775, when the present parish church was built.

[2] Irvine, formerly written Irwin, Irwine, and Irwyn.

[3] Rivers Garnock, Irvine, and Anack.

[4] In 1760 Irvine was the third port in Scotland.

[5] 'The Seagate Castle is a ruinous fabric of considerable antiquity. It belongs to the Earl of Eglington, and is supposed to have been intended as the jointure-house of the Dowager Ladies of that family.'—Robertson's *Top. Ac. of Cunningham.* See forthcoming vol., 'Irvine,' *Ayr and Gal. Arch. Assoc.*, twelve plates by W. Galloway, F.S.A. Scot.

[6] Founded about 1285. On its site stands the present church, built in 1774.

half way at Thornton, and saw Lord Eglington's house, with fine plantations about it, two miles north-east of Irwin, and near Kilmarnock to the south Cubringtown,[1] I suppose the same as Carpentown in the map, a fine old castle belonging

Doorway at the Mansion-house at Irwin.[2]

to Sir John Cunningham. Kilmarnock is situated on a rising ground at the confluence of two rivers. There is a tolerable square, but the streets are narrow, and the houses thatched, though adorned with stone cornices as in many other parts. They have two good churches, that on the site of the Parish Church as well as the other being new built. They have a

[1] Caprington.   [2] The arch is segmental, not circular.

great manufactory of carpets, woven Scotch bonnets, serges, shaloons, narrow cloaths, and some broad cloath. When we came to the town all the shops were shut, nor would they sell anything, and almost all the people were at church, being the Fast Day before the Sacrament. The carpet manufacture has

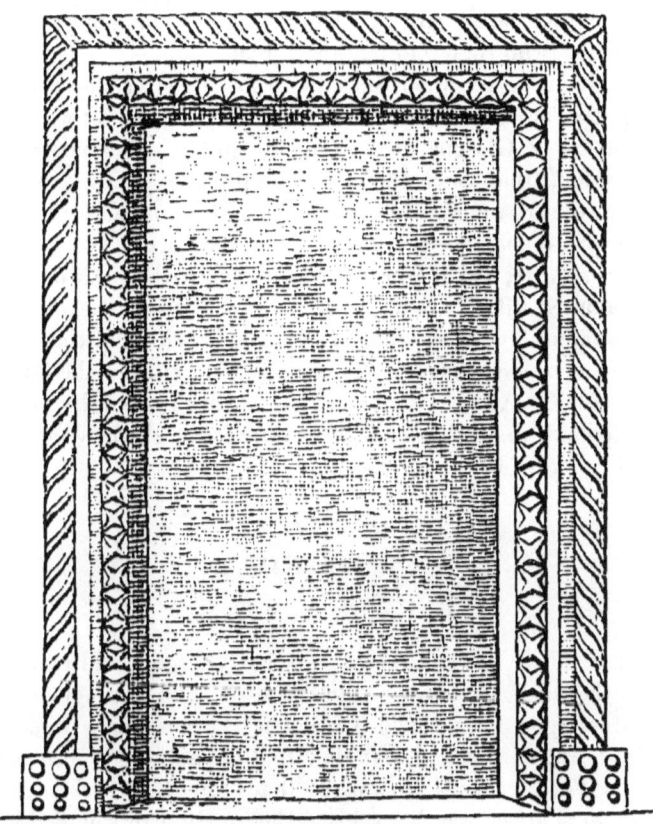

Window at the Mansion-house at Irwin.

been settled here about a dozen years. A little higher up the river is Castle Loudon, the residence of the earl of that name. Near the river of Aire they have a quarry out of which they get whetstones.[1]

[1] The celebrated Water-of-Ayr hones.

I set forward, and observed about a quarter of a mile from the town a head of land made by the river to the east, and a valley to the west. The south end of it has been fortified with a fossee drawn across the north side. Just without this is Kilmarnock Castle,[1] now belonging to the Earl of Glencairn, who never lives there. A mile further we passed by a very good mansion-house called Crawford Land,[2] belonging to one of that name, who they told me was abroad.

The road was for about six miles near the river, and part of it up the mountain, and having travelled ten miles we came within six of Glasgow at the summit on the other side called Haslewood, from which there is a fine prospect of Glasgow, and all the country round. On this height is a stone set up on end, as a mark, it may be, of an ancient burial-place. We came to the river Carte, which runs in a deep glyn with rocks on each side adorned with trees, and soon arrived at the castle of Cath Carte, opposite a little village called the Brayhead of the Carte, where we crossed the river. This castle gives title to the Earl of Cath Carte. All the country we passed through is full of coals, and abounds in a black kind of granite in which there are very small grains of white sparr.—I am, &c.

LETTER XII.

INVERARAY, *June* 2d, 1760.

DEAR MADAM,—On the 30th I left Glasgow, and travelled near the river by several country seats, and through a fine country, eight miles to Old Kirkpatrick,[3] where many think the wall of Antonine ended, but they told me nothing is seen of it here. They see some remains of it towards New Kirkpatrick.[4] Here St. Patrick was born, his father, a Roman who fled into this country from the persecution of the Emperor, for many Christians settled here on this account. It is conjectured that his ancestor was a Patrician.

---

[1] Dean Castle, now the property of the Duke of Portland. For illustrations see *Trans. of Ayr and Wigtown Arch. Soc.*, vol. iii. p. 112 ; also *Castellated Arch. of Scotland*, by Messrs. MacGibbon and Ross, 1887, vol. i. pp. 401-408.

[2] Crawfurdland Castle.   [3] Old Kilpatrick.   [4] New Kilpatrick.

A mile further is Douglas Castle,[1] on a rock, three sides of which are covered by the water of the river. There are some fine hewn stones in it, and enquiring here about the wall, they showed me a mound in a garden which they said they took to be part of it, and that a little further, at a channel for water from the hill, which is made under the road, they found a part of the field very stony, which they thought was part of the foundation of the wall. This old castle, which was small, is in ruins.

About a mile further is the curious castle of Dumbarton, which is Alcluith mentioned by Bede, and to the north of Clyde the Scots from Ireland settled under Reuda, their leader. This castle is situated on a high rock, with the water on three sides of it. I was at it in 1747. The entrance is at the east side, from which one ascends by a winding way on the south side. On this side there is a very good house. The road up turns round to the west side, where towards the summit are other buildings. There is a wall from near the top, on the north side, and along part of the west side where it is weakest.

On the other side of the river, as between the two castles, is a seat which stands finely, having a view of both the castles, of the town of Dumbarton, up and down the Clyde, and up the river Leven towards Lough Loughman, and further down is another seat adjoining to an old castle in much the same kind of situation.

The town of Dumbarton is on a flat peninsula formed by the winding of the Leven. There was a collegiate church in it, founded in 1450 by Isabell, Countess of Lenox and Duchess of Albany, and dedicated to St. Patrick, who they say was born in Lenox.

The coach way is by Dumbarton ferry, but is two miles about, so we went up the foot of the hill, and soon came to a most charming place, Leven Side, Mr. Campbell's, being finely situated and commanding a view of the windings of the river both ways. From this we soon came to Bonille[2] ferry, where we began to have a view of Lough Loughman,[3] and crossed over the

[1] Dunglass Castle, the ancient stronghold of the Colquhouns. Erected in 1380; garrisoned till near the close of the seventeenth century.
[2] Bonhill.
[3] Loch Lomond, derived, according to Dr. MacLauchlan, from Laoman, one of the heroes of Celtic antiquity. *Vide Celtic Gleanings*, pp. 130, 131.

Leven, which runs out of it into a most charming, romantick country, with a great number of streams that divide the hills covered with wood, all having good bridges over them. We first had a large island[1] in view, and two smaller to the northeast, the first appearing in different shapes according to the places from which we saw it. Then other islands open to view. One or two of them are large, and several small ones—all covered with wood, as well as the hills to the west.

At last we saw the Castle of Lus: to which there is adjoyning a good mansion-house. It is on a peninsula which points to the north, having a small creek to the west of it, and is a most charming situation, inhabited by a baronet of the family of Grant,[2] who takes his name from this place, which has a more particular denomination.[3] We came to the inn at Lus, between which and the castle is the church and parsonage house. A long island lies before it as in the middle of the Lough, and another most beautifull one stretches from the south, covered with woods of firr and other trees of different greens, with a smaller island to the east. The top of a larger appears over it, towards which the foot of the eastern mountain, beautifully broken, extends to the south, and these mountains are covered with several spots of corn as well as wood and rock, and cascades falling down all round after the great rain. I went on by the military road made from Dumbarton to this place, and so along over the lake to Torbut, and from that place to Fort William which is 63 measured miles from Torbut. Near Lus they have very good slate quarries.[4] This road was made by blowing up the rocks in several places. The miles are marked on the rock, and three miles from Lus is this inscription—

COLONEL LASCELLES regiment, May 1745: that regiment being employed in this part of the road.

There are no islands on the lake from Lus to Torbut, and

---

[1] Inchmurrin (the largest and most southerly). On it are the ruins of an old castle, which once belonged to the Earls of Lennox.

[2] Grant of Grant married Ann, heiress of Luss, and by an ante-nuptial contract it was settled that in certain events (which happened) the oldest son should inherit the estate of Grant, the second Luss—the Colquhoun estates,—and assume the name and arms of Colquhoun.

[3] Ross-dhu, the seat of Sir J. Colquhoun, Bart.

[4] Camstraddan.

it appears like a river being about a mile wide. Half a dozen islands appeared opposite to Lus which were not seen before. Some of them indeed are only rocks. The road is extremely pleasant, trees growing beautifully on each side, and after the rains streams of water, rushing down the rocks, are seen in beautiful cascades through the trees almost every hundred yards all the way.

After three or four miles we came to Lower Inver Douglas,[1] where the Douglas passes under a bridge, having formed a cascade above it which falls down the rocks about 10 feet. Here is a tumulus, and before this place is a beautifull flat promontory. Just beyond Torbut,[2] the lake not being above half a mile broad, the land locks in, so that it appears like the end of the Lough. From Torbut the road goes off to Inveraray to the west, another military road going northward to Fort William 63 miles.

I took a boat and went eight miles to the north end of the lake, where the river falls into it, near a little hillock which appears like a tumulus. There is an island[3] opposite to Torbut, and four more higher up, which are all small except one which contains about an acre, and it is entirely covered with wood as the others are, and there is an old house on it in which a late Laird of Macfarlin lived to whom all this country belonged. In one part is a beautifull high head[4] which makes into the lake from the east, and appears like an island.

They have in the lake perch about eight inches long, pike, trouts, and powens,[5] which are a sort of white fish, a kind of fresh water herring, and not very good.

I went ashore to go to the redoubt commonly called the fort of Inversnade. It is a mile from the mouth of the River Snade, and the soldiers have made a road to it. It holds two companies, and is fortified against anything but cannon. There

---

[1] Inveruglass.   [2] Tarbet.

[3] Eilean Vhou, on which are the ruins of a stronghold of the Macfarlanes.

[4] Ben Lomond seemingly did not attract the attention of the Bishop, or what is more likely, the noble mountain might be enveloped in mist when he passed. See note 5, p. 68.

[5] The Powan, *Corregonus Cepedii* (Gaelic, pollag or pollac). A rare freshwater fish peculiar to Loch Lomond and Loch Eck, akin to the Irish pollan and the vendace of Lochmaben.

is a horse road this way to Sterling, which is 18 miles distant. The river Snade falls down in different cascades at least 300 feet, some ten feet, some more, but the last falls in three streams divided by the rocks, and one of them a little lower divides into two. The fall is between 30 and 40 feet and extremely beautifull, and highly adorned with rocks and trees.

Opposite to this on the other side they told me is Lough Slowie, I suppose the same as Lough Sloy[1] which they told me is a mile long and half a mile broad, in which there are small trouts.

They have limestone in Glan Traun[2] to the west, and in the country of Buchanan to the east. At Clefton,[3] 22 miles in the way to Fort William are lead mines belonging to Lord Broadalbin. A road goes off from this road at the end of the Lough to Killin at the west end of Lough Tay, which is 15 miles from Taymouth.—I am, etc.

Letter XIII.

Lochness, *June 5th*, 1760.

Dear Madam,—On the 2d we set out for Inverary, and in two miles passed by the Laird of McFarlin's house[4] a very pretty place at the head of Lough Long which is a bay of the sea. Going on by a river which falls into it, we came up to a semi-circular seat made in turf, on which is this inscription on a stone—"Rest and be thankful, 1748."[5]

We descended to Glyncrow having passed several beautifull cascades. We then came to a small Lough, and to a less below it, out of which rises a river that falls into Glynfine. In Glyncrow I had observed that the slaty rocks were in the figures of the members of architecture, as on Lough Foyle in

---

[1] The rendezvous and battle-cry of the Clan MacFarlane. It was also the motto of the chief.
[2] Glen Fruin limestone, parish of Row.
[3] Clifton, near Tyndrum.   [4] New Tarbet.
[5] At the top of the hill is a seat with this inscription, Rest and be Thankful. Stones were placed to mark the distances, which the inhabitants have taken away, resolved, they said, 'to have no new miles.'—Dr. Johnson's *Journey to the Western Isles*, 1773.

Ireland and in some parts of Errig in that country; and on this side of Lough Louman, I had seen much of the white flint in patches between the rocks as well as in the fields, and it is in many parts.

This by the map is the head of the river Kinglas which falls into Lough Fine at Carndow,[1] to which we came, and went round the end of Lough Fine.

We had been in the country of the Damnii, but this is the country of the Epidii, Cantyre being called Epidium Promontorium as the Lough or bay was the Lelannonius Sinus.

On the west side of it we passed by veins of limestone, one of which is of a greyish marble, and there are veins of slate and other stones that come in between them.

When we came round the head of the land to another part of the bay of Lough Fine, I was most agreeably surprised with the sight of Inverary, the grand castle[2] built by the Duke of Argyle,[3] and the beautiful hill[4] to the north of the town with two heads, on one of which a turret is built, and both covered with wood. To the east of it—a fine glyn, with a rivulet running through it, which forms a lake, into which salmon, sea-trouts, and other fish are brought up by the tide. One goes over this river on a fine bridge of one arch adorned with a ballustrade [built] by the Duke of Argyle. Inverary is on the west side of the Lough, which is 24 miles long and winds to the south-east.

The Duke has built a bridge at the mouth of the Aray with circular piers, designs to adorn an old bridge which is a little higher, and is building a third bridge above this. The two upper bridges lead to the castle, and the lowest towards what is designed to be the new town. The castle is a most magnificent Gothick building with a round tower at each corner about 14 feet in diameter within. The house is lighted by seven windows in one front and five in the other. In the former is a gallery the whole length, which is 110 feet. The

---

[1] Cairndow Inn, opposite Ardkinglass.
[2] Illustrated in Pennant's *Tour*, 1769, Pl. xxi. p. 238.
[3] Archibald, third Duke. This is the present castle, begun 1744, finished 1761. It stands on almost the same site as the old baronial castle, built in the time of the first Earl (1453-1493).
[4] Duniquaich (*Dun Chuaich*).

other front is not so long by about 15 feet. There is a fosse round the house, and all round the outside of that arched offices about 15 feet wide in the clear, and to this fossee the windows of the offices open under the house. The grand floor is over that, having three rooms on each side, a hall in the middle, with large Gothick windows rising above the rest of the building. There is a stone staircase on each side of it, to which there is an arched opening, so as to give some light to the rooms. There is an attick story, and rooms over them for servants as in the roof, lighted by skylights. All the windows are turned with Gothick arches. The house is built of St. Catherine's stone, which works like chalk, growing hard in the weather, and is of a lightish green. There is another sort also which comes from another quarry. Some of the rooms are finished, and all the others are going on with the utmost expedition. The Duke is building the farm offices round a court some way off to the south-west, and designs the stable offices half a mile to the west to be built to the kitchen garden wall. To the north of that is a Gothick building on four arches over a mineral well of steel and sulphur, and this is near the hill on which the turret is built, round which there is a coach way up to the top, and from it the castle appears very grand. The Duke designs to make some additional buildings to it. To the west on an eminence is a building made to appear like a ruin, which is the dairy. All the ground to the west is finely planted, the Aray running through it, which gives name to the town—Inverary (the inlet of the Aray).

The old town which is to the east of the castle, is to be pulled down, and a new town built to the south of a little bay, where the townhouse and the Inn now are, between which there is to be a street [1] to the south, and another will be built to the east of them along the Lough. In the old town is a small cross adorned with carvings which was brought from I-Colm-Kill, as was another that is set up at Campbelltown,[2] but there are no characters on this.

---

[1] For this street a beech-tree avenue, a mile long, was substituted. Duke Archibald did not live to see his designs carried out.

[2] The crosses are still standing. Dr. Pococke's informant mistakingly venerated those commemorative or memorial High Crosses as Iona relics, through

There are large woods to the south, with ridings cut through them, and a Gothick arch is built over a well in one part of the wood where a spring of fine water runs out of the rock. In another part a beautifull cascade falls down the rocks between the trees. The rocks here for a considerable way to the south and west are of a red granite of small grains, which promises to polish very finely. On the opposite side of the Lough is another stone of a more mixed colour. To the west of the great hill is a small ridge of a mountain that consists of a limestone.

Mr. Cumin, a very ingenious person in experimental philosophy and mechanics (who, I have been since told, is making a clock to regulate time by the stars as well as sun,) gave me the following process as to the qualities of the stone of St. Catharine, which appeared to me to be much like the harder kind of soapstone in Cornwall. It is soft when dugg, and may be cut with a knife; hardens in the air; if burnt in a moderate fire it becomes almost impenetrable, and loses near a third of its weight, but if the heat is encreased it melts into a substance like bottle glass; if oyl is rubbed on the stone, it becomes black; burning turns it brown; rubbed with Sperma Ceti it looks like a deep coloured serpentine.—I am, etc.

LETTER XIV.

ISLE OF MULL, *June 7th*, 1760.

DEAR MADAM,—On the 4th I set out westward from Inverary and went by the Millitary road which is continued five miles to the west on the side of the hill over the Aray, where in all parts the Duke is enclosing the woods with a dry wall, and cover'd with sods. They have a great number of

ignorance of their local historic value and association. They date about 1500. For a description, etc., of the Inveraray Cross, see Stuart's *Sculp. Stones of Scot.*, vol. ii. p. 22. The Campbeltown Cross is 11 feet high, 19 inches broad, 4 inches thick. On a square panel on the shaft of the cross is the following inscription: HEC : EST : CRVX : DOMINI : YVARI : M : HEACHYRNA : QVODAM : RECTORIS : DE : KYL : RECAN : ET : DOMINI : ANDREE : NATI : EIVS : RECTORIS : DE : KIL : COMAN : QVI : HANC : CRVCE : FIERE : FACIE : BAT. An excellent cast of this cross is a prominent object in the Museum of the Soc. of Ant., Edinburgh.

Roe Deer[1] here which are about as big as an Antelope—but not so delicate, as I think being longer behind. They are great destroyers of the growth of young trees—as well as hares. I came to bad road for about two miles and a half over the hill, till we arrived near to Lough Awe, which lake is 24 miles long and fresh water. We went two miles to the south to Port Sonachan ferry. Here the hills are common whin or fire stone. Towards the north end of the lake is Castle Culhorn[2] on an Island which was the first seat of the family of Broadalbin; and eight miles to the south is Inch Chonnel Castle[3] on another Isle the first seat of the family of Argyle. Where we turned to the south at Ardbrache[4] they lately found a vault with an urn and bones in it.

We crossed this Lough in a Boat, which holds only two large horses, and they put Boughs at the bottom to preserve the boat which is slight; it is about a mile over; we went on six miles to Lough Etive, where a river from Lough Awe falls into it which is called Inver Awe (the outlet of the Awe). I crossed this river to see what I took to be a camp which had something of the air of a Roman fortification, but it was occasioned only by the straight sides of the Bank on the eminence, and there was no sign of any entrenchment any other way, so that if any fortification it was probably British.

Over this is Cruhaun[5] Mountain something less than 1445 yards which is the height of Benevis[5] near Fort William.

We returned and crossed over Lough Etive about half a

---

[1] In the MS. on the page opposite to this reference to Deer are two notes written by different hands. 'I made great enquiries about the Roe-Bucks in this and other parts of the Highlands, but could never hear of them being plentifull anywhere except near Castle Grant. The Red Deer of the Highlands are by no means so large as those in the English parks—some of these may be seen in the D. of Athole's Park at Blair.—[Initialled] D. B.' See note, p. 69.

The following is evidently a rejoinder: 'Roes in vast plenty near Invercauld and all parts of the wooded country of Inverness.—[Initialled] T. P.' Can this note be by Thomas Pennant? *Vast plenty* is a frequent expression of his, and he may have had access to Bishop Pococke's MSS. when preparing his *Tours* for the press. See note 5, p. 85; also note 3, p. 86.

[2] Kilchurn or Caolchurn Castle, the property of the Marquis of Breadalbane. The ruins are based upon a rock, which tradition says was once an island.

[3] Ardchonal Castle, or Inischonel, the ancient seat of the Lords of Loch Awe.

[4] Ardbrecknish (Rock Hill).

[5] The respective altitudes of Ben Nevis, Ben Cruachan, and Ben Lomond are

mile broad in the same kind of boat. Here the Rocks are grey granate. We had to the right beautifull wood on the rocky hills and in about 3 miles came to Ardchattin, Mr. Campbell's house built on the site of an old priory of Cistercians of Vallis Catrium.[1] The west end only of the Choir is remaining and is Saxon architecture. The other part is new modelled. It was founded by Duncan MacLoud from whom the McDouglas's of Lorn are descended. It was annexed to the Bishoprick of Argyle by Jas. VIth in 1617. In 1573 Jno. Campbell the Prior was made Bishop of the Isles.

On a hill over this priory is the Old Parish Church which on account of the saint it is dedicated to is had in great veneration. His name was [M]Hoiden or as 'tis pronounc'd Voidan being call'd Bailim Voidan.[2]

We went on in the same beautifull country having Lough Etive to the right, and came to the end of the mountains which terminate in a perpendicular rock exactly like the ancient Anxur now called Terracina in the way from Rome to Naples. This rock was called Dun Vallin Re (the Hill of the King's town) and by the Cromwelian soldiers Craig Nuke, and this is the entrance, so that ancient city rock seems to have been called Vallin or Ballin Re (the City of the King). In the new map of Scotland it is called Berigonium, and seem'd to have been anciently the Chief City in Scotland, and I was told that Buchanan gives it that name. Cambden calls it Beregonium,[3] a Castle wherein the Courts of Justice were anciently kept, but what foundation there is for this name I cannot form any

4406, 3611, and 3192 feet. In the MS. the following note has been written: 'I cannot conceive that Crohaun Mountain is of this height as I was very near it. It seems extraordinary that Bishop Pocock should not have taken notice of Ben Lomond, which is directly opposite to Tarbet, where he appears to have been. It is certainly the 2nd Mountain of the Highlands, and I never heard any other than Ben nevis compared to it.—[Initialled] D. B.' See notes, pp. 63, 68, 113.

[1] Vallis Caulium. The priory was founded in 1231 by Duncan M'Coull, supposed ancestor of the Lords of Lorn—MacDougalls.

[2] Baile-Mhaodain, church of Bal-maodan or Modan. Abbot or Bishop Modan flourished early in the sixth century. Several churches were dedicated to him.

[3] 'The famous city of Beregonium was situated between two hills, one called Dun Macsnichan, "the hill of Snachan's son," and the other, much superior in height, is named Dun bhail an righ, "the hill of the king's town." A street paved with common stones running from the foot of the one hill to the other is still called Straid mharagaid, "the market street;" and another place, at a little

judgment. This rock consists of large pebbles and stones cemented together, and there seemed to me to be some Iron ore in a sort of Dust between them. Just within it is the Church dedicated to Saint Columbus and being called Kill[1] gives name to the Hamlet near it.

A quarter of an English measured mile to the west is a Rocky hill extending a furlong from South to North and close to the Sea, this is called the Dun McSneam[2] (the Fortress of McSneam), all over it are marks of the foundations of Buildings. In the Castle, etc., they show the place where the well was, and it is now so moist, that Flaggs grow about it. From the other Rock to this is an Elevated Bank which is supposed to have been a street, and is called the Salt market, there seem to have been houses towards the sea and to the north; there being a sort of terrace on each side; and to the north is a small bog which might have been a pond to supply the town with water. There is a long stone on the south side of it. Before I came to the first rock called Ballin Re I saw two Carns[3] consisting of heaps of stones. From the north end of this on the edge of a bog are signs of another street extending about a furlong to the west, towards another rocky hill, and this is called the meal Market, which might be a suburb of the town. The sea seems to have left this place, for the ground between this

distance, goes by the name of Straid namin, "the meal street." About 1780 a man, cutting peats in a moss between two hills, found one of the wooden pipes that conveyed the water from the one hill to the other at a depth of 5 feet below the surface.'—*Old Stat. Ac.*, 'Ardchattan,' vol. vi. p. 180.

For the Beregonium theory see the late Dr. R. Angus Smith's charming dialogue *Loch Etive and the Sons of Uisnach*, 1879. 'We know of no *Bere*gonium before Boece, and whether it is connected with *Reri*gonium in Galloway or not is not quite proved. . . . The evidence for Beregonium breaks down, and the destruction of the civilisation follows' (pp. 137, 138).

[1] Kilcolmkill or Kiel. Traces only of church dedicated to Columba are all that can be seen.

[2] The Dun of the sons of Uisneach.

[3] 'It would be endless to enumerate all the Druidical monuments in the parish of Ardchattan. Many cairns and heaps of stones are to be seen; one, in particular, near the centre of a deep moss about 3 or 4 miles in circumference. In different places are stones rising 12 feet above the surface, all of them one single stone, and, at a small distance, a number of large stones from 20 to 22 feet in length, of an oval figure.' By Rev. Ludovick Grant; *Old Stat. Ac.*, vol. vi. p. 180. Dun Macsnichan or *Dun-mac-*Sniachan is held to be identical with the Selma of Ossian. This whole district is full of Ossianic legendary interest.

last street and the sea consists of such pebbles as are on the beach. They have a tradition that the Scots from Ireland landed here.

From this place to the passage over to Sr Duncan Campbels, it is about a mile, but when the Tyde is in, it is a mile further to the West. This seat is situated on a head of Land a Peninsula, which extends to the South about a mile and is divided by little vales into four or five long narrow hills covered with wood. The Highest of them is to the West on which on a rock covered also with wood and projecting to the East, Lady Campbel built a square tower in 1754 consisting of four arches on a basement formed into three steps; it is about fifty feet high, and a wall is built on each side between the piers with a semi-circular window in the top of each, to give light to the staircase. There is a fine prospect from it of the Isles to the South, and of the mountains to the North, and it has a most beautifull effect as one approaches from the East. At this Tower we saw the Isle of Kerera where there is a fine harbour, on which, at Oban on the Continent opposite to this Island they are building a Custom house to facilitate the export of herrings, and other Salt fish and provision, the Custom house being now at Fort William. South east of that we saw the Isle of Scarba between which and Jura is the gulph of Cory Beckan,[1] where there is a whirlpool which has an effect on ships and the common people say they have been sunk in it.

To the west of Jura, Colonsa, where there was an Abbey of Canons Regular brought from Holyrood House, and founded by the Lords of the Isles. At the Isle of Eysdal,[2] is a slate quarry, and on the Continent near it at Ardmaddy is the quarry of White and Liver coloured marble, belonging to the Earl of Broadalbin, which I have mentioned before.

Sir Duncan's place was called Ardmuckmish[3] (the height of the morning) [?] because the morning sun comes on it, but Sir Duncan has given it the name of Loughnell from a part of his Estate which is near it. This peninsula is much dressed by

---

[1] Coryvreckan.   [2] Easdale.
[3] Ardmucknish or Lochnell House. It was greatly added to by Sir Duncan's son, General Campbell. In 1850 it was destroyed by fire.

Sir Duncan who has cultivated the land and preserved the wood. He has a very good well finished house, and a staircase and back stair very well contrived at the back of it in a bow which consists of five sides; nor must the Hermit's garden be forgot among the Curiosities of this place. I here saw a head and horns[1] which I take to be of the Urus I have seen abroad, and is mentioned by Cæsar in his Commentaries; this Creature being a native of the furthermost part of Germany, Poland, and Hungary. It was found with the bones in a bog at Lismore Island, two of the bones of such an animal found in another bog there I took with me. In Lismore was the seat of the Bishop of Argyleshire, so that probably some Bishop having seen this animal when he was going to Rome, might bring two of them to Lismore.

I saw here the Area Theophrasti[2] which bears a round fruit, and is falsely called the Service tree.—I am, etc.

Letter XV.

I-Colm-Kill, *June the 8th* 1760.

Dear Madam,—On the 6th I sent my horses to Fort William about 24 miles and went by water about two Leagues to Dun Stafnige[3] (Stephen's hill or Fort) where there is a Castle, formerly a palace of the Kings of Scotland, which disputes antiquity with Inverlochy. It is built round the edge of an irregular high perpendicular Rock, with Towers, which are

[1] The *Bos primigenius*, described minutely, with measurements, in article 'Lismore,' *Old Stat. Ac.*, vol. xxi. p. 426.—See *Proc. Roy. Phy. Soc.*, vol. ii. p. 112.

[2] *Pyrus Aria*, Ehrh., White Beam. 'Sorbus sylvestris, Aria Theophrasti dicta. The wild Service, called Aria.'—Parkinson's *Herbal* (*Theatrum Botanicum*), London, 1640, p. 1421.

[3] Dunstaffnage Castle. For particular plans and views of the castle and chapel, see *Castellated Arch. of Scot.*, 1887, by MacGibbon and Ross, vol. i. 85-93. The legendary history appears to have been gathered from Camden and Buchanan. The description corresponds very closely with that given by Mr. Pennant (*Tour* 1772, pt. i. p. 409), who was also entertained twelve years after Dr. Pococke by the same proprietor. Both travellers deemed the 'figure of ivory' worthy of drawings, doubtless after being duly impressed with its supposed antiquity and object—that of commemorating the coronation chair of Scotland, or as a memorial of a particular coronation. There can be little doubt that it was simply a chessman. See p. 75.

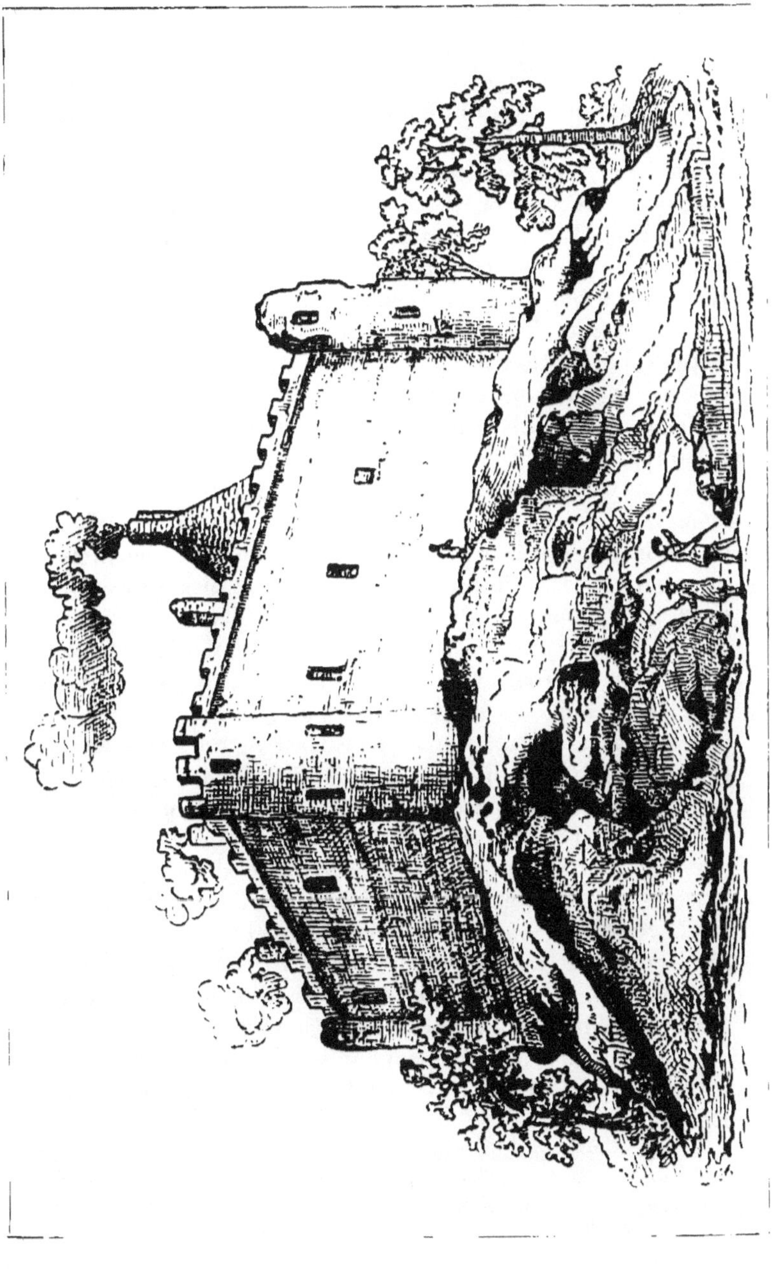

DUNSTAFFNAGE.

The Castle of Dunstaffnage.

round within. The way to this Castle is by a Drawbridge, and the appartments were to the South. It belongs to a Campbell, whose family has enjoyed it for many years. He showed us a very curious piece of Antiquity found not a great many years agoe in the Castle; It is a figure of Ivory sitting in a Chair as supposed of a King of Scotland, about four Inches and a half long with a Crown on the Head and a beard, the robes hang rather clumsily; a drawing of the figure and chair are on the other side; what is very particular his hands are laid on his Knees, as in the statue of Memnon,[1] and as the Grand Signior sits at this day when any one goes to Audience. The tradition is that this Castle was built by King Ewin 100 years before Christ. A view of it is here seen [see p. 73]. They have a red stone here which seems to have iron in it.

To the south of the Castle is the Chapel in which they say many of the Kings of Scotland are buried in a vault, there being no memorial of them. It seems to be an old Church tho' it has been altered. About 30 yards from this Church is a perpendicular rock, it may be 20 feet high which turns to the south near opposite to the west end of the Chapel. If any one goes about 20 yards behind this rock to the south and directs his voice to the South wall of the Church, and you stand at the rock about opposite to the middle of this wall, though the person speaks low yet you hear his voice by the Echoe and by the Echoe alone, and it seems as if it came from the Church.

We went on and saw Castle Dunolly two miles to the South which is the Castle of the Physitian, where as they say the Physitian of the Kings of Scotland lived; a little to the south of which is Oban where the Custom House is building.

The wind turned so that we could not get to Ahan Craig[2] in Mull, and therefore we went to Douart Castle,[3] an oblong square building of which nothing is remaining but the outer walls; it is strongly situated on a rock over the water. Here is a barrack for one company of soldiers and there is one always here on Duty. We went three miles round Lough Don to Ahan Craig.

---

[1] Bishop Pococke saw this statue during his Eastern travels. It is described and figured in the first vol. of his great work, *A Description of the East and some other Countries*, 'Observations on Egypt,' 1743, p. 102, Pl. xxxvi.

[2] Auchenacraig.   [3] Duart.

DUNSTAFFNAGE, DUNOLLY.

A King of Scotland (?).[1]

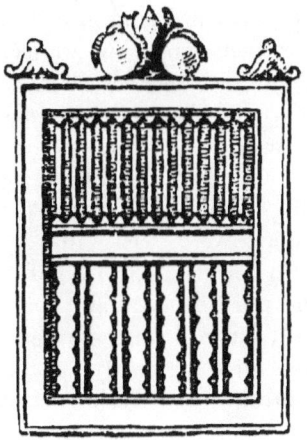 

Back and Side View of the Chair.

[1] More probably an antique chessman. See note 3, p. 72.

On the 7th we set out on the Horses of the Island for I-Colm-Kill; these beasts are small and never shod, very sure footed in bad road, but they say not so sure on plain ground however I found them excellent Horses in all roads; They are very hardy and go through great labour, and are fed only on grass, they are indeed hard mouthed, turn only with a stick directed to their head, and sell for about £4 apiece; they send 300 of them most years out of the Island.

The miles[1] are double the length of the English, and they seem to measure their miles by straight lines on the map, whereas the roads wind much from this part to the place opposite to I-Colm-Kill. They compute it 24 miles, and it is certainly double.

In three miles we came to Lough Spelve which is a good harbour and winds so that the opening is not seen, which extends to the South East.

We then went two miles through a pleasant wood of Hazel, Birch, Quicken, and Alder: and a mile further having heathy hills on both sides and the same turning to the South, and came to three lakes one over another, out of which rises a rivulet.[2] In these parts are great plenty of Mineral waters which seem to be Iron. We then turned round by degrees to the west and passed a lake with a small Island in it, incircled with stones; out of this rises another water; and we had near a mile of bad road into that plain in which Loch Sekreidan[3] is situated, which is a very large bay of the sea with some good harbours in it. We came to Rossal at the head of this Bay; from this part a road goes to Aras[4] eight miles, being on the East side on the Sound of Mull, where there is an old Gothick tower of an extraordinary figure with very thick walls.

I was told that opposite to Mr. Campbel's old house, between it and the sea, on the right-hand, to any one who is on that road to I-Colm-Kill, is a low rock with a hollow Cleft in the top in form of a Cross directing nearly to the four cardinal points of the heavens in which if a Mariners Compass

---

[1] The Scots mile was 320 lineal falls (each = 6 ells), so that the Scots mile = 1·123, or 1⅛ English mile.

[2] River Lussa, which falls into Loch Spelve.

[3] Loch Scriden. [4] Aros Castle.

was placed to any of these points, it turned to the contrary point, and when placed on the middle it veered about and did not settle, tho' at four feet Distance above it. The rock has been lately broke and I could not be enformed if this has made any alteration. These are the words of the Description that was given me. It is probable that there is Iron Ore or loadstone here.

From Aras it is 12 miles to Achen Craig a good road, Salt Calas hill being half way: from Arras to Knock is three miles, and from that to Rossal we were at, 5 miles: At Rossal is a Druid Temple which seems to have consisted of seven stones, six of them remaining at five yards distance, and there are two at the Distance of two yards to the west, and seven yards apart as opposite to the supposed entrance at the West. They are from five to eight feet high, the two lowest being to the East; three of the stones in the Circle are lying on the ground. they are of the light blue stone with white specks, and rather of a soft kind, in which the Country to the East abounds.

Here we dined, and went on, having the Bay to the right, and low hills with some wood on them to the left, from which several beautifull cascades fall down after rain in narrow glyns of rock and wood, we came in seven miles to Ardschrinish to the house of Mr. Neill MacLeod[1] the Minister, a very amiable man of the Isle of Skey: and came three more to Benissan[2] where I lay. Here they have very fine Oysters.

On the 8th we went 3 miles to Ferryport, and were rowed over to I-Colm-Kill. I observed for about two miles the rocks are all of a bright red granite; and towards the little Islands and rocks near the Shoar. I also took notice of several hills about Ardscrinish which resembled the Giants Causeway in irregular Pillars, mostly of four sides, with several Joynts, and are much like the rocks between Ballintory and the Giants Causeway in Ireland, and it would be curious to know if there is anything of this kind in Ila which is directly opposite to the Causeway.—I am, etc.

---

[1] Rev. Neil Macleod, described by Dr. Johnson as being 'the clearest headed man that he had met with in the Western Islands.'—*Fasti Ecc. Scot.*, pt. v. p. 84.

[2] Bunessan or Bonessan.

LETTER XVI.

ISLE OF LISMORE, *June* 10*th*, 1760.

DEAR SISTER,—At I-Colm Kill I met Mr. Campbell the Bailif of the Isle of Terri-I, who with great complaisance attended me in seeing everything.

I-Colm Kill is about three miles long and a mile broad. Bede informs us that in the year 605 Columba a priest and Abbot famous for the profession of Monkery came out of Ireland into Britain to instruct those highland Picts in the Christian religion, who by the high and fearfull ridges of the Mountains were sequestered from the Southern Countries of the Picts. He had founded a Monastery in Ireland,[1] called Dearmach (The field of Oaks) because it was in a wood. As he succeeded, Bridius the King of these Picts gave him the Island Hii or I or Y, that is the Island now called I-Colm Kill; it is called Iona if I mistake not by Buchanan; he founded a Monastery here and was himself the first Abbot. Bede says that his monks differed from the Church of Rome in the keeping of Easter, and in the Tonsure till the year 716. They were at first regular Canons, but the Monastery being destroyed by the Danes, it afterwards was inhabited by the Benedictines of the order of Cluny,[2] who not being capable of holding Cures, those which they had in Galloway were given to the Canons of Holy Rood house in Edinburgh. This Abbey was annexed to the Bishoprick of Argyle by James the VI. in 1617. The Scotch Historians say that St. Columb crowned Aiden the 49th King of the Scots. The Abbot of this Monastery seems to

---

[1] 'Durrow, anciently Dairmagh, paraphrased by Adamnan as Roberti Campas, or plain of oaks, was one of the earliest and most important of St. Columba's foundations in Ireland. It is stated in the *Annals of Tighernach* that Aedh, son of Brendan, King of Teffia, gave Darmach to Columcille. Aedh became lord of Teffia in 553, and St. Columba removed to Iona in 563, so that the monastery must have been founded between these dates.'—Anderson's *Scot. in Early Christ. Times*, 1881, p. 144. *Vide* Reeves's *Adamnan*, p. 23.

[2] Dr. Skene, in his critical *Notes on the History of the Ruins of Iona*, conclusively argues that this could not be a Cluniac monastery, but belonged to another order of reformed Benedictines, viz. those called Tyronenses.—*Proc. Soc. of Ant. Scot.*, vol. x. p. 200. See also Dr. Skene's chapters on the Monastic Church of Iona in *Celtic Scotland*, vol. ii.

have exercised Archiepiscopal Jurisdiction over the Bishops of Scotland or at least of this part of it, for all of them being sent from this Monastery, 'tis supposed they did not look on themselves to be freed from the Jurisdiction of the Abbot when they were made Bishops; and if any of them had not been Bishops, it would be a superiority of their Jurisdiction and not of Order, as A-Bp. Usher observes, who cites the Annals of Ulster to prove that a Bishop always resided in Hy; and Lloyd proves that Columba was ordained Bishop of Meath by Finlan, so that at first sight it seems as if Bede was mistaken in saying that their first Teacher was not a Bishop, and the Saxon Chronicle that there must be in Hy an Abbot[1] and not a Bishop. From History we collect that the Bishop of the Isles resided in the Island of Hy, and that before St. Columb founded the Monastery, even in the year 360, 'tis said that the Bishop of the Isles had three places of Residence, the Isle of Hy, Man, and Bute, but it is to be questioned whether at the same time. It is also affirmed that the Cathedral of the Isle of Hy being dedicated to our Saviour, in greek *Soter*, the See took its name from it Sotorensis[2] and Sodorensis, and I have read or heard that this part of the Island is or was called Sodor.

The Isle of Man was subject to Scotland, but the Danes and Norwegians about 1065 taking advantage of the troubles occasioned by Macbeth's usurpation, conquered the Isle of Man, and sett petty Kings over it. In 1097 Donald Bruce[3] the usurper

---

[1] 'That island [Iona] has for its ruler an abbot, who is a priest, to whose direction all the province, and even the bishops, contrary to the usual method, are subject, according to the example of their first teacher, who was not a bishop, but a priest and monk.'—Bede's *Eccles. Hist.*, Book III. Chap. iv., Bohn's 3d ed., p. 114. 'Now in Ii there must ever be an abbot, and not a bishop; and all the Scottish bishops ought to be subject to him, because Columba was an abbot and not a bishop.'—*Anglo-Saxon Chronicle*, Anno 565, Bohn's 3d ed., p. 313. The confusion in Dr. Pococke's mind seems to have arisen from failing to recognise the distinction between a territorial and a non-territorial episcopacy, distinctions which have given rise to much controversy on Church government. See Goodall's Pref. to Keith's *Cat. of Scot. Bishops*; Bishop Lloyd's *Hist. Acc. of Church Government.*

[2] Should be Soter and Soterensis, the derivation being not Greek but Norse. The Norsemen divided the Western Islands into Nordreys and Surdreys—the northern and southern islands.

[3] Donald VII., surnamed Bane.

The Church of I-Colm-Kill.[1]

[1] A view of the church is shown in the article 'Iona,' by the Earl of Buchan *Archæologia Scotica*, vol. i, p. 240; the imprint is given thus; 'The South-East view of the Cathedral in Icolmkill, done from the original drawing, which was taken on the spot A.D. 1761.' Bishop Pococke having made his drawing in 1760, it is probably the earliest sketch in existence.

gave the Western Isles to them for assisting him; they brought the See to Man, and then they were called Bishops of Sodor and Man. In about 200 years the Scots recovered the Western Isles, and Alexander the 3d in 1266 the Isle of Man. In the time of David Bruce, Edward the 3d took that Isle, and soon after there was a distinct Bishop of Man, who still retained the title of Bishop of Soder and Man; and the other Bishops had the title of Bishops of the Isles.

Wymundus was the first Norwegian Bishop in 1113, and became Suffragan to the A-Bp. of York who consecrated him. There having been 13 before him, a Bishop of Sodor residing at the Isle of Hy. There were 14 Bishops before the Scots reconquered the Isle of Man, having as said a little before, conquered the Western Isles. From this to the conquest of Man by the English there were six Bishops. Then the Bishops of the other Isles were called Bishops of Soder, which name was in no long time after lost in the title of Bishop of the Isles. However on the whole from Bede's authority it seems as if the Abbots and Bishops were distinct persons, tho' some of the Abbots might be Bishops, and that the Abbots had for some time had a superiority, as mentioned, of Jurisdiction, and were invested with all the privileges of an Arch-Bishop, as the Guardian of the Holy Sepulchre at Jerusalem is at this day.

The Church, as I was informed by one who measured it, is 144 feet long. In the quire are three arches on each side, the Capital of one of the pillars is adorned with Gryphens and other beasts something in the roman taste, another with monkish conceits, and in the north side is a Capital adorned with Laurel leaves, it is of an octagon form on a round pillar. In the transcept on the Saxon round pillars divided by fillets into four equal parts, are figures on the Capitals in the same monkish taste, on one Adam and Eve, on a second the Devil tempting Eve, on another the salutation, and on a fourth a man driving a Cow and the Devil behind him. (A view of the South Side of the Church is here seen.)[1] To the north of the

---

[1] For the architecture of the Abbey Church of Iona, see Messrs. Bucklers' illustrations and measurements in 'The Cathedral of Iona, and the Early Celtic Church and Mission of St Columba,' by the Right Rev. Alex. Ewing, D.C.L., Bishop of Argyll and the Isles. 1866 and 1872.

Choir is a vestry. The Body of the Church is a very mean Building, in the North part of the Transcept are three very old Saxon Arches, in the middle arch is a figure sitting, in relief, and in this part are remains of the foundations of a pulpit [1] and of the steps leading to it. A hole is shewn at the North West angle into which they say St. Columb used to retire to prayer. At the East end of the Church is a stone which is supposed to have been laid on the Altar ;[2] it is of a white veined marble like Cipolino and seems to be the Marble of Terre-I. The common people break pieces off from it, which they affect to use as a Medicine for man or beast in most Disorders, and especially the flux. On the North side of the Quire is a very entire Monument of Abbot MacPhingone; he is represented on it with two lyons at his feet, and one on each side of his arms; on it is this inscription: + Hic + Jacet + Johannes MacPhingone Abbas de Y + qui Obiit Anno Millessimo quingentessimo, Cujus Animæ propitietur Altissimus.[3]

On the other side is a monument in freestone for Abbot Mackenzie, but the inscription is Defaced. In a small building [4] South of the Church is the Monument of Abbot MacPhingone's father with this inscription: +Hæc est Crux Lancelani MacPhingone et ejus filii Johannis Abbatis de Y facta anno Domini MCCCCLXXXIX.[5]

Near it on another stone much worn is this inscription: + Hic Jacet Angutius filius Angutii Maic Domhuil Domini de Ila.[6]

[1] More probably an altarage.

[2] When Pennant visited Iona in 1772, only a very small portion of the Altar Slab remained, and even that (he says) 'we contributed to diminish.' The last fragment, 4 in. × 3 in., is now in the centre of the altar of St. Andrew's Episcopal Chapel, Willow Acre, Glasgow.—Gordon's *Iona*, p. 29.

[3] Pennant illustrates this tomb, and gives almost the same inscription, *Tour Scot.*, 1772, Pt. I. Pl. xxiv. p. 290. The inscription is now much effaced ; it is given by Drummond ; . . . [IOH]ANNES MACFINGONE ABBAS DE Y QVI OBIIT ANNO DNI MILLESIMO QVIN[GENTESIMO].—*Sculp. Mon. in Iona*, etc., Pl. xlv.

[4] A small burial-place, with remains of three stone coffins, now empty and without covers ; also several flat tombstones.

[5] This inscription corresponds very closely with that given by Pennant, *Tour Scot.*, p. 286. In Drummond's illustration it reads : HEC : EST : CRVX : LACCLANI : MEIC : FINGONE : ET : EIVS : FILII : JOHANNIS : X : ABBATIS : DE : IIY : FACTA : ANNO : DOMINI : M°CCCC°LXXX°IX.—*Sculp. Mon.*, Pl. xxxvi. Also see Stuart's *Sculp. Stones*, Pl. xlvii. p. 27.

[6] Given by Pennant, *Tour*, p. 287. Illustrated by Drummond : HIC · JACET · CORPVS . . . FILII · DOMINI · ANGUSII · —MAC DOMNILI · DE · ILA. —*Sculp. Mon.*, Pl. xxv.

This person was called Iunus or Angus Oig the chief of the Macdonalds in Scotland, who lived under Robert Bruce, and was in the Battle of Bannockburn in the 14th Century.

On the North side of the Church are remains of the Cloyster [1] built with very ancient narrow Saxon Arches, on the East side of it is an arched building with four flat Niches on each side with arches turned over them, which I judged was the Chapter house; the Abbots Seat having been probably at the further end. To the North is the refectory, and a building near it which seemed to have been the Kitchen; at the South West corner of the Cloyster is an ancient Cross in bas-relief sett in the Wall, and near it a broken Mezzo-relievo of a figure which seemed to have belonged to a tombstone. On the North side of the entrance to the Church is an oblong square hole with a wall round it, and a flat plain tombstone on the south side of it under which they say St. Columb's body lay. Near this is an entrance to a vault which is now filled up and they say led to a subterraneous passage.

The following inscription was given me as near this place :—[2]

+ Hic Jacet Johannes Betonius M'Lenorum familiæ medicus qui obiit

        Ecce Cadit Jaculo Victrici Mortis iniquæ
        Qui toties alios solvit ipse Malis.

On the South side of the Church is the burial-place [3] of the M'Clean's with several reliefs [4] of them in armour on the stones which lye on the ground; and on the South west part of the Church yard lye several stones on the ground, which they say

---

[1] These cloister arches are now entirely gone, but many of the capitals and other remains of the building are preserved in the charter-house mentioned, which is the only part of the whole structure still carrying a roof.

[2] The memory of the famous old Doctor of Mull . . . is preserved in these words : HIC JACET JOHANNES BETONUS MACLENORUM FAMILIÆ, MEDICUS, QUI MORTUUS EST 19 NOVEMBRIS 1657. Æt. 63. DONALDUS BETONUS fecit, 1674.'
    'Ecce cadit jaculo victricis mortis iniquæ ;
      Qui toties alios solverat ipse malis,
          Soli Deo Gloria.'—Pennant's *Tour Scot.*, 1772, Pt. I. p. 28.

[3] St. Oran's burial-ground, connected with St. Oran's Chapel.

[4] Drummond's *Sculptured Monuments of Iona*, Pls. xxxvii., xxxviii., xxxix., xli., xlii.

84   TOUR THROUGH SCOTLAND, 1760.

are the tombs of the Kings of Scotland buried there, 48 in number; four Irish Kings, and eight Danish or Norwegian Kings, one King of France.[1] At the head of them is a stone[2] sett upright in which is an inscription in Eirshe (Irish) characters which is the name they give the old Language that is spoken here, in Ireland and Wales, which I attempted to copy, but was given me more perfectly taken by one who understands the Character and Language—

+ᴏʀ ꙅᴘᴍꝙɔ ʟꜰ ǫ ᴛ ǫ ʜ ⸍, ᴄ

[+ OR · DO · MAI   LF   AT   A   R   I   C]

and he interpreted it thus, Coramac Ulfhada hic est situs. He saies ulfhada means long-bearded, from ulla (a beard) and fad (long); so it is long-bearded Coramac.[3] Dr. Keeting in his history saies Coromac McArt [4] one of the Kings of Ireland was buried here in 213, which date does not correspond to this place.

Among the tombs is a relief of an odd figure with crooked

---

[1] 'About 70 feet south of the chapel is a red unpolished stone, beneath which lies a nameless king of France.'—Pennant's *Tour*, 1772, p. 287.

[2] The Maclpatrick Stone. Bishop Pococke's informant was in error in translating it Coramac, etc. The inscription is supposed to commemorate the Bishop of Conner and Dalaradia, mentioned in the Irish Annals of 1174. Maclpatrick O'Banan, a venerable man, full of sanctity, meekness, and purity of heart, died in righteousness in Hy-Columbkille at a venerable age. Stuart's *Sculp. Stones*, vol. ii. p. 31. 'The little rude slab in the Reilig Orain at Hy, bearing an incised cross, with the inscription, ορ δο mαιλρατάμπε, "A prayer for Maclpatrick," may be commemorative of him. In the interval between July 1852 and July 1853, when the writer visited Hy, part of the slab (which is of red sandstone), bearing the last part of the inscription, had exfoliated and disappeared. The inscription, as well as the other Irish one in the Reilig Orain, has been a fruitful source of speculation to native antiquarians' (see *Ulster Jour. of Archæol.*, vol. i. p. 84). Concerning the Bishop, see Reeves's *Eccles. Antiq.*, p. 243; Reeves's *Adamnan*, p. 408. See also *Christian Inscriptions*, edited by Miss Stokes, p. 174, and Errata note at end of the vol. This *mica-slate* slab was removed by the Duke of Argyll to Inveraray, and is now carefully preserved within the Castle.

[3] Illustrated in Stuart's *Sculp. Stones of Scot.*, Pls. xl., xli., p. 26.

[4] 'Lord Buchan speaks of "long stones which seemed to have had long inscriptions;" one of them has on its edge, says he, the following antique inscription in the British character:—Cormac Ulfhadda, hic est situs: *i.e.* Cormac Barbatus, or Long-bearded, lies here. Cormac M'Aird, one of the kings of Ireland, who, according to Dr. Keating in his *Notitia Hybernia*, was buried here.'—*Hist. Acc. Iona*, by L. Maclean, 2d ed. 1833, p. 108. *Vide* Article 'Iona,' by Earl of Buchan, *Arch. Scot.*, vol. i. p. 240.

leggs, which they call an Abbot, and say it is Crooked-legged Henish [Hamish].

At the west end of the Church is a Cross[1] called St. Martin's, and to the West of that a higher, about which they bury unbaptized children. All of them are adorned with running lines as the Cross at Inverary,[2] and I suppose that of Campbelstown, both of which were taken from this place, and said to be inscribed with Irish Characters.

In the Church yard to the south of the great Church is St. Ouran's Chapel, a Saxon building called Rollic Ouran,[3] it is sixty feet long and twenty-two broad. Here they shewed me the tomb of a Macdonald of Clonronnel in a Coat of Mail, and here they say is buried Paul a Duibne called Paul-na sporran Knight of Lochow, who was Purser or Treasurer to one of the Kings of Scotland. Here also is a stone with this inscription :[4]

Hic Jacent Quatuor Priores una.

To the North east of the Church is a small house called the Bishop's.

A quarter of a mile to the North east of the great Church, on a piece of ground which is at present morassy, are two stones about seven feet high with a stone laid across at top, and some other stones near it set up on end, which they say were the first buildings St. Columb erected here; but I take them to be the remains of a Druid Temple,[5] and the rather, as this isle was anciently called Inish Drunish,[6] or the Isle of the Druids.

About 300 paces to the East are the remains of the Nunnery

---

[1] See 'The Crofters,' *Eng. Ill. Mag.*, 1885, p. 717.   [2] See note, p. 66.
[3] Reilig Ourain, the burying-ground of St. Oran.
[4] Plate xxxv., Drummond's *Sculp. Mon.* :—HIC : JACENT : QUATUOR : PRIORES : DE : Y : ER : UNA : NATIONE : V : JOHANNES : HUGONIUS : PATRICIUS : IN : DECRETIS : OLIM : BACALARIUS : ET : ALTER : HUGONIUS : QIU : OBIIT : ANNO : DOMINI : MILLESIMO : QUINGENTESIMO.
[5] Cladh an Diesart. The trilithon (all that remained of the inclosure) was seen and sketched by the late James Drummond, R.S.A., and as the first plate in his *Sculptured Monuments in Iona* forms a most picturesque illustration. The upper stone has since been removed and broken up.—*Proc. Soc. Ant. of Scot.*, vol. x. p. 614.
[6] 'Bishop *Pocock* mentions, that he had seen two stones seven feet high, with a third laid across on their tops, an evident Cromleh : he also adds, that the *Irish* name of the island was Inish Drunish.'—Pennant's *Tour in Scot.* 1772, Part I. p. 295.

of the Cannonisses of St. Austin, Dedicated to St. Oran and said to be founded by the Benedictines who were settled in this Abbey. It is reported that they continued here in their Dresses several years after the reformation; and I was told that the last Abbess died here after she had sold the lands. The Church was small; the refectory and the Abbesses lodgings are remaining and one sees the side of the Cloyster. In the Church yard are some stones adorned with lines as the Crosses are. I could not see the tomb of the Prioress, described as having a relief of her on it in black marble with this inscription in which the latter part is remarkable: + Hic + Jacet + Domina Anna Donalda Tertetis filia quondam Priorissa de Iona, quæ obiit anno Millessimo quingentessimo & undecimo; Cujus Animam Abrahammo Commendamus.[1]

About a quarter of a mile to the south of the town is a little Bay where bodies were always landed which were brought to be buried, and till within this six years Women were always buried in the Nunnery, and Men in the Monastery. To the west of it are the foundations of an enclosure about twenty yards square, which they call the Druid's Burial-place.

I went to the South west part of the Island and in half a mile passed by a fine small green hill,[2] called Angel Hill,[3] where they bring their Horses on the day of St. Michael and All Angels, and run races round it; it is probable this custom took its rise from bringing the Cattle at that season to be blessed, as they do now at Rome on a certain day of the year.

A mile further is a small Bay called Port i Charich or

---

[1] Given by Pennant, *Tour Scot.*, 1772, Pt. i. p. 282. Illustrated in Drummond's *Sculp. Mon.*, Pl. xliv. . . . FILIE QUONDAM PRIORISSE DE IONA QUE OBIIT ANO M⁰¹D⁰XI⁰III ET [ANIM]AM ALTISSIMO COMENDAM[VS]. Also see Stuart's *Sculp. Stones*, Pl. lxi. p. 31.

[2] Cnoc nan-aingeal.

[3] 'On my return saw, on the right hand, on a small hill, a small circle of stones, and a little *cairn* in the middle, evidently druidical, but called the *hill of the angels*; Cnoc nar-aimgeal; from a tradition that the holy man [St. Columba] had there a conference with those celestial beings soon after his arrival. Bishop *Pocock* informed me, that the natives were accustomed to bring their horses to this circle at the feast of St. *Michael*, and to course round it. I conjecture that this usage originated from the custom of blessing the horses in the days of superstition, when the priest and the holy-water pot were called in; but in latter times the horses are still assembled, but the reason forgotten.'—Pennant's 1772 *Tour in Scot.*, Part I. p. 297.

IONA.

Curich[1] (The Port of the Curicle or boat) because they say St. Columba landed there from Ireland in a Curricle as they call it; and at the bank the shape of it is marked out and a stone set at each end of it, but it is I believe forty or fifty feet long.[2]

On this bay they find transparent pebbles mostly green, and some white which are the best, and they make sleeve buttons of them which look like agats. Here I found a beautiful sea plant with smooth thick leaves, and small blew flowers, of which I brought away a specimen.

On the high beach, composed of Pebbles, are several heaps of them, which some conjecture to have been made by Pilgrims by way of Pennance.[3]

The rocks at this end of the Island are of red granite some of which is mixed with green veins. The rest of the island consists mostly of a black firestone, the soil of the plain part between the rocks is very fruitfull. The Sand on the Beaches round the Island is remarkably white.

There are about 36 families on the Island who live in the Village at the Churches. I-Colm Kill is in the district of the neighbouring Minister in Mull, who performs service here once a Quarter in a private House.

From the part we were at, in clear weather the isle of Terre-I is seen, that is the land of I, for it belonged to this Monastery. It is about eight miles long, and three broad, and is a very fine flat fertile spot of ground, and one part, the Common, is the finest pasturage. It is the property of the Duke of Argyle and there are about 300 houses in it. They

---

[1] 'Strangers visiting Iona, who have time to do so, should take a boat from the landing-place to the Port-na-Churaich—the creek where Columba landed. In passing along this part of the shore with its successive bays and creeks, a fine view is obtained of the contorted stratification; and the colouring of the rock near the Port itself, seen through the clear ocean water, is singularly beautiful. It is, perhaps, vain to speculate—and yet a geologist cannot fail to do so—as to the nature of those "metamorphic" agencies which have converted matter, once consisting of soft marine deposits, into rocks so intensely hard and so highly mineralised. The beach of the Port-na-Churaich, which consists of fragments of these rocks rolled and polished by the surf, is almost like a beach of precious stones.'—*Iona*, by the Duke of Argyll, 1870, pp. 129, 130.

[2] See Publications of the Iona Press. Iona, 1887.

[3] Pennant says: 'The penances of monks who were to raise heaps of dimensions equal to their crimes: and to judge by some, it is no breach of charity to think there were among them enormous sinners.'—*Tour*, 1772, Part I. p. 297.

have a Minister but no Church. When a stranger lands they leave off their work, and come to attend him all round the isle wherever he goes. They are remarkable for horses, smaller than those of the isle of Man, as I was told about five hands high, and sell them for twenty shillings. They have a white Marble in this island and some of it with grey veins, something like the Cipolino. This place is managed and governed by the Duke's Agent, who is a Justice of the Peace and settles all differences between them. This Isle as to Spirituals belonged to the Dean of Lismore who was called Dean of Terre-I but this it is probable was after the reformation. The largest Cod and Ling are caught about these Islands.

They hand down from father to son the large two handed sword and the Helmet of the family.

In I-Colm-Kill when I went into a poor house with the Bailie of Terre-I a woman brought in a wooden vessel of new Milk and drank to the Bailie, who performed the same ceremony to me and so it went round. After we had viewed every thing I was conducted to a house where Eggs, Cheese, Butter, and Barley Cake were served, and a large bowl of Curds.

Going through Mull, I met one of the chief ladies of the Island riding home from a great burial where they had staid some days; before her went a lad bareheaded, as they all go till they are above twenty, and held up a stick in his hand; behind her at a little distance walked her maid. This leads me to speak of a singular custom there, and I believe in most of these parts. They spend commonly three days at funerals, one before and one after, and often more, especially those who are related and have any Buissiness to do, and those who come from far; and this time is spent in eating and drinking very plentifully; and the widow and children danced with others round the Corps till very lately.[1]

The notion of the second sight prevails very much in Mull, I-Colmkill, Terri-I and Col, which is a subject I may consider in another place.

The Inhabitants of Terre-I are esteemed great natural geniuses, especially for Poetry, chiefly of the Lyric kind, in

[1] See Garnet's *Tour through the Highlands*, 1798, p. 119.

which they are rather exceeded by those of the Isle of Skye. Mr. M'Pherson[1] of that Island a Minister there who gained reputation in writing against Mr. Laws, has composed several very fine Poems mostly in Latin, some of which are printed in the Scotch Magazine.

In Morvern on the sound of Mull is a good freestone quarry.

I returned to the Isle of Mull to Mr. Campbell's of Cromakery, and on the 9th came to Achancraig the same way. There are three Justices of the Peace in Mull.

They have several burial-places, where there are no signs of Churches, but probably there were Churches at most of them. Any one who rents a Village and has tenants under him is called a Gentleman, and sometimes they keep publick houses. The best houses in the island (a very few excepted) are only thatched Cabins built of large stones, and form a semi-circle at each end. They have neither hares, partriges, nor the Roe Deer; but plenty of red Deer, the black game and grouse. There are near 1000 houses and about 4000 souls[2] in Mull.

In this island and other parts they chew the root[3] of an herb called Charnicle [? Charmele], a sort of wild liquorice, and it is said when they drink whiskey it keeps them from being intoxicated.—I am, etc.

[1] Rev. John MacPherson, A.M., minister of Sleat, Skye. Died 1765, aged fifty-six. 'He gave testimony to the authenticity of Ossian's poems, was himself a scholar and Latin poet of no mean order, so that the great English lexicographer was constrained to admit "it does him honour ; he has a great deal of Latin, and good Latin." Publications : *Critical Dissertations on the Origin, Antiquities, Language, Government, Manners, and Religion of the Ancient Caledonians, their Posterity the Picts, and the British and Irish Scots*, Lond. 1768, 4to ; " Latin Ode to the Memory of Mr. Norman M'Leod," minister of Duirnish ; "The Song of Moses, paraphrased in Latin Verse" (*Scot. Mag.* i., ix., xi.) ; " Letter to the Author of a Treatise on the Second Sight in 1759" (*Miscell. Scot.* i.)'—*Fasti Ecclesiæ Scoticanæ*, Pt. v. p. 129.

[2] Pennant gives a higher population twelve years later : 'near four thousand catechisable persons.'—*Tour*, 1772, Pt. I. p. 407.

[3] 'The Natives [of Mull] . . . chew a Piece of Charmel-root, when they intend to be merry, to prevent Drunkenness.'—*Tour through Great Britain*, 1753 (by Daniel Defoe), vol. iv. p. 273. See also Martin's *Western Isles;* Pennant's *Tour*, 1769, p. 310 ; *Flora Scotica*, by Lightfoot, 1776, p. 388 and p. 1132 ; *The Scottish Gael*, by Logan, vol. ii. p. 158 (new ed.) and p. 167 ; Jamieson's *Scottish Dictionary*.

Letter XVII.

Ardes in Argyleshire, *June 12th*, 1760.

Dear Sister,—On the 10th I went by water eight miles to the Isle of Lismore, and two more along the south east side of it, where we landed. We saw young Whales swimming round the bay and making a great noise when they blew.

This Isle is esteemed the finest spot of ground of all the islands. It is a beautifull rock adorned all round with trees and shrubs, and though there are rocks almost all over the Island, yet the soil between them bears excellent Barley and Oats, being a limestone, and they have plenty of Marle. It was the See of the Bishop of Argyle containing the Countries of Argyle, Lorns Kintyre, and Lochaber, with some of the western isles. Molocus was their tutelar saint whose day is kept on the 10th of April; he lived about 1160 and his bones were brought to this place. John the Englishman Bishop of Dunkeld was an excellent man, lived about 1200 and requested the pope to take this See out of Dunkeld, and the Bps. were called Episcopi Lismorenses, tho' they have been called Ergadienses, and Ergalienses.

Going up towards the Church I saw a Rivulet which turns a Mill, and rises out of a beautifull lake which is in a deep bason and is about half a mile in length and a furlong in breadth and is edged with wood. Nothing remains of the Church but the Quire, the doors, and seats for the officiating priests; they are of the most plain and simple Saxon architecture I ever saw, which is a mark either of the Antiquity of it, or of the want of art when it was built, supposing the Fabrick is of no longer date than the See. At the reformation this See was removed to Dunon[1] between Lough Fine and the Lake Heck[2] as the most convenient situation for the Diocese. About 3 miles to the south west I saw the old Castle which commanded a view of the sound of Mull, and was the Bishop's house.

[1] Dunoon.   [2] Loch Eck.

I observed many veins of white Flint running through the Marble. Such veins when they are of Sparr are a sign of Ore.

We passed by a Danish fort on an eminence encompassed with a round wall of loose stones.[1]

There are 200 families in this island and near 1000 souls.

From this Island we crossed about a league to Ardes the seat of Campbell, Laird of Ardes,[2] a very pleasant place near a low hill, to the east covered with wood, commanding a view of the great bay to the South, and the islands in it, and of Linnhe Lough to the North West which extends up to Fort William. The name of this Lough or bay in Eirshe, is Lochy, and it is the river Longus of Ptolemy, for the Romans doubtless gave names which had some resemblance to those of the inhabitants. It is also situated very near to Lough Creran at the mouth of which is the Isle called Ireska, I was told the tyde does not ebb to the north of the isle, and so that way it is always passable.

A plant grows on the shore here which they call Spinage and is most excellent in the garden, where they are sure to have plenty of it, if they manure with sea weed which conveys the Seed. It is a plant that is in great abundance in most gardens; in gathering it they take care not to destroy the root, and it continues to shoot out for a considerable time.

I here procured two bones of the leg and thigh of the Urus found at Lismore.[3]

Here I was also presented with an ornament of Brass in an oval shape adorned with Mosaic Embosements in several compartments; there was one on each side of the breast of the skeleton, and they are supposed to have been ornaments on each side of the shield, for the irons to fix it remain in part— a Drawing of it is here given; with this skeleton was found a pin about four inches long, and a brass needle two inches long, which, 'tis supposed fastened some parts of the garment. It was found in the Isle of Sangay[4] between Wist and Harris a place much frequented by the Danes.

---

[1] Tirefoor.   [2] Airds.   [3] See note 1, p. 72.

[4] Norwegian Oval Bowl-shaped Brooch; *vide Scotland in Pagan Times*, by Jos. Anderson, LL.D., 1883, p. 43. Dr. Pococke's brooch is evidently the one referred to and engraved in the *Vetusta Monumenta* of the Soc. of Antiq. London, vol. ii. Pl. xx. Figs. ix. and x.; Explanations, p. 2. 'An oval brass ornament of chased work, somewhat like the embossment of a horse-bit. It was

TOUR THROUGH SCOTLAND, 1760.

I shall now give some account of the Western Isles as to the things which are most remarkable, some of which I have been informed of, but have most of them from Authentick writings, which on enquiry have been confirmed to me.

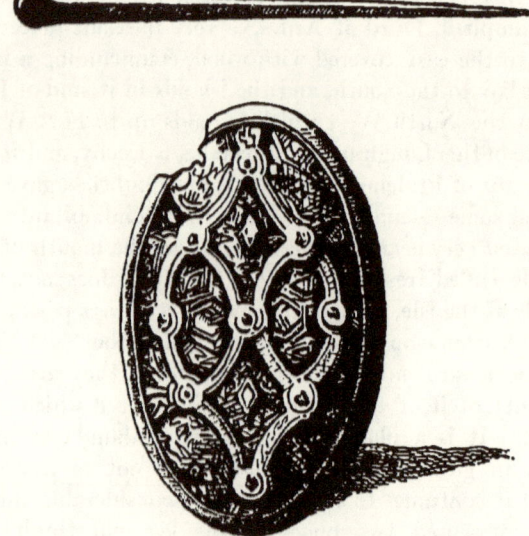

An Ornament found in a Sepulchral Cell [in Lingáy Island].[1]

At Avona[2] near Cantire is a good Harbour to which the Danes used to come when they possessed these Isles.

At Gigaia[3] is a mineral water; two sea weeds for dying grow on the stones there, Corkir for Crimson, and Crottil for Philamorte, which is a yellow Brown, the colour of dead leaf.[4]

found, together with a long brass pin and a brass needle, one on each side of a skeleton, in the Isle of Sangay, between the Isles of Uril [Uist] and Harris, to the west of Scotland. Exactly the fellow of it is in the British Museum.' The evidence appears conclusive that the writer in the *Vetusta Monumenta* must have seen Bishop Pococke's MSS., for here we find the origin of the mistake Isle of *Sangay*—doubtless Lingay Island, and the MS. might be read Langay. Also on the MS. has been written the following note, probably by the same writer: '*Exactly the fellow of it is in the Museum* from Sr. Hans Sloanes collection.'

[1] See note 5, p. 93.   [2] Isle of Sanda, the Avona Porticosa.   [3] Gigha.
[4] Highland dyes. 'Crottle Corkir Fine, white variety, ground into powder and mixed with urine; dyes Crimson. Crottle, a coarse kind of Lichen; dyes Philamot—Yellowish Brown (colour of a dead leaf.)' Article 'Highland Dyes' in *N. N. & Q.* by A. Ross, Inverness, vol. i. p. 10.

In Jura they have a mineral water good for the Stomach and stone; they live to a great age. One of the name of M'Clain died here in the last Century who had lived 180 Christmasses in the same house—a fact that ought to be enquired into before it be fully credited; and they live also to a great age in the Isle of Scarba.

In Ila[1] there is plenty of Lead and Limestone.

In Lough Finglan,[2] in the middle of it, lived Macdonald King of the Isles, the ruins of whose Castle is still to be seen. Here is a mineral water.

In Oransa there was a monastery dedicated to St. Columbus.

In Colonsa I was informed there was a monastery Dependant on I-Colmkill.

It is supposed that on the north end of Canney[3] is Iron or Loadstone, because the Needle does not answer there.

In Egg are several Mineral waters. It belongs to the Macdonalds, and all the inhabitants are roman Catholics as they are in South-Wist, and Barra, Kismul and Benbecula, and there are many in the shire of Inverness.

In Skye are seven parishes and great remains of the Druids. Opposite to Skye at Bernera in Glanily are two round towers,[4] they are about 60 feet in Diameter, and built with double walls between which is a winding ascent without steps as I was informed, but find they are the same as some others which I shall describe in Sutherland. They are engraved in Gordon's Journey over Scotland who describes them, and saies there have been winding stairs up to the top, that they are 33 feet high, the two walls and passages twelve feet and they are divided into four stories. Here they dry fish without salt, and in some islands, near the Sea they salt sea fowl with Kelp ashes. Ambergras has been found on some of these Coasts.

In Lingay[5] they have Swans, and salt their beef in skins, which they say keep it fresher than wood.

---

[1] Islay. [2] Loch Finlaggan, on an islet in it are the ruins.
[3] Canna, Compass Hill.—*Vide Old Stat. Ac.*, vol. xvii. p. 287.
[4] Castles Troddan and Tellve, Gordon's *Itin.*, Sept., Pl. 65, p. 167. See Anderson's *Scot. in Pagan Times*, 1883, pp. 181, 182, for description of these Brochs in the Valley of Glenbeg in Glenelg, miswritten Glanily.
[5] Lingay Island, north of Uist, written Sangay on p. 91.

At the North end of Harris Island they have a greater variety and more beautifull shells than on any other Coast.

In the isle of Lewis there is a most remarkable Druid Temple.[1]

About twenty leagues to the west of these islands is the isle of St. Kilda, of which I learnt the following particulars; for other things I refer to what Martyn has wrote in his treatise on the Western isles, who travelled several years agoe, and took most of what he writ, from the report of others. He had a pension from the Government, I think in the time of Charles the 2nd to enable him to undertake that work. About eighty years agoe they were without a Minister, and after some time an imposter[2] went among them, who at last behaved improperly to their Women, and was sent off; and when they were visited by a Minister some years after, they were found very ignorant, and had little more than the name of Christians. They were about 160 souls, but the small pox coming among them the infection of which was brought in some cloaths, a great number of them died, so that now there are not above 70 or 80 souls. They are subject to the scurvy, and many of their children dye: for they live chiefly on seafowl, fish, and eggs, and are dextrous in taking the Eggs, being let down the rocks several feet by a rope. They marry early, the women at 14, the men at 19, and have a particular dress. The sheep commonly bring 2 or 3 lambs, and they make small Cheese of their milk, much in taste like those of Cyprus in the Levant. They have but one road to go in, and that so bad that they are obliged to draw the boat up the rock, for there is no anchorage. It belongs to the Laird of Macloud who sends one of his relations there, and they pay their rent, in cows, sheep, butter and cheese; for they have no money. This is brought to the Continent to be sold; and they themselves have no trade. The Scotch Society for propagating Christian Knowledge sent a minister to them, who is returned, and he gave this account of them.—I am, &c.

[1] The Callernish (or more properly Classernis) groups of stone circles near Loch Roaig. The most remarkable one having lines of stones in cruciform position. See Defoe's *Tour*, 5th ed. (1753), vol. iv. p. 285; Dr. Wilson's *Prehistoric Annals of Scot.*, vol. i. p. 166; Dr. Ferguson's *Rude Stone Mons.*, p. 259. Dr. Anderson's *Scot. in Pagan Times*, 1886, p. 120.

[2] 'An Account of one Roderick,' Martin's *Voyage to St. Kilda*, 1753, p. 68.

Letter XVIII.

Fort William, *June* 13*th*, 1760.

Dear Sister,—On the 13th I left Ardes going by land, the wind being contrary: and crossing a stream which extends to the East, in a mile came to Karn-vain[1] (the White-Kern) which is very large. On the west side of it a little way up is a very difficult entrance which leads to a cell about two yards long and one and a half broad, and this by a sort of door place to another about the same dimensions. I observed in some parts the stones on the sides are laid flat, in others edge way, and a little sloping, and large stones are laid across on the top: To the north of it is a low heap of stones, in which three mouths of entrances are very visible, and there seemed to be two more; these were probably for different Branches of the family; the large one is twelve yards long at the top and about a yard broad: It is not improbable that these Cells were built all round and several stories of them one over another. They are something in the style of the Picts houses but the entrance in the Cells of those were at the Bottom.

Opposite to this is a curious structure of the Castle kind, situated on a rock, of which it takes up near the whole surface, there are stairs on the outside to the upper floor, as may be seen by the Drawing. They can ford over to the Island at low water. It was built by James the Vth probably for a hunting lodge as it is called Tene Stalcar[2] (The house of the Hunter).

In half a mile we came to Detersunt[3] the uninhabited place of a Stewart, with fine plantations about it and commanding a

---

[1] Carn bān, or White Cairn, probably at Port na Crois, on the east side of Loch Laich bay.

[2] Tigh na Stalcaire, written phonetically by the Bishop Tene Stalcar, on Island Stalker, or Eilean an Stalcair—the Isle of the Falconer. 'The founder was Duncan Stewart of Appin, who built it for the accommodation of James IV., who used to frequent these parts on hunting expeditions.'—*New Stat. Ac.*, Argyle, vol. vii. p. 240.

[3] The Bishop's amanuensis may have miswritten Detursunt for Letersuna, or (?) Letershuna. Lettirschewnay is the name of lands which formerly belonged to the Stewarts of Appin. Thomson's *Abbrev. Retours of Scot.*, vol. i. (1811), for 1633, Nos. 42-53.

charming view of the Lough, the Hill being covered with wood all the way to the Ferry, and the ride mostly in sight of the Water.

In half a mile more we came to a height from which I saw all the opposite Islands and those on each side of this Bay.

Castle of Tene Stalcar.

In two miles we came to a rivulet and bay where is the ruined Church of Kill Columb Kill said to be built by St. Columb; and a little further is a stone set up on end which seems to have been worked into form. They give such stones the name of Carr. This is about 8 feet high.[1]

This country belonged to Stewart of Appin who forfeited

[1] At Duror.

in the late rebellion, and the Inhabitants are Episcopal Non jurors. Those Estates are in the Government and given for publick uses, but they are so charged by allowing large salaries to factors and by debts due on them, that little as yet is got by them, but the Crown has great influence by having them in their hands. We passed by a place where the factor of this Estate, who was displacing some of the old tenants, was shot dead ; some say by a servant of Stewarts who fled ; some suspect his son ; but a natural son who harboured the person that fled, was hung in chains on a hill over the ferry we passed at Lough Leven.

We came to that ferry, there is a hill to the South of it, which much resembles Mount Tabor[1] on which our Saviour was transfigured, except that the surface of Tabor is smoother, but this is covered with trees and fine verdure in the same manner.

Two miles higher on the south side of Lough Leven is Glenco, famous for the Massacre[2] by a command under an officer of King William, who, 'tis said, required them to take the Oaths, wch not being complied with, some say for want of a Justice of Peace, he executed his order in that case (as 'tis said) from a great person, but as it could not be entirely fixed.

Lough Leven is seen from the hill winding beautifully to the North, and the tyde comes in here with great rapidity.

---

[1] 'Left *Fort William*, and proceeded South along the military road on the side of a hill, an aweful height above *Loch-Leven*, a branch of the sea, so narrow as to have only the appearance of a river, bounded on both sides with vast mountains, among whose winding bottoms the tide rolled in with solemn majesty. The scenery begins to grow very romantic ; on the West side are some woods of birch and pines : the hills are very lofty, many of them taper to a point ; and my old friend, the late worthy Bishop *Pocock*, compared the shape of one to Mount Tabor.'—Pennant's 1769 *Tour in Scot.*, p. 229.

'A beautiful high hill, green to the very Top, and Wood almost to the Summit. . . . This hill is called Benvheir. . . . Dr. Pocock admired it much, and said it resembled Mount Tabor more than any Hill he had ever seen, from which Lady Ballachelish calls it, for the most part, Mount Tabor.'—*Bp. Forbes's Journals*, by the Rev. J. B. Craven, p. 311.

[2] In the MS. the whole reference to the massacre is cancelled in ink, thus V, whether by Dr. Pococke or a later hand cannot be determined. It is however extremely likely to have been the Bishop's cancellation, for he appears to have believed in the divine right of kings, and wished that even his timid account of the infamous act should be expunged.

On the North side we passed by a very good Slate quarry, and a little further we came to a vein of grey Marble at Blair Chalisty; we then turned to the North having a pleasant hill covered with wood to the East, and a view of Lough Eil and of high rocky Mountains to the West of it. Between them we saw a Vale, called I believe Inversaddell, in which there is a very grand high mountain with a broad top.

On a green flat point about two miles below Fort William, if I mistake not, on the south side of the Vale, the Pretender first set up his Standard[1] in 1745 from which place they marched behind the mountains to be covered from Fort William towards Achnacarry, Lochiels place which was their head quarters of Rendevouz.

I came to Fort William which was built by King William to bridle the highlanders: It is a weak fortress, but they have put high Pallisadoes along the fossee which would prevent any sudden assault. It was besieged in the late rebellion but the Siege was raised on the approach of the Duke of Cumberland, tho' 'tis said they could not have taken it with the train of small Artilery they had against it: It is an irregular pentagon. There is a very poor town at Fort William.

A little to the North of this is a very small Lake, called Loughaber, which gives name to that part of the Shire of Inverness. This Loch, says a certain Writer,[2] is noted for Banco the Thane of this country about 1050, who was here murdered by Macbeth the Tyrant, on account of a Prophecy that his family should enjoy the crown for a long series of years, which so happened; as his son fled into Wales, married the Daughter of the Prince of North Wales and was afterwards Stewart of Scotland, from whom the Royal family of Stuart is descended; on which story Shakespear founded his Tragedy of Macbeth.—I am, &c.

[1] The Standard was first set up at Glen Finnan, at the head of Loch Shiel, about 16 miles west of Fort William.
[2] Buchanan's *Hist.*, B. vii. ch. x.

Letter XIX.

FORT AUGUSTUS, *June* 15*th*, 1760.

DEAR SISTER,—I left Fort William on the 14th in the afternoon and came in a mile to the Castle of Inverlochy[1] which is about 40 yards long and 30 broad with a round tower at each corner, that to the North west is about 25 feet in diameter within, and the wall near ten feet thick, which is called Cummin's tower, the name of a great Clan here; the other three are about ten feet less in diameter. It is said to be one of the oldest Castles in Scotland, and it is not determined whether Dunstafnage is older or not; they talk of this as built 200 years before Christ. It was formerly a place of Trade and was Destroyed by the Danes and Norwegians.

In the field to the South east of it the Marquis of Montrose in the time of King Charles the first, engaged with the Earl of Argyle and defeated him.

We went on in the Military road, in which the Number of Miles from Edinburgh . . .[2] and from Fort Augustus 28 are marked, and went 8 miles to high bridge over the river . . .[3] which here falls beautifully down the rocks. We had the high Mountain Benevis to the South, on which the Snow lies in holes fronting the North the whole year.

We went about two miles travelling to the North, and turning again to the North east, we saw Achnacarry the site of Lochhiel's house to the north which was destroyed after the Rebellion was suppressed. It was on a hill over the River that runs from Lough Ark[4] into Lough Lochy which we had now to the North west of us; and over this Lough we went in a road on the side of a hill for about eight miles; this road is very pleasant being adorned with wood both above and below. We then travelled through a Vale for about two miles and came to a beautifull narrow lake called Loch Oich, with two or three very small Islands in it covered with little clumps of trees.

---

[1] For plan and views, see *Castellated Arch. of Scot.*, by MacGibbon and Ross, 1887, pp. 73, 78.

[2] 130 miles *via* Stirling.   *Vide* Government Map, 1776.

[3] River Speyon or Spean.   [4] Loch Arkeg or Arkaig.

Lough Garry falls into it by a river from the west; on the South side of which on this Lough stands Invergarry Castle which belongs to M'Donnald and is commonly called Clongarry.[1] This Estate was saved, as the Lord of it was taken in a ship with a Commission from the King of France; but the Duke blew up a corner of the Castle, and a new house is built near it. His younger son brought the Clan into the field with the Pretender.

On the road near opposite to this is a Kern about sixty feet in Diameter being a circle of stones round a plain spot.

In two miles we came to the river[2] by which this lake empties itself into Lough Ness, and saw up the Mountains to the right the entrances to the Copper Mines which are rich, and 'tis said that there is some gold in the Ore, but so little I suppose as not to be worth extracting.

We came to Fort Augustus[3] at the north west angle of Lough Ness. It was built under the direction of General Wade (when he was making this great road) in order to defend the Country against the Highlanders, and to be a Bridle on them. It was given up to the Rebels, as 'tis said, when it might have very well held out: they blew it up, but it was repaired at the expense of £10,000 and is a very handsome regular building consisting of four bastions.

On the 16th I sett out with Governour Trappeau[4] in a boat on Lough Ness. They have a gally[5] here of about twenty tons belonging to the King in order to supply the Fort with stores which are brought to the other end of the Lake; for the river of Inverness is very shallow, and not navigable even for small boats.

We first sailed to Glanmorrison on the North side of the

---

[1] Glengarry.   [2] River Oich.
[3] A splendidly built Roman Catholic Monastery now stands on the site of the old barracks.
[4] Dr. Johnson and Mr. Boswell, thirteen years later, also experienced Mr. Trapaud's courtesy.
[5] 'Some time ago there was a vessel of about five-and-twenty or thirty tons burthen built at the east end of this lake, and called the *Highland Galley*. She carries six or eight pattereroes, and is employed to transport men, provisions, and baggage to Fort-Augustus, at the other end of the lake. . . . When she made her first trip, she was mightily adorned with colours, and fired her guns several times, which was a strange sight to the Highlanders, who had never seen the like before—at least, on that inland lake.'—Burt's *Letters from the Highlands*, vol. ii., Letter xxvi.

lough, in which the river Morrison runs and gives the name of Invermorrison to the place where we landed. They say the river rises 16 miles off; by the Map its sources are near the Western Sea towards Skye, in its way it forms Lough Cluny. The Laird of Glenmorrison has a house here; and at this place there is a very fine linnen Manufactory, built out of the forfeited Estates. They teach 40 Girls for three months to Spinn, and then they take in forty more; they buy flax and employ six looms. They buy also yarn from the Country people, who raise a large quantity of it. It consists of the principal Building, and an office, for the Manufactures on each side. There are two more, one at Lough Carran, the other at Lough Broom, both to the West.

From this place we went on and came to Foyers on the South side belonging to a Frasier, but now in the hands of the Government for a debt due to Lord Lovett. Almost all the Estates on both sides were forfeited except this, Glencarry, and Glan Morrison. Here is a most beautifull narrow glyn with high rocks and wood on each side, and a very fine water fall in one sheet about ten or twelve feet wide, and as I conjectured a fall of near 100 feet. The opening in the rock perpendicular over it, for near 50 feet as I guess, is so narrow that when there is a great flood the fall is by so much the higher, and is, they say, then extremely fine.

A little beyond this is the half way house to Inverness called the General's Hutt,[1] where General Wade lived in the summer when the roads were carrying on. The Rebels blew it up, and the Duke after the battle of Culloden encamped near Fort Augustus, the house of the Fort being destroyed; and at the Fort Lord Lovett was kept, untill he was sent to London.

We proceeded in our voyage, and came on the North side to Urquhart Castle[2] wch belonged to the Cummins, and was

---

[1] 'The General's Hut . . . is now a house of entertainment for passengers, and we found it not ill stocked with provisions.'—Dr. Johnson's *Journey to West. Isl.*, 1773. This old inn has entirely disappeared; it stood a short distance west of the old churchyard of Boleskine.

[2] See *Transactions of the Gaelic Society of Inverness*, vol. vi. p. 152, for a paper by Mr. William Mackay, Inverness, on the 'Early History of the Glen and Castle of Urquhart.' Mr. Mackay is now writing an exhaustive history of the United Parish of Urquhart and Glenmoriston, including the Castle.

destroyed by Edward the first: It is built round the edge of the rock which consist of two summits one on the west is very narrow and high, the other which seems to be the original castle is lower and here the habitable tower stands. A view of it is here seen.

I have heard of a famous inscription here since I left that country.

Castle of Urqhuart.

There is a beautifull Vale here between the hills. We went on and landed at the end of the Lough not far from the river, where the Governor's post-chaise met us and we went towards Inverness and passed by a Druid temple[1] about ten paces in Diameter, consists of flat stone about a yard above the ground set close together. Six paces from this is a circle of seven stones, some of which are fallen, they are nine paces apart, about a yard broad, and five or six feet high. General Pole and his Lady came out in their Post chaise to meet me and we came to Inverness.—I am, &c.

[1] Possibly the Stone Circle at roadside near Scaniport, being Circle No. 27, described in *Proc. of Soc. Antiq. Scot.*, vol. xviii., 1883-84, p. 356, Article 'Stone Circles,' by James Fraser, C.E., Inverness. The measurements, however, do not agree; it may be Circle No. 26 at Aldourie.

LETTER XX.

INVERNESS, *June 17th*, 1760.

DEAR SISTER,—Inverness is situated on the river of that name, the meaning of which is, that it is the outlet of Lough Ness, and is the Vararie Æstuarium of the New Map. The Land on each side of this river for some way up makes a very extraordinary appearance in regular high steep banks, that look like ramparts, and the same for a considerable way beyond Inverness to the East, as if they had been formed by the Sea coming up to them. The Town of Inverness is on a flat below the high grounds; and all that flat ground is very rich. It is a pretty good town of two Streets. They have a trade in imports, and an export of Salted Salmon Caught in the river Beaulieu, and also near the town in the river Ness. They had an export of Malt to Holland but it is at an end, and all the Malt houses are in ruins. The Salt Salmon of Scotland is sent in great quantities to London; and a new trade is lately opened of exporting it to the East Indies. There was here a Convent of Dominicans,[1] founded by Alexander the second in 1233, wch I suppose was at the present parish Church, where there are marks of some ruins, but nothing appears of any great Antiquity; one part of the Church is used for the English Kirk, and another for the Eirshe Kirk, and when a Chaplain was here they had Church of England service in one of them at another hour. The Castle is finely situated on an eminence over the Town; the Old Castle is a square tower in the Common way of building of those times; the inside has been new modelled into a Barrack, and General Wade built a Barrack on each side, which with the Governour's house in front formed a Court: Before the old Castle to the West are the remains of the Chapel which the Rebels in 1745 blew up with part of the Castle. Some of the

[1] 'The Dominicans had their monastery and chapel dedicated to the Blessed Mary, with its cemetry, on the site of the present chapel-yard. The Franciscans' convent occupied the ground still named the Greyfriars'-yard. Both were settled here by Alexander II. about the year 1232.—*Edward I. in the North of Scotland* [by Dr. Taylor of Elgin], 1858, p. 232. See paper on 'Old Inverness,' by Alex. Ross (Inverness Field Club, 11th August 1882).

Kings of Scotland formerly resided here. There was an irregular pentagon fort at the river built by Cromwell, and destroyed by Charles the 2ᵈ. At a basin to the West of it is a handsome Quay of hewn stone, but 'tis a bad harbour to come into.

General Poole with great politeness would show me Fort George whilst he was at Inverness—it is seven computed and thirteen measured miles to the East of Inverness.

In about six miles I passed by two Druid Temples, one of them like that described before I came to Inverness; the other about 100 yards East of it, not having the Outer Circle of Stone;[1] A little further is Castle Stewart belonging to the Earl of Murray. Fort George is situated at the end of that Sandy point which is opposite to Fortrose. They first thought of building at Inverness on the site of the old Fort, but this place was thought more proper to defend the Harbour; it not being a mile across: it was begun about eleven years agoe and is the design of Colonel Skinner, who showed me the Fort: It consists of two Bastions to the South and a ravelin; of a flat Bastion on each side, and two Demibastions to the North. The foundation was made on the Sand with large stones well cemented by Mortar. There are fine Casemates. Three sides of a Court for Barracks are finished: There is to be a large building in front but not joyning to them; and on each side is to be a grand pile of Building for Stores: near the Entrance are to be the houses of the Governor and Deputy Governor: There are Sluices to let in the Sea Water on the South Side, and make it an island: A thousand men may defend it for some time but it would take 2000 for a long siege; it can be attacked at the same time only on one side: Some of the large Canon of the Toudroiyant are brought to this place; it will be finished in 3 or 4 years:

I saw two such Druid Temples in the way to Culloden house as those in the way to the Fort, and exactly in the same position; the place is from them called Stony field.[2] Culloden

---

[1] Stone Circles, probably at Allanfearn and Culloden Tile Works, Nos. 32 and 33 (or they may be Nos. 34 and 35, a little further east), described in *Proc. of Soc. Antiq. Scot.*, vol. xviii. p. 358, by James Fraser, C.E.

[2] Stoneyfield of Raigmore. There is only one Circle there now, No. 31, *Proc. of Soc. Antiq. Scot.*, vol. xviii. p. 358.

house stands very low near the bay and is entirely encompassed with wood. It is built somewhat in the Castle way, and was the Estate of the late President Forbes, and now of his son. I then went to the Field of battle: the Pretenders Army was stretched from the wood of Culloden to the South East to a wall of an Enclosure: The several clans forming distinct Columns for above half a mile; the Horse were behind on each side; and some bodies of reserve behind them; and beyond the summit of the hill entirely out of sight was the Pretender and his attendants, with a large body of reserve behind, as by the plan[1] on the other side, which is said to have been found in the pocket of one who was slain in the battle. Our forces to the left were drawn up on a rising ground much lower than theirs; Stretching beyond their right line with a small shallow valley and the bed of a winter stream between them; it extended across the vale up the hill on which the Enemy was drawn to a Cabbin where there is a large Rock[2] on the top of the Hill; we had twelve Canon in front, four at each end, and four in the middle; The Duke was behind the first line towards the right, and behind the first line our Cohorns played; 'tis said the Enemy intended to wait our attack, but our whole Artillery played so briskly on them and galled them so terribly, that their right, some say, without order, advanced with great fury in a highland trott in a deep column and in an unsoldierlike manner firing without order and moving sideways with their targets and broadswords as to stretch out to the length of our left wing; we kept our fire till they were near; but notwithstanding, they broke the first line of Barrell's regiment on our left, and being let in, they were flanked by them, and met by the second line in front, who 'tis thought by their fire killed several of Barrell's mixed with the Enemy; the left wing of the Enemy advanced, but the Duke ordering Pultney's to shoulder, 'tis said they went back, fearing the fire reserved for them, as they would have attacked, if we had parted with our fire; but 'tis most probable they were stopped by the general rout, for 'twas all over in five minutes.

[1] For another plan, showing both armies as they were drawn up when the attack began, see *Guide to Culloden Moor and Story of the Battle*, by Peter Anderson, Inverness.

[2] A large boulder, the 'Cumberland Stone.'

Order of Battle of the Rebel Army at the Battle of Culloden 16 Apr 1746.

Lord John Drummond.

Duke of Perth.

Glengary	Clanronald		Mathans	Macleods		Farquarsons		Lovats			Appins	Lochiel		Atholl
600	300	250	100	100	300	200	400	500	300	200	600	500

++++ a Cannon. ++++ a Cannon. ++++ a Cannon.

Keppochs Macintoshes Clunys Lord George Murray

Lord John Drummonds FitzJames's Horse.

Pinquets with B Stapletons.

The Pretender.

Kilmarnocks Guard to those of the above who have only Guns.

Lord Lewis Gordon & Glenbucket to succours when needful.

Colonel Roy Stuart to those of the above who have only Guns.

The Duke of Perth & Ld Ogilvys Regmts met to join without position who is to keep close as a fresh Corps de Reserve.

Abstract

First Line   4350
Right Flank   400
Left Flank   400
1st Column   800
2d Column   800
3d Column   800
Corps de Reserve 800

Total. 8350

The Duke had in the movement ordered Poultney's to the right, instead of the Scotch fusileers; 'tis said also that they threatened an attack on the middle, but it is probable both the one and the other were advancing on the general route, which they say was occasioned by our Argyleshire men breaking down the Wall for the horse to go round; and perceiving themselves encompassed by the Horse the general rout ensued; the flight was towards Inverness, Culloden Wood, and some went off towards the bay; the other horse, whether for want of order or whatever cause did not pursue so quick.

The Pretender soon rode off towards Lough ness and got to the house of a Frasier,[1] where Lord Lovett was, and so went through the Highlands to the Isle of Skye.

Where the action with Barrel's was, just on the other side the fossee in the vale, I saw several bodies had been burried from 50, as supposed, to 100 in a hole: 'tis said half a Battalion only (about 500) were engaged: The horse pursued every way; a Detatchment was ordered into Culloden Wood, and they pursued through Inverness into the highlands.

To Inverness the Duke went and lodged in the same house[2] where the Pretender had laid, and our Army partook of all the good things they were preparing for them on the victory which the people supposed was sure. They say it was a fine sight to see the fleet and transports with provisions sail as our army moved, and cast Anchor every night, and brought provisions ashore to our Camp.

On the 15th we were encamped on the side of the river Nairn, and being the Duke's birthday they thought to attack very early the next morning, and sent out in the night parties to reconnoitre, but two who had appointed to meet missed each other, and we came on next morning in a cold mist: but it cleared up, and the Duke had often practiced a very fine movement: we marched in four Columns, and by the ruff of a Drum formed instantly into order of Battle. At the same time a man of war came up the bay and cannonaded:

[1] At Gorthleg.
[2] Lady Drummuir's House, about the middle of Church Street, on the west side. In *Reminiscences of a Clachnacudin Nonagenarian*, 1842, Lady Drummuir remarked, 'I've had twa kings' bairns living with me in my time, and, to tell you the truth, I wish I may never hae another' (Anderson's *Guide to Culloden*, etc.).

I saw for half a mile the graves where they fell: They were all instantly stripped by the Women who went loaded with Spoils to Inverness, and the bodies were soon naked all over the field. It is said the few that fell of our Soldiers were not stripped: those in the field of Battle were killed by Musket Shot and Cannon Ball; the others by the broad sword. Thus ended this day of such consequence to the British Dominions, and Crowned the Duke with immortal Lawrels.[1]—I am, &c.

LETTER XXI.

FORT GEORGE IN INVERNESS SHIRE,
June 18*th*, 1760.

DEAR SISTER,—On the 20th we went a mile by boat across the bay, and a little way up the river Beaulieu to the Northern bank, where the ferry boat crosses the river, and where we met our horses: We went eight miles to the river which falls into the Frith of Cromarty, having a view, up Lough Beaulieu, *i.e.* the broad part of the river Beaulieu, of the Country called Aird in which Beaulieu is situated on this river, which is a fine country that belonged to Lord Lovett, and where he lived. Our road was mostly over a very coarse Stony Heath, many spots of which were cultivated and bear good Oats by picking up the Stones and ploughing it: The river is commonly fordable, but after Rain they go over in a ferry boat:

Travelling about two miles to the East we came to Dingwall,[2] a town with one long street, but the houses mostly thatched, they have here some linnen Manufactory: It is a royal Borough, but its Priviledge of sending members to parliament, with some other towns is suspended; for some Male practices as 'tis said: but is recoverable as I was informed by taking out a new patent; There is a church here, the East part of which is ruinous, it was covered with a Gothick Arch,

---

[1] For a less biased account see Anderson's *Guide to Culloden Moor and Story of the Battle*.

[2] 'The bishop of *Ossory*, when travelling through this country, stopped at *Dingwal*, and said he was much struck and pleased with its appearance, for the situation of it brought *Jerusalem* to his remembrance; and he pointed out the hill which resembled *Calvary*.'—Cordiner's *Antiq. N. of Scot.*, 1776, p. 64.

and secured by a pointed Covering of hewn Stone: At the Angles and where it joyns to the Church are pilasters which make part of the Segment of a Circle, with sort of Doric Capitals; In an old Chapel is a tomb stone of a person in bas relief with a sword hanging down and girt to his left side, and he has a pointed staff in the right hand: To the South of the Church is a stone enclosure in ruins but fenced with a Ditch which is the burial place of the family of Cromartie: There is a handsome Obelisk[1] erected in it of hewn Stone; the pedestal is about twelve feet high and six square; and the Obelisk on it crowned with a Cross without the apex, may be about 30 feet long.

We went on to the North, and turning to the East, we had a fine view of a most beautifull Country to the West called Strapeffer, being a Vale about half a mile wide, and a mile Deep; to the South are two rough hills; to the North a most beautifull gentle Declivity from the hills, as if laid out by a line, and it is finely improved; at the end, exactly in the Center, is the Earl of Cromartie's Castle[2] with woods about it, and three small valleys extending from the End of this Vale, and under Corn.

We went on and in three miles from the ferry passed by Fowlis Sir Henry Monroe's, near the bay of Cromarty, which Horsley makes the Tuaesis Estuarium of Ptolemy, but I should rather think it to be Muray Firth, if so be Nairn be Tua as

---

[1] The Right Rev. Robert Forbes, M.A., in his Journals of Episcopal Visitations of the Dioceses of Ross and Caithness in 1762, only two years after Bishop Pococke had travelled through those counties, records having been entertained with several interesting reminiscences of his lordship. He writes:—

'We came to the Town of Dingwall . . . and visited Baillie [Colin] Mackenzie. . . . He conducted us to the Pyramid, a Square or four-sided Figure, ending in a sharp point at Top, upon the Burying-place of the Earl of Cromarty, of about 50 feet high, all of cut stone, which makes a grand Appearance, and was much admired by Dr. Pocock, the Bishop of Ossory, in Ireland, in his travels through Scotland in 1761 [1760].'—*Bishop Forbes's Journals*, edited by the Rev. J. B. Craven, Incumbent, St. Olaf's Church, Kirkwall, 1886, p. 162.

George Mackenzie, the celebrated first Earl of Cromartie (1630-1714) was buried here, and to his memory this obelisk was erected. In 1875 his coffin was found with the letters G. E. C. on it. The monument was thrown off the plumb towards the north-east by an earthquake in 1816. According to recent measurement the central point of the top is 3 feet 9 inches out of its true position, or 9 inches outside the base or pedestal. The south-west side is bound by several iron straps for its preservation.

[2] Castle Leod.

he makes it, but the Æstuarium might comprehend both: And I should think that Alata Castra was somewhere about Inverness, where there are so many fine natural situations for a Roman town, and I imagined I saw something like a roman road in the way to Fort George. Since the above was writ the new Itinerary and Map came to my hands by which it appears plainly that Vara Æstuarium is the Fortu of Inverness: Ptoroton or Alata Castra, the town of Inverness.

We came two miles further to Culcarney[1] Mr. Monroe's in the bay directly opposite to the Castle of Craighouse, which was a Country seat belonging to the Bishop of Ross. When we crossed over from Inverness, we came into Rosshire which extends from East to West across Scotland, and was the Entire Diocese of Ross. The Cathedral was at the Chanoury of Ross to which the parish of Rose Market[2] is annexed called formerly Fortrose. There are marks of Coals in the Mountains to the North; and the late Sr Robert Monroe had specimens brought to him from them of two or three sorts of ore, but the Veins were not pursued. I saw here Stones of Granite mixed with red, blew and white: But they have no limestone in this part of Ross Shire: near Beaulieu Lough I saw freestone,[3] and some of it mixed with pebbles, but believe they were brought from some place about Fortrose. More probably from the quarry hereafter mentioned near Cromarty.

Near Culcarny they lately found a Cave under a Kern, the Mouth of it was covered with a stone; when Mr. Monroe went in, he saw Dust in the middle in the shape something of the trunk of a Body; in one corner an Urn with Dust in it: in another the shape of a broad Short Spear or Instrument which looked like iron, but was all in dust. In the Mountain towards Fort Augustus they have found the Caper Keily[4] (Cock of the Wood). They are now very rare. I saw the skin of one stuffed, they are about the size of a Turkey, the head like a Grouse or Moor Fowl, entirely black, except that the Belly is spotted with white, and it is white under the Wings.—I am, &c.

---

[1] Culcairn. See Letter xxxv.   [2] Rosemarkie.

[3] The sandstone of Tarradale quarry, near Muir of Ord Station, answers to this description; also, at an earlier date, Redcastle quarry.

[4] See *The Capercaillie in Scotland*, Illustrated, by J. A. Harvie-Brown, 1879.

EASTER ROSS, EDDERTON.

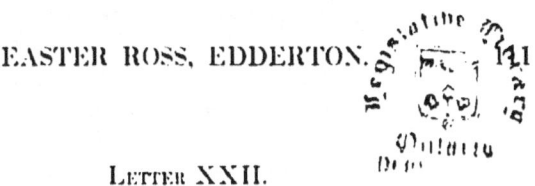

LETTER XXII.

DINGWALL IN ROSSHIRE, *20th June* 1760.

DEAR SISTER,—On the 21st we went three miles to Milcraig[1] (Mr. Cuthbert's), a fine situation on the foot of the hill, commanding a view of the river and the country below. Near it is a deep glyn in which their runs a mountain torrent.[2] The banks of it are green and most beautifully adorned with wood. We saw three or four kerns as belonging anciently to the heads of the several villages, for their burial-places. But on seeing the Picts' houses since, I doubt whether they might not be the habitations of those people. In three miles from Millcraig, going over very disagreeable heathy mountains, we came to a rivulet, and continued on about two miles, passed another mountain torrent, and came into the fine country which is on the Frith of Dornock. I saw a small Druid temple with two or three stones in the middle near the rivulet, and a little further some remains of another. Here I observed grey granite in large spots of white and a darker colour.

We came to Ardmore Mr. Bailey's, near the river, where we staid two hours, the family being at Rosehall. In these parts they find beds of shells at a little distance from the sea, but not petrified, and they are used for manure. We went westward and soon came to a large Kerne, the entrance to which about half-way up is visible with a large stone over it. If the entrances are not on a level with the ground I look on it as a mark that they were burial-places; if there are great ruins, that they were castles; and if covered over with green sod, that they were Picts' houses.

About a mile farther we came to Odonaliskey or Doniskaig, a very curious Pictish round castle.[3] (See plan next page.) The walls at bottom with the passage between take up

---

[1] Near Alness.   [2] River Alness.
[3] The name of this Broch is variously written—Dun Agglesag. Dun-alishaig. Done-Alliscaig, etc. See Maitland's *Hist. Scot.*, 1757, vol. i. p. 145; *Ancient Monuments and Fort. in Highlands*, by James Anderson; *Archaeologia* (Lond.), vol. v. p. 248; *Antiq. North of Scot.*, by Cordiner, 1780, p. 118; *Scot. in Pagan Times*, by Dr. Joseph Anderson, 1883, p. 185.

twelve feet and a half in thickness. Over the door, which is about three feet wide, is a stone in shape of a pyramid; what remains is about fifteen feet high. Eight feet and a half from the outside is an entrance on each side two feet broad; that to the right leads to a room which is a kind of oval, five feet wide in the broadest part, and sixteen feet long, to which

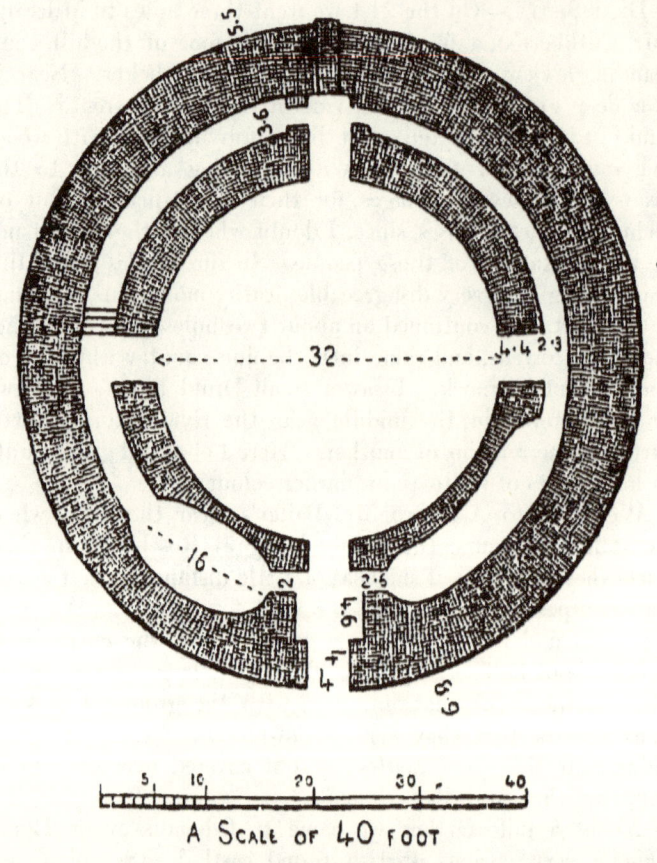

Plan of an Antient Castle.

there seems to have been another entrance at the other end, and from that a passage is continued round to the entrance opposite to the gateway; this passage is two feet broad. Opposite to this entrance, I observed on the outside, there had been a square hole, now filled up with stone, merely to give light; continuing round there is a passage three feet six inches wide, with four steps down to the middle on the other side, where there is another entrance from the court, and from this I suppose there was such an apartment as on the other side. The court is about thirty feet in diameter. The building sets in and lessens every tier on the outside, and it seemed to me to be strait up within. There is no mortar on the building, but the stones are fine and laid so as to bind one another. The round castles at Bernera are of this kind, which are engraved in Gordon.[1] We came in three miles to Kincaron,[2] where there is a church, and passed the river called Spatts Carn,[3] which was deep. There is a boat that carries over one horse, but we forded it. We passed several little torrents and had a very pleasant ride in sight of the river, which as far as the tyde goes they call a kyle,[4] the hills in many parts being covered with wood; so that ascending a height we had a most delightfull view of a very fine country, and of the winding of the river, which was then full after the rain, and appeared most beautifull.

We crossed over to Rosehall in Sutherland in a boat to Mr. Bayley's,[5] allied to Lord Reay's family, sending our horses to cross two rivers[6] that meet here. These two rivers rise within eight computed miles of the western sea, that is about sixteen measured miles. They have no miles here different from the English in measure,[7] but the acre is five perches more than the English.[8]

[1] The Brochs of Glenbeg, near Bernera. See p. 93.   [2] Kincardine.
[3] Strath Charrain [River], i.e. the Strathcarron River.
[4] Strathkyle; south side of the Kyle of Sutherland. The Bishop must have passed near the remains of the Broch or Pictish Tower at Birchfield, Strathkyle. The inside is still standing, 5 or 6 feet in height and 33 feet in diameter. The outside diameter was about 65 feet.
[5] Mr. Baillie of Ardmore and Rosehall was married to Janet, eldest daughter of Col. Hugh MacKay of Bighouse. Col. Hugh was the second son of George, Lord Reay, and came to the estate of Bighouse by marrying Elizabeth, daughter and heiress of George MacKay of Bighouse.
[6] Rivers Oykell and Cassley. The Cassley rises within 3 miles of Loch Glencoul, the head of Edderachylis Bay; and the Oykell within 6 miles of the same loch, and another branch of it within 5 miles of Loch Broom.
[7] On the MS. is written, 'I think the Highland miles are not above the proportion of 2 to 3 as in England.—[Initialled] D. B.' See notes, pp. 68, 69, 76, 118.
[8] The Scots acre is to the English acre as 1·2612 to 1; or the Scots acre = 202 English poles, the English acre = 160 poles.

Roshall is a pleasant situation about the place where the tyde ends. There are fine meadows on each side. I walked out from the most northern of the two rivers, and about half a mile from the mouth of it there is a fine waterfall after rain. The first fall[1] is about ten feet, it then runs some way and tumbles down by several falls and declivities for forty or fifty feet in a large stream, and two smaller on one side of it. Over it is a burial-place, where probably was a church or chapel belonging to an oblong square castle near it, called Dun Agharn Eski[2] (the castle of the field of the cascade), and near it is either a kern or Picts' house or a ruined round castle. They catch salmon here by holding nets and driving in the salmon as described at Kilmare in Kerry. On the river is a castle or two of the kind described at Duniskaig, and one or two more to the south of the mountain; one is at Glanmick on a morass on the river Cartigo, and two at Arsbrook and Douney, on the river Carran. There is a road to the south-west to Lough Broom, where there is another spinning school of the kind of that mentioned at Glanmorrison, and there is another at Lough Carran. About eight miles south of this place is the mountain called Scarre in Lappik,[3] on the top of which are several sorts of shells, mostly of the welk kind, and not petrified; there is also a white stone said to be almost transparent, which I conjecture to be the white flint. They have a different species of trout in most of their rivers here. At a place called Craighalian,[4] at Coleray,[4] by which we passed, the Earl of Montrose was defeated by Colonel Strahun, and escaping to the house of M'Cloud[5] at Assunt to the south-west, he was sold for £1000, on which account the family became infamous, dwindled to nothing, and are no more. This, they say, is the only instance of a Scotchman betraying one of his

[1] The Falls of Cassley, near Roshall House.
[2] The broch Dun Achadh- or Ach'-an-Eas, Achness.
[3] Scurr na Lapaich, south of Loch Monar. Height, 3773 feet.
[4] Creag-a-chaoinidh, the Rock of Lamentation or Mourning, west from Culrain; or possibly an older name, Creag Chailliun, Rock of Woods.
[5] See Appendix to Bishop Pococke's *Tour through Sutherland*, 1760, for Privy Council Records relating to Macleod of Assynt. Ed. by D. W. Kemp, 1887.

own country; though, I believe, there is another that is more remarkable.[1]

The Frith of Dornock, called by Horsley the Frith of Tayne, is supposed to be the old Vara Estuarium of Ptolemy, but it is certainly the Loxa of the new map; and here, when we crossed over, we came from the Caledonia to the east, and from the Sylva Caledonia to the west from Rosshire into Sutherland, the Cantæ of Ptolemy, having been in those countries ever since we came to Ardes, except that at Inverness we just entered into the country of the Vacomagi. In the west, to the north of Mull were the Creones, falling in with the north part of Argyleshire and the west part of Rosshire; to the north of these again were the Carnonacæ, being the west part also of Rosshire; opposite to the two first is the isle of Skye, the ancient Dumna. Loch Ewe in Rosshire is supposed to be the river Itys of the Creones; Lough Broom is probably the Volsas between the Creones and the Carnonacæ, and Lough Ennard the river Nabaus, between the Carnonacæ and the Catina, who inhabited the north-west part of Scotland, now the north-west part of Sutherland.—I am, &c.

Letter XXIII.

ROSEHALL, IN SUTHERLAND,
22d June 1760.

DEAR SISTER,—On the 22d I went towards Lough Schin, eight miles distant, and in the way, at a rivulet, came to Dun Cor,[2] another such stone fortress, but destroyed; it was thirty feet in diameter within, and the walls six feet thick. We came at the end of Lough Schin to Mr. Monroe's,[3] having passed by a place a mile from it, where they say there was a battle in very ancient times; and there are two or three small stones set up on end, which they say is the tomb of a great man who

---

[1] The betrayal of Sir William Wallace.
[2] Doir-a-Chatha, or Durcha, north of Rosehall, below Cnoc-a-Choire.
[3] Mr. Munro of Achany.

fell. I went on the lough to an island,[1] where we saw the nests, eggs, and young of the gulls;[2] and one nest and eggs of a smaller sea-bird.[3] This island is frequented by wild geese and ducks. We went about two miles on the lake, and came to such another stone fortress on a height. It is about thirty feet in diameter within; the walls seemed to have been about eight feet thick, except in front, where they appear to have been twelve, and where there is such an oval room on each side as described,—nine feet long and four feet broad; and on one side I could see some signs of a passage between the walls, there seemed to have been an outwork before the entrance. About a quarter of a mile to the south is another, rather smaller, and much ruin'd, the walls of which seemed to have been thicker at the entrance, but no sort of sign of any rooms in it. Here we went into a Highland cabbin, in which there were five apartments, one at the entrance seemed to be for the cows, another beyond it for the sheep, and a third, to which there was an entrance only at the end of the house, for other cattle; to the left was the principal room, with a fire in the middle, and beyond that the bed-chamber, and a closet built to it for a pantry; and at the end of the bed-chamber, and of the house, a round window to let out the smoak, there being no chimney. The partitions all of hurdle-work so as one sees through the whole. A great pot of whey was over the fire, of which they were making Frau.[4] They have a machine like that which they put into a churn, with stiff hairs round it,[5] this they work round and up and down to raise a froth, which they eat out of the pot with spoons, and it had the taste of new milk; then the family, servants and all, sat round it, and eat, the mistress looking on and waiting. She brought us a piggin of cream, and drank to me, and we drank of it round. The dairy is in a building apart. This was contrived that I might see the Highland manners. They have here a great number of foxes and hares, the skins of which are very fine;

[1] Eilean Donuil, or Donald's island.
[2] The Great Black-backed Gull, *Larus Marinus*, L.
[3] Grey Lag Goose, *Anser ferus*, L.
[4] Fro' or Froth, still made in some districts. Frau [omhan], whisked cream, is or was a Christmas dish.
[5] A whisk of horse-hair; Gaelic, *loinid*.

the hares are of a light colour on the back, and the bellies are quite white. I was told there are some all over white in the winter. A few swans[1] come here every year in the hard weather; and a great number came in the year 1738, when the winter was very cold, but it is difficult to shoot them. They have great plenty of red deer, and of the roe deer. Mr. Monroe shot in the upper part of the Kyle of Dornock an extraordinary sea-bird,[2] which dived very readily. It is as big as a goose, and much like it, except that the bill, about four inches long, is pointed; it is black with a spot of grey under its throat, and one on each side about the middle of the neck; it is spotted down the back with a streak of brown on each side, there are larger spaces towards the wings, which are also spotted, except that the long feathers are black; the belly is whitish, but with yellow streaks up round the broad part of the neck, it being all black on the back of the neck between these streaks; the spots on the back are mostly of an oblong square figure, and of a dirty white, the grey of the neck being formed with such streaks. This is the only bird of the kind that had been seen. There are many spots of fine ground in this country, mostly on the side of rivers and streams, and some large ones up the sides of hills. They breed much young cattle and sheep, but not so many I think as the ground wou'd bear. At night they house the sheep all the year, and the poorer people shear in May and November, who have not grass for them abroad. On this side of the Kyle of Dornock they have a whin stone and grey granite. I this day met an aged person, who had much the look of a gentlewoman. She had about her shoulders a striped blanket, and saluted us genteely. She was followed by a maid without a cap or fillet,[3] with a bundle at her back; this was a sort of decayed proprietor, who, I suppose, was going round a-visiting; and as they are very hospitable to all, so they are not uncivil to such unfortunate persons.

On the 24th, I set out and went near the south end of the

[1] The Hooper or Wild Swan, *Cygnus musicus*, L.
[2] The Black-throated Diver, *Colymbus arcticus*, in summer plumage.
[3] On the MS. is written, 'A woman without any cap, but only a ribband round her hair, professes herself to be a maiden in the High'ands of Scotland.—

lake, passed by one of the same ruined castles which they call
Dunes, and saw another at a distance to the south. They are
as common here as Raths in Ireland, and probably there was
one to every village. I crossed the ferry over the river by
which the lake empties itself into the kyle, and went half a
mile to the house of one Mr. Mackay,[1] the minister of Larig.
who has an extent of parishes thirty English miles in length on
both sides of the lake, and only £50 a year, but the land is
commonly let rather cheap to the minister. He had sent to
invite me to his house; he brought cakes and a bottle of wine,
and desired me to bless the entertainment. Having asked if
we had breakfasted, as we had, he went on with me. We came
to a large brook[2] which falls from the north-east into the lough,
we crossed it often, and went often into it to avoid the cutts
made by the floods; from this river we ascended over the foot
of Ben Clibrig,[3] the Earl of Sutherland's forrest. Here it was
like the month of November; we saw a breach that was made
by a spring like a flood gushing out at the side of a mountain.
We came to another rivulet and sat down in a sheltered place
half a mile beyond some sheelings or huts, to which they come
in the summer with their cattle. We asked about the
accommodation, which as it did not please us, we went on as
mentioned. We here took our repast; some boys came near
with their cattle, and afterwards two others; we invited them
to take share, and when we were going away, they said their
mother was coming with some refreshments, and immediately
she appeared at a good distance; she carried a piggin of cream,
and her maid followed her with a small tub covered, which was
warm whey. She drank to us, and we took it round and tasted
of the whey; the minister conducted me across a hill to another

[Initialled] D. B.' See note, p. 113. Sir Walter Scott adorns Ellen of Loch
Katrine with the silken riband—

> ' A chieftain's daughter seem'd the maid;
> Her satin snood, her silken plaid,
> Her golden brooch, such birth betray'd.
> And seldom was a snood amid
> Such wild luxuriant ringlets hid.'
> *The Lady of the Lake,* Canto i., Stanza 19.

See also Canto iii., Stanza 5 (end).

[1] Rev. Thomas Mackay, Lairg. See Pref. to *Life of Gen. Hugh Mackay*,
by John Mackay.   [2] River Terry.   [3] Ben Clibrec.

rivulet where they joyn, and running towards the mouth of it between deep rocks adorned with trees, it falls into Lough Naivern[1] four miles lower; I observed on the bottom of it and on each side fine flags lying a little sloping from the perpendicular; I came to another rivulet which runs through fine marshes into this lough, to which the salmon come up. It falls by a river into the North Sea at the Bay of Farr; we came to Mowdale. The mountains here abound much in red deer; the roe deer frequent more where there are woods, and always bring two fawns, as I was told, but doubt of it. The males of the red deer are distinguished by different names in Eirshe and English according to their ages.[2] The first year a fawn; second, Procha (Pritchet); third, Kiligavir, that is two branches; fourth, Ostoun; fifth, Dougolag, that is two at top. I was told they were not further distinguished by name, tho' an antler is added every year till the twelfth, when they are called in Eirshe, . . . , in English, Harts. When I came to Durness, I observed besides the shells common to most shores, that large shells of Echine are thrown ashore, small Trochi, a large cockle, bright, red, yellow, and white chamey, and a large white one about five inches long which are very rare, and the limpet called the fool's cap, some with the point at one side, others nearer the middle, the former are very rare. There are also on the coast fine small pebbles of different colours. They find also, drove ashore here, a tender spunge in branches some-

---

[1] Loch Naver or Navern.

[2] Dr. Pococke has preserved to our Gaelic vocabulary distinguishing names for deer, some of which are obsolete, if not altogether forgotten. His spelling, as usual, is phonetic.

Procha, Procach; 'Damh feidh òg, a year-old stag.'—*Rob Donn's Poems*, Glossary, p. 357. Also in the hunting song, 'Soraidh na Fridhe'—

> 'Theid sinne gu socrach
> Air ionnsuidh nam Procach,
> 'S o neamhnuid ar 'n acfuinn,
> Bithidh 'n asnaichean dearg.'—*Rob Donn*, p. 17.

Kiligavir, probably Gille da mheur, or Gille da bhior, the two-fingered one.

Ostoun, probably Osdoun, the dun stag. 'Os' occurs in the old unpublished hunting songs of Sutherland ; also in Ossian's poems.

'Lean-sa 'n os bhallach air Cromla.'—*Fionnghal*, D i., line 137.

Doulgolag (or it may read in the MS. Dongolag), probably Donn da lub, the double-looped dun one ; or Don-gobhlach, the forked dun one.

Blank in the MS. Cabrach, or Udlach. See *Rob Donn*, Glossary, p. 360.

what resembling the ends of stags' horns, and I have seen other spunges since that time in these shapes, which show in what manner the spunge grows, and in other seas to greater perfection. They often see large whales[1] not far from the shoar.

They have great plenty of venison of red deer in this country, so it is commonly brought to table in most houses, and even when it is not fat, is excellent food minced and dressed like a hash, which they call Minced Collop. It is said that there are no rats[2] in Sutherland, except in some places near the sea, where they have been brought by ships.—I am, &c.

Letter XXIV.

Durness, 26th June 1760.

Dear Sister,—On the 25th I set forward, and soon came to a lough which seems to be Lough Culset[3] in the map, which they call four miles long; there are about a dozen islands in it, and it winds and appears like a beautiful river, and if I mistake not falls into Lough Loyal; the distance between this and Strathmore and Mowdale seems to be made too great in the map. After travelling near the east of this lake, we came soon to the ascent over the hill which leads to the river Strathmore, to which we descended. The river Strathmore rises out of

---

[1] For an account of various captures of whales of different species on the Sutherland coasts see *A Vertebrate Fauna of Sutherland and Caithness* (in the press), by J. A. Harvie-Brown, Esq., and J. E. Buckley, Esq.

[2] 'Ther is not a ratt in Sutherland, and if they doe come thither in shipps from other pairts (which often happeneth), they die presentlie, how soone they doe smel of the aire of that cuntrey. And (which is strange) their is a great store and abundance of them in Catteynes [Caithness], the verie nixt adjacent province, divyded onlie by a litle strype or brook from Southerland. Ther are manie wild catts in Southerland, which the inhabitants doe hunt among the rocks and mountains.'—*The Earldom of Sutherland*, by Sir Robert Gordon, written 1630 (first published 1813), p. 7. See Franck's *Northern Memoirs*, 1658, Edinburgh, ed. 1821, pp. 217, 218; Capt. Burt's *Letters from Scotland*, 1728, vol. i. Letter iii.; *Old Stat. Ac. of Scot.*, vol. iv., p. 76; vol. x. p. 269.

[3] Loch Coulside—not Culset—falls into Loch Loaghal; but Dr. Pococke here describes Loch Meadie, which was directly in his route from Mudale to Strathmore.

Mount Coarness,[1] where it forms a large sort of a theatre some way up the hill there; here the late Lord Reay used to have a grand hunt every August. They compute a thousand red deer in that country, and that four or five hundred of them have been drove into this part by about a hundred men who drive the mountains, and they have shot sixty of them in a day. The river Strathmore rises to the west, and after it comes out of this glyn it turns to the north, where a stream falls in from the Glyn Bellachnamerlach[2] (the Glyn of the Lough of Theives).

From this it is not above eight of the computed miles (that is, sixteen English) to Lough Schin; and here is the line that seems most convenient for a road through the kingdom to go south by Rosehall, then to Lough Broom, to which there is a tolerable road now. The way afterwards seems to be most easy by Lough Vrine, Lough Tanide, by the river to Lough Clair, to Lough Contin up that river, and to cross the mountains to Bernis Water to Lough Glasletir, to get to the river that falls out of Lough Assarig, from that to a small stream that falls into Lough Cluny, which crosses the road from Glenmorrison to Bernera, opposite to the Isle of Skye, to go down Lough Cluny river to that which comes to Lough Loyne, and so by that into the road to Fort Augustus from Bernera, and then there are roads to Fort Augustus and Fort William; which line would be of infinite advantage to the kingdom, as they would make roads into it from many parts, both from the east and west; and the most eastern parts would go to the road which is tolerable all along the eastern coast.

We stopped at Strathmore, and travelled by that river to Doundor, called in the map, Dundor Nadilla; it is the most entire round castle I have seen, seeming to be perfect in one part about thirty feet high. Every tier of stone sets in on the outside about an inch. The top is crowned with long even stones; it consists of two walls. There is a set-off within of one foot three inches, where the inner wall is three feet six inches thick; the outer wall four feet three inches at bottom, but both of them lessen to two feet five inches; and the space

---

[1] Coir-an-essie, or Coir nan cas (Coirean casach of Ordnance Survey).
[2] Gleann Beallach na meirleach.

between the walls is two feet five inches; the court within is twenty-six feet six inches in diameter. It is divided by the stones laid across into three stories, and opposite to the entrance, it is open for about two feet and a half in breadth, divided in three parts by the floor. In the middle on the left hand it is the same, as it was probably in the right, which is now ruined. These seem to have been below as entrances, and

View of a round Castle [Dun-Dornadilla].

above to give light; and being divided in this manner into four parts to each story, there might be twelve separate places for twelve families for lodgings in time of danger, and they might have some light doors to them. However, it seems not to have been very strong except at the bottom, and now the support of the circle being lost, as it is ruinous, it is in a very tottering condition. It is built on an eminence over the river, on which side the foundation is ten or twelve feet lower than in the other part, as it is laid near the bottom of the hillock. A view of the inside and outside are here seen.[1]

The hill we crossed to Strathmore is a foot of Benhope.

Inside view of a round Castle [Dun-Dornadilla].

Under the foot of this mountain we travell'd, which is a fine natural slope, with perpendicular rocks over it, resembling ruined buildings. This continues on all under the mountain

---

[1] These sketches of Dun-Dornadilla, or Dun-Dornigil, are the earliest known. For Views see *Archæologia* (Lond.), vol. v. p. 216; Cordiner's *Antiq. North of Scot.*, 1780, p. 105; Henderson's *Agric. of Sutherland*, 1812, App., p. 172; Logan's *Scottish Gall.*, 1831, vol. ii. p. 26; Anderson's *Scot. in Pagan Times*, 1883, p. 185; Pococke's *Tour through Sutherland*, edited by D. W. Kemp, Appendix. See also Pope of Reay's Acc. in Pennant's *Tour*, 1769, p. 341; Pennant's *Tour*, 1772, p. 393; *Archæologia Scotica*, 1883, vol. v. pt. i.; *Sutherland Brochs*, by Rev. Dr. Joass, pp. 95-118.

itself with a sort of terrace on it, from which the mountain rises most beautifully, being divided by several pyramidal risings with little hillocks between them to the number of above twenty, in which little cascades of water fall down after rain in a very beautifull manner. And before we came to this part we saw a sheet of water falling down into a hollow about a hundred feet, and 'tis said falls fifty more out of sight. All the cascades after the morning showers appeared very beautifull. A little lower, Strathmore falls into Lough Hope, which is fresh water, and empties itself by a river into Lough Eribol to which we crossed over a foot of a mountain. I here sent my horses back to Strathmore, and so round about to Tongue to avoid the bog of the Moan, and so to Thyrso. Over that Lough Eribol we ferried, and Lord Reay's horses met me, and I rid three miles to Durness, Lord Reay's house, which is situated at the south-east end of Durness Bay, where there is a fine strand bounded to the north by Farout Head, the end of which is in the degree of 58.45. To the west of this head are two little points which appear to have been fortified.—I am, &c.

LETTER XXV.

TONGUE, IN SUTHERLAND,
July 1st 1760.

DEAR SISTER,—I crossed the bay from Durness to a strand to the west, in order to go to Cape Wrath. Above this strand, to the south, is the Kyle of Durness, into which the river[1] Durness falls, having formed near its rise the Lake of Dinart[2] on the other side of the mountain out of which Strathmore rises. On the north side of this strand are fine cliffs and a beautifull head of marble with white streaks in it, and red spots, it seems to be black. Here the herd's boys were fishing for *Cudines* of a beautiful mixed brown colour, about eight inches long, and eat like trouts.

We went on to the west, and soon came to hills of bright red granite in large spots, we passed by a little stream where we found a fawn of the red deer about a week old, that had

---

[1] River Dionard.   [2] Lake Dionard.

been killed by an eagle; probably two of them shared in the prey, for there were two great holes on one side of it. The herd moved it from the place, and covered it with heath, in order to come and take it for the use of his house, and they say it is excellent food; it was as big as a calf, and the skin streaked with yellow. The hinde on this occasion runs about and stamps with her foot and cries terribly. But the eagles will, they say, kill a hart [1] by seizing them about the neck and fluttering their wings in their eyes. There are two kinds of eagles, the large which keep in the cliffs and feed mostly on fish, and the small black eagle which live in the rocks of mountains, and prey on fawns, lambs, hares, &c. We passed by some lakes, and saw stags feeding at a distance.

After travelling three computed miles, we came to Kerwich Bay, a small strand with rocks to the east, which are a sort of composition of very small pebbles, and some of it looks like the granite of the Statues of Memnon.[2] On the other side the rocks are of a bright red granite, and so all the way to Cape Wrath, to which we went, passing by two lakes in which there is no kind of fish visible, no stream running into them; we ascended two or three heights before we came to Cape Wrath, which consists of two points, that to the north-west is the lower; before the other are two high rocks of red granite, encompassed with water, where there is an aery of eagles, and we saw the two eagles which belong to it flying over the point and very near the ground; they sometimes fight for fish on the strands and kill one another.

I saw from this head a great part of the Isle of Lewis, and the Isle of Ronon,[3] which is about three leagues off, I was told that there are about seven families on it, and that a minister from the Isle of Lewis visits them sometimes once a year. Six

---

[1] An account of a desperate struggle between an eagle and a stag was graphically described in the *Scotsman* of 11th Dec. 1884. See *Sport in the Highlands and Lowlands*, by T. Speedy, and 'The Eagles of Loch Treig,' in *Scot. Church Mag.*, Jan. 1886, by 'Nether Lochaber,' the Rev. Dr. Alex. Stewart.

[2] *A Description of the East and some other Countries*, by Richard Pococke, D.D., LL.D., 1743, vol. i. p. 102.

[3] Islands Rona or Roney and Soulisgeir or Sula Sgeir. See Articles by Mr. Swinburne in vol. viii. pp. 51-67, and Mr. Harvie-Brown in vol. ix. pp. 284-299, *Proc. Royal Physical Soc.*, 1883-86.

leagues to the north of White Head, which is the head of the Moan,[1] is a very small rocky island called Scalisker, which island is in no other map but Buchanan's; to it the people of Orkney go once a year to catch seals, of which they make oyl, and they come all along the coast. In this island the solan geese breed, which is the same as the gannet I saw in Kerry. A herd[2] lives at Kerwich Bay to take care of the sheep and horses, and another near the bay where we landed. To this head and peninsula of Cape Wrath they have sometimes drove the red deer in order to shoot. They have a great number of the adder kind here; and I was told in the middle parts of Scotland that goats do actually kill and eat them, which I could not believe untill it was confirmed to me here in such a manner that I could not withold my belief of it, and, 'tis added, that they make a great noise when they kill them.[3] It is mentioned in some books that the red deer do kill them, but of the truth of this I could not be informed, but they say swine certainly do kill and eat them.

Another day we went eastward to the Cave of Smoo.[4] It is

---

[1] The Moine (or Moss).

[2] The herd at that time may have been *Rob Donn*, the Sutherland bard. He was at one period Lord Reay's herd at Kearvaig or Kerwich.

[3] This was well known in the Highlands. Hence the saying, 'Itheadh na gabhair air an nathair,—ga h-ith' 's ga caineadh.' See also Sheriff Nicolson's *Collection of Gaelic Proverbs and Familiar Phrases*, 1881, pp. 294, 295—

'Itheadh na goibhre air an nathair.
The goats' eating of the serpent.

'It is believed, in some parts of the Highlands, that goats eat serpents, and that they eat them tail foremost, first stamping on the head. It is said that while the goat is thus engaged it utters a querulous noise, not liking the wriggling of the adder. A verse in reference to this is:—

'Cleas na goibhre 'g ith' na nathrach,
'G a sior-itheadh, 's a' sior-thalach.
*The goats' trick with the serpent,
Eating away, and still complaining.*

'Be this as it may, it is positively affirmed by persons of experience that serpents disappear where goats pasture.'

[4] Sir Walter Scott, in his *Diary of a Cruise in the Pharos*, in 1814, describes most graphically, but perhaps too imaginatively, his visit to the eerie caves of Smoo. See Lockhart's *Life of Scott*, ed. 1837; *Uamh Smowe*, vol. iii. pp. 209-216; *Two Months in the Highlands, Orcadia, and Skye*, by C. R. Weld, 1860, p. 225; *Guide to Sutherland and Caithness*, by Hew Morrison, 1883, pp. 107-9.

very beautiful, with high rocks on each side. Into this cave a stream falls, and runs through it. The cave is forty yards broad and fifty long, and it may be forty feet high. From one side of it a water comes from under the rock, which is open for some way above. A boat was sometime agoe put in, and a small lake was found underground, formed by a cascade of water a few yards to the south, which falls down in a sheet from a rivulet, it may be thirty feet, and runs along the rock into this lough; and the light from that part at noon, when the sun shines on it, has a very extraordinary effect. There is a long opening over the cave, as for an oval cupola, and altogether it is a most singular curiosity. I went another time to the west, where there is a deep hole, into which the sea comes underground for about a hundred yards, like those to the south of Waterford in Ireland, and it must be sixty feet deep.

The sand here has covered a great quantity of good ground, and is gaining on a lake near adjoining; for there are many lakes in this tract which have communication one with another, and that partly underground; and in a valley near one of them I observed rocks on each side, with a harder kind of marble between the strata, which remained proof against the weather, for about two inches in thickness, and is of a black colour, whilst the stone above and below was worn by the weather. I rid up by the Kyle of Durness, which in one part appears like a large triangular lake.

The people here live very hardy, principally on milk, curds, whey, and a little oatmeal, especially when they are at the sheales in the mountain, y^t is, the cabins or hutts in which they live when they go to the mountains with their cattle during ye months of June, July, and August. There best food is oat or barley cakes. A porridge made of oatmeal, cale, and sometimes a piece of salt meat in it, is the top fare. Except that by the sea, they have plenty of fish in summer, and yet they will hardly be at the pains of catching it but in very fine weather. They are mostly well-bodied men, of great activity, and go the Highland trot with wonderfull expedition. The post travels on foot in four days and back again to Dornock, sixty computed miles, which cannot be less than a hundred

English, that is fifty miles a day, and seem to make nothing of it. A boy ten years old goes post from Ratter to Thyrso, eight computed miles, and back again by eleven in the morning. When they were in vassalage they paid their rent in cattle to the landlord for the land they held, and for the cattle's sustenance he gave them what corn they wanted, and they were oblidged to work whenever he required them. Of grain they have only barley and oats, with both of which they make cakes. They are not yet come into the use of potatoes, but are making a very small beginning; in the middle and south parts of Scotland they are in plenty.

The people are in general extremely hospitable, charitable, civil, polite, and sensible. In the north-west part I met with the greatest hospitality and politeness in Lord Reay's family.[1] The ancestor of this house in the time of Charles the First was going to Gustavus Adolphus with a regiment of Scotch. Just as he was embarking with a recruit of a thousand men he received an account of the death of that monarch, with whom he had been for some time. He had spent and mortgaged great part of his estate (to Lord Sutherland's family) in military expeditions, having a strong passion for military glory. On his return home he offered himself to the Swedes, and not being accepted he went into the service of Denmark, where he soon died. This is one of the loyal clans, the head of which has a pension[2] from the Crown of £300 a year.—I am, &c.

[1] 'HOUP [HOPE], *Saturday, 5th July* 1760.—Most of last week taken up with a conspicuous stranger, Dr. Pocock, Lord Bishop of Ossory in Ireland, who after a course of travels through Europe and Asia came at length to Scotland, which he means to pervade thoroughly, and accordingly came to this north-west point of it, and stayed with Lord Reay from Wednesday till Monday. He seems to be curious, ingenious, and judicious, and I hope our country may not be the worse of his visit, which has probably rubbed off prejudices *hinc inde*. It was on Monday he came over the water [Loch Erriboll] in his way to the eastward, when I also came from home.'—*From the unpublished MS. Diary by the late Rev. Murdo Macdonald, Minister of Durness, Sutherland, 7 vols., in the private Library of Mr. Hew Morrison, F.S.A., Scot., Edinburgh.*

[2] This pension appears to have been paid in varying amounts to various branches of the Reay family from 1707 to 1831. The last Lord Reay in receipt of it was Lord Erick.

Letter XXVI.

Tongue, in Sutherland,
July 1st, 1760.

Dear Sister,—On the 30th we set out by the way we came, and cross'd the bay of Eribol to a place about a mile lower, where Mr. Mackay had sent horses for me, to whose house we went, two miles, crossing over Inverhope, where there is a large salmon wear of Lord Reay's; and we had a fine view of Lough Hope. But ye mountain Benhope did not appear so beautifull with its pointed top as when it was covered with a cloud. We took some refreshments at this gentleman's house, and were met by Mr. Forbes, who conducted me six miles to his house over the Moan, a morassy country, impassible except to their little bog horses. Coming to the bay of Tongue, we had a more pleasant country in view, in which there are many fine spots of ground, and especially Lord Reay's estate of Tongue. Here I was shown the place where a Frenchman had been buried who fell in an engagement in 1746, when the Sheerness man-of-war "Captain Obrian" had chased the "Hazard" sloop,[1] which had on board 150 men and £13,000 for the Pretender about three weeks before the battle of Culloden, the want of which lessened their army, as it deprived them of purchasing provisions. After they had run ashore accidentally on the point, they fought for a short time. Mr. Forbes attacked them with about eight men, and led them up the mountain, now and then giving them a volley, till the country and part of a regiment of regular troops cantooned at no great distance came in, to whom he had sent for aid; and then they immediately laid down their arms, and were carried off on board the man-of-war.[2]

[1] The French appear to have immediately replaced this sloop by another bearing the same name, and which was equally unlucky:—'*Le Hazard*, a French privateer, of 6 carriage-guns, 8 swivels, and 48 men, taken betwixt Tain and Dornoch, by the *Experiment*, Captain Farmer, in company with the *John* and *Margaret* of Leith, George Stiel. The Privateer is brought to Leith.'— *Scots Mag.*, 1747, p. 453.

[2] This narrative was doubtless communicated by the Rev. Murdo Macdonald, the minister of Durness, and corresponds very closely to the notes in his MS. Diary. See Note 1, p. 128.

The ground we had passed was the foot of Benhope, at the several heads between the rivers stretched out from the mountains which lye to the south.

On the 1st of July, Mr. Forbes and Mr. Gordon, a student of Aberdeen, set out with me, and we passed by a kern of circular stones, and in a mile and a half came to Tongue, a seat of Lord Reay's, calling by y^o way on Mr. Ross the minister, who came with us to that place, where the late lord had made a handsome terrace and bowling green between the house and the bay, and a kitchen garden behind the house planted with all kinds of fruit except peaches, apricocks, and plumbs. Cherries and apples are planted against the walls; and in the middle of the kitchen garden is a pillar entirely covered with dials. The Master of Reay, the lord's eldest son, usually lives here. There are large plantations of wichelm, ash, sycamore, and some quicken or mountain ash. On the opposite side on a height saw Dunbar[1] Castle, where the Mackay family did formerly sometimes reside. We went on and soon came to the foundation of a round castle on an eminence now entirely destroyed. To the south is a fine craggy long mountain called Ben Loyal, on the other side of which is Lough Loyal, near which we had passed in the way to Strathmore from Moudale. So we were here on the foot of Mount Loyal which makes Torrisdale Head.

A little before we came to the Bay of Farr we stopped at the house of Captain Mackay a half-pay officer of Holland, and met with his brother there, who was actually in that service. We were entertained with cake and a glass of Malaga, and came on to Farr Bay, to which some fine rocks extend in perpendicular veins of a black slaty stone, and whitish granite with some mixture of very pale red. This bay near a mile over consists of soft sand on which we rid, not without some apprehensions to a stranger, tho' all was safe. Here we crossed the water which comes from Loch Nevern,[2] near which we travell'd about Moudale, and from this lake and river the whole country to Caithness is called Stranevern.[3]

---

[1] Dun Bar or Dun Varrich or Berovik.   [2] Loch Naver or Navern.
[3] Strathnaver.

SUTHERLAND.

We came round the hill to Farr Church,[1] where on a stone [2] about three feet wide and six high, a short cross is cut in a circle in bas relief, and many ornaments of lines round about it so as to cover that side, which the common people imagine to be inscriptions. Hear the sea at some distance. In a strong situation is the ruined castle of Farr,[3] the ancient residence of Lord Reay's family, who were called lairds of Farr, being made peers in the time of Charles the First, when the lord I have mentioned mortgaged all this eastern part of the estate, which was afterwards sold to the Earl of Sutherland.

At Tongue near the house is a vein of sparr, which being examined by a miner he said it was tin ore, but so small a vein that it is not worth the working.

We here dined with Mr. Monroe [4] the minister, who heard of our coming. We proceeded in bad stony roads, and passed by several little loughs, in which there are trouts and eels. The last are eaten here only by the common people. We saw two kerns near Farr, and soon found ourselves in a boggy country, and crossed the river Armisdale.[5]

We then came on the land which makes Strathy Head, supposed to be Virvebrum Promontoricum, which seems to extend from Ben Maddy, that is near the Loughs Strathy and Buy which are to the east of Lough Nevern. The new map makes this point as stretching out to due north, so as at first view to appear like the north-east point, but then was call'd Dumna, and the Mainland of the Orkneys, call'd Thule Ult. Ins., lye pretty well to it, whereas the Orcades stretch out towards *Epidium Promontorium*, now Cape Wrath. Torridale [6] Head seems to be Orcas Promontorium of that map, unless Strathy Head should rather be Orcas and Vervedrum the head,

---

[1] The present church dates from 1774; the former one was a small thatched building.

[2] This cross is described and figured in Stuart's *Sculp. Stones of Scot.* Pl. xxxv. p. 12. The stone is very hard, and differs entirely from any of the rocks in the district.

[3] Farr or Borve Castle, near Swordly. See *Guide to Sutherland and Caithness*, by Hew Morrison, F.S.A. Scot.

[4] Rev. George Munro, minister from 1754 to 1779. He was the paternal grand-uncle of the Rev. Gustavus Aird, D.D., Free Church, Creich.

[5] Armadale.   [6] Torrisdale.

to the east of Thurso. But in this case Virubrium, the northeast point, is too far from it in that map. This part we went over is the worst of all, consisting of many guts, over which the horses must leap, and sometimes so near one another that we continued in a gallop over them; whereas Moan is soft and shaking, tho' dangerous only to very heavy horses, but my horses, I was told, leaped over this part very well.

We came to a most charming vale between the bogs called Strathy Bay on Avon Strathy. It belongs to Captain Mackay, now in the Sutherland regiment [1] and laird of Strathy, being an apenage from the lairds of Farr before they were enobled. Here is a good house and offices, and I was received with great politeness by Lady Strathy. This is a fine country situated between a foil of black bogs that hang over it, but between the house and the sea there are beautifull hills which have fine downs on their summitts.

We set out on the 2d, and came about four miles over another course of bogs, under which is a yellow freestone, and crossed the Avon Hollowdale, which rises to the south out of the Paps and Ben Grim, and passed by Bighouse, another apenage of the house of Reay that descended to the present lord's half-brother by his marriage of the sole heiress.[2] This is a beautifull vale of considerable extent. Ascending such another tract, we came to a flaggstone set up on end, some say, in memory of a victory obtained here, tho' probably it is an ancient sepulchre.

We crossed a stream on the top of this hill into Caithness. Sutherland seems to have been inhabited by the Caroni to the west, by the Mortie to the east, by part of the Conavii to the north, and part of the Cantie to the south. Caithness was inhabited to the east by these two people, and by the Logi

---

[1] A letter from a gentleman in Inveraray to a gentleman in Edinburgh dated Aug. 4th 1760 has the following paragraph:—'On Friday last arrived here in their way to the Roads, eight miles from this place [Inveraray], 100 sturdy fellows of Lord Sutherland's highlanders, commanded by Lieutenant James Mackay of Skerray; though after a fatiguing march, they made as fine an appearance as any troops I ever beheld, and though they are but a young corps, there is scarce a regiment in his Majesty's service better disciplined.'—*Caledonian Mercury*, Aug. 13, 1760.

[2] See note 5, p. 113.

between them. We soon came down near to a large bay, and to Sandside, Mr. Innys,[1] near the west hill of it, and a little to the west of Reay, from which the family take their title, and where the first lord built a small house. Here we saw a fine country, a good house, and everything in great order and elegance. Here I also viewed the remains of a Picts' house and part of the outer wall of the gallery round the cells, which seemed to have been supported on the outside by earth. They have here freestone, limestone, and thin flags, used as slating for their buildings, and there are rocks of grey granite. Over the bay in the middle of the sands are two kerns, in which they have found bones.—I am, &c.

LETTER XXVII.

July 1760.

DEAR SISTER,—On the 3^d I set out; the Laird of Sanside Mr. Innys, sending a Gentleman with me. We went a mile to the south of Thyrso to see a Picts house at Giese, in which I discovered only an entrance about four feet wide, and a segment of a circle that might be about 25 feet in diameter, and probably a wall was built within this to make a circular passage which led to the small appartments in the middle, about 8 feet long and 4 feet wide, which answers to the description of them. From this I came to Mr. Murray's,[2] near Thyrso, and

---

[1] Mr. Innes of Sandside.

[2] 'Mr. James Murray of Pennyland, Surveyor of the Customs, told me [Bishop Forbes] he desired the Bishop of Ossory to visit the Clet, but he was in haste, and could not think of walking so far, as it is two long miles from Pennyland, where his Lordship had dined and ate heartily of fried chicken, and liked it so well that he desired to have a receipt for dressing of it, as there is no such dish in England or Ireland. There was another Dish, which he took to be Enammelet, but it happened to be toasted Ears. "Toasted ears!" said he; "what is that?" "Why," said Mr. Murray, "the Ears of a Calf toasted on Bread." He liked it much. But what surprized him most of all was the fine Wheat-Bread he ate here, of which he said he had not got any since he came into Strathnaver, through which he travelled in his way to Caithness; and he begged to know how they came by it. When they told him it was baked in a Pot, he was amazed, insomuch that it behoved them to assure him it was so before he could believe it; and he declared he had never ate better all his Life; and so

embarked at that town for the Orkneys. Thyrso is pleasantly situated on a bay and a river of the same name, which rises out of several loughs to the south-east towards Dunbeath ; It is but indifferently built ; and is chiefly supported by the salmon fishery. They also export some corn, and have an import for the use of the gentlemen of the country. About half a mile to the west are ruins of a castle which belonged to the bishops of Cathness, whose See was at Dornock, and it contained this county and Sutherland. Helburn Head to the west of this, is esteemed a very fine head of land. On the 3^d, about seven in the evening, we took boat for the isle of Walls, pronounced Waies, one of the Orkneys.

We landed about 11 in a rocky Creek that had a very frightfull appearance, and would have been dangerous, if it had not been perfectly calm. We walked a mile to Captain Moody's house ; this is a most charming situation on an eminence which commands a view of the sea to the East, and of a most beautifull bay to the North that locks in and appears like a lake ; the land between it is cultivated, and if the hills were planted it would be a perfect terrestrial paradise.

On the 5th we took boat on this bay, which to the West for about half a mile is divided from the North Sea by a narrow beach. We rowed on for about four miles to the North West[1] and by West, having Waies on both sides, but afterwards we turned to the North West, having Hoy Waies to the west, which is the name of that part of the island, as that to the South of the bay we came in, is called South Waies. We saw to the East the small isle of Switha, and rowing on had Flota to the East, and saw beyond it the isle of South Ronaldshaw : we had a view of Kirkwall Church across the neck of Land of the isle of Pomona commonly called the Mainland : We went on and had Fara isle to the East, and then the isle of Risa, and beyond that Cava.

plentifully did he take of it, that Mr. Murray jokingly said, "Stop, my Lord, else your Lordship will raise a Famine in ye Country ;" which pleased him so well, that he called to his own Servant, "John, pray, give me t'other cut of that fine Loaf." And, when he came to Wick, he desired his Servant to see if he could have a Loaf baked in a Pot to take along with them. He had two Servants, viz., a Valet and a Groom.'—Bp. Forbes's *Journals*, by the Rev. J. B. Craven, p. 200.

[1] Should be north-east by east.

We saw two or three of the golden Eagles flying to the Cliffs: they are the large kind, and lighter than any I have seen in Ireland; tho' I saw of the largest kinds, which I believe are all black in Ireland. And I have some doubt whether these are not of the Vulture kind: I was told they measure from the end of one wing to the end of the other six feet; It was to these Cliffs that an Eagle brought a Child four miles, from Houton Head on the Mainland, as mentioned by Sr Robert Sibbald in his Natural History of Scotland which is so remarkable (tho' almost incredible) that I insert it in his own words. . . . Infantulum unius anni Pannis involutum arripuisse, quem Mater tesselas ustibiles pro igne allatura momento temporis deposuerat in loco *Houton-head* dicto cumque deportâsse per quatuor milliaria passam ad *Hoiam*; quâ re ex Matris ejulatibus cognitâ, quatuor viri illuc in Navicula profecti sunt, & scientes ubi Nidus esset, Infantulum illæsum & intactum deprehenderunt.—L. 3. c. ii. p. 14.[1]

We came to the vale which is to the South of Hoy Hill, where over the Sea cliff is a Picts house, & we walked a mile and a half by the vale to the foot of the hill on the South Side of the Vale, where we saw that famous stone commonly called the Dwarfe Stone,[2] it is 28 feet long, 14 feet 7 in. broad, 6 ft. 3 in. deep: into which a room is cut, the middle is a sort of passage 3 feet broad about seven feet long and two feet six inches high, to the right is a place as for a bed 4 feet 11½ inches long with a rising three inches high and seven inches

---

[1] 'An eagle carrying away to his nest an infant in its swaddling-clothes. Dr. Matthews MacKail, a doctor of Aberdeen, informed me that there are many eagles in the west part of the mainland of the Orkneys, called Pomona, as well in the Island of Hoy, and he said that one of these had seized an infant of one year old, wrapped up in its swaddling-clothes, which its mother had laid down for a moment at a place called Houten-head, while she went to gather dry fuel for the fire, and that this eagle carried the infant for four miles to Hoy. When the occurrence became known from the cries of the mother, four men set out to the island in a little boat, and, as they knew where the nest was, they rescued the infant safe and sound.' Vide *Scotia Illustrata sive prodromus Historiæ Naturalis*, etc., by Sir Robert Sibbald, 1684. This incident is referred to by Sir Walter Scott in his notes to *The Pirate*; but it must have occurred at an earlier date than there indicated.

[2] See Note P. to Sir Walter Scott's novel *The Pirate*. Dr. Pococke's measurements correspond very closely with those given by Mr. Tudor in his large work *The Past and Present State of the Orkneys and Shetland*, 1883, p. 323.

broad so as to lay the head on it, and a very little hollow in
the middle, as if designed for the back part of the head; on
the other side is a Compartment with a division 3 inches broad
and about the same height from the passage, the Compartm^t is
two feet wide, and three feet four inches long with a round
hole over it which comes a few inches over the passage. This
seems to have been the hearth, & the hole to be made to carry

A Hermit's Cell in the Dwarfe Stone.

off the smoak; The stone at top of this hole is seven inches
thick. Drawings of it are here seen. This stone must have
fallen down from the hill, and was without doubt the habitation of a Hermit.[1]

There is great plenty of Grouse here, and they have the
black game, but neither Deer, hares, foxes, patriges, Pheasants
or quailes.

We went on and it was curious to see the birds following
the Shoals of fish, supposed to be young Herrings. We saw on
a point of Hoy a pidgeon house formed out of the chamber of

[1] 'The common tradition among the people is, that a giant with his wife lived
in this Isle of Hoy, who had this stone for their Castle. But I would rather
think . . . the retired Cell of some melancholick Hermite.'—Brand's *Description of Orkney*, 1701, edition 1883, p. 63.

a picts house with some additions made to it; that room is eight feet long and 4 feet wide: The Hill of Hoy is a fine red hill probably abounding in Iron; and Hoy head to the North of it, is a very grand and beautifull cliff. We rowed along to the west of Gromsa,[1] a fine isle of about 300 acres, and brings near £100 rent, it belongs to Mr. Honeyman who has his title of Gromsa from this island. A Bishop[2] of Orkney anno 1664 was of this family: He received a shot in his Arm by a poisoned ball which was designed for A: Bp Sharp as he was getting into the Arch Bp's Coach which much impaired his health.

We passed in sight of Orphir called Orpher in Dorrets Map of Scotland; Here is a Rotondo Chapel[3] built as they say long before the Cathedral of Kirkwall, and was entire in 1757 but wanting stone for the Church of Orphir, they much defaced it; however as it was of freestone & the mortar proving excellent Cement it did not answer to separate them, and soe it was not entirely destroyed; It is 20 feet in Diameter and 15 feet high, is vaulted, with a hole in the top to give light, and there is a small window in the East End: Orphir was the chief seat of the Danish governors till Romuald[4] Earl of Orkney who succeeded Paul, built the Cathedral, and then Kirkwall became the Seat of Government. Torfæus p. 103 in the life of Earl Paul, in the beginning of the 12th Century speaks thus of this building. In Iorfiara magnificæ ædes in præcipite colle stabant; . . . Ingens triclinium, convivisq,; excipiendis [capacissimum Jorfiara estabat,] inpariete australi prope angulum orientalem, qvi latera committit, fores erant, ante qvas tem-

---

[1] Gremsay.

[2] Andrew Honyman, Archdeacon of St. Andrews, afterwards translated to the Bishopric of Orkney.

[3] 'We must look to Orkney for the only specimen in Scotland of a circular church—that at Orphir, now only a mere fragment. This interesting ruin has been adduced as an example of the development of a church from the early dry-built circular or beehive dwellings of the native inhabitants; but it is on record that the Norwegian Earl Hakon, who had his residence at Orphir, made the pilgrimage to Jerusalem in expiation of the murder of St. Magnus, and as the church is plainly one of the well-known twelfth-century imitations of the Church of the Holy Sepulchre, it was more likely to have been erected by him than by any one previous to his time.'—Anderson's *Scotland in Early Christian Times*, 1881, p. 29.

[4] Earl Rognvald.

plum magnificum, ad qvod ingressus à triclinio per devexa patebat.[1]

We came to Stromness town, situated something like Kingsale in Ireland, about half a mile in length, on the side and foot of the hill on the Sea, but very irregularly built. They are all (except one Factor), Publicans and shopkeepers; There are above 200 families in the town; the women are great knitters: most ships going Westward or Northwards touch here, but the chief are 4 large ships which goe every May to Hudson's bay with all kinds of Sortments of goods, and bring back bever skins for hats, & Marten's for Muffs and Tippets, which last are brought only by the Sailors & sell here for about five shillings a piece; the bevers for . . .[2] They also bring Sea horses teeth which are about 18 inches long, and are very fine Ivory—of these, among other uses, they make artificial teeth—fish, oyl, the Skins of the Mouse, and of Deer, & Elk. The first I was assured answers to the description of the Urus: They are five weeks in their voyage to the Entrance of Hudson's bay and four weeks more to the furthest factory. When they arrive they fire a gun which is a notice to the Natives to bring their goods. The Askeomies are those round about the outer parts of the Bay: The Indians are in the inner parts: These are always at war, and 'tis said the former eat the latter when they Kill them in Battle, as no Quarter is given on either side, except to the Children which they breed up as their own. The Askeomies use the long Canoe covered with Seal Skin, and a hole in it large enough for one person, about which they lash their garment, so as that water cannot come in; the Indians use a Canoe made of the bark of a tree; and both manage them so well, that they will remain near a ship (till their turn comes to go aboard) for a considerable time in very bad weather. They admit into the ship about a dozen at a time, not choosing to

---

[1] From *Rerum Orcadensium Historiæ*, by Thermodus Torfæus, 1697, lib. I. cap. xxiii. 'In Iorfiara a great castle stood on a steep hill. In it there was a large banqueting hall, the most commodious in all Iorfiara for receiving guests; and in the south wall, near where the east corner unites the sides, there was a door, and in front of this a great temple, to which entrance opened from the banqueting hall by means of a flight of stairs.' See also Popes' translation of Torfæus, and notes, pp. 107, 108.

[2] Blank in the MS.

be outnumbered by them. The teeth and oyl they bring floating and fixed to the Canoe. The Sailors give them beeds, red coats for the Chiefs, adorned with tinsel lace, and many trinkets in exchange. The Askeomies prostrate on the face to do obeisance, and are afraid of Canon, which if fired they fall prostrate; whereas the Indians take the fire of Canon as a Compliment: They wear a Jacket and Capuchin over their heads of woolfs or bearskins, and trousers, which cover their feet and legs: of the same, a sort of broad Sandal of Mouse hide with an ornament turning up before, and these are convenient to walk with on the Snow. The Chiefs wear, as before mentioned, a red Jacket, and have purses of Seal Skins adorned with glass beeds, on which they set a great value.

The principal trade of the island is at this place, which consists in an export of Barley, Kelp Ashes, Fish oyl, Salt beef, and butter. They also send out Oatmeal, Malt, hams, dryed geese, tallow, Cod, Ling and the Skins of Calves rabbits and foxes, goose feathers, coarse frizes, fine stockings, knit gloves, and linnen: But they say the fishery has failed of late, whether for want of fish or Industry I cannot say. They have apples and pears against the walls, and say they will not do as standards, nor grow above the walls: the horses are like those of the highlands: They have a very small hog with long Bristles which lookes like a Hedge hog; it seems to be a mixture with the wild boar. They are not bigger than the Chinese hog & the bodies not so large; they have little huts for them in the Commons to keep them from the Corn. The Sheep are very small and in this island they pull off the wool,[1] which bruises them in such a manner, that if it happens to be wet afterwards they often dye. In Waies they sometimes sheer them, and oftener cut off the Wool with a sharp knife in a very dextrous manner; but in that Island the sheep are mostly wild; they have marks[2] on them, and an officer who is a kind of Constable,

---

[1] 'The process of *rooing* (or plucking) is said not to be so cruel as it would seem, the wool, when the sheep is ripe for the operation, coming away very easily.'—Tudor's *The Orkneys and Shetland*, p. 155.

[2] Sheep-marks were general in the Orkneys until about 40 years ago, and when registered with the bailie of the parish, under the old Country Acts gave hereditary rights. The following are three examples: (1) A hole in the right lug, a lap before on the left lug, a teen in the left nostril; (2) A shear on the

when they want to catch them, points to them and the dog
brings out the sheep he desires: But as they eat of the Sea
weeds, they are not good till fed for a few days on grass, having
a disagreeable taste. In the winter the Snow bird comes,
which is about as big as a bunting, the body is of ash colour
with white wings, it eats like a lark. They have also the Chac
which is of an ash colour with black wings as big as a sky lark.
The Lyar seems to be the Puffin, they let down people several
fathoms by a rope to take them on the ledges in the rocks,
where they have their young in holes. The herrings come
from the North in the beginning of Summer in great quantities,
and proceed along the East and West coast, and are not so
good as those caught here. The whole Bay through which we
sailed is a very fine harbour, but especially that part of it which
is between Hoy Waies and South Waies: the entrance between
Gromsa and Stromness is narrow. The largest ships anchor
within Gromsa to the North West; and two points make out,
and form a Beautifull Bason under the town, where the small
shipping come in: And this passage is much frequented in
order to avoid Pentland Firth where the tydes and currents
are very difficult for strangers; and so they sail to the
East of Duncansby head the North East point of Scotland.—
I am, &c.

Letter XXVIII.

Kirkwall in Orkney, *July 4th, 1760.*

Dear Sister,—On the 6th we took horses at Stromness and
travelled to the North West; we had in sight the Lough of
Stenhouse and Circles of Stones, and came in about 4 miles to
the Sea Cliffs which are very fine perpendicular rocks, with

right lug, a piece behind the left lug, and a crook before burnt on the face;
(3) A shear on the right lug, two holes on the left, and oowed on the face.
Explanation of terms:—*lap*, a bit taken out of the edge of the lug (ear); *teen*, a
slit made in the nostril, the effect of which was that it became larger than the
other; *shear*, the upper part of the lug clipped off in a slanting direction; *piece*,
a small bit taken out of the edge of the lug at the root; *crook*, a larger piece
taken out of the middle of the lug; *oowed*, the flesh on the face cut to the bone,
and the flesh twisted round so that it rose like a wart or mole. Ear-marks are
still common, and recognised by large sheep-farmers throughout Scotland. See
also Tudor's *The Orkneys and Shetland*, p. 154.

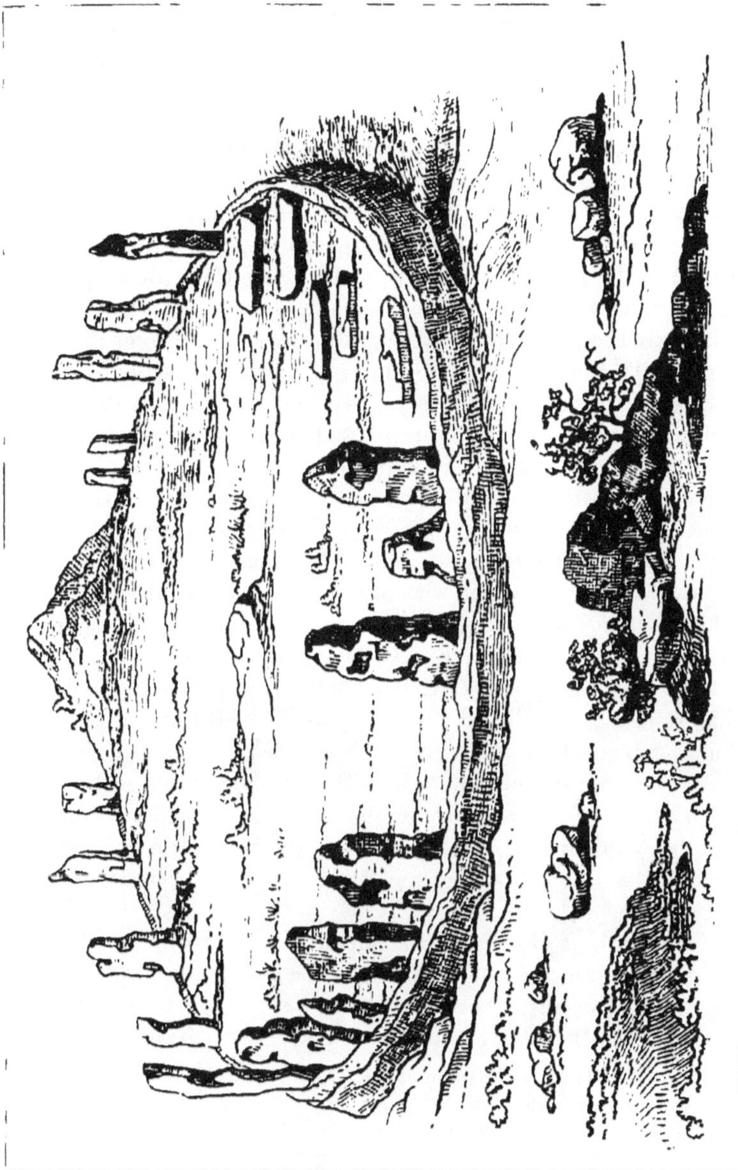

ORKNEY.

View of a Druid Temple (Stennis)

several coves in them, these rocks consist mostly of thin strata of stone each about 6 or 8 inches thick and then a Ruble stone for about ten feet: the thin strata are joyned in several figures, and these joynts commonly continue through them. They mostly consist, each of them, of three kinds of Stone of Different Colours and sometimes four, which are different as to their hardness, the middle and outside yellow, and that between blewish. There is a softer stone between them, which wears away, and the others resisting the force of the waters, they form figures round in the shape of the stone, and in some there are three of them, besides the middle stone. Many of them are triangular, which are beautifull, some in shape of a Needle, and some rise in a small dye of a Uniform substance ; The Cliff extends to a head near which there is a small lake. To the North of this about 5 miles in Birsa, is the old Country Seat of the Earls of Orkney built round a Court in a Circular form, the rooms being high : Here also are the remains of Christs Church the first Christian place of Devotion built in this island. We came Eastward two miles to the glebe or as they call it the Manse of the parish of Sandwick, where we dined with Mr. Terrè :[1] we passed by a lake which is the rise of a river that runs a little way and makes another lake, and running a little further it forms the great lake of Stenhouse, which extends about six miles to the South, and is near a mile broad ; it then passes between two heads of Land, extends four miles to the North West, and falls by a large opening to the South into the Sea, and is said to be 25 miles round, of which I have no doubt ; to the North is a ridge of hills, between which and the hills to the South is a fine Vale, beyond this is another ridge and there is a most beautiful vale between them.

The parish of Birsa,[2] and the parish of Eva,[3] to the north of these make another fine spot on the Sea : we had a most pleasant ride between the two parts of the Lough, tho' the Country is mostly heathy, & we came to a very grand druid temple,[4]

[1] Rev. James Tyrie, minister from 1747 to 1778. [2] Birsay. [3] Evie.
[4] The large stone circle at Stennis is 366 feet in diameter. Thirteen stones are still standing; ten others are prostrate, and the stumps or fragments of thirteen more bring the number still recognisable on the site to thirty-six. *Vide* Anderson's *Scot. in Pagan Times*, 1886, p. 118, fig. 129; Barry's *History of Orkney*, p. 217, 2d ed.

some of the stones of which are 15 feet high and from three to six feet broad, and fifteen feet apart. There were about sixty

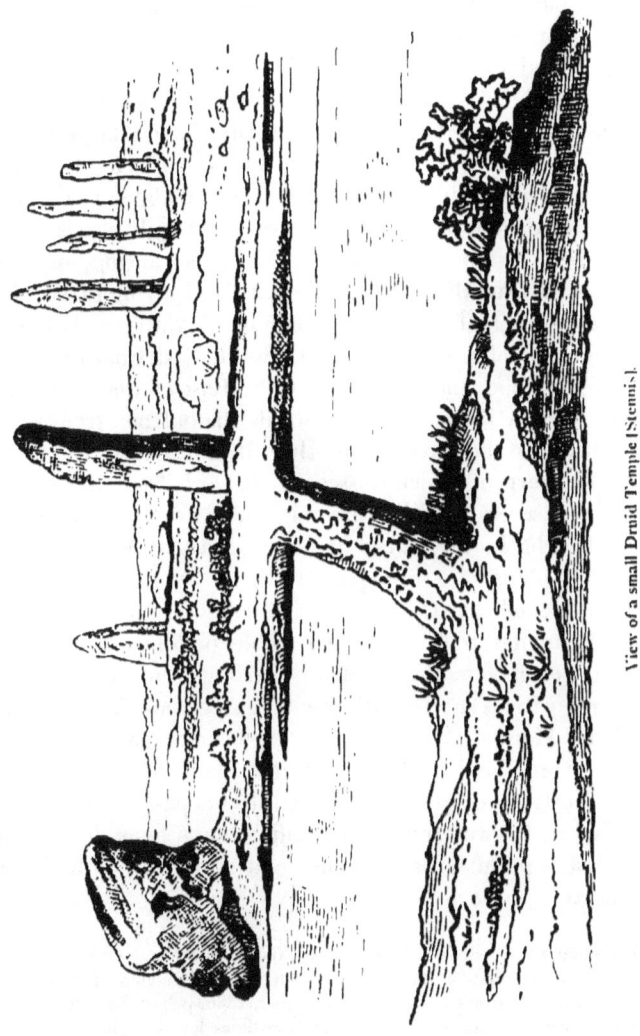

View of a small Druid Temple (Stennis).

of them but many lay on the ground, and there are cavities wherein most probably some of them stood. There is a single pillar about 50 yards to the North East, and a barrow to the

North and South, one to the South West and another to the North East, and what is singular, at the distance of ten yards is a fossee all round the Circle about ten feet deep. A view of it is seen on the other side [page 141].

We crossed over the narrow pass which joyns the two parts of the Lough on stones laid like a wier. I was assured there were no Salmon in the Lough, but they have a large kind of trout,—soon afterwards we came to another Circle of Stones[1] which are 15 feet high, six feet broad, the Circle is about 30 yards in Diameter, and the stones are about eight yards apart; There are two standing to the South, one is wanting, and then there are two standing to the West, a third laying down, then two are wanting, there being a space of 27 yards so that there were eight in all: Eighteen yards South East from the Circle is a single stone, and 125 yards to the East of that is another with a hole[2] in it on one side towards the bottom, from which going towards the circle is another 73 yards from the fossee, the outer part of which fossee is 16 yards from the Circle: There are several small barrows chiefly to the East, which might be the burial places of the Druids. A view of the Druid Temple is here seen [page 143].

We came on by the Kirk of Stenhouse, to which there is a semicircular tower, and the whole building seems to be without Cement, or at most with Clay between the stones and is covered with Thatch. We went near a beautifull small isle called the Holm of Ghimbuster[3] very near the land, and such another North East of it called Damsa, both of them in a bay to the North, and crossing over a hill we passed by a linnen Manufacture for weaving and bleaching and a house for Drying which last is peculiar to Scotland; and soon come to Kirkwall. —I am &c.

---

[1] The smaller stone circle at Stennis is 104 feet in diameter. Only two pillar-stones remain standing, a third lies prostrate, and the stump of a fourth is visible. *Vide* Anderson's *Scot. in Pagan Times*, 1886, p. 119, fig. 130.

[2] The Stone of Odin, or Woden. In later times lovers plighted their troth by joining hands through the hole in the stone. It was destroyed in December 1814. See *Notes on Orkney and Zetland*, by Alex. Peterkin, 1822, p. 20; notes to *The Pirate*, by Sir Walter Scott.

[3] Grimbister Holm, in the bay of Firth.

LETTER XXIX.

KIRKWALL, *July* 6*th*, 1760.

DEAR SISTER,—Kirkwall is pleasantly situated on a flat up on the North side of a strand which is divided from the bay by a beach, with an inlet to the West: The town is near a measured mile long; excepting a few houses, it is ill built, the streets are paved with irregular flags, and 'tis computed that there are above 300 families in it: it has been more flourishing, but now decayed and the Decay seems to be owing to the neglect of the fishery, for now throughout the island they are farmers, or go to sea, and the former only go out to fish when they want food. They catch a great many fish here of a beautifull mixed colour of brown and of a gold yellow; they are called Keaths[1] by some, by others Cudins, they are about six inches long; in the first year they are called Sillacks and are four inches long, the third year and after they are called Seaths from eight inches to thirty long; in England they are called Colefish; It is said that all other fish have deserted this place, as they have part of Shetland, tho' there they have still a great Cod and Ling fishing, and also Tursk, which is about 30 inches long, and they say is excellent when salted, or dried as stock fish.

The Church of St. Magnus the old Cathedral[2] here is entire. Views of the West end with the Bishop's house, and of the East end are here inserted. It was built by Roynoald[3] Count of Orkney in 1138 and seems to have been designed and first executed near to a Greek Cross entirely in the Saxon Style; The Nave or body now consisting of five arches on each side;

---

[1] Cuithes or Cuths.

[2] 'It is curious that we should have to look to the distant Orkneys, and to the work of an alien people, for the best preserved example of the Romanesque in Scotland. The Cathedral of St. Magnus, designed by the Norwegian Kol, and commenced by Earl Rognvald in 1137, contains "the greatest amount of Norman work of any building in Scotland," and in its internal aspect, according to Mr. Muir, is "nowhere equalled by any interior in Scotland."'—Anderson's *Scot. in Early Christian Times*, 1881, p. 29. See Tudor's *Orkneys and Shetland*, p. 233. Sir Henry E. L. Dryden's Description of the Church dedicated to St. Magnus, and the Bishop's Palace.

[3] Rognvald. See *Orkneyinga Saga*.

View of West End of Kirkwall Church and of the Bishop's House.

KIRKWALL. 147

The Choir only of three, one of the pillars in the Choir on each side is round with an Octagon plain Capital, the other square with a semicircular pilaster to the West, and there was a large pier for about the space of one arch to the East, to which probably a Skreen was built between the Altar and the isle, which

East End of Kirkwall Church.

according to the Ancient way might go round, and so make the Quire part equal to the body; for there is an isle on each side, and three arches are added to the East of the pillars composed of several pilasters which form a segment of a Circle, and have what I call the Corinthian Gothic Capital of curled leaves. It appears that opposite to the Western arch of the old building on each side was a door from the North and from the South, a view of the Church from the West and of the East end are on the other side [pp. 146, 147].

The Choir is much in the same state as it was fitted up in 1593 by Patrick Earl of Orkney, particularly the seat of the Earl and Bishop, who according to the best information I could get, sat together, but this inscription [1] and the Earl's Arms on it has given rise to the story that the tyrant Earl who was beheaded, dispossessed the Bishop—

$$P.E.O.$$
$$SIC\ FVIT$$
$$EST$$
$$ET\ ERIT$$
$$1593$$

And opposite is a Gallery which now belongs to the Stewarts with the same date, and probably was the Seat of the Earl's family.

In the Vestry which is one of those Chapels from the Transept are two very large brass dishes for collecting alms, on both of them is Adam and Eve, and round one is this inscription: Had Adam Gedaen Gods woort Wys soo Waer Hy Gebleven Int Paradys Anno 1636.[2]

There are three bells[3] in the Church the two large ones are old and are those given by Bishop Robert Maxwell of 1521. He also beautified the Quire with Stalls of carved work: Bishop Robert Reid of 1552 the last Bishop of the Church of Rome, it is said, added a porch to the Church, and tho' there is no tradition of it there, yet there seems to have been a porch to the Middle door; he also built a Seminary which joyns on to the Bishop's house at the West side of it; it is said also that he beautified the Church, and added to the number and Revenues of the Chapter.

---

[1] This panel is now in the possession of the Earl of Orkney.
[2] Had Adam obeyed God's words, so had we then lived in Paradise.
[3] The date on one of the bells is 1528. See account of the bells of St. Magnus by Sir Henry Dryden, Bart., in Anderson's *Guide to Orkney*, App. p. 161.

The Bishop's House was to the south of the Cathedral on one side of a Court. It is built of flat stones with window and door cases of the red freestone: There was one large room in it: But it is said that Patrick Earl of Orkney built the grand house on the upper side of the Court with fine bow windows to a large room and handsome Gothic Chimney pieces in that room all of light coloured hewn freestone. About the doors and Windows, and on the Chimney pieces are his Arms and the Initial letters P. E. O. On his death it was restored, as it is said, to the Bishop, and I am inclined to think that the Bishop's principal house stood there, as there is a covered way from it to a Chapel, all built with the same kind of materials as the house below. It is reported, that Bishop MacKenzie lived privately in the Building of the Seminary which is now an hospital.

To the North West of the Church and on the other side of the Street, are remains of a strong small Castle built in 1379 by Henry Lord Sinclair the first Count of Orkney of that family. The opening before the Church is handsome, the best houses are near it, and particularly the town house and jayl, which were built out of a Fine for some misconduct: Towards the further end of the town is an Hospital: And a furlong to the north of the town is a small fort with ramparts of Earth and two small irregular bastions to the sea, made by the order of Cromwell; where they used to have some Canon, and one still remains.

We walked up a hill to the South of the town in which are several very small barrows, which are often found three together, and under them are commonly four stones set up on end covered with a single stone, and they generally find a single urn with burnt bones in it. From this hill we had a fine view of all the Northern islands, except North Ronaldsha, which they say is the most beautifull, and entirely covered with Corn; Westra is rather rocky. They are all within sixteen miles of Kirkwall, except Ronaldsha and Papa Westra; and these are very near the others. They are all most beautifull spots in summer, when the corn is green: And they never give the land rest, but make a Compost of Earth, Sea Weed, Horse dung and the like for the crop of bare-barley, and the next year take a crop of Oats. On Westra is an old Castle commonly said to be built by Earl Bothwell, but I was assured that the Shell was finished before it came into his possession. Patrick, Earl of Orkney, commonly called the Tyrant, was natural son of Robert Stewart[1] one of the base sons of James 5th, he underwent a Trial for his tyrannical acts, and ordered to sett all things right, and James the 6th having bought his estates, which were mortgaged and taken possession of, the Earl sent his natural son John to take the possession, which he accordingly did, as well as of the Castle of Kirkwall in which the Earl was taken, condemned for Treason, and beheaded in 1614.

The Earl of Moreton has the chief influence in the Orkneys, he has an estate of 500 £ a year in them, and the Crown having given him the Earl's lands for an old Debt due to him from the Government, he obtained an irredemiable right in them by an Act of Parl.^t and he has improved them so as to bring in 1500 £ a year. He has also the Bishop's lands that are let also at a fixed rent of £500 a year which is every year remitted to the Earl.

The Earl of Galway [2] owns Flota and another island, and part of Bursa.

I had a letter to the provost of Kirkwall, who chose to visit me with two of the Corporation in his public Capacity, and if I had staid another day, it was signified to me that they intended to present me with the freedom [3] of the town, which they afterward pressed by a Message, but I was obliged to depart: The wifes and Daughters of most of the better sort are of the Church of England, and do not go to the Kirk; but read prayers to themselves at home: And I found it would have been very agreeable to them if I could have staid there some days. Keith in his history of the Bishopricks of Scotland saies, that the people of these islands would not at first attend the Services of the New Established Religion.—I am, &c.

---

[1] For account of the Stuart family, see Chap. ii. Peterkin's *Orkney and Zetland.*

[2] Earl of Galloway.

[3] The Kirkwall Corporation Minutes for this period have been lost. Mr. W. Cowper, Town-Clerk, writes: 'For some reason unknown the Minutes of Town Council meetings between the years 1743-64 have never been recorded in the Minute-Book, nor are there any Draft Minutes of meetings during these years among the Burgh papers.'

Letter XXX.

Wyck in Caithness, *July* 15*th*, 1760.

Dear Sister,—On the 8th I left Kirkwall which might be made a pretty town by establishing a fishery and trade and making a flood gate to keep the Sea out of the Strand which is to the West of the town. We came over the heathy hill four miles to the South part of the island to Mr. Graham's of Gromshall [1] situated on a bay near the South East point of the island, and on a fresh water Lough, in which there are trouts and Eels; it has an Outlet into the Sea, and a small rivulet falls into it; here is a fine spot of tillage and pasturage, and from the hill over it we had a view of many of the southern isles; no tree will grow here above the walls, and they plant gooseberries as well as apples against walls. We spent most part of the day here, and set out in the even with a contrary wind, and rather too high, but rowing near the islands of Lamen [2] and Glimsholm we came in two hours and a quarter two leagues under the Lee Shoare of the Calf of Flota belonging to Lord Galway,[3] as well as Flota; rowing near the islands of Burra and Hunda we were under shelter; and going by Flota we were somewhat exposed till we got under the shelter of Fara and Risa and soon came into the Bay called Long Hope, and at the end of it came again to Melsetir Captn Moodie's house from which I set out.

This Gentleman's Ancestors with three others were anciently the chief proprietors, but whether of the Orkneys or this island I cannot recollect. His father was Captn of a Man of war, and Commodore [4] of a number of Ships which relieved

---

[1] Græmeshall.   [2] Lambholm.   [3] Earl of Galloway.

[4] Commodore Moodie received a Sword of Honour. It was sold about 1817, and was purchased by Mr. Donald Moodie, and is now supposed to be in the possession of his son, Mr. Dunbar Moodie, late Magistrate at Ladysmith, South Africa. Queen Anne granted an augmentation of Arms to the Commodore—a Naval crown, with lion holding a pennon *or*, charged with an eagle with two heads displayed *sable; motto*, 'The Reward of Valour.' When an old man, he was assassinated by the Stewarts of Burray, and their adherents, in the streets of Kirkwall. Melsetter is now the property of Mr. Heddle, who is a descendant of the Moodies. See p. 134.

Denia in Spain when besieged; on which Charles the 3d, afterwards Emperour, presented him with a batoon, and writ a letter in his favour to Queen Anne with his own hands in french, both which I saw, and gave him leave to wear the black Eagle in his pennant, which was given likewise by Lyon King of Arms under his Seal, with other Armorial Ensigns. This Gentleman was most barbarously murdered by Sr. James Stewart,[1] who provoking him to fight before the great Church at Kirkwall, made a signal to persons to come upon him and put him to Death: Stewart being deeply engaged in the rebellion in 1746, it happened to fall to the share of Capt Moodie's Son to take him, who from the Cutter delivered him on board a Man of war; He was conveyed to London lodged in Southwark Jayl, and to prevent the forfeiture of his Estate, 'tis thought he poisoned himself, being found dead in the Jayl, and swoln to a very extraordinary degree.

There were six gentlemen in this island in the rebellion, in which it was exactly computed in 1746 that there were 33,800 souls:[2] They have taken lately many of all degrees for the Sea service, so that probably the people are not at present more in number than at that time: Their genius lyes entirely to Navigation. They dress like Seamen, and never in the Scotch dress, except that the women wear the plad like a hood, on their heads, and brought over their arms like a short scarf, there is now no Norn or Norwegian spoken but all English with the Norwegian accent, which differs from the English no more than one County does from another: but they have particular words and manner of expression: And they are in general a good kind of people, who must have every Necessary of Life within themselves, for there are no Markets. In this bay of Waies they have plenty of Lobsters and of very large Oysters: They have Scollops with two hollow shells, and pectons with one flat shell both large; they roast them and also pickle them. In this bay also they have banks of Cockles with which at Spring tydes they load their boats and put them in an

---

[1] See *The Orkneys and Shetland: Their Past and Present State*, by John R. Tudor, 1883, p. 232.

[2] The estimated population of the county of Orkney and Shetland in 1755 was 38,591. The census of 1881 was 61,746.

enclosure where the Sea comes in; to serve them for the whole month: The spawn must be very numerous to keep up the bank which never fails, and they find them no bigger than a pin's head.

The Tydes here and in Petland or Pentland Frith are very extraordinary and in the Frith the Tydes run so high that there is no such thing as stemming them; they must cross with the tyde; And the Seas run as high in the Frith as in the bay of Biscay. For the nature of these tydes I referr to Mackenzie's or Cade's, who examined them most exactly. The post comes over from Ratter every Tuesday when the weather permits, lands at South Ronaldsha, crosses to the North End of it, ferrys over to Burra, then goes North and embarks for Gromshall Ferry house, and so goes to Kirkwall, from which place the bag is sent to Stromness and the letters are dispersed to the different places; And a boat on Monday takes the bag at the Ferry house and so it goes in the same manner to be conveyed to Ratter by the boat that brings over the letters.

These isles (some little ones excepted) are about forty in number: In the isle of Waies near Capt\u{n} Moody's the rocks are of a yellow freestone, but at a little distance to the West on a bay is a broad vein of a red freestone which crumbles at top but is hard below; it is full of pebbles, and little veins of Spar intermixed some of which are incrusted with a red stone as if caused by water running from Iron Ore.

From North Ronaldsha it is about seven leagues to Fair Island, and from that to Shetland about five more, if I mistake not; Shetland, with the isles about it, have a great trade with Hamburgh: They carry Cod, Lyng and Torsk, and bring back Spirits and Dutch Tobacco and many goods they want in those islands as Apparell &c. They differ from the people of Orkney, chiefly among the better sort, in their dress, in which they affect to be fine and have much of the German manners, are very decent and observers of form, extremely hospitable and civil to Strangers; They are very sociable among themselves, but are rather apt to go to excess in drinking, and Deal very much in Spiritous Liquors; They have a small breed of Horses 7 or 8 hands high as I was informed. They have one town which is called Ylesbury [1] which is a good Harbour.

The largest island is called also the Mainland and affords the same Game as in the Orkneys, except that they have not the Grouse, and the reason assigned is that the Heath does not blow there, which is their food: These islands, with the Orkneys form one County and are under a Depute Sheriff, who has a substitute in Kirkwall and in Shetland, where he himself at present lives. . . .[2] Leagues . . .[2] off Shetland are the Faroe islands belonging to the King of Denmark. Wormius saies a fossil wood or bituminous fossil is found in the isle of Faro, that it does not easily take fire but shines like the Gagates,[3] is found in the joynts of the rocks, and is taken out in lamina or splinters three or four inches thick. He saies also there are fossil strata like wood [4] in Iceland. See Horrebow's Acc[t] of Iceland.

They produce a small but strong breed of Draft horses about 13 hands high, of which as I was told, the King of Denmark sent a present of a yellow sett to the King of England: The export of them is strictly prohibited. These and fish are the only productions which Denmark avails itself of;

[1] Islesburgh on Islesburgh Voe—Northmaven. It is not quite apparent why this small place should be mentioned, possibly a hasty conclusion from the termination burgh: or Scalloway, which was then the only important town, and being just inside the Burra Isle, may have given rise to the name, *Islesbury*.

[2] About 58 leagues north-west from Shetland.

[3] 'Iceland produces two sorts of agate. The one will burn like a candle, and is in fact a species of bitumen. The other, which the Icelanders call Hrafntinna (black flint stone) does not burn. It is harder than the former, and will break into flakes, which are very transparent, and not unlike glass.'—*The Natural History of Iceland*, by N. Horrebow, 1758, ch. xvii. 'Obsidian—This stone, which is found in Peru and Quito, the Spaniards also call Piedra de Galinazzo, or Raven Stone, which is the signification of the Icelandic Hrafntinna.'—Henderson's *Iceland*, 1818, vol. i. p. 178.

[4] 'A very extraordinary sort of wood, which they call sorte brand, or black band, very hard, heavy and black, like ebony, is found somewhat deep in the ground [in Iceland] in broad, thin, and pretty long pannels or leaves, fit for a moderate size table. It is generally wavy or undulating, and is always found between the rocks or great stones, wedged as it were, quite close in. At first, on considering its situation, I was very doubtful whether it was wood or petrifaction, but as it could be planed and managed in every respect like wood, the shavings also having the appearance of such, I was induced to think that it is nothing but wood.'—Horrebow's *Nat. Hist. Iceland*, 1758, ch. xx. p. 33.

Iceland also is under the dominion of Denmark. In the inland parts of which island, they live in Caves, and are not Christians—Pagans? and bring down skins of black Cattle and deer, and Tallow to exchange for fish, but live chiefly on their Cattle. Those on the Sea deal in these Commodities and fish, and they sell also white fox, and squirrel skins: The King of Denmark suffers no one to trade with them, but sends two ships loaded with Corn every year, who truck for these Commodities; and he has two ships also cruizing all the summer to hinder any ships from trading, or taking away any of the people; and when he is engaged in war, he obliges them to furnish men both for land and sea service: They have plenty of hay, but no Corn, and with that they feed their Cattle in Winter.

The Faroe islands are in much the same situation, except that their people are not so strictly prohibited from going out of the islands. A governor resides at Iceland. The Greenland whale fishery is between Lapland and Greenland; several ships go from England and Scotland every year, and touch mostly at Shetland; They often go ashore in Summer at Greenland, and kill a great many animals for their Skins.—I am, &c.

LETTER XXXI.

DUNBEATH, IN CATHNESS,
July 16*th*, 1760.

DEAR SISTER,—On the 11th we crossed over in two hours to Ralter in Scotland to Mr. Sinclair's. We rid in the afternoon to the east, and in a mile came to Sir James Sinclair's (a branch of the same family), pleasantly situated opposite to the middle of a bay. In all this coast the rocks consist of a fine flagstone, dipping from south-west to north-east. It being a fine evening, we saw a great number of boats fishing. We passed by the Parish Church of . . . ,[1] and towards Dungsby Head (the Virubrium promontorium of the new map), we came to 'Johnny Grott's House,' which is in ruins, and from a quondam inhabitant of that name, gives the appellation to this angle of Scotland. There are on this strand a great number of the small

[1] Canisby.

striated Buccinum shells, and some of the very small shells striated likewise, of that kind which are called the porcelain shell,[1] and are here named 'Johnny Grott's *Buckeys*,' probably from some confusion of the name of the other shells; We ascended a height at the Head to view the Eastern sea, and, returning, the dairyman's daughter brought us a bowl of milk by way of refreshment.

They bring to this place limestone from Stroma, the direct passage to which is not above a mile; And it is about as much more from that to. . . .[2] isle; In the latter are about a dozen families, and it lets for about £15 ster. a year, being a mile round. Stroma is two or three miles round. There are about thirty families in it, and it lets for a hundred pounds a year. On the east point of it is a small building over a burial-place, where the bodies remain entire,[3] and the skin does not corrupt, owing to the nitre in the air, which preserves equally with salt when applied to animal bodies.

Part of our way led us over what appeared to be fine green sod, like a down, but when we came upon it the horses sunk into it, and we were obliged to trot on fast, & it was very disagreeable: In wet weather it must be almost impassible.

I walked out from Mr. Sinclair's house half a mile to the west, to see a Pict's house[4] in a mount on the sea cliff; I found two cells, three yards apart, and the mouth about a yard wide; The passage to one is destroyed, and, as I apprehended, two yards of the other; It is three yards into a bend, and then two yards more; The cell within is two yards wide and five yards long in a sort of an oval, and at the entrance is a sett in of three quarters of a yard, and on the other side it forms the narrow end of the oval, the sides are straight for a yard high, and set in for another yard to three quarters of a yard in width at top, which is covered with flags: There are two or three small holes as convenient recesses: The other cell is only a yard and a half high. At the end is a hole, half a yard above

---

[1] See Calder's *History of Caithness*, 1861, p. 10.   [2] Swona.

[3] 'Stroma, famous for its natural mummies.'—Pennant's *Tour*, 1769, p. 197. 'The mummies are now destroyed, and the chapel is unroofed and mouldering into ruin.'—*Old Stat. Ac.*, 1793, vol. viii. p. 165.

[4] See *Pre-Historic Remains of Caithness*, by Laing and Huxley, 1866.

the floor, about two feet six inches high, three feet long, and three feet broad, lessening by a set in of three quarters of a yard, and this was probably a chimney, as there seemed to have been an opening to the top. Both the cells and passages have without doubt been in some degree filled with earth, for it is with difficulty any one can get in by the passages, which are

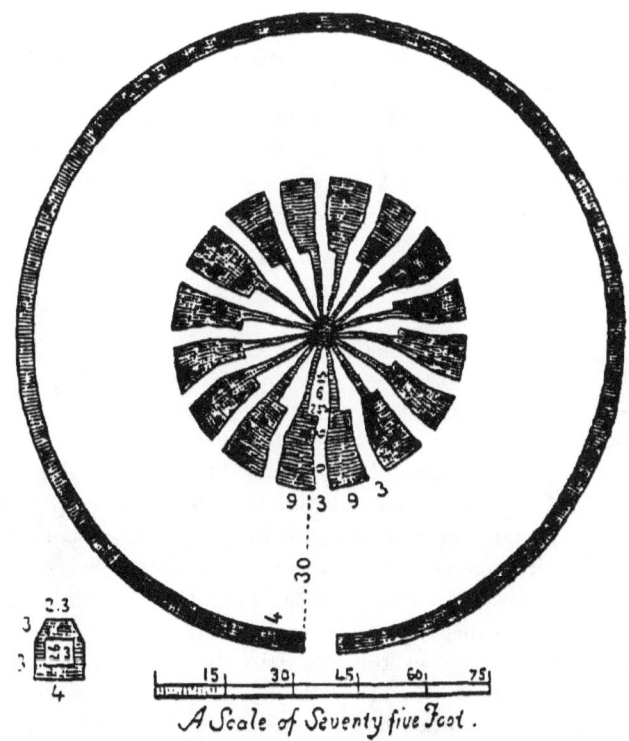

The Plan of a Pict's House.

about a yard high. From the supposed end of the entrance I measured ten yards to a wall, which is the segment of a circle; so that I imagine this was a way all round; from which they entered to the cells, and it being about eighty yards round, allowing four yards to each cell, and the space between, there might be twenty cells for so many sleeping places, or whatever other use they were put to: Part of such circular passages I found in other Picts' houses; and they have all a terrace round them, where probably these circular passages of communication were; And as they might be used as places of defence as well as mansion houses, when the enemy intended to destroy them as lurking places, they might do it by breaking down these circular passages, and so formed these terraces; & this confirms the opinion that the passages were high enough for proper entrances, as they must have been as low as the bottom of the circular passages. (As this gallery was thirty feet wide, it is to be doubted whether it was covered.) Into this gallery round the cells they might drive their cattle for security as well as shelter.—I am, &c.

Letter XXXII.

July 21st, 1760.

Dear Sister,—On the 12th I proceeded on my journey, and came six miles west to the Earl of Cathness's house of Myrtle,[1] situated on the sea-side in a very fine corn country, and in the afternoon went four miles to the south-east to Sir Patrick Dunbar's, situated near two loughs[2] made by the rivers which fall in at Wick, and rise a little above the western lake, on each side of which there is marl; and there is also limestone in most parts of this country: in the nearest lake is an island, in which the sea-gulls breed. The water runs in half a mile to another larger lake; there are trouts and eels in both of them. There are but nine parishes in Cathness, five of the churches are on the northern coast, & the three eastern parishes talk English and no Eirshe, and also two others in this part. One would suppose them originally to be a colony either of Danes or Norwegians, or from the Orkneys. The Sinclairs are certainly from Orkney, & in the Orkneys, many of the families are descendants of governors of the

---

[1] Murkle.   [2] Lochs Scarmclet and Watten.

Isles, either Danish or Scotch. But the Sin Clairs or St. Clairs were originally either Normans or French, as were the Frasers, Boswells, Mowbrys, Montgomerys, Campbells, Boises, Betons, Tabziours, and Bothwells: The fugitives who were received by Malcolm in the time of William the Conqueror were the Lindsays, Towers, Ramsays, Prestons, Sandilands, Bissets, Wardlaws, Maxwells, Fowlis, and Lovetts; & about the same time several came from Hungary at the request of Queen Margaret: These were the Creightons, Fotheringhams, Bothwicks, Giffards, Melvils, unless the two last may be rather thought to be Normans. D. Scot's 'History,' p. 141. I saw two more churches in the neighbourhood, not above three miles from the North Sea, Wyck is the eighth, and that in which Dunbeath is situated is the ninth. Caithness is 30 miles long from north to south and 20 miles broad from east to west, but the breadth must be much more in measured miles. When we came to the summit over Sir Patrick Dunbar's house, we had a most uncommon prospect of the broad vale in which his house stands, of another separated by low hills or eminences, with a great number of gentlemen's seats, and two churches in view, two large lakes, the fine mountains of the Paps, and that ridge which bounds the county, and the ground rising gently on all sides; but what is most singular spots of corn all over the county, contrasted with such a mixture either of heath or pasturage as rendered the face of this northern country very agreeable.

They have here, and as I was told, in the Orkneys also, a very uncommon way of preserving barley, which they must thresh in order to have straw to fodder their cattle. They make a foundation of loose stones five feet in diameter, lay chaff on it, and add a heap of corn in the middle, then they sett up straw on end all round the stones, and put in more corn, and as it fills they bind it round with straw ropes, and so continue raising the straw untill it is about eight feet high, & they finish it in the shape of a cone, covering the top well with straw, and bind it round with such ropes of straw as they lay over their thatched houses. They have also a neat way of dressing their thatched houses in the roof within, I mean people of some condition. For about four feet of the lower part they lay flags, then on to the top ropes of straw close together and drawn tight; On others they lay the sods and then the thatch;[1] There are two ways of laying straw, either regular as they thatch in England, or laid loose and kept down with straw ropes, in which last case it is renewed every year. They make near the sea a compost of sods, seaweed, and dung, move it once, and then shred it off very thin to lay on the lands.

This is the country of the Sinclairs, under their antient head the Earl of Cathness, and there are but three or four other names in the county, two of which are the Dunbars and Murrays.

On the 14th, I travelled eight miles, mostly near the river, to Acright,[2] Sir William Dunbarr's, situated close to the sea by a fine old castle. I went to see the castles of Carnigo and Sinclair,[3] the first situated on a rock over the sea, and separated from the land by a deep fossee, over which there was a draw-bridge. A view is here seen [p. 161]. The other is close to it, built for an elder son; in both of them are several appartments, and beyond the first are several little courts on the rocks: Sinclair was built in the time of King Charles the Second, and the King's Arms are on it; a view is here seen [p. 162]. This Sinclair was the last Earl of that line. From this place I went to see the Slate Quarry, which produces a large blew slate, but rather thick and heavy.

On the 15th I came two miles to Wyck, a small borough town pleasantly situated on a little bay which is no harbour: They have an export of Corn, Salt Beef, Salmon, hydes, butter and tallow, but on the whole, it has but small trade. In the Church they shew a tomb under a Nich which they call S^t . . . .[4] to whom the Church is dedicated; the hands are joyned as in a praying posture. It was probably the founder, restorer, or improver of the Church. This is the only borough in Cathness. Passing two or three miles further we called at the house[5] of Mr. Sinclair the provost; where I took leave of Mr

---

[1] See Sir John Sinclair's *Northern Counties of Scot.*, 1795, pp. 193, 211.
[2] Ackergill Tower. See Calder's *Hist. Caithness*, title-page.
[3] Girnigoe and Sinclair Castles. See Cordiner's *Antiq. North of Scot.*, 1780, p. 82, Pl. 17; and for views and plans, MacGibbon and Ross's *Castellated Arch. of Scotland*, 1887, vol. ii. pp. 307-313, and Calder's *Hist. Caithness*, Frontispiece.
[4] St. Fergus.
[5] Provost Sinclair then resided at Thrumster House.

CASTLE GIRNIGOE.

Castle Carnigo (Girnigoe).

William Dunbarr; and then the Provost and another gentleman[1] went with me 5 or 6 miles to Mr. Sinclair's of . . . .[2]

Castle Sinclair.

where I dined; and the master of the house and one Mr. Sinclair desired to meet me, they accompanied me allmost to Dunbeath, Mr. Sinclair's, the Sheriff's Deputy of Cathness and Sutherland, the former returning. This place is sixteen miles from Wyck, the country for the most part heathy, with patches of corn about it and particularly near the rivulets. The Castle

[1] 'Mr. William Sutherland of Wester, is a gentleman of reading, and had been bred to the sea, whereby he had visited many foreign Countries; particularly he was once nigh to the city of Jerusalem, but some Incident or other had prevented his seeing of it. These particulars made his conversation extremely acceptable to the Bishop of Ossory; for they compared Notes together as to the Places they had both been in, and their accounts of them tallied exactly. Wester gave him the Convoy till he came near to the Castle of Dunbeath.'—Bp. Forbes's *Journals*, ed. by the Rev. J. B. Craven, p. 209.

[2] Lybster.

of Dunbeath was built by one of the branches of the family of the Earl of Cathness; it is on a rock which projects into the sea, but there was no drawbridge to it; the rock continues for a hundred yards behind the house, having a narrow fossee to the south above thirty fathoms deep, with perpendicular rocks on each side, and the sea to the north: In the cliffs are several strata of different kinds of stone, among which are freestone and limestone; & there are patches of limestone all over this country; some of the strata coming near the surface; though it has not been found out twenty years. The Marquis of Montrose in the Civil War spent twenty-six days in besieging this castle,[1] where there was deposited a considerable sum of money, and part of his followers thinking he was gone by sea, did not meet him on the Kyle of Dornoch, which was the cause of his defeat.—I am, &c.

LETTER XXXIII.

DUNROBIN, 17th July 1760.

DEAR SISTER,—On the 16th the Sheriff and Mr. Sinclair accompanied me, and we travelled to the south mostly over heaths, diversified here and there with several spots of corn. We passed by the remains of a Picts' house in which part of the circular wall remains, and in it an entrance stopped up. We came to a beautifull romantic vale, through which a rivulet runs that is formed a little higher by two branches which pass through such vales. They are called Berrydale: and this river seems to be the Ila of the new map, which was the bounds between the Carnabii and the Logi. We soon reached the foot of those hills, out of which all the rivers rise that run to the east, north, and west.

This famous pass is called the Ord: and Berrydale river is difficult to pass in winter, when the torrent has brought down great stones, which are moved away in the summer to make an easy passage across that stream. The ascent to the Ord is

---

[1] See *Civil and Traditional Hist. of Caithness*, by James T. Calder, p. 151.

steep, and the road over the steep hill is frightfull to those who have not been used to such kind of roads; but is not in the least difficult, only it is more pleasant to walk rather than ride over some parts of it. It seems to be the Ripa Alta of the new map.

Having passed the principal heights we came to a rivulet called Navidale, which is the bounds between Cathness and Sutherland. We soon after got to Hemsdale,[1] where there is a salmon fishery. Here the tyde being in, we crossed in a coble in the shape of a boat cut in two, and our horses forded over half a mile higher. By this dale there is a pretty good road towards Mowdale, which we passed in the way to Durness.

We soon came into the beautifull country of Loth. It is not easy to determine whether it had its name from the ancient Logi, situated here, or from some loughs. Loughs that have been drained, one part being called Lothmore (the great lough), another part Lothbeg (the little lough). A rivulet runs through it, formed by two streams which unite a little higher up. It is a fine narrow strip of arable ground, with several beautifull hillocks near the foot of the hills, and the supposed banks of the loughs are visible. Loughmore was situated towards the sea; Loughbeg is to the south-west. We took some refreshment at the house of Mr. M'Cullogh,[2] the minister at Lothkirk. He went with us to Lothbeg, where the banks of the lake are very plain, as well as the outlet that was made at the rocks towards the sea.

We here ascended to a Picts' house[3] covered with stones. In two or three parts of which are stones set up on end to denote the entrances, which might be closed on some occasions. One cell is open. We went about nine feet in the passage. Then one passage is about eighteen inches lower, and nine feet

[1] Helmsdale, in older maps written Hemsdale.
[2] Rev. Robert M'Culloch. In addition to his charge, he held the chaplaincy of the 2nd or Sutherland Fencibles. *Fasti Eccles. Scot.*, Part v.
[3] 'There is one of them entire in the parish of *Loth*, which the Bishop of *Ossory* visited and examined. . . . At the desire of the Bishop of *Ossory* I measured several of them, and saw some quite demolished.'—Rev. Alex. Pope of Reay, in Pennant's 1769 *Tour in Scot.*, p. 337. 'Near the miln of *Lothbeg* is the entire *Pict's* house, which the Bishop of *Ossory* entered.'—*Ibid.* p. 359.

more brought us into the oval appartment,[1] seven feet and a half long and high, and six feet broad. We saw the light through the top, where some stones had probably been taken away, and at the end is a little hole as for a convenient recess. There is a great stone over the inner entrance, and another at the end. To the north of the entrance of this cell is a broad stone set up on end, and just before it a small circle of stones set close together, and in the middle of it the mouth *as of an entrance* made with flat stones, and to the north of it a small square sort of a foundation. There are two more in Glyn Loth, which are called Uagbeg and Uagmore.[1]

From this place we return'd to the road, and struck out of it again near the house of Clyne to the south-west, to a ridge of very low hills, where there are small quarries of a loose slaty limestone,[2] in which there are petrified large oyster shells, the small Cornu Ammonis, the Gryphites, and cockles, also the pecten, of most of which I brought away some specimens.[3] From this place we descended to the Brora, where to the west of the bridge is a beautifull natural cave [4] opening to the river. We then went a little way to the south-west, to what is called the Dals,[5] which is a most beautifull bason of a lake that has been drained, with an island in the middle of it. The flat is entirely covered with corn.

From that place we came to the sea-cliff, and descending, we afterwards ascended about fifty feet up a steep way to a

---

[1] Probably a sepulchral mound or chambered cairn. The names, too, are suggestive—Uagmore, the large tomb ; Uagbeg, the small tomb, from the Gaelic *uaigh*, a grave or tomb. Pope says : ' In Glen Loth are three [cairns], and are called by the country people *Uags*.'—Pennant's *Tour Scot.* 1769, App. p. 338.

[2] Oolitic fossils from the strip of Jurassic rocks on the shore between Golspie and Helmsdale. *Vide The Geology of Sutherland*, by H. M. Cadell, B.Sc., 1886.

[3] ' On the top of a small hill, near the house of *Clyne*, is a lime-stone quarry ; and in the heart of the stone, all sorts of sea-shells known in these parts are found. They are fresh and entire, and the lime-stone within the shell resembles the fish. The Bishop of *Ossory* employed men to hew out masses of the rock, which he broke, and carried away a large quantity of shells.'—By Rev. Alex. Pope of Reay, in Pennant's *Tour Scot.* 1769, p. 357.

[4] ' Near the Bridge of *Brora* there is a fine large cave, called *Uai na Calman*. The Bishop of *Ossory* admired it, and said there were such caves about *Bethlehem* in *Palestine*.'—By Pope, in Pennant's *Tour Scot.* 1769. p. 357.

[5] The Doll of Brora.

grotto in the rock, where art has been used in cutting a bench or two, and about three feet higher is an inner appartment, which is worked out in a rough manner, with a large short kind of pillar between the two entrances, and opposite to the northern entrance is a part of it in which one may stand upright. As brambles and weeds grow upon the mouth of the outer cave, they have a beautifull effect, and the view of the fine strips of corn below and of the sea is most delightfull. This was probably the retreat of some hermit.

Coming along the coast near a mile to Dunrobin, Lord Sutherland's castle and house, we were surprized at seeing half-a-dozen families forming so many groupes—viz., the man, his wife, and children, each under a coverlit, and reposing on the shoar, in order to wait for ye tyde to go a-fishing.

We arrived at Dunrobin, twenty miles from Dunbeath. This castle is finely situated on the end of a hill, which is cut off by a deep fossee, so that it appears on the south side, and next to the sea, like an old Celtic mount. Between it and the sea is a very good garden. The castle did consist of two square towers and a gateway. One tower only remains now, to which the house is built. There are good appartments in it, tho' some have been destroyed by fire. The present earl has begun to plant the hanging ground from the house, and proposes to carry it on, which will make it exceeding fine. This castle was built by the first Earl of Sutherland.

A small mile to the north-west is a part called the old town and ye remains of a Pictish castle,[1] which must have been the residence of the Thanes of Sutherland, under which name they have been famous in history, and more especially in the time of Macbeth. The court of this castle is about thirty feet in diameter; there was a terrace on the outside twenty-one feet broad, and round that are the foundations of a wall six feet thick; this also is a mount cut off from the hill; on each side at the entrance was a sort of Cell; that to the right small and something of an oval, being six feet long and a yard and a half broad; the other is of the same breadth at ye entrance, and only a yard broad at the other end, and the

---

[1] For a description of some Sutherland Brochs, see paper by Rev. Dr. J. M. Joass in *Archæologia Scotica*, vol. v. p. 95.

passage from it half a yard, as I conjecture, to the opening on that side. The outer wall is seven feet thick, and the inner three feet. From this we went half a mile further, to the ruins of a much larger castle on a mount which may be thirty feet high, into which mount cells seem to have been made, and there are two stories of terraces in different parts, according to the shape of the hill; that at the top going all round, the lower terrace being only a segment of a circle to the east and west. From the latter there is an ascent to this fortress, which is in ruins, as the other was, untill the present earl cleared away a great part of the rubbish. The first I suppose was the winter fortress; the other, as the stronger, was for the summer, being the time of most danger, and as it is in a higher and cooler situation, and nearer the hills, which are more practicable in that season. In the rivulet below, which is a mountain torrent, is a pretty waterfall (as I was inform'd) after rain.

We came on towards Dornock, and observed a spot of ground very much resembling a Roman road, with entrenchments and outworks; but it is nothing more than the different beaches which were formed by the sea as it lost ground, which it has done very visibly in these parts. We crossed the ferry at the river . . . [1], which rises towards Lough Schin, and they say it is most part of the way a fruitfull vale, and so it appeared as far as we could see.

We travelled over a sandy head of land, and came to the cross[2] set up there in memory of the defeat of the Danes (when they landed here in 1263) by William, Earl of Sutherland, and Gilbert Murray, Bishop of Cathness. On the north part are the Sutherland arms; on the south were the bishop's, which are worn out. On the top of ye stone is a circle with a cross cut through it, which is the arms of the See of Cathness. A stone is said to be near the cross, which I did not observe, under which it is reported the Danish general, slain in the battle, was burried.

We came to Dornock, which is pleasantly situated on the head of land not far from the river of that name, called the

---

[1] The 'Little-Ferry' across the river Fleet.
[2] The Cross is still standing, but much dilapidated.

Kyle of Dornock, near which I went to Rosehall in my way to Lord Reay's. There is very little trade in this town, and no manufacture but spinning of linnen yarn. The church here is the body of the old cathedral [1] which belonged to the Bishop of Caithness.[2] It seems to be pretty near a Greek cross, tho' in the eastern part, now uncovered, there are four arches on each side supported by round pillars, with a kind of a Gothic Doric capital. In the body or nave are only three plain Gothic windows on each side ; but what is most remarkable is a round tower within *jiyning* to the south-west angle [3] of the middle part. It is built for a staircase, and is about ten feet in diameter, with geometrical stairs. The bishop's house [4] is a solid high building, consisting of four floors above the arched offices on which it was built. They show also the dean's house, and it is probable several other houses now standing near the church did belong to the members of the chapter. These were granted with other parts of the church estate to the Earl of Sutherland. This is a royal burgh, of which they made me a burgess.[5]

In two miles we passed by Siderhall,[6] a fine situation, now belonging to Lord Sutherland, but was an apenage from the

[1] The Cathedral, as probably seen by Bishop Pococke, is engraved in Henderson's *Agric. of Sutherland*, 1812. The imprint describes it : ' East end of Dornoch Cathedral, erected by St. Bar Bishop of Caithness in the 11th Century and enlarged by Gilbert Murray, Bishop of Caithness in 1280 ; burnt by John Sinclair, Master of Caithness in 1570, and repaired by Sir Robert Gordon, Tutor of Sutherland Anno. 1630. The west end was since repaired, and is now the Parish Church Anno. 1808.' See note 4, p. 12. *Vide* Sir Robert Gordon's *Earldom of Sutherland*.

[2] See ' Two Ancient Records of the Bishopric of Caithness from the Charter-room at Dunrobin,' *Bannatyne Club Miscellany*, contributed by the Duke of Sutherland, 1848.

[3] The staircase is in the north-east angle.

[4] For view of the Palace of Dornoch, see MacGibbon and Ross's *Castel. Arch. Scot.*, 1887, vol. ii. p. 337.

[5] Mr. Donald Taylor, Town-Clerk, has been unable to find any Burgess Roll ; the Council minutes, which date from 1729, contain no reference to such matters. The Magistrates for the time being were—Provost, the Earl of Sutherland (the ' good Colonel,' father of the Duchess-Countess) ; Bailies, Kenneth Sutherland, ' Ensign ;' Wm. Sutherland, yr. of Sciberscross (wadsetter, grandfather of the present Provost, Wm. Sutherland Fraser, Esq.); Kenneth Sutherland, jr. ; David Sutherland of Cambusavie, wadsetter.

[6] Now written Cyderhall, formerly Siddera, Sytheraw, from Siward's Hoch (Sigurd's haug).

family. Here a gentleman carries on a manufacture of flax in order to prepare for spinning; gives it out, and sells the yarn. A mile more brought us to Skibo, the seat of Mr. Mackay, half-brother to Lord Reay, and member of Parliament. It was a castle and country seat of the bishops of Cathness, very pleasantly situated over a hanging ground, which was improved into a very good garden, and remains to this day much in the same state, except that there are walls built, which produce all sorts of fruit in great perfection, and I believe not more than six weeks later than about London.

On the 18th I went in the afternoon over the river into Ross-shire, and came soon to Innerchasley,[1] the seat of Mr. Ross, situated on an eminence at a little distance from the river, with some fine plantations of firrs behind it. Under Siderhall I saw on this side several acres of the finest flax for the manufactory I ever beheld. From Innerchasley there is a beautifull view[1] both up the river and down to the sea, as well as of the towns of Dornock and Taine.—I am, &c.

Letter XXXIV.

CROMARTY, *July 20th,* 1760.

DEAR SISTER,—On the 19th we came a mile through a rich country to Taine[2] pleasantly situated, about a quarter of a mile from the sea. They have here a Manufactury for preparing Flax and for spinning—are mostly Country people and Shop-keepers,[3] and it is but a poor town. I was met at the entrance by the Magistrates and Minister,[4] who would have presented me with the freedom of the borough if I could have staid.

---

[1] The Bishop appears to have crossed the Meikle-ferry into Ross-shire, and gone on to Invercarron. From Invercassley (which is west of Rosehall) 'the towns of Dornoch and Tain' cannot be seen.

[2] See *History of Tain, Earlier and Later,* by Rev. Wm. Taylor, M.A., 1882; article 'Tain,' by Provost Vass of Tain, in *The Ordnance Gazetteer;* and *Orig. Parochiales,* vol. II. pt. ii. pp. 416, 417, and footnote, p. 426.

[3] The town, it would appear, could boast of a Music School. See note 4, p. 12.

[4] The Magistrates and Minister of Tain in 1760 were David Ross, Advocate, younger of Inverchasly, Provost; Hugh Ross, Donald Munro, David Ross, Bailies; John Reid, Dean of Guild; George Miller, Treasurer; the Rev. John Sutherland.

They shewed me the Collegiate Church;[1] it is built of hewn freestone and was founded in 1481 by Thomas Bishop of Ross at the Instance of James the 3d in honour of St. Duthac for a provost eleven prebendaries & three Choiristers: The north side consists of small narrow windows which are not high, but on the north side, and at the East End are Gothic windows of the newest fashion with square mullions. About a quarter of a mile to the South East of the town on a little Eminence is the old Chapel of St. Duthac,[2] which was had in such great esteem that James the 4th[3] rid in two daies from Stirling on a pilgrimage to make amends for what he thought wanted an attonement; (viz.) the being taken away at sixteen years old by the Nobility and placed at the head of the Army against his father, who, 'tis supposed fell in battle, and was never found.

We passed over a heighth, and came into that fine plain country which extends all the way to Dingwall, and so on to Beaulieu: and in about three miles we came to the Abbey of Fern founded by Ferquhard first Earl of Ross in the time of Alexander the 2d they were præmonstratenses of the rule of St. Austin. It was annexed by King James the 6th to the Bishoprick of Ross. Mr. Patrick Hamilton Abbot here when the reformation first began, was burnt at St. Andrews in 1527 for heresy, being among the first that suffered. Nothing remains but the Church and Chapels adjoyning to it, wch are of fine hewn freestone inside and outside with a handsome cornice. There are four long narrow windows at the East End, and on each side of the Quire, and three on each side of the body; those to the South being very small: There was a considerable

---

[1] Occupied as the Parish Church until 1815, when it was relinquished for the large new one which had been built. Thereafter the Collegiate Church, now known as 'Old St. Duthus' Church,' was allowed to fall into great disrepair, almost ruin; but it has in recent years been quite restored, its windows filled in with stained glass designs, commemorative of eminent citizens, and the church is appropriated and preserved for monumental and memorial purposes.

[2] In 1306 or 1307 the Queen and daughter of King Robert Bruce sought refuge 'in the girth of Tane.'—*Origines Paroch.* vol. ii. pt. ii. p. 428.

[3] From 1496 to 1513 King James IV. made seven pilgrimages to 'Sanct Duthois Chapel quhair he was borne' (*Origines Paroch.* vol. ii. pt. ii. p. 433). The *New Stat. Acc.*, 'Ross,' p. 288, says James V. made a barefoot pilgrimage to St. Duthus, but the *Origines Paroch.*, vol. ii. pt. ii. p. 433, question it.

addition to the Church at the West End, but not as high, as there is a Gothic window above that building, and a like Gothic window is practiced over three windows at the East End: On the South Side is a large Chapel in which is a handsome monument, a kind of broad Nich in the wall richly adorned with Sculpture, with this inscription:[1] Hic Jacet Finleus M'Fayd quod Abbas de Ferne qui obiit an. M.CCCCXXXV. There is a couchant statue of the Abbot with his feet resting against a Lyon, on each side near to the East End is a small Chapel; the larger is to the North in which arches are turned about five feet apart and end in a point, & on these flag stones are laid about six feet long and two feet broad one over another like slates, the Arches being about two feet wide; and the large Chapel was covered as it is to be supposed in the same manner; part of the Arches remaining on each side, which seems to be a method to save the expense of a wooden roof.

A most extraordinary accident happened here in the year 1742. There was a sudden hurricane in time of Divine Service, and about 600 Souls in the Church, the Couples all of a sudden gave way, and the roof of Deal slipped off on the North Side, and brought off the outer Casing of the Wall with it for some feet from the top, and the whole roof to the South fell in, the Canopies of the Seats saved them much, but 36 were killed and twelve[2] died afterwards of their fractures and bruises. A great number were stunned and had not the least recollection of what happened; The minister whom I saw, was found with his head pinned[2] to the desk by the speaking board over him, and did not recover his senses untill the next day. They heard the Slates tumbling off, and looking up, the roof instantly fell without any notice.

They built a Kirk close to this, which together with the glebe house and offices took up most of the materials of the old Abbey. The Abbots Lodgings joyned on to the end of the

---

[1] 'Hic jacet Finlaius M'Fead abbas de Fern qui obiit anno MCCCCLXXXV.'—*Origines Paroch.* vol. II. pt. ii. p. 441.

[2] 'Eight more died soon after.'—*Old Stat. Ac.*, 'Fearn,' vol. iv. p. 296. The details of the accident to the minister, the Rev. Donald Ross, do not appear to have been previously recorded. 'He was seriously injured by the falling of the roof of the Abbey Church, . . . and was seized with palsy in 1767, which deprived him of his memory and faculties.'—*Fasti Eccles. Scot.* pt. v. p. 312.

Southern Chapel, in which there is an opening where he might occasionally attend Divine service.

From this place we kept on Eastward to the end of the beautifull head of Land to the house of Hugh McLeod Esqr. at Geanies, which is a most charming situation near the end of the Country called East Ross; the Head of which to the Sea is called Tarbat Ness & seems to be Penoxullum Promuntorium of the New Map.

From this place I went to Catboll the seat of Roderick McLeod Esqr.:[1] I waited on this gentleman who is of the Epis-

---

[1] This Cadboll, Roderick Macleod, being implicated in the '45, was abroad for several years; and being a man of superior parts, as well as, if report be true, of petulant temper, employed his time in collecting a valuable library of old books, a collection of coins, etc., and on his return to Scotland had them stored at Cadboll in rooms he built with stone-arched roofs to keep them *safe from fire*. He had planned to arrange the coins in tin boxes, but died in 1771 before anything was completed. The coins, together with the library, were removed to Invergordon Castle (the old one) about the year 1787. In 1805 or 1806 the castle was burnt with almost the whole of its contents, and thus was lost that large, valuable, and unique collection. A few coins have been found among the ruins.

The Duke of Athole lately gave R. B. .E. Macleod, Esq. of Invergordon Castle (the present Cadboll, and great-grandson of Roderick Macleod), a letter, dated 1771, relating to the coins, etc., which had been found in his Grace's chests at Blair Castle, written by the then Duke's Factor. '*Edinburgh*, 20th *Novr*. 1771.—My Lord [His Grace the Duke of Athole], In obedience to the commands your Grace was so good as honour me with, I some time ago enquired at Mr. Swinton about Cadbol's Medals. He told me they were not to be sold, but could give no final answer whether there was a catalogue of them, or if they could be sent your Grace to peruse them, till Mr. Macleod, another of the Guardians, came to town. He arrived yesterday, and I spoke with both to-day. They agree the medals cannot be sold, and there is such anxiety in Cadbol's settlements concerning them that they cannot be moved from his House in Rossshire. They told me there was no Catalogue, but that any person commissioned by your Grace should be welcome to see them, and Mr. Macleod would attend himself on that occasion when he went to the country. The Collection I understand, is numerous, Cadboll having prepared three hundred Tin Boxes to contain them, but he had only arranged about twenty Boxes when he died. . . . My Lord, your Grace's most obedt., most obliged, and most humble servant, ALEXR. MURRAY.'

Cadboll, being on bad terms with his cousin, the Macleod of Geanies, he mustered his tenants (very small holdings in those days), and piled up the earth, until it formed a great mound, for the purpose of looking down on his cousin's lands. Geanies thereupon planted a belt of trees to block him out, which it effectually does to this day. The mound is quadrangular, built in steps, and may be some 60 feet high.

'He [MacLeod of Cadboll] is a great Antiquarian and Medalist, having,

copal Church, & a person of great learning, especially in the Scotch History and Coins, of which he showed me a curious collection, the gold he bought of Keith the nonjuring Bishop. And he presented me with some very valuable Coins in gold and silver: His land is on the highest ground of this Promontory called Tarbotness, and on that spot, he has raised a pyramid of Sods exactly on the model of the Egyptian pyramids; it is on a basis which at a medium may be about seven feet high and forms a terrace, I believe, about two feet wide all round it. It consists of seventeen steps each of them eighteen inches high, and about two feet wide; it is at top about two yards by three, & is one way twenty one yards at the steps. It has been raised by degrees, that is two or three steps every year by his Tennants.

We went on and came to the side of a low hill near the sea about two miles to a Curious monument[1] of Christian Antiquity, said to be erected in memory of a Victory over the Danes, and

perhaps, the best Collection of Scots Coins, Copper, Silver, and Gold, from the first Penny of each down to the present Time, of any Gentleman whatsoever; and, to complete the character, he has an excellent Library of Books. The Bishop of Ossory, spying his Mount at some distance, asked what it was, and would by all means take a View of it. When upon the Top of it, he admired it greatly, and said it behoved the Gentleman who had contrived and effected it to be a curious Person indeed; and then he made particular Inquiry about him; for so poorly and indifferently had his Lordship been directed, that he had never heard that such a Man existed, though he had lodged a night within a mile of Cadboll's House, which being pointed to him at length from the Mount, he went directly to it, spent about two Hours with Cadboll, and was agreeably surprised to find the Scots Coins to be much older than what he had supposed, Cadboll giving him presents of some, of which he had Duplicates. In a word, he plainly declared he would have been very sorry if he had miss'd seeing such a Gentleman, as being one of the greatest Rarities he had ever met with in all his Travels; and so much was he taken with what he saw or heard at Cadboll, that, in token of his singular pleasure, after his Return to London, he sent Cadboll a present of his 4 Vols. of Travels in Folio, elegantly bound, with a copy of his Sermon at Magdalen's Hospital, and of a Pamphlet giving an Account of its Foundation, etc. A polite Letter accompanied the handsome Present, which I saw read, and in which his Lordship said, among other Things, that he had attended a Sale of medals at London upon Cadboll's [account], but that he saw nothing there worthy of one of his Taste.'—*Bishop Forbes's Journals*, Ed. by the Rev. J. B. Craven, p. 172.

[1] Monument of Sandwick (Shandwick: Nigg), engraved in Cordiner's *Antiq. North of Scot.*, 1776, Pl. xii., p. 65. See also Stuart's *Sculp. Stones*, p. 10, Pll. xxvi. and xxvii.

they say that the Eldest son of the Danish King is buried there who died in Battle: it is a yard broad about ten feet high and eight inches thick. The East side is all adorned with lines in knots and with beasts in bas relief, and Different Compartments. From the top and about half way down is a Cross consisting of two rows of round nobs like those which are in embossed plate ornaments, & look very rich, on each side above the transept of the Cross, is an Ornament so defaced that I could make nothing of it: below it on both sides is St. Andrew on the Cross; below this on one side is a Lyon, with something in his mouth which I could not distinguish; on the north side an Elephant which is the order of Denmark; beneath which is a Compartment of lines &c. as above, the whole being adorned to its utmost basis. This is the richest and finest of the kind I ever saw.

A little way beyond this hill we came to Ancherville, formerly the seat of one of the name of Ross, who from a very low beginning went into the service of Augustus of Poland, and being the only person who could bear more Liquor than his Majesty, got to be a Commissary, came away with plunder of Churches &c. in the war about the Crown of Poland, purchased this Estate of 100£ a year, built and lived too greatly for it, was for determining all things by the Sabre; and died much reduced in his Finances between twenty and thirty years agoe.

Half a mile more brought us to a bed of fossil shells[1] not petrified, but very tender, it is about a quarter of a mile from the vale which is a Morass, and high spring tydes do some times come into it, where in all probability it formerly did pass and make this place an island: The ground I conjecture to be about 50 feet above this Vale, the bed is about a yard from the Surface and near a foot thick, it consists chiefly of Oyster Shells; there are many Cockles, and limpets, winkles and muscles, the last are the most tender: There are also trochi, the Buccinnū and pectens. This bed is most admirable Manure for Corn.

Half a mile more brought us to the house of Duncan Ross,

---

[1] The shell-bed near Ankerville may, at the earliest, be a formation of the 25-feet beach. See Hugh Miller's *Sketch-Book of Popular Geology*, p. 280.

CROMARTY.

Esqr., at Kindeace, who had met me at Geanies. After we had taken our repast Mr. M'Leod of Geanies, and Mr. Mackay took leave, and Mr. Ross went with me to the ferry of Cromartie: from this part we saw Torbut which was the seat [1] of Lord Cromartie, a most charming situation and delightfull place, finely wooded near the Sea.

To the North East is Balyguineon [2] the seat of the Ross's, of which family was the late General Ross, who is buried in the Abbey Church of Fern with a most elegant inscription on his monument, in which his father is called, *Rossavanagentis Regalus*.

We crossed over to Cromartie which is situated on an exceeding fine harbour in so much that it was called Portus Salutis, and seems to be the Loxa of the New Map. The entrance a mile wide is made by two heads, called the Suters, and may be about a mile in length: it widens to the North two miles. The good harbour extends six miles to Invergordon, in which space 120 of the largest ships might Anchor, and as the Deep Harbour is two miles in breadth, it is thought that three lines of shipping might ride in that space: on a flat to the West of the head, the town of Cromartie is situated, which may have 200 houses in it. Their trade is only accidental from such ships as touch there, except that 3 or 4 ships come in a year from London with groceries, hops, &c. They prepare some flax and spin much more, which they sell to the Company at Edinburgh: They had a herring fishery, but since it has failed they apply very little to fishing.

To the East, the head, covered with Corn rises like Mount Olivet over Jerusalem; [3] and over the North East angle of this flat at the End of the town, and to the South of it, the eminence is naturally fortifyed to the East, West and South, by a deep fossee: on this most beautifull spot an old ruined Church is situated to the East, with the remains of a handsome building to the west of it, the base of which, of hewn stone, remains over a burial vault belonging to the family who inhabited the house,—*the house to* the west, in which the situation does not receive all the advantages it might from the building,

---

[1] Cromarty House, Tarbet.   [2] Balnagown Castle.
[3] *Vide* Dr. Pococke's *Travels in the East, Palestine, etc.*, Lond. 1743-5, 2 vols.

having fallen into the hands of one Mr. Urquhart who had commanded a Spanish Gally, and died a Convert to Popery; which slip his Son, now eighteen years old, has in some degree recovered, by conforming to the Church of England. This situation appears in every view most delightfull. There are very imperfect remains of a Church[1] on the Shoar to the East which is called the Old Kirk: Where the present Church is, they found lately in pulling down a wall an old font and some stones of the old Church.—I am, &c.

LETTER XXXV.

NAIRN, *July* 24*th*, 1760.

DEAR SISTER,—I set out from Cromarty and came about six miles by the Shoar near to Inver Gordon ferry, passing soon after I left Cromarty by a quarry of a sort of Coarse red freestone, with which fort George is supplied by Sea. We went by New Hall the seat of Mr. Gordon (brother to Sr. John Gordon) who is an Advocate in the Courts; it is a large house built by one Mr. Urquhart out of an imaginary South Sea Estate. This gentleman is improving his fine situation in a very good taste by planting: we came on having a very pleasant hill all along near the Frith of Cromarty and by the Bishop's Castle[2] opposite to Kulcarran,[3] where I was at Mr. Monroes on the other side: Having been mostly during this ride in the small County of Cromarty, we came into Invernesshire forded the river and passed through Dingwall to Foules Sir Henry Monroe's, pleasantly situated about a quarter of a mile from the river, and finely planted by his father Sir Robert, and continued by this gentleman. Sir Robert[4] and his brother were killed at the battle of Falkirk:

---

[1] St. Regulus's Chapel.   [2] Castle Craig or Tigh-na-Craig.
[3] Culcairn of Novar, see p. 110.
[4] See paper on 'Sir Robert Munro, 6th Baronet and 24th Baron of Fowlis, who fell at Falkirk,' by Alex. Ross, Alness (*Trans. of Gaelic Soc. of Inverness*, vol. xi. pp. 199-209).

and the present possessor was taken prisoner at the battle of Preston Pans. Here I saw the picture[1] of a servant maid who died in 1758 and came as a servant with Sir Henry's Great Grandmother a Mackenzy to this house in 1658, when it is supposed she might be about sixteen years old.[2]

They have here a fine freestone something of a green colour like that at Inverary, and they abound in mineral waters; A little beyond it to the North East is a Kern with two stones set up before it; in a cell there made with five stones, they found some bones:

I went beyond it to the Burne called Aldgrant[3] (The Ugly Burne). It rises two or three miles up in the mountains, and running about a mile above the road between the rocks covered with Trees, it has worn the rock down at a bridge which we went over, as conjectured 150 feet deep; 'tis said below that, it is much deeper some say even to fifty fathom, which they

---

[1] This portrait is not now at Foulis Castle, having been sold with other pictures in 1826 by the late Sir Hugh Munro.

[2] 'At Foulis Castle, the seat of Sir Harry Munro, Katharine Mackenzie, aged 118. She had been a servant in the family for 103 years, and was able to walk a mile a few days before her death, Dec. 24th, 1758.'—*Edinburgh Magazine*, Oct. 1759.

[3] Allt grannda. Bishop Forbes, in company with Mr. Mackenzie of Inchcoulter, the proprietor, visited, in 1762, the Water of Aultgrad (the ugly burn), and most graphically describes the river and scenery in his *First Journal*, pp. 163-165. He also records that 'the Bishop of Ossory viewed this august and grand wonder of Nature; but, I am told, he took his Observations on the south side, where he could not discover the tenth Part of its Grandeur, the Bank being so steep and slippery in many places that there is no attempting to get near the Verge of the precipice. Inchcoulter, happening accidentally to meet his Lordship on the Highway upon his coming from Ault-Grad, made up to him in a very polite manner; and the Bishop, after Compliments, told him he had been viewing that Wonder, and that he admired it much, as one of the greatest he had ever seen in all his Travels. To which Inchcoulter said in return, "Well, my Lord, that same wonder is the property of a Mackenzie, every inch of it, and as I have the good fortune to be the Owner of it, your Lordship will do me much Honour by a visit at my House (pointing to it) qch is hard by here." But his Lordship begged to be excused, as he was in haste to be gone at present. So they parted with mutual Bows. Inchcoulter's kind Invitation, after so seasonable a Memento, was a home-thrust to his Lordship, as, remarkable as it is, he did not visit one Mackenzie in all Ross-shire, tho' it be the well-known Country of the Clan Mackenzie. A Gentleman [Dr. Sinclair, at Thurso], a Sinclair by name, and, I have reason to think, a Whig, too, told me that Ossory was surely a narrow-thinking Man, and gave the above Omission or Neglect as a strong proof of it' (Bishop Forbes's *Journals*, by the Rev. J. B. Craven, p. 166, 1886).

affirm some person descended by the help of a rope and found the bottom with a pole 12 feet deeper.

They here make bread of pease, mixed with barley or Oats and sometimes with pease alone, and they sow Oats with Rye and make bread of them together. About Dingwall they have great plenty of beans and make bread of it alone.

On the 21st I left Sir Harry Monroe's who did me the honour to accompany me from his house to Dingwall, and crossing the ford higher up than when we first came this way, Dr. Frasier[1] met me and we soon saw Brahan Castle the Earl of Seaforth's, a fine situation on the North side of the river, and abounding in wood, and to the West Fairburne house, on a high hill at the foot of the mountains, which belongs to a Mackenzy.

In about two miles we came to Beaulieu Priory[2] very pleasantly situated on the river Beaulieu; The shell of the Church remains almost entire, which was a very plain oblong square building; In a tomb of one of the Earl of Seaforth's family is the body of a Lady—part of the skin remains entire like leather, and the hand is also entire but dried like a Mummy.[3] There are remains of other buildings, and of the Kitchen with a Chimney as wide as the room. Reid, Bishop of Orkney repaired several parts of the Priory, and his arms are over some of the doors. It was a priory of the order of *Vallis Caulium* reformed from the Cistercians & founded by James Bisset of this shire in 1230.[4] We crossed the river Beaulieu and went a mile Eastward to Kirkhill Church, from which we had a prospect of Beaufort,[5] the late Lord Lovett's Seat, and of

---

[1] Of Achnagairn.

[2] Beauly Priory: see Cordiner's *Antiq. North of Scot.*, Pl. xi. p. 61; *Trans. Inverness Scien. Soc. and Field Club*, 1880, vol. i. p. 358.

[3] 'Said to be the Body of Anne Ogilvie, Lady Kinchuldrum; the Right Arm of which, up to the Elbow, is still entire, with the Skin only up to the Shoulder. Half of the Fore Finger is broke off, but the Nails of the Thumb and the other Fingers are still entire, and all the Joints quite distinct. The Skin is brownish, and the Body is reckoned to have lain there for about 70 years' (Bishop Forbes's *First Journal*, 1762, p. 222; ed. by Rev. J. B. Craven).

[4] See Anderson's *Hist. of Family of Fraser*, p. 29.

[5] Beaufort Castle, built close to the site of the ancient fortress of Beaufort, or Dunie, of Alexander I.'s time. The castle has lately been built anew in a beautiful style.

the beautifull country about it, to whose ancestor Hugh Lord
Fraser of Lovat the last Prior alienated it, and the late Lord,
marrying the heiress, as it is said, forceably, fled abroad, but
making his peace with the Government after her death, he
came home and got possession of the Estate: to which event
this remarkable Epitaph alludes, which he inscribed on his
Father's Monument in this Church:[1]

> To the Memory
>
> of
>
> Lord Thomas Fraser of Lovat, who
> chose rather to undergoe the greatest
> Hardships of Fortune than to part with
> The ancient Honours of his house,
> And bore these hardships with an undaunted
> Fortitude of Mind.
>
> This monument erected
> by Simon Lord Fraser[2] of Lovat his son,
> who likewise having undergone many and
> great vicissitudes of good and bad fortune
> Through the Malice of his Enemies, He, in the end,
> At the Head of his Clan, forced his way to his
> Paternal inheritance with his sword in his hand,
> And relieved his kindred and followers
> From oppression and slavery;
> And both at Home and in foreign Countries,
> By his eminent actions in the Warr and State,
> He has acquired great honour and reputation.
>
> Hic tegit ossa lapis Simonis Fortis in Armis.
> Restituit pressum nam Genus ille suum,
> Hoc marmor posuit Cari Genitoris Honori
> Ingenus afflictum par erat ejus Amor.

[1] The monument, being inside the old church, is still in good preservation. Anderson's *Hist. of Family of Fraser*, p. 156.

[2] 'Sir Robert Munro, who fell at Falkirk, being on a visit to Lord Lovat, they went together to view this monument. Sir Robert, upon reading the inscription, in a free manner said,—Simon, how came you to put up such boasting romantic stuff? To which the wary old Lord replied,—The monument and inscription are chiefly for the Frasers, who must believe whatever I, their chief, require of them: and their posterity will think it as true as the Gospel.'—*The Highland Note Book*, by R. Carruthers, 1843, p. 82, note.

From this place I went to Dr. Fraser's,[1] situated very near the Church, where Sir Harry Monroe and Mr. Ross of Keandace[2] left me, and the Dr. went on with me to Inverness; opposite to this place, I saw a very pretty box[3] built on the side of a hill by Mr. Fraser, the Author of the life of *Konlikan*, who purchased that Estate and built the house after he had made a small fortune in the East Indies. His MSS.[4] in the Indian Language of the Moguls Country were sold by his Widow for £500 to the Trustees for Ratcliff's Library in the university of Oxford. The agreeable variety of wood and beautifull fields up the side of the hills have a most charming effect in the prospect. I returned to Inverness by . . .[5], a fine well-timbered Estate of the late Lord President Forbess's, which is in a most delightfull situation on Lough Beaulieu.

In the New Itinerary from Ptorotone or Inverness through this middle of the island to Varis 8 miles in the first place which might be at Farr in the map or at Cornburgh[6] 10 m. The next is Tuessis or the Spey 18, probably at Ruthven of Badenoch, the next is Tamea 29, which falls in with Dalnacardoch as to distance by 24 Computed miles, which may be but 29 measured through the mountains where the miles are commonly short. The name of the next place is lost, the distance 21 which falls in with Mulinearn 15 m. computed. In medio is nine about Dunkeld, next is Orrea which may be Scone on the East side of the Tavus or Tay in the New Map. The distance of Victoria is 18, which may be Kinross 10 from Perth and 12 from Scone, Abernethy is much too near where Horsley places it. Then follows Advallum 32 and Queens ferry is 18, and consequently it is further to the Wall which did not come so far east, and 18 computed may be 24 measured. The next Luguballia Carlisle, 70.

I came on the 23d to Fort George, and crossed over in a boat to the Chanonry of Fortrose 8 miles from Cromarty

---

[1] Dr. Duncan Fraser of Achnagairn. See Shaw's *Hist. of Province of Moray*, vol. ii. p. 374, ed. 1882.

[2] See p. 175.   [3] Reelick.

[4] The Fraser MSS., Sanskrit, Arabic, and Persian, are in the Bodleian Library. It is doubtful if any part of them have been published. See Prof. Aufrecht's catalogue.

[5] Bunchrew.   [6] Corrybrough.

which was the See of the Bishop of Ross founded by David the 1st about 1124.

The Church is entirely destroyed excepting one chapel to the South of it, in which there is a burial-place of Ld. Seaforth's family, and it has been in service since the reformation, but is now in ruins, it is a well-built Gothic fabric of hewn stone inside and outside. The foundations of the Church appear, which was large. To the West of the Church in the present town stands the shell of the Bishop's house a very poor building. In the yard are finely cut on a large stone the Arms of the King, and under that of the Bishop: Lord Seaforth has a ruined house in this place: It is a poor small town, but beautifully situated on a fine flat spot of ground under the hill. They have some little manufacture of linnen yarn and a small fishery. I passed four miles on the great military road which leads to Sterling, and went a mile to the North West of it, mostly through a wood to Mr. Ross's of Killrack,[1] a large house built to an old Castle over the Nairn, the Country rather rough, but there is a fine wood near the House: Here is a granite runing in small red and blew veins: between the stones is a sort of green Cement, which has Copper in it.—I am, &c.

Letter XXXVI.

Elgin, *July 26th* 1760.

Dear Sister,—On the 24th Mr. Rosse's Eldest Son, Dr. Robinson and Mr. Brody the minister came with me to Calder, where I took leave of Governour Trappeau who had brought me to Kilravock[2] in his chaise. Calder is the seat of a family of that name who were the Thanes of Calder; it now belongs to Mr. Campbell who lives in Pembrockshire, to whose family it came by the marriage of the heiress of Calder. It is a good house built to an old Castle[3] of one room on a floor; there is a

---

[1] Rose of Kilravock (pronounced locally Kilrack).

[2] For 'A Genealogical Deduction of the Family of Rose of Kilravock, 1290-1847,' see the Spalding Club Pub. 1848.

[3] For views and plans of Cawdor Castle see *Castellated Arch. of Scot.*, by MacGibbon and Ross, 1887, vol. ii. pp. 314-323.

Drawbridge to it, and the Stables were in vaults under the new house, and so is a very fine Kitchen; they say that the Thanes lived in a wooden house probably built with a Wooden frame on a low Mount about half a mile to the North East near which I saw the ruins of a Chapel, and that this Castle was built about 300 years ago round a Hawthorn tree, the body of which we saw standing, and concerning it there is some family Tradition.[1]

The Castle stands on a brook, which is a great torrent in winter, and runs between Rocks, that a little higher, are fifty feet high, adorned with trees and very beautifull. We came by the banks of the River Nairn which is a tremendous torrent after rains, to Nairn, a town of one street about a quarter of a mile long and may consist of 100 houses. It is very pleasantly situated on an eminence between the Sea and the river; over the river was the Castle of the Constable; there is a good bridge across it, here is a salmon fishing after rains, but when the water is low there is no visible outlet. I was told since I left it, that the river did run into the Sea directly South, close to the East End of the Town, and that there was a Pier at the mouth of it, the remains of which have been taken for the ruins of a Castle which are seen only at very low water. Nairn is a Royal borough and I was presented with my Freedom,[2] & I set forward toward Forres.

We passed by Brodie[3] the Seat of Brodie late Lord Lyon,

---

[1] 'The tradition is, that the original proprietor was directed by a dream to load an ass with gold, turn it loose, and, following its footsteps, build a castle wherever the ass rested. By and by it arrived beneath the branches of a hawthorn tree, where, fatigued with the weight upon its back, it knelt down to rest. The space round the tree was cleared for building, the foundation laid, and a tower erected; but the tree was preserved, and remains a singular memorial of superstition. The trunk of the tree, with its branches, is still shown in a vaulted apartment at the bottom of the principal tower. Its roots branch out beneath the floor, and its top penetrates through the vaulted arch of stone above, in such a manner as to make it appear, beyond dispute, that the tree stood, as it does, before the tower was erected.'

[2] The burgh records of Nairn are very incomplete. Mr. Wm. Laing, the Town-Clerk, writes:—'The minutes of that period are not in a state of good preservation, and I fear that the part applicable to the year 1760 has either gone amissing or been destroyed.'

[3] For the Diary of Alexander Brodie of Brodie, 1652-1680, and of his son, James Brodie of Brodie, 1680-1685, see the Spalding Club Pub. 1863.

which is finely planted, and came to Tarnaway[1] the Earl of Murray's, a fine situation on an eminence granted to Randolph Earl of Murray by King . . . The Earl used it as a hunting seat, and built only a very large hall, in which they show Randolph's Carved Chair of Oak.[1] I was told that underground Rooms had been taken from it by raising the floor, and consequently its height is much lessened. To Tarnaway Castle a large house has been built in the Castle style, and there are fine woods with ridings in them.

It is situated over a rivulet, which falls into the Findhorn a terrible torrent after rains, across it we forded, and in about two miles came to Forres another small town consisting of a handsome broad street, and about 150 houses; it is well built and most delightfully situated in view of the river, the sea, and a very fine country; A beautifull situation at the West end of the town belongs to Sir William Dunbar; it was the site of an old Castle, on which a Modern house was begun to be built.

This is a Royal borough & the Provost Mr. Cummin the head of that very ancient family came to town on purpose to give me my freedom,[2] but the town Clerk was absent, and it was sent after me.

A little to the East of the town is Clover hill,[4] round which about halfway up is an old entrenchment probably of the Danes who gained a great victory over the Scotch near this

---

[1] Darnaway Castle. Randolph, Earl of Moray, was Regent during the minority of King David II., but the castle appears to have been at least partly built by Archibald Douglas, Earl of Moray, about 1450.—*Exchequer Rolls for* 1456-58. A view of the carved oak roof in the hall is shown in MacGibbon and Ross's *Castellated Arch. of Scot.*, 1887, vol. i. p. 305. ' Randolph's oaken chair, on which are coarsely carved the bearings of his office and arms, weighs about 60 lbs., and differs little from the coronation chain in Westminster Abbey.'—*Old Stat. Ac.*, vol. xx. p. 224.

[2] Mr. Rob. Urquhart, Town-Clerk, Forres, writes:—' There is no record of this presentation in the old Minute-Books of the Council. After the minute of the 26th June 1760 there is a blank of more than half the page, which has probably been left for the purpose of filling up, on the Town-Clerk's return, the minute as to Bishop Pococke's admission as a burgess. The next minute is dated the 31st July 1760, and seems to have been the last subscribed by Provost Cumming of Altyre.

[3] Cluny Hill.

place, where a pillar[1] is set up about 20 feet high : on one side is a long cross, and a compartment below it something like a Coat of Arms ; on the other side are about ten compartments of figures some of men, others of horsemen, and some of beasts ; this is the East side, which being the rainy quarter is much defaced. I have been informed that a Traveller ought to go from this place to Strath Spey to Castle Grant, three miles North West of which is Roeth[2] an old castle, & at Cord na Thesu or Abernethy is another old Castle,[2] & Iron forges & furnaces built by the York building Company :[3] From that place down the Spey to Keith or Gordon Castle & Garmouth the land is yearly increased by the stones brought down by the Spey.

We went on a mile to the Abbey of Kinloss[4] or Kean Loch (the head of the Lake) founded by St. David in 1150 ; the Cistercian Monks were brought to it from Melross : Edward Bruce Commendator of it was made Baron Bruce of Kinloss by James the 6th the Church is entirely destroyed but there is a ruin on the North Side of the East End of an arched room and another over it, I at first imagined there might be a tower on each side of the East End ; there are Shallow Niches on the west side of it which seem to be part of the Cloyster ; The Chapter house is in a line with the tower which consisted of three arches supported by two rows of small octagon pillars three in a row ; to the North of the Cloyster is a grand gate finely adorned with Carving, and to the East of this is a broad

[1] Sweno's Stone, or the Forres Pillar. It has been frequently figured. Gordon's *Itinerarium*, 1727, Pl. lvi. p. 159 ; Cordiner's *Antiq. North of Scot.* 1780, p. 55 ; Alexander's *Sketches of Moray* ; Anderson's *Scotland in Early Christian Times*, 1883, p. 279.

[2] Probably Castles Roy and Lochindorb are meant, but the localities reversed ; or Rate Castle—a stronghold of the once powerful Cumins.

[3] The enterprise carried on at Abernethy, and its connection with the forfeited estates, is well described in a pamphlet, 'The York Buildings Company ; a Chapter in Scotch History,' 1883, by David Murray, M.A., F.S.A. Scot. See also 'Paper on The Early History of the Iron Industry,' by D. W. Kemp, in *Trans. Royal Scot. Soc. of Arts*, 1886 ; 'Notes on the Ancient Iron History of Scotland,' by W. Ivison Macadam, F.C.S., *Proc. Soc. of Antiq. Scot.*, 1886-87.

[4] Founded by David I. in 1150, and confirmed by Papal Bull in 1174. See *Record of the Monastery of Kinloss*, with illustrative documents. Ed. by Dr. Stuart, 1872. The stones of the building were largely taken for the construction of Cromwell's Fort at Inverness in 1650. The son of the first Baron Kinloss was created Earl of Elgin in 1633.

Arch, which is a small segment of a circle and I take to have been the Cistern for washing the hands at the Entrance of the refectory, of which there are now no signs; but to the North of the supposed site of it, are large buildings of three stories which might be the Abbott's Lodging, but I rather think to be more modern, on the west side of the wall of the Cloyster are arches in the wall supported by pilasters that might be part of some Chapel belonging to the Church.

I here visited the Minister[1] who went on with me near to Sir Robert Gordon's; we crossed a large Strand. Here they find turf under the Sands a considerable way out, and about the river Findhorn, hills of Sand are frequently raised in one night, & sometimes blown away in the like space of time. We came to Bruff or Brugh-Sea, a poor fishing village at the East End of the strand: To the North of it is a small Promontory of about two acres of ground called Brugh head: This was fortified first with a deep fossee by which the Sea came in, and made it an Island, and then by three more fossees: the high part to the west forms a Triangle, washed to the west by the Sea, and seems to have been defended by Walls now ruined and appear as a heap of stones; tho' I don't recollect I saw any Mortar:[2]

To the East is a flat strip of ground not much above the Sea which was also fortified, but now it appears like a Rampart of Earth, here were houses for Women and Children, for this was a place of Arms for the Danes, when they landed in 1108 and staid till 1112. There must have been here considerable buildings, as they find large beams of Oak about a foot square which were worked so as to be used for buildings. The Danes fought a second time at Mortlick—ten miles South of Elgen and were defeated; Gordon[3] thinks the stone at Forres was set up on that Victory. Mortlick is in the Shire of Banf twelve miles from the mouth of Spey, and three miles from that river, between the Castles of Balveny and Auchin Down, and 36 miles from Aberdeen: on the Victory Malcam III. founded a see

---

[1] The Rev. James Munro.

[2] 'The ramparts, with their dry stone building, more nearly resemble the brochs of the North; and it is worthy of note that the place is to this day called "The Broch" as freely as it is called Burghead.'—*Trans. Inverness Scien. Soc.*, 1878, vol. i. p. 164. Anderson's *Scotland in Pagan Times*, 1883, p. 279.

[3] Gordon's *Itinerarium Septentrionale*, 1727, p. 159.

there in 1110 which in 1206 was removed to Aberdeen.[1] They were beat a 3d time at Barry near Dundee, and last of all at Crudin in Buchan, and were all permitted to go off on taking an oath they never wou'd return more.

We came on about two miles to Duffus near the West end of Lough Spigny, to the South of it, on a Mount near the Lough, are the remains of the Castle of Duffus the Seat of the Lords of that name, one of which forfeited for Rebellion(?) and was afterwards an Admiral in the Swedish Service; We came on half a mile to Gordon's toun,[2] the Seat of Sir Robert Gordon a large house of seven windows in front which would have made a good appearance if clumsy offices had not been built on each side with a very high roof of three sides resting against the wall of the house.

About two miles more brought us to Kinedder where Bp Archibald built a large house about the year 1290 and, I suppose, a Church in form of a Cross the foundations of which are seen as well as of the house, and of the wall of the enclosure. Some say the Bp's See at first was fixed at Bernie, then removed to Spigney, and describe this as a Country house, but others say, that they had no fixed See, but resided sometimes at one place and sometimes at another, which seems to have been the truth; for Bishop Bruce of the family of Douglas, represented to the Pope, that they had no fixed place of residence and desired that the See might be fixed at Spigny.[3] And this has frequently been the case where Bishops have their titles from a Country, & not from the town of their residence. Kinnedder is near the Sea, and we came to the East End of the Lough of Spigny, there is a great appearance that this was an island to the North, that the Sea first gave way to the West, there being a large beach at the West end of the Lough, and Banks to the South which seem to have been the bounds of the Sea; for to the North, and running from East to West, are a great number of old beaches of gravel

---

[1] See note 3, p. 204.
[2] See Rhind's *Sketches of Moray*, p. 121.
[3] See *The Parish of Spynie*, by Robert Young, 1871; and 'Extracts from the Register of the Regality Court of Spynie,' *Spalding Club Miscellany*, vol. ii. pp. 120-146.

that appear like plough furrows, and seem to have been made successively as the Sea retired: There is the same appearance of Sand banks and gravelly banks of the Sea all the way to Pluscardin, so that it seems to have formed a sort of Lough between the land untill it retired some ages after the flood.

I came to the Castle of Spigny,[1] finely situated over the South Side of Lough Spigney: It originally seemed to have consisted of a Chapel[1] on one side, with a small strong square tower to retire to in time of Danger, and a hall on the other with a high building of seven apartments to the East of the gate: but Bishop David Stewart having been threatened by Alexander Lord Huntley built that noble Castle, which with a little more building adjoyning to it, and what was built before, encloses the whole court, the walls are ten feet thick; it consists of six floors about 24 by 40 feet with several closets practiced in the Walls which range all round; at top there is an Arch, & one over the ground floor, and one over the highest room but one; all being covered with a roof: it is built of hewn freestone inside and out: over the Entrance to the court are the Bishops Arms with a Crosier for the Crest: On the Tower are the Arms of the Royal family, with a Ducal Coronet resting on the back of a Couchant unicorn; under this are the other arms, there is a Mitre on one of them, if not on both.

On the Height to the North West are remains[2] of a Church which they say was the Ancient Cathedral, and afterwards a parish Church.

This Lake[3] is four miles long and half a mile broad, there are swans always on it which breed in the Islands and there are very large pike in the Lough.—I am, &c.

[1] For plans and views of Spynie Palace, see MacGibbon and Ross's *Castellated Architecture of Scotland*, 1887, vol. i. pp. 439-445.

[2] The last of the remains, a Gothic gable, fell about 1850, and now all trace of the old Cathedral is gone.

[3] Loch of Spynie is now drained. See the interesting account of the reclamation in Young's *The Parish of Spynie*, pp. 5-36.

Letter XXXVII.

Elgin, *July* . . . 1760.

Dear Sister,—From Spigny we came two short miles to Elgin situated between low hills on the small river Lossie; The town chiefly consists of a broad street half a mile long; in the middle of which is the large parish Church dedicated to their Patron St Giles whose figure is the Arms of the town. There are about 3000 Souls in it, they have a manufacture of Linnen yarn, and some linnen, blankets, and coarse cloath, mostly for home consumption. They have also a good Market and Shops.

Bishop Andrew of the Duffus family, obtained from Alexander the first the ground on the river to the East of the town for the site of a Cathedral which he built, and it was consecrated in 1224. The Towers are at the West End, & the Transcept seems to be of the old building, being of a plainer and heavier Gothic Architecture than the rest of the building. For in 1390 Alexander Earl of Buchan, called the Wolf of Badenoch, burnt the town of Elgin, particularly the Cathedral, St. Giles's Church, the Maison de Dieu, and 18 houses of Canons and Chaplains; for which when he was absolved from his Excommunication, he made the best restitution he could: when Bishop Leighton came to the See in 1414 he gave a third of his Bishoprick to build the Cathedral Church, and 'tis said all the Chapter did the same: And then it is to be supposed this beautifull Cathedral[1] was begun, the Ornaments of which show that Arts had begun to revive. The west door is extremely fine, consists of thirty members of round pillars, fillets and flutes; There are two door places in it which are all adorned inside and outside with most elegant open carved work; over the middle is a compartment in which they say there was a Crucifix, there is a Nich on each side, and one over each of them. 'Tis said in these were the statues of St. Peter and St. Paul, and over the point of the arch in the middle compart-

---

[1] See Shaw's *History of the Province of Moray.* 1775; Pennant's *Tour*, 1769, p. 162; Cordiner's *Antiq. of Scot.*, 1776, p. 57; Forsyth's *Survey of the Province of Moray*, 1798; Rhind and Alexander's *Sketches of Moray*, 1839.

ment there seems to have been some ornament probably an Emblem of the Trinity to which the Church was dedicated, for on a house near adjoining there is a head carved in Stone, with three faces: The body of the Church seems to have consisted of three windows and a door on each side, so that to the west there was a porch, and the towers have been raised higher in this elegant style; the Buttress in which the Staircase is formed, appearing a modern work: The middle tower which 'tis said was very grand, fell down not long since, occasioned by digging a grave near the foundation: From this spot about half the Quire is plain wall, except an opening to a Chapel in which the family of Gordon are buried; in this part the stalls seem to have been, for it is distinguished from the East part by a compounded Gothic pillar on each side crowned with three tiers of pyramidal Carved Ornaments. On each side and at the East End are fine single windows adorned within with three small circular pilasters and two flutes between them, on the outside with two pillasters and one flute, all the flutes being covered with carved works in roses, as beautifull as the finest roman or greek ornaments: over these on each side, and over the plain part are single windows, under them on the North Side are the four Niches for the persons who administered, and a Nich for the Elements, on the North Side is a large Nich probably designed for the tomb of the founder, and on that side is the door that leads to the Chapter house; which is an Octagon about thirty-six feet in Diameter, the Arch of which is adorned with Coats of Arms, and supported by a pillar consisting of several pilasters, every stone going entirely through; at the upper end is a Seat for the Dean and two on each side of it for the dignitaries, there was a bench all round, and a window in each of the right sides; and here the Ornaments are in the same fine taste.[1]

The four dignitaries seem to have had their houses to the North of the Church, the Archdeacon had his to the South, and probably the prebendaries; most of the names of the five first are retained. All was enclosed by a high wall of a large

---

[1] In the *Edinburgh Architectural Association's Sketch-Book*, 1887, vol. i., New Series, there are ground-plan of south transept and exterior elevation, also Triforium plan and interior elevation, by Mr. James C. Watt.

circumference, which Close was called the Colledge. Near the wall to the South was an hospital commonly called Maison Dieu and in the records Domus Dei de Elgin, a wall of the Chapel remains: To the west of this is the Grey Friers, which I suppose was the monastery of the Observantines, founded by John Innes in 1479; The walls of the Church remain entire; it is a very plain building; Towards the west gate on the South Side was the Monastery of red Cross which are supposed to be the Knights of Jerusalem; but I find no mention of them in books.

To the North of the Castle hill in a field, are some slight remains of the foundation of the Church of the black friars or Dominicans, founded by Alexander the IId in 1233. Two Chapels also are mentioned, one of the Trinity, the other, if I mistake not, of the Virgin Mary, Mr. Innes's house is on the site of one of them to the North East of the Cathedral. They have here one Kirk, a Meeting house of Seceders, and a Chapel of the Church of England,[1] built on the site of the Chapel of St. John.

There is a large house[2] in the town built by the Murray and Duffus families with some fine appartments in it, and there are many good houses in the town: On the Castle hill to the West called also Lag hill are ruins of an old wall; it commands a fine view of the Country.

I went four computed miles to the south west, and by west, to the Priory of Pluscardin[3] situated between the hills on the rivulet called Lochty, which falls into the Lossy, it is in a fine flat spot which (as the name of the river imports) seems to have been a Lough; It was a very grand Monastery; The body of the Church is destroyed. There were fine Gothic windows to the Quire, and at the North End of the Transept

---

[1] 'Bishop Pococke was the only Bishop of the Church of England, since the Revolution, that preached and confirmed in Scotland, when Episcopacy was there abolished. . . . He preached and confirmed in the English Church in Elgin; and continued to do so in every other of that persuasion which he had occasion to be near.'—*The Cambridge Chronicle*, 5th October 1765. See Note 1, p. 51.

[2] Thunderton House, the ancient house of the Sutherland family of Duffus, illustrated in *Sketches of Moray*, by Rhind and Alexander, p. 55.

[3] See Macphail's *History of the Religious House of Pluscardyn*, 1881.

a beautifull round window twenty feet in Diameter. There are two Chapels on the East side of the Transept, and a small Chapel on each side to the East of them, in which most of the Stones of the Arches are of one Stone laid from Mullion to Mullion; over the Northern Chapel is a building which might be a Chapel to the Prior's appartment that might joyn to the refectory on the same floor; under the refectory was the Chapter house and the Kitchen, the arches of both are supported by pillars, with a passage between them, and over the Kitchen is another arched room. Whatever fate befell the Monastery after the irregular Monks were chastised, and it was made a Cell to Dunferling: It appears that the opening from the body to the Transept was walled up, and in each of the fine windows of the Quire is built a plain Gothic window probably that it might serve as a parish Church. It is built of very fine yellow hewn freestone inside and out brought from the hills called Quarelwood,[1] from which Elgin was also supplied with Stone.

We came within two miles of Elgin to Birney, to see the Church[2] which was probably the first Cathedral of the See of Moray founded in the Eleventh Century (as 'tis said) by King Malcolm IIId. It is a small plain Church with a Chancel; The windows on each side are narrow & turned with true arches; and the Arch and pillars that support it leading to the Chancel are plain Saxon Architecture with singular capitals, the whole is of hewn stone within as well as on the outside. On the hill to the South are some marks of foundations called the Castle, which by tradition was the Bishop's house.— I am, &c.

Letter XXXVIII.

Cullen, *July 28th*, 1760.

Dear Sister,— On the 29th the Gentlemen who had visited

---

[1] Now called Quarrywood. 'Quarrelwood, so called from a rich quarry of freestone in the adjacent hill.'—*Shaw's Hist. of Moray*, 1775, p. 79. 'In old writings it is written Querelwode, Correilwood, and Quarelwode, and as it had this name before there were quarries in the hill, it may be somewhat difficult to ascertain the meaning of the word.'—Young's *The Parish of Spynie*, p. 62.

[2] There is a saying associated with this church which has become proverbial: 'You have need to be prayed for thrice in the church of Birnie, that you may either end or mend.'

me accompanied me out of town: The Master of Forbes returned home, and near the Church of Urquhart, I was met by Sir Harry Innys who showed me the Church. It is of the old Saxon Architecture with narrow windows. Going a quarter of a mile North of it, I was shown the field in which stood the priory of Urquhart which was a Cell of Dumferleng[1] founded by David the first, to the blessed Trinity in 1125, nothing appears except a spot, not cultivated, which might be the site of the Church.

From this I went to Sir Harry Innys's; From whose house[2] Lough Spigney and another Lake appear like a large river at a Distance: I proceeded on my Journey, taking leave of all but Dr. Brodie and Mr. Chamler who travelled on with me. Sir Harry Innys came with me near to the Spey, which we forded: here it is a red earth and freestone on both sides: They have a boat for Horses, when there is a flood in the river, which is a terrible wide torrent. It is supposed to be the Tuessis of the New Map.

The King's Army in 1746 passed about a mile lower; it is said that some of this Country were afraid[3] to pass but being led on by Mr. Brodie a very zealous person of Elgin, and Father of Dr. Brodie of Elgin, others followed, and those who flinched were kept for the rear: Tho' the waters were high, yet there were but very few drowned; among them were two or three women. The rebels determined that the troops could not stand our [? their] artillery in opposing the passage of the Army: and so concluded to have the chance of a pitched battle.

Near the East side of the river is Fochabars, a small town that chiefly subsists by the Salmon fishery, which is very great

---

[1] Dunfermline.   [2] Innes House, now the property of the Earl of Fife.

[3] This story may be paralleled by 'the following anecdote, with regard to the Earl of Sutherland's regiment of Highlanders (now arrived from the northern counties to Aberdeen) we copy from the *Aberdeen Journal* of last post. On arrival of the first division on the western bank of Spey, the ferry-boat was not just ready; and that way of passing the river seeming very dilatory, they took immediately into the water (tho' considerably increased by rains in the highlands), and above sixty of them actually passed it without the least disorder or concern; and the whole would have followed, had they not been restrained by their officers, upon the inhabitants representing that the river was still rising—a notable instance of the natural temerity and hardness of our yet brave and ineffeminated countrymen.'—*The Edinburgh Evening Courant*, Wednesday, May 28, 1760.

in this river: There is a little place near the Mouth of the river where they salt most of them. This place or Fochabers might be the Site of Tuessis. Castle Gordon is very near the Town, with a small park belonging to the Duke of Gordon.[1] Most of the way to the Spey was heathy and so it is for about three miles from the Spey. We passed by an Episcopal Chapel which was in use till of late, that the people did not care to support it for alternate service with Elgin; the most of the Duke of Gordon's Tenants having been papists came over with the present Duke's grandfather to the Church of England. Here they manure with a rotten stone, and near this place they have a reddish Marle and a blewish near Brockley Mills.

We visited Mr. . . . .[2] took some refreshment there, and came on through a fine Country to Cullin, a small town where the Earl of Finlater is endeavouring to establish a linnen Manufacture.

A little to the North East of the house is a sort of a Danish Mount, which seemed to be worked into two terraces: and all along the Coast are small Mounts which they say were made for beacons; but about Urquhart I observed some very small mounts, which I was informed were certainly made to Caw hawks, and near that place I saw the remains of a small Circle of Stones about 5 feet high, they were large, and I was told there was another near it: About the river of Nairn above Kilroack[3] are several, they say above twenty, within the space of three or four miles, and there are many in the Country of Bueghan,[4] in Aberdeenshire.

I went to the Earl of Finlaters,[5] in whose house there are some good apartm^{ts} and pictures,[6] particularly one of James 6th wth a strong Character in his face of that smile which attended his facetious conversations. His Lordship has built a bridge over

[1] Now the property of the Duke of Richmond and Gordon.
[2] Blank in the MS.   [3] Kilravock.   [4] Buchan.
[5] Earl of Findlater, now merged into the title and estates of the Earl of Seafield.
[6] 'A full length of James VI. by *Mytens*: at the time of the revolution, the mob had taken it out of Holy-Rood House, and were kicking it about the streets, when the Chancellor, the Earl of Finlater, happening to pass by, redeemed it out of their hands.'—Pennant's *Tour*, 1769, p. 151. See *George Jamesone, the Scottish Vandyck*, by J. Bulloch, 1885, p. 174.

the river to his woods and Demesnes on the other side, which is 84 feet wide and sixty high, from which on each side are pleasant winding Walks through the wood, partly in sight of the river, and partly at a Distance, with a walk likewise over the high ground. The fields are planted, as are the hills to the West, which will appear very beautifull when the firr trees grow up.

On the 29th I left this place, and came in four miles to Portsoy a little town and Creek with a mole built to shelter small vessels: They export Corn here and some fish: To the West of the town are two perpendicular veins of Marble, which run about two miles into the land, and may be from 15 to 20 feet broad. They are of that deep green streiked and another kind mixed, & some with a mixture of a Deep reddish Cast all which are called the Scotch green and sometimes the Scotch Serpentine for it resembles that soft stone called Serpentine, which is found in Saxony.

I came four miles further to Banf, near the Town is a yard for bleching linnen yarn[1] of which a load is sent off every three weeks to Edinburgh, and from that place is carried on to Nottingham by Land. Banf is a well built small town pleasantly situated on a rising ground, and on a flat to the west of the river Devin;[2] at the mouth of which a basin is made by two piers in which a ship of a hundred Ton can lie with safety: And they have a Salmon fishery in the river: The town subsists by this linnen yarn and Shops.

There are a great number of the Church of England here, the wife often going one way and the husband another: So that there is no sort of animosity in the Town upon the account of religion: Here is an Episcopal Chapel to which about 600 souls resort of the town and the adjacent Country.

Lord Despert[3] has a small house on the site of the old Castle over the Mole; this precinct of the Castle was about 100 f. square, and a small part of the Enclosure remains. He has formed a Lawn before the house and a beautifull walk round another lawn below, and it is a Delightfull Summer Situation.

A little way from the town to the South, the Earl of Fife, a

---

[1] For an account of the thread and linen manufactures, see Cordiner's *Antiq. of Scot.*, 1776, p. 50.
[2] River Deveron. [3] Lord Deskford.

peer of the Kingdom of Ireland (his Ancestor Lord McDuff having forfeited) built a house of four floors and six rooms on a floor with tower at the Angles in which there are Closets, and back Stair Cases: It is all of hewn freestone, brought by sea ready worked (as I was told) a great part of it in boxes from the Frith of Forth. The two middle stories of the towers are adorned with one tier of Corinthian pilasters in the style of Lord Carlisle's house at Castle Howard in Yorkshire, and the attick, with composit Pilast^{rs}. To the three middle rooms every way are arched windows and pediments over them. The Chimneys are brought into the tower to what appears like a large pedestall on the coved roof of each of them. The Attick story in the fronts being above the pediments which with an Entablature crowns the other stories. The under-story is rustic; the ascent in the front to the South is by winding steps on each side, and leads to a Saloon over which is a room of a Cube of thirty feet: Excepting the towers it consists of seven windows in a story, and is within, an exceeding good house of thirty-four rooms and sixteen Closets; it is now inhabited by Lord McDuff, Ld Fife's Eldest Son who is married to the sole Heiress of the Earl of Cathness.

A little to the South of the Town over the river towards a Mount called St. Leonard's hill was a Convent of Carmelites entirely destroyed; it was dedicated to the Virgin Mary. James the 6th granted the Estate to the old College of Aberdeen. I was told that near Banf are some fine Caves in the Sea Cliffs.

We Rid six miles through a very pleasant country in the way to Aberdeen, to Forglan[1] Lord Banff's, late Sir Alexander Ogilvye's. It is near Turriff and is very delightfully situated over the river[2] with large plantations about it, and there is a most pleasant walk both up and down the river through the wood, the river appearing full and very beautifull.

The river Deven or as some Maps have it Dovern—supposed to be the ancient Celnius; Selina is 19 miles from the Spey which may fall in with Turriff—rises in Aberdeenshire, and is here the bounds between Banffshire and that part of Aberdeenshire called Buchan, because it belonged to the Earls of that name. The Spey bounds Banffshire mostly to the West, which is a fine Country. The next thing mentioned in the New

[1] Forglen.   [2] Deveron.

Itinerary[1] is Ituna which I suppose to be the Ythan ; the next is Devana, 24 m. Aberdeen ; Fluv. Tina Inverberry 23 m. ; ad Æsica, South Esk (it may be at Brechin), on which stands Montrose, 8 m. ; Tavum or the Tay, 23 m. it may be at Dundee ; Orrea, Schone, 19 m. ; Ad Itunam, the Erne probably at Ardite, 14 m. ; Victoria, Kinross, 9 m. ; Alauna, Alva or some other passage over the Forth, 9 m ; Ad Vallum, it may be about Falkirk or Lithgow, 12 m. Afterwards the Itinerary is very doubtful. Corio is the next & all are without miles. This seems to be Coria Damniorum supposed to be at Kirkurd to the North West of Pebles, & is in the road. Gadanica is next mentioned, & answers to Colanica, which if it were not placed to the North of the Mountains might be Blatum Bulgium. The next is Trimontium, Anan. & so to Lugu Vallis, Carlisle.
—I am, &c.

Letter XXXIX.

. . . , *July*, . . . 1760.

Dear Sister,—On the 30th I set forward to the East and soon came to Turriff, on an Eminence over a Stream[2] which falls into the Deven: There was a Church of Eng^d Chapel which is still kept in repair, but has not been in Service since the late Act passed. We travelled by this Stream and going over some high ground we soon came to the rivulets which run eastward & fall into the river Ugie that empties itself into the Sea at Peterhead. This County of Buchan is a fine Corn Country, abounding in small hills like Northhamtonshire, which Country it would much resemble, if it were as well planted with trees.

We came to a little village called New Deer, and in about four miles more to Old Deer. Half a mile west of it I saw the ruins (on the river Uggie) of the Cistertian Abbey of Deer,[3] which seems to have been a very plain building ; it was founded by William Cumming, Earl of Buchan in 1218, and the Monks were brought from Kinloss. Some of the Sheriffs of the Earl Marshall's family had been Abbots of this place, and James 6th created Robert Keith a younger Son of that Earl a temporal

---

[1] Richard of Cirencester's *Itinerary*, see note 4, p. 26.
[2] The Burn of Turriff, which falls into the Deveron.
[3] *The Book of Deer.* Spalding Club Pub. 1869.

Lord of this Abbey by the title of Lord Altrie, which title fell into the Earl of Marischal.

There is a Chapel at Old Deer with a Congregation from the adjacent Country of 1000 Souls. It is only a village and near it is the seat[1] of Mr. Ferguson, a famous advocate, who is esteemed a great Lawyer. It is adorned with fine plantations of firr and other trees.

We came eight miles to Peterhead, pleasantly situated on a fine bay formed by this Cape and Boddom head on which there is a ruin of a house of a Baronet of the name of Keith, in this bay a harbour is formed by a narrow head that stretches out into the Sea, and two piers built to Defend the Shipping, in the harbour a Vessel of 200 Tons may lay: The east side is formed by the isle of Keith, the North by the passage to it, the West by the Main land, and the South by the two piers, between which is the narrow entrance into the harbour, there is a good road for anchoring in the bay when the weather is fair. The town consists chiefly of one broad well built street, the rocks here are of red granite, and many of the houses are built of this Stone hammered, which is very beautifull when it is well squared: There is a Chalybeat Spaw[2] here which is well frequented, it seems to be stronger than Tunbridge Spaw, but not so strong as the German. The Freemasons have built a bathing place adjoyning to it, into which the sea water is to be pumped; and there is a long room over it that is to be let for the use of the company; it is fronted with the granite, very well executed: They have a trade here in an import of Norway Deals and Iron, and of French wine and brandy, and other wines, and an export of oyl meal and barley; and also a small manufacture of linnen yarn, & of thread and woorsted Stockings and Gloves. About ten leagues off there is a rock on which there is a good fishing, but they neglect that, as well as the lobster fishing: They have great plenty of fish whenever they please to take them; the Cod fish, the Holybut, and Skait in great abundance. The Easterly winds here bring rains, and in Summer foggs, which often come on early in the Evening, continue all night and sometimes for whole days, and are very disagreeable tho' no way unwholesome, except that by their moisture, they are apt to make people catch cold if they do not take care.

[1] Pitfour.   [2] The Wine Well.

I came eight miles through a country which is a mixture of corn and heath to Slanes the Earl of Errol's, who finding the weather foggy had sent his post chaise for me, having had Intelligence of my intention to wait on him by one of his family: This house, built round a Court, is situated over the Sea Cliffs which are not very high, but the rocks appear in beautifull figures like Gothick workmanship: This Earl is son of Lord Kilmarnock and inherited the title and Estate of Earl of Errol from his Aunt about two years agoe; Having been bred in the Army and was in the King's Service in 1745.

A mile to the North of this place is a remarkable hole into which the Sea comes, it is about 100 yards long and 50 broad, being in a long triangular form: it may be about 100 feet deep, & a boat can go into it, the passage being short: Nearer the house, close to the sea cliff, is a high rocky small island with two tops, one is joyned to the other by a very curious natural bridge;[1] Here the Gulls and other sea birds breed, and make a beautifull appearance when they fly about the rocks: The young of some of them are good Food, and the Country people feed on their Eggs. Three miles to the South, is a Cave in which there are curious Stalactites,[2] and tho' of the Alabaster kind, there are some in small ramifications like those which are formed by droppings from freestone. Inland they have here a red granite, but not of so good a colour as that of Peter Head.

The Earl gave me a piece of red Jasper which is divided by spars, something in the manner of the Ludus Helmontii, it is about 2 inches in Diameter & was found in the middle of one of these Stones. His Lordship also gave me a petrification of the Cave with a pidgeon's Egg in it, being a Stalagmite formed by the water dropping on the Egg.

At Frazerburgh is an old Castle,[3] and between it and Peterhead, is a very fine rid of ten miles, four or five of which is over beautifull Downs. Kynairds head must be Taixalorum Promontorium of the New Map, & Taizalum of Ptolemy. —I am, &c.

---

[1] Bullers of Buchan. The Pot of Buller's Buchan. The Rock of Dunbuy. The Bow of Pitwartlachie. Dr. Samuel Johnson was entertained at Slains Castle, and in his own graphic way describes the castle and the Buller of Buchan. Vide *Journey to West. Islands Scot.*, 1773.

[2] Dropping Cave, or the White Cave of Slains.   [3] Cairnbulg.

LETTER XL.

ABERDEEN, Agst 2, 1700.

DEAR SISTER,—On the first of August I set out in Lord Errol's postchaise, and crossed near his Lordship's house a stream, which soon falls into another, on each side of which stream there is a most beautifull Kitchen Garden on the ground which rises gently on each side. This river is placed at Bowness in Dorret's Map five miles North of Slanes; we came in eight computed miles through the same kind of country eight miles in the whole to Ellen[1] a small town on the river Ythan, supposed to be the Ituna of the New Map close to which town Lord Aberdeen has a large old House,[2] and a great plantation of firr trees: There was a Cross match in this family with the late Duke of Gordon, the Dowager Dutchess being Sister to the Earl, and he married to the Duke of Gordon's sister.[3]

We crossed the river and came to Pitmedden, Sr Wm Seaton's House where there is a quarry of Marble resembling Cipolino; to the South is an old Castle with good improvements about it; it belongs to . . .

Between the Ythan and the Don a black grey Granite of small grains abounds, and between the latter and the Dee a very light grey granite with large white spots.

We came to the road from Banff to Aberdeen; and in a mile (nine miles in the whole from Ellen) to old Meldron,[4] the Country of the Urquharts; here is a great market for yarn stockings from 8^d to 5 shillings a pair. It is a small town. We passed near the field of battle fought[5] in 1411. And crossed

---

[1] Ellon.   [2] Udny Castle.
[3] William, second Earl of Aberdeen, married, for his third wife, Anne, daughter of Alexander, second Duke of Gordon; while his daughter, Catharine, by his second marriage with Susan, daughter of John, Duke of Athole, married Cosmo, third Duke of Gordon, and son of Alexander, second Duke. Thus the Earl married his son-in-law's sister.   [4] Old Meldrum.
[5] The battle of Harlaw. See *Inverurie and the Earldom of the Garioch, a Topographical and Historical Account of the Garioch to the Revolution Settlement*, by John Davidson, D.D., 1878.

the . . . ¹ which falls into the Don we came to Inverury, and saw to the East Kintore, both royal boroughs, tho' poor Villages: Near the former a battle was fought in 1309 between Robert Bruce and . . . ² the camp of the enemy was on the hill above Kintore the latter gives title to the Earl of Kintore, which title and estate will come to Lord Marischal, lately Ambassador in Spain from the King of Prussia, and Governor of Neuschatel at present in England, his attainder being taken off but his title not restored. He is next heir to the present Lord of Kintore who is lunatic. The Family Seat, Keith Hall, is near the town where the fields appear in a very beautifull manner between the firr trees.

At Inverury we came into the road from Elgin to Aberdeen, but soon leaving it, we travelled westward, & passed by Keminay[3] a seat of the Burnets; the famous Bishop of Sarum being of the family of . . . towards Aberdeen, and his father was one of the Lords of Session.[4]

We came by several plantations of firr trees on the hills to Monymusk the Seat of Sr Archibald Grant a gentleman I was desirous of seeing, as he is very curious in all the Branches of Natural History, & has a considerable collection in that way as well as in English and Scotch Coins. He is also a very great improver[5] in the farm and garden: About two miles from his house to the west he has made a fine plantation; first you come into an orchard, then to an avenue of firrs with parterres on each side: there is also a pleasant walk by the river; and the hills to the south are covered with trees: on the Mountain to the west an open Arcade is formed in Wood which still beautifyes the Scene. The Mountain called Benachie[6] (m^{tn} of ye Pap) has a high top on which they find Chrystal; They find also Iron Ore on Kern William[7] which yields twelve and a half out of twenty:

[1] Ury.   [2] The battle of Barra, between Bruce and the Comyns.
[3] The family of Burnett have possessed Kemnay since 1688.
  'Mind Kemnay's seat, how beautifully placed,
  With shady woods and flowery gardens graced.'—*Don: a Poem*, 1655.
[4] Burnett of Leys. Gilbert Burnett, the author of the *History of His Own Times*, and son of Robert Burnett of Crimond, afterwards Lord Crimond.
[5] See Paper on Monymusk Improvements, *Spalding Club Miscellany*, vol. ii.
[6] Bennochie is the mountain referred to in the song—
  'I wish I were whaur Gadie rins,
   At the back of Bennochie.'
[7] Cairn William.

About ten miles to the West on a mountain called Noth[1] are all the signs of a Volcano from the burnt stones and Cinders which appear on it, and on Kern Vorn,[2] They have brown chrystals. I saw one which was almost an entire pillar and is about four inches in Diameter. They find a few yellow, and harder than common Chrystal, and some of other colours.

The Parish Church of Monimusk was the Church of the Augustinian Canons regular of St. Andrews. This Priory was built by Gilchrist Earl of Mar in the reign of William the Lyon, and dedicated to the Virgin Mary; it was annexed by James 6th in 1617 to the Bishoprick of Dunblane; The Church appears to have been much ruined, but is now in service and the Saxon Arch remains leading to the Chancel supported by Semicircular pilasters. The Convent is entirely destroyed and was within the enclosure of Sr Archibald's Demesne.

On the 2d in the Evening I came 12 miles to Aberdeen great part of the way in sight of that river[3] which forms Lough Skene, and falls into the Dee on which Aberdeen is pleasantly situated near the Sea, being a tolerable harbour, into which the Ships come up under the Castle, almost close to the town:

The Dee is the ancient Deva, and the town the ancient Devana Texalorum: From the Spey river to this river being the Country of the Texali:

The New Town was burnt by the English in [1336] in the Disputes between Bruce and Baliol, and when it was rebuilt it was called the New Town. The other town which seems to owe its rise to the Cathedral being founded there was then called the old town: The New Town is about half a mile long from North to South, & a quarter of a mile broad, finely situated on an Eminence which ends near the Harbour & taking in the Gardens on the side of the hills is not less than two miles in Circumference; The Castle hill is on the East Side, from which to the South end of the town there is a hanging ground: Catharine hill is to the South which has its name from an

---

[1] For descriptions of those vitreous remains on the Tap o' Noth, see article on 'Vitrified Fort,' by Prof. Pirie, in *Trans. of Aberdeen Philosophical Society;* also 'Notes for the Excursion of the Aberdeen Phil. Soc. to Kildrummy Castle and Tap of Noth, 27th June 1855,' by A[lexander] C[ruickshank], LL.D.].

[2] Cairngorm, celebrated for its beautiful rock crystals.

[3] A small stream or burn.

ancient Chapel: The rest of the town is built on a long hill[1] with fine falling ground on each side of it.

St. Nicholas Church[2] is on the West side, under which are some old Chapels turned into a plumber's shop: It is a plain Gothic building with round pillars and short Capitals of leaves. To the west end of it they have added a New Church in the Pallatian Style designed by Gibbs a native of this town, being built with the pediment and half pediment on each side on the site of the body of the Church; it is of freestone from the Frith of Forth; the foundation being of the grey Granite. It cost £5000 and would have cost more if it had been built of that granite as it is so hard to work. The pillars within are solid square pillars covered with pilasters of the Doric order with galleries all round. At the west[3] end is the seat of the Magistrate, and both the Churches are very well fitted up within. They have a sermon every Tuesday and Thursday at 8 in the morning.

There is a congregation of Seceders, two of nonjurors, and one of papists who meet privately in the night. The English Church have two Chapels, one is the Chapel of Trinity house: The other St. Paul's, built on the London model, with galleries supported by Doric pillars, the pillars above are of the Ionick order, there is a Cupola or small Dome in the Middle, it is decently furnished, and they have a congregation of 1000 people, the other being about 500. Supported only by the collections; but at St. Paul's two ministers have £60 a year each; which the people make up by the collections as at most other places in Scotland.

The Trinity house now called either the Traders[4] Hospital or Beadhouse is said to have been the palace of William the Lyon and Alexander the 2d, the former having founded here a Convent of red friars or Trinitarians: It now serves for the

---

[1] The Gallowgate.

[2] For a lengthy account of this Church see *The Selected Writings of John Ramsay, M.A., with Memoir and Notes*, by Alexander Walker (his literary executor); Portrait and Illustrations by George Reid, R.S.A.; Aberdeen 1871. *Ye Paroch Kirk of Sanct Nicolas of Aberdeen*, by Alexander Walker, 1876 (privately printed). Article and Illustration, 'St. Nicholas Church and Churchyard,' by A. M. Munro, in *Scottish Notes and Queries*, vol. i., July 1887.

[3] Should be east end.

[4] See *Merchant and Craft Guilds, a History of the Aberdeen Incorporated Trades*, by Ebenezer Bain, in the press.

Companies of the Town; They have a large hall[1] in it furnished with old wooden Chairs curiously carved; Beyond this in the fields was the Carmelite Convent, of which there are no remains; it was founded in 1350 by Philip de Arbuthnot ancestor to the present Viscount, and dedicated to the Virgin Mary.

On the site of the Dominican Convent is built Gordon's School or Hospital[2] as it is called for sons of Burgers and Tradesmen; above 40 are lodged clothed, dieted, taught and apprenticed. The founder raised his fortune and left it all to found this house, which is a handsome building in a very fine situation; adjoyning to it is the Latin School and further out of town a large building for an infirmary.

The Grey friars or Observantines was on the spot of the Marischal College, and the Church remains entire; it was founded by the citizens of Aberdeen about 1450. And was afterwards called the Marischal College, as it was founded under James the 6th at the expence of the Earl Marischal.[3]

The fine oblong square called the Cross is from 142 feet to 158 feet broad and near a furlong in length, & is for the most part well built, on one side is a grand old house which belonged to the Earl Marischal; near opposite to it is the town house and the Jayl with a tower over it; and answering to the Town house is a fine inn, all which are built of the grey granite. There is a handsome Conduit[4] in the square, consisting of 16 sides adorned with pillars which support a sort of Entablature, in the freeze of which are Medaliones of the late Kings, and in the middle above is a pillar, if I mistake not, of the Corinthian Order, finely carved and crowned with a gilt capital: beyond that is a part of the Square paved with broad stones, which serves as by way of Exchange for the Citizens to walk on:

It is a great pity that a town which is so finely situated, should be so ill laid out in other parts as to its streets; It was

---

[1] The hall was abandoned in 1847 for the handsome building at the south-east corner of Union Bridge, erected by the seven Incorporated Trades, which are now very wealthy.

[2] See *Robert Gordon, his Hospital and his College*, 1886, by Alex. Walker. In recent years the scope of the Endowment has been much enlarged. See Endowment Commissioners' Report.

[3] George, fifth Earl in 1593.

[4] The Cross in Castle Street, the finest and best preserved Cross in Scotland. See *The Book of Bon-Accord*.

made a Royal Borough[1] in 878 by King Gregory, and King William in 1165 enlarged its privileges. It is computed that there are about 9000 souls in this town, and in the old town and in the Suburbs to both about six thousand.

They show in a Nich made in the wall of a house, an alto relief[2] of the famous Champion Wallis in Armour, and with a sword in his hand.

They have here a great Export of Knit Stockings, Oat Meal, barley, Salmon, and some pickled pork, but not so much as formerly. They make very fine Knit Stockings of all prices, those that are very large, even to five Guineas a pair. They have good Shops to supply the Country round to a considerable distance, especially to the North. And the University spend a considerable sum of money here, there being in both Colleges besides professors about two hundred Students. Ships of 100 Ton come up to the Quay and of 200 into the harbour. The old Town is near a Mile Distant from the New, but most of the way is between houses.

All the Country round the Town is extremely pleasant, being uneven ground, and covered with Corn or garden Stuff and there are several Citizens houses within a mile or two, of the place: The old Town doubtless owes its site to the Bishops' See and the College. The former was first founded at Mortlick[3] in 1010 by King Malcolm on his Victory there over the Danes as observed before. Bp. Nectanus in 1106 removed the See to old Aberdeen and it was enriched by King David; Bp. Henry de Cheyn[4] having taken part with the Cummins, in the dispute about the Crown on their being worsted fled to England, but when things were settled he was very acceptable to Robert Bruce, and out of the arrears due the See, built the fine Gothic bridge of one arch over the Don 72 feet wide and 60 high: Bp. Gordon[5] built the fine bridge of seven arches over the Dee

---

[1] A rather apocryphal antiquity. The probable date of the earliest charter is 1179. The first charter, granted by William the Lion, is to be reproduced in photo-lithography, as the frontispiece to the Burgh Charters which the Town Council are printing under the editorship of Mr. P. J. Anderson, M.A., LL.B.

[2] An old unknown recumbent figure set on end, certainly not Sir William Wallace. The name Wallace Tower is a corruption for the Well-house.

[3] The tradition of the earlier bishopric at Murthlach is now discredited as without historical support.

[4] Henry Cheyne, nephew of John Comyn.

[5] The Bridge of Dee was finished by Bishop Dunbar, not Gordon.

which had been designed by Bp. Elphinston: Bp. Patrick Forbes of 1618 writ a comment on the Revelations:

The body only of the Cathedral[1] remains, which is a very plain Gothic building with two Towers crowned with Steeples at the West End, built very much in the Castle fashion. The Arms of the Bishop and benefactors are blazoned in the Soffit with their Names, and Inscriptions[2] round as in the freeze, which together with the Monumental inscriptions are here inserted.

(North Side.)

I Nectanus II Eduardus III Mattheus de Kynenmond IIII Johannes Prior de Calco V^{to} Adam Clericus Regis Willmi VI Matheus Cancellarius Gilbertus Strivelin VII Radulphus Lambley VIII Petrus Ramsay IX^9 Richardus Potcocht X^9 Hugo Bentrame XI^9 Henricus Chenie XIJ^9 Alexander de Kynenmond XIIJ^9 Willms de la Deyne XIIIJ^9 Johannes de Raite XV^9 Alexander Kyninmond XVI^9 Adam de Tyninghame XVIJ^9 Gilbertus Greynlaw XVIIJ^9 Henricus Lychtoun XIX^9 Ingeramus Lyndesay XX Thomas Spens XXI^9 Robertus Blacater XXIJ Willms Elphynstoun Universitatis et Collegii Conditor XXIIJ^9 Alexander Gordon XXIIII^9 Gavinus Dumbar XXV^9 Willms Steuart XXVI^9 Willms Gordon XXIJ^9 . . .

(East Side.)

Imperatorie Majestatis	Pont. Rom.	Regie Celsitudinis
Fracorum Regis	Sanctiandr Archepi	Sanctissime Margrete
Hispanorum Regis	Glasgueñ Episcopi	Albanie Ducis
Regis Anglorum	Dunkeldeñ Episcopi	Marchiarum Comitis
Regis Danorum	Gavini Aberdoneñ	Moravie Comitis Radulphi
Regis Hūgarie	Moravien Episcopi	Duglasie Comitis
Regis Portugalie	Rossen Episcopi	Angusie Comitis
Regis Aragonie	Brechieñ Episcopi	Marrie Comitis
Regis Cipre	Cathanen Episcopi	Suthurlandie Comitis
Regis Navarre	Candide Case Episcopi	Crasurdie Comitis
Regis Sicilie	Dumblaneñ Episcopi	Huntlie Comitis
Regis Polonie	Lismoren Episcopi	Archadie Comitis
Regis Bohemie	Orchaden Episcopi	Erolie Comitis
Ducis Burbonie	Sodorensis Episcopi	Mariscally Comitis
Ducis Gilrie	Prioris Sancti Andr	Bochtuile Comitis
Veteris Aberdonie	Alm$^{eh^s}$ Universitatis	Nove Aberdonie

(West Side.)

(South Side.)

Murchtlakeensem et Aberdonen ecclesias Cathedrales respective Condidere pro quibus in hac sacra Ede fundati obligantur orare Macolmus Kennedi qui Murchtlakeensem ecclesiam pris Constituit anno Mil^o quarto Cui Successit Duncanus Cui Macolmus Canmoir Anno M^o lvi^b Cui Edgarus Cui Alexander Cui David Seus anno M^o C^o xxiiij qui Murchtlakeensem Ecclesiam ad Aberdoniam transtulit Cui Macolmus Virgo Cui Willms Cui Alexander II^{dus} Cui Alexander 3' Cui Robertus Bruce Anno M^o CC^o quadge^o VI° Cui David Bruce Cui Robertus II^u Cui Robertus III^u [Cui Jacob I Cui Jacob II Cui Jacobus 3 Cui Jacobus IIII Cui Jacobus V Cui Maria Regina].

---

[1] Among the publications which the New Spalding Club, of Aberdeen, has undertaken, is a monograph on the emblazoned ceiling of St. Machar's Cathedral, with coloured reproductions of the escutcheons and other illustrations, edited by Principal Geddes and Mr. Peter Duguid.

[2] The inscriptions were copied by Mr. James Paterson, master of the ancient music school, Old Aberdeen, and appear in Kennedy's *Annals of Aberdeen*, 1818, vol. ii. p. 341. In the main Dr. Pococke and Mr. Paterson agree, but neither is correct.

Epitaphs on Monuments in the Cathedral Church at
Old Aberdeen.

Hic jacet bone Memorie Henricus de Lychtoun[1] utriusq; juris Doctor qui ad Ecclesie Moravien regimen olim esset assumptus ubi Septennio prefuit demum ad istam translatus fuit in qua xviij annis rexit presentisq; Ecclesie fabricam a choro [Statione] scorsum usq; ad summitatem parietum plene astruxit A.D. M°CCCCXL.

   Hic Jacet Nobilis domina Joneta de Lychtoun
   de . . . Mater domini H. ecclesie
   hujus Episcopi qui obiit quinto die februarii
   An° d¹ MCCCCXXXVII) etatis sue lxxxxiiii

Hic Jacet Nobilis vir Walterus[2] . . .
. . . . canonicus licentiatus
qui donavit xxl annuatim Capelariis in choro servi-
entibus pro Missa in vi ferie Celebranda . .
qui obiit . . die Julij . . . anime propiciate Duom amen

   Duodecim pauperibus domum hanc
   Reverendus pater Gavinus Dumbar[3] hujus
   Alme sedis quondam pontifex edificari Jussit
   Anno a Christo Nato 1532 OEΩ ΔΩΞA

Isthuc Oraturus [Deum] Memor precor sis anime salutis Gavini Dumbar Alme Sedis Aberdonensis quondam pontificis hujus Cellule pauperum fundatoris qui apud Sanct. Andream Nature debitum persolvit Sexto Idus Martij Anno a Christo Nato trigesimo primo sesq; Millessimo. At homines quibus alimenta dedit orare tenentur.

   Gloria Episcopi est pauperum opibus providere.
   Ignominia Sacerdotis est propriis Studere divitiis
   Patientia pauperum non peribit in finem.

There is a fine carved pulpit of wood in the Church of the old town : A small part of the cross isle remains, in which are the tombs of some Bishops : There was a large enclosure for the

---

[1] In the north side, or Saint John's aisle, are the remains of the tomb of Bishop Lychtoun, who died in the year 1440. Kennedy's *Annals of Aberdeen*, 1818, vol. ii. p. 345.

[2] There is an effigy neatly cut in stone of a prebendary, in a recumbent position, with an inscription much defaced. Kennedy's *Annals, Aberdeen*, ii. 346. Hic jacet honorabilis vir magister Walterus Ydil— | cancellarius cathen et Brechynen canonic et licenciat | in decretis qui donavit xx sol. annuatim cappellarius in choro | mitibus pro missa in VI feria celebranda qui obiit II | die Julij anno sexagesimo octavo cujus anime propi | ciatur Deus.' Amen. See Orem's *Old Aberdeen* for above inscription and English translations.

[3] For Sketches of the Tomb of Bishop Gavin Dunbar, by Mr. James C. Watt, see *Edinburgh Architectural Association's Sketch Book*, 1887, vol. i. new series.

houses and gardens of the Ecclesiasticks: The Bishop's house was at the East End of the Church, but there are not the least remains of it.

At some little distance to the South of the Close of the Cathedral Bishop Elphistoun founded a College, called the Kings College, but it now commonly goes by the name of the old College; There is a handsome Church belonging to it: The top of the tower is adorned with a Crown, and from the ground near Gordon's hospital it appears like an Ornamental Arch on a hill, no part of the tower being seen: The Church is an oblong square and the body is divided from the Quire by a fine Carved Skreen and Gallery, with a pulpit in it, and under that are two Carved Seats; on the South Side is a small Gallery as for Musick and Covered with a Carpet; The Stalls of the Quire are of the same beautifull Gothic carved Work; Toward the upper end is the founders raised tomb, without inscription, made of plain black stone: and here also is the Monument of Bishop Scougal's Son; who writ the treatise called *The life of God in the soul of man*. He and his father the Bishop, left their books to the Library. This Church is not used except for giving degrees: In the room where they hear Morning and Evening prayer, is a large desk hung with a fine Carpet in which the King's and Bishop Elphinston's arms are worked: They have a very handsome hall where the Students eat who live all in the College, as they do likewise in the New College: They have a good Library, in which are some M.SS. as Hygini Chronicon translated into Latin by Trevisa, Ovid's Metamorphosis and some Church books: They have also a printed book in folio with the Initial letters illuminated, the Type is not very clean; it is Plutarchs lives translated into Latin by Arretinus, some other modern lives are added to it, & there is no mention made of the printer. Doctor Frasier whose picture is in the Library, was a great benefactor by building some parts of the College, as mentioned in an inscription; and here is Johnston's[1] picture, the rival of Buchanan in the translation of the psalms into latin.

In the New College there is likewise a hall to eat in, A

[1] Dr. Arthur Johnston, M.D. See Chambers's *Lives of Eminent Scotsmen:* also *George Jamesone, the Scottish Vandyck*, by John Bulloch, 1885, pp. 61, 100, 119.

'The first in painting, Jamesone shall shine,
As Johnston does in poetry divine.'

library, And a room for giving degrees hung with pictures, and the Names of those gentlemen of fortune who have taken their degrees, and contributed something to the College.[1] In the Library they have some Church M.SS. and a Hebrew Bible with points finely writ, of what age I know not, but by the Ornaments it must have been since Arts revived. The Professors of both Colleges were so polite, as to come in a body and conduct me to their Colleges and the Cathedral, and in the New College I saw Keith's Curious Collection of Silver Scotch Coin which he gave to the College.

The following are the Professors in each College, those who are marked * I had the pleasure to see.

List of the Members of King's College Aberdeen.
 * Doctor John Chalmers Principal.
   Mr John Lumsden—Professor of Divinity.
   Dr James Catanach Professor of Civil Law.
 * Dr John Gregory Professor of Medicine.
   Mr Alexander Burnett Sub-Principal & Professor of Philosophy.
   Mr Thom^s Gordon Professor of Humanity.
   Mr Roderick Macleod } Professors of Philosophy.
 * Mr Thom^s Reid[3]
   Mr John Leslie Professor of Greek.
   Mr George Gordon Professor of Oriental Languages.

List of the Members of the Marischal College.
 * Mr George Campbell Principal.
 * Mr Alexander Gerard Professor of Divinity.
   Mr. Francis Skene Professor of Philosophy.
 * Mr. William Kennedy Professor of Greek.
   Vacant } Professor of Philosophy.
   Vacant } Professor of Philosophy.
   Dr. Alexander Donaldson Professor of Medicine and also of Oriental languages.
   Mr. John Stuart Professor of Mathematics.

Professor Gerard has published a fine treatise on Taste, and

---

[1] Selections from the Records of Marischal College, 1593-1860, — *Fasti Academiæ Marischallanæ,*—by Mr. P. J. Anderson, is expected to be an early volume of the New Spalding Club.   [2] Translated to Edinburgh University.
[3] Translated to Glasgow University; author of *Inquiry into the Human Mind.*

most excellent Sermon on the influence of the Pastoral Office on the Character, in answer to Hume.

Principal Campbell has printed some sermons and Professor Gregory is the 15th of his family who have been professors, almost all of them of Astronomy.

In the New College in the Town I saw the following inscription found on the Roman Wall[1]—

> IMP. CAESAR
> TAELIO HAORI
> ANO ANTONINO
> AVG PIO. P.P.
> VEXILLATIO IQ
> LEC·XX· VA L·VIC·P
> PERMIL P. III

From the Cathedral I went to Seaton, Mr. Middleton's, which was part of the Bishop's Demesne. It is a most delightfull place, the hanging ground about it being very fine. The entrance is by a Walk with a hedge of Elm on each side, through which are some Vistaes opened into the Meadows of the Dairy, and from thence to a branch of the Don, which is here very considerable, also a view of the house, and of the hanging ground covered with wood to the right and left: Over the latter is a Mount planted with firrs on which is a Dome supported with six pillars that belongs to Hermit hall a little tower to the right, the ground is adorned with flowering shrubs, and flowers on each side of the Walks, there being a flat spot below, through which the road winds to the house from the grand entrance to the East, on the other side of which are meadows: There is a hermit's Cell on the hill to the North from

---

[1] 'A stone of the legionary class, measuring 38½ × 34 inches. It was discovered at least 150 years ago, and was for a long time in the possession of the Keith family, at Dunnottar Castle, near Stonehaven; it subsequently became the property of Marischal College, Aberdeen, whose professors presented it to the University of Glasgow in the year 1761.'—Stuart's *Caledonia Romana*, 1852, p. 364, P. xv. Also Hübner's *Inscriptiones Britanniae Latinae*, 1873, p. 205.

which there is a walk to a Kitchen Garden, and a little beyond that is a good view of the Gothic Arch over the River Don. We crossed the road to the Arable part of the farm which is very beautifull.

I saw a Print[1] at Aberdeen relating to a most extraordinary event which happened at the beginning of this Century. At St. Andrews, three Students, two apprentices, and two Schoolboys, took a boat, went on the Sea, and were drove out: The people of St. Andrews could get no boat there, or at Crail, or in any other place, so as to overtake them, they saw the fishing boats, but the fishermen did not see them. They went out on a friday, and thus climbed up on rock to get to some houses for help, and came into Aberdeen on friday following. A Bakers apprentice had taken two roles in his pocket, which helped to support them. And the father of one of the lads being a Silver Smith in Edingburgh, had the Story engraved very handsomely on a Copper plate. They had suffered much in their feet and legs by the Salt water. The two boys were carried ashoar alive, but died soon after.

The Lord Provost of Aberdeen came to see me, and would have Engaged me to dine in their townhouse, but as I could not stay, they insisted on my supping with them, and presented me with the freedom[2] of the town. The Managers of the Established English Church also Entertained me at Dinner, in Return for the offices I had performed in their two Churches. —I am, &c.

[1] This print is preserved in the Municipal Buildings.

[2] Mr. W. Gordon, advocate, Town-Clerk, Aberdeen, has been successful in finding a minute recording the admission of Bishope Pococke as an honorary burgess of Aberdeen (see notes, pp. 3, 47, 168, 182, 183, 253). The Lord Provost was John Duncan of Mosstown.

'Aberdoniae Quarto die Mensis Augusti Anno Domini 1760, In praesentia Magistratuum.

'Quo die Reverendus admodum in Christo Pater Richardus Miseratione Divina, Dominus Episcopus Ossoriensis, Municeps et Frater Guildae praefati Burgi de Aberdeen, In deditissimi amoris et affectus ac Eximae observantiae Tesseram quibus dicti Magistratus illum amplectuntur, Receptus et admissus fuit.'

Thirteen years later Dr. Samuel Johnson was presented with the freedom of the city. He says—'The parchment containing the record of admission is, with the seal appending, fastened to a riband, and worn for one day by the new citizen in his hat.'—*A Journey to West. Islands of Scot.*, 1773. When Dr. Pococke had the freedom of Glasgow conferred on him in 1747, he wore the burgess ticket in his hat (see p. 4).

Letter XLI.

MONTROSE, *Aug^{st} the 6th*, 1760.

DEAR SISTER,—On the 5th I left this most agreeable place Aberdeen alone, which I had not been for above seven weeks. In about two Eng^{sh} Miles I came to the Bridge over the Dee, and after I had ascended the hill for about a mile, I had a fine road through a very stony country for about three miles, and saw the remains of a small Druid temple, and a mile further two more near each other, the stones are about four feet high.

I passed by a Kern and came in twelve miles to Stonehive,[1] a small well built town of about 150 families; I remarked in the way hither first red granite of small red grains and afterwards larger, and a sort of firestone in uneven veins running like Cipolino: The small rivers fall in near the Town in this bay, and there is a pier into which a ship of 100 Ton can be brought: If in bad weather they miss Peterhead which is the most convenient harbour in this part of Scotland, they are brought in here, of which the pilots make considerable profit: They have a Salmon fishery and catch Sea fish, Especially at Cowie, which they lay on places paved with stone in order to dry them without Salt: They Knit Stockings, and have some linnen manufacture. There is an English Chapel and a Congregation of about 300 Persons in and near the town, for it was the Estate of the Earl of Marischal. Barclay a quaker, descendant of him who writ the famous Apology, lives near this place.

On the Sea cliff about a mile from the town is the singular Castle of Dunnotter[2] which belonged to the Marischal family: It is built on a detatched rock of large pebbles cemented together; the Sea does not come to the West side of it; but it might easily be sunk so as to make it a wet fossee at low water. The

---

[1] Stonehaven or Stanehive.

[2] From its situation and extent, Dunnottar Castle forms one of the most majestic ruins in Scotland. Blind Harry has immortalised Wallace's achievement there, when, besieging the castle, he burnt 4000 Englishmen in it. For several views, plans, and historical sketch, see MacGibbon and Ross's *Castellated Arch. of Scot.*, 1887, vol. i. pp. 562-573.

ascent is very steep up to the part where the Wall is low enough to be battered to any purpose from a level on the opposite ground: On each side of the Entrance is an arched room together with some other rooms from which there is an ascent up to the square tower, which is the oldest part; within this is a head of rock extending to the South, on which in the last Civil War they had a battery opposite to that of Cromwel's on the other hill, which we saw with two Embrasures; To the East of this is another building of two rooms on a floor; and beyond that a Room with a large Chimney which extends the whole breadth of it, this is called the Mint and might be also a forge. And in the middle of the Court there is an Entire house as if designed for a part of the family: but the grand and most Modern building is a half H consisting of a brewhouse, bakehouse, Kitchen with a Chimney, likewise the whole breath of it: above is a grand room, a Drawing room & another room from which to the South there is a gallery which extends for about 100 feet in length and 18 broad, over one of the doors to a vault is this inscription—. . . Andrew Barklay.

This Castle did belong to the Crawford family who Exchanged it with the Earl Marischal for a Seat in Fife.[1]

I proceeded through a fine Corn Country to Inver Barvy,[2] Commonly called Barvy, observing an old Church over the Sea Cliff a mile North of the town: here the linnen Manufacture begins and the woolen of Stockings ends: The linnen Manufactures to the North being mostly of Linnen yarn brought from Banff and sent as before mentioned to Nottingham; This is a small Royal borough under Lord Arbuthnot who lives near: it is situated on an eminence over the bay and the river Barvy; it is no harbour, and they have only two or three boats for the Salmon fishery, which is considerable; We saw the porpuses following the Salmon half a league from the Shoar.

We went on the 6th, and came through a fine Country six miles to North Esk which we forded, but after rain it is a rapid river and broad; it rises out of the Mountain of Benochieh;[3] we came two miles to Montrose on South Esk which rises out

---

[1] The exchange was made between Lord Lindsay of Byres, and Sir William Keith, about 1382-92, for Struthers in Fifeshire.

[2] Inverbervie.   [3] See note 6, p. 200.

of the same Mountains, the Town of Brechin being situated on it, we travelled most of the way on an old beach which seems to have been made by the Sea and the western Strand that might anciently have been much deeper than it is at present. Montrose is most pleasantly situated on an Eminence that falls every way in a beautifull manner, one street about half a mile in length, extending along the heighth of it from the gate down to the Pier, there being only two or three lanes that stretch from it to North and South, the Street is broad and well built except that most of the houses are in that bad style of building with the Gabel Ends to the Street. They have one Church; and in the green to the East is a handsome Chapel for the Congregation of the Church of England, which consists of about 1000 Souls. The Seceders are here of two sorts called Burghers and Antiburghers and each have a separate Meeting house. There was a Convent of Dominicans or black friars here founded in 1230 by Sr Alan Durward.

It is said that the friars were translated to an hospital near the City built by Mr. Patrick Panter, and enquiring for the Convent I was informed that it was a little to the north of the town at Muir Montrose which is a house belonging to Mr. Kennedy where foundations of buildings have been discovered, and under the threshold of a Door, an Urn with a utensil of gold worth about twelve pounds, which from the Description answers to the fibula in this shape the like of which has been often found in Ireland.[1]

This I conclude to have been the hospital from which they were brought to their old Convent by permission of parliament in 1524, a piece of history probably not to their honour.

They have here an export of Corn and Salmon, and three vessels employed in the herring fishery, which I have been assured does not succeed, no more than the Whale fishery, and

---

[1] In 1757, Dr. Pococke communicated 'an account of some antiquities found in Ireland' to the London Society of Antiquaries; and in 1773 (eight years after his death) it was published in the *Archæologia*, vol. ii. pp. 32-41, Pl. iii. Fig. 2, together with plates of twe ve of these articles. *Vide* article on 'Antique Gold Ornaments found in Ireland prior to 1747,' by W. R. Wilde in *Trans. Royal Irish Academy*, 10th Feb. 1862.

that both will be laid down, as carried on in the East and North, and they do affirm the same as to any other fishery in the East. But since I left the North, great shoals of herrings came on that shoar:

They have fine granaries here, and such malt houses as I never saw elsewhere, they are round, about twenty feet in Diameter, and roofed in a particular manner so that the segment of a circle ends at top in a point on two sides, and on the other two sides it is a roof which forms an inclined plain in the common way. They have small buildings called Cobles in which they wet it, made up with thin flag, with which their houses are covered.

They have here a manufacture of sail cloth and other cloth, and linnen yarn. Especially dyed threads, and for these purposes, they import a great quantity of flax from Riga and Narva in Russia: The Castle hill is to the West of the town near the river and there is another hill to the North of the piers which was made by the Cleaning of the harbour. They have some curious pebles at Alessis haven,[1] two miles South of Montrose.—I am, &c.

LETTER XLII.

GLAMIS, *August 7th*, 1760.

DEAR SISTER,—I left Montrose in the afternoon and crossing a skirt of the strand came into a most beautifull Country, and passed by a fine grove of Firr trees belonging to Colonel Scot whose house[2] is happily situated on the Eminence. We then rode by Mr. Erskins's of Dun much the same situation, and came to Dun Quarry, which is a mixture of limestone and sand, and as I apprehend a Marl or rotten stone good for manure. At the end of the Strand I saw what was called old Montrose and New Magdalene's and near it is a Baronet of the name of Kennedy:[3] I think there is a great probability that the Sea has left these parts, and that anciently Montrose was here situated, and the river below, a good harbour.

[1] Usan, formerly called Ulysses-haven. [2] Hedderwick House.
[3] Sir D. Carnegy, Bart., Kinnaird, great-grandfather of the present Earl of Southesk.

MONTROSE, BRECHIN.

We came to Brechin five miles from Montrose finely situated with Glyns on three sides, and to the South of one of them, is Lord Penmure's house [1] on the height over the river with trees growing out of the perpendicular rocks: it commands a beautifull view of the windings of the river and of the bridge: A large house and offices were built to an old Castle by the late Lord, who forfeited in 1715, and the present Lord who is a General in the Army has been made an Earl of Ireland.

This was a Bishop's See but first a Convent of Culdees, and K. David about 1150 founded the See: The Cathedral is situated over the glyn between the Town and Lord Penmure's. The Choir seems to be coeval with the first foundation having narrow Gothic single windows and semicircular pilasters between them, and one on each side of them half the way down: Here is a round tower [2] like these in Ireland at some distance from the Quire, but the body of the Church is built to it so as to cover about a quarter of it: a step appears as a basement to it within the Church, which is only three inches and a half broad, and probably there was one if not two more: a door is

The Round Tower at Brechin.

[1] Lord Panmure, Brechin Castle, now the Earl of Dalhousie's.
[2] The Brechin Tower has been frequently figured. See Gordon's *Itinerarium Septen.* 1727, p. 165, Pl. 62; *Archæologia*. vol. ii.: Pennant's *Tour Scot.*,

broke into it from the Church, and the first door is built up: a view of it is here seen; two bells hang in it, and there are six ladders to as many floors which are laid only half way over and fixed on the projections at every story; the door way lighted the ground floor, and that next above; a window on the East side lighted another floor: one above that lighted two other together with the four windows in the top part. The door is made with a plain moulding, the Lintel is adorned at each end with Sculpture, and about the middle on each side is a figure of a Saint: on the Crown of the Arch is a Crucifix, and there are about 80 tiers of hewn stone to the Apex, which is an Octagon, and the Angles of the base of it project; There are four upright pointed windows in it, and I suppose this pyramidal part is made by the stones projecting within and cut in an inclined plane in the same manner as the Steeple of the Church is, according to the information I had as I observed the same, at the small spire at Restennot,[1] the top part of which is solid for some feet and it is also an Octagon.

There is an English Church here consisting of 350 Souls in and about the town: There was a nonjuring Congregation and now that there is a licenced Minister, many of them come to the Chapel: There is a Congregation of Seceders here. They have a manufactory of linnen and several shops, & it is the great thoroughfare to the North: The town is much improving in buildings of freestone. In all these parts they cover their houses with thin flaggs. They have a town house and a Modern Cross,[2] for sale of Corn, both of hewn stone: It is a royal Borough under Lord Penmure.

Here is a Clergyman of the Church of England Mr. Norman Seivwright[3] who has composed a book of the Theory of Church Musick, and another of the practical part with psalms set to tune; and is writing a hebrew grammer both which he proposes to publish; he is a Native of Aberdeenshire, and a man of great genius and application.

I set forward on the 7th and came in a mile to the Esk which

1772, part 2, p. 161; *Hist. of Brechin*, by D. D. Black, 2d ed., 1867, p. 239; *Scot. in Early Christian Times*, 1881, by Joseph Anderson, LL.D., p. 38.

[1] Restenet.   [2] Removed in 1767.
[3] Seivewright left five MSS.—a Hebrew Grammar; Supp. to *Eccles. Hist. Scot.*; *Church of England Defended*; and two musical pieces.

we forded. I was shewn to the North a hill situated between two lesser hills; it is called Catherthun;[1] by way of a rampart, there is a heap of stones round it; it is in an oval figure about 80 yards long and 35 wide. There are signs of a wall in the middle, and a fossee all round the hill as I was informed: We saw also a pleasant place called Caristown the seat of Mr. Skene of Skene.

This country is very fine, the plain being about three miles wide; we crossed a hill which ends about two or three miles to the west, and then the plain may be about six miles wide. On the hill we saw Aberlemno Crosses;[2] two of which are adorned with Sculptures: on one is St. Cathern's Cross with some ornaments of Sculpture (viz.) Angel on each side of it; on the back part men on horseback hunting a stag are represented: They are said to be erected on some Victory over the Danes as was Camus Cross between Glames and Lord Penmure.

We came down to the Monastery of Restennot[3] which belonged to the Cannons Regular of St. Augustine; It is a peninsula formed by a Lough and Morass: This Lough[4] and that of Forfar abound in perch, Jack and Eel.

Here is a fine Saxon Square tower which seems to have been a Detatched building; for the body of the parish Church is evidently built to it; an octangular spire is practised on it, in a very peculiar manner; there is a Cornice round it, from which each of the two sides forms an inclined plane in a line with the Spire, which is built on it, and the other sides are formed by taking off the same breadth from the Square, and ending in a point where the regular Octagon is formed, at which place there is a window answering to the middle of each side of the square tower. The Quire is on the model of that of Brechin, there is very likely more of this Church remaining. The records and valuable effects of Jedburgh Abbey were kept here, it being defended as 'tis said by a drawbridge.

I came in a mile to Forfar a poor illbuilt small town of farmers, innkeepers, and linnen Manufacturers: A great

---

[1] White Caterthun Hill-Fort,—more probably the Wirren Hill.
[2] Figured and described in Anderson's *Scot. in Early Christian Times*, 1881, pp. 56 and 57.
[3] Priory of Restenet—a ruin. [4] Loch now drained.

quantity of flax grows in this Country, especially towards Glames: The people spin and sell the yarn to the weavers who vend the green unbleached coarse cloth to the Merchants: they export it to London, and it is mostly sent to North America: Here is a Church with a Saxon door and small narrow windows tho' but a mean building.

Two miles more through an exceeding rich Country brought us to Glames which is a poor market town: They have a pretty good Manufacture of Linnen: This place is remarkable for the grand Seat of Lord Strathmore: It was given in 1376 by King Robert the first of the Steuarts with his Daughter to John Lyon Lord Glames Chancellor of Scotland: It seems originally to have been a Castle[1] only of three floors in shape of an L. Patrick Lord of Glames in 1686 added two wings, and the round tower in the Angle with a hollow pillar in the middle of it, in which the clock weights hang, and the stairs round it are about 7 feet long, so that in front it makes this shape, the Castle part being two stories higher than the wings: There is a good hall in it, and many Rooms. From the leads, there is a very fine prospect, and to the North East in a little Vale between the Mountains, is a hill, the top of which has been fortified,[2] it is called the Law of Denune: We saw also into that Glyn between the hills in which Dunhold[3] stands, that is sixteen miles distant. At all the Angles of this house are sort of projecting Closets practiced like towers, which are mostly crowned with round pyramids, and so are two round towers on the outer arches of the Whole, which gives it a most uncommon Gothic appearance. There is an avenue to the house of four or five rows of trees, three quarters of a measured mile long: the first row being firr trees, and the second Lime. The fields on each side are divided by rows of trees after the manner of St. James's Park; and the plantations have a very grand appearance: The present Lord's Uncle was killed in battle for the Pretender in 1715 after he had entertained him here in his house, his death in battle saved his

---

[1] Glamis Castle. See Pennant's *Tour Scot.*, 1772, part 2, p. 170; MacGibbon and Ross's *Castel. Arch. of Scot.*, 1887, vol ii. pp. 113-125.

[2] Denoon Castle.

[3] Dunhead, a stronghold near the ravine's Black Den and Den of Gwynd.

estates. This Earl's Grandfather, if I mistake not, was made first Earl of Strathmore having his title from this great Vale, which is reckoned to extend from Stonehive to Sterling.

It is supposed that all the great Vales of Scotland extend in parallel lines from North East to South West as this does.

The Great Glyn at Inverness & the Kyle of Dornock are the principal. And that of Inverness is in a straight line & not a curve as represented in the old Maps, & from the hill at Inverness I saw the whole length of it.

The present Lord is travelling abroad and is at present in Spain. They show an arched room in the Castle in which they say Malcolm the 2d was murdered; and near the Church is a stone eight feet high and four feet broad with a Cross[1] cutt in relief, and the figure of two men with hatchets or other implements with which 'tis supposed Malcolm was killed and on the other side a fish, as an emblem of the lake, in which they say the Murderers were drowned, when they fled; and that this stone was erected in memory of this Event.

There is Marl in the bottom of the Lough, which they raise and carry off in flat bottomed boats.—I am, &c.

Letter XLIII.

DUNDEE, *August 9th*, 1760.

DEAR SISTER,—On the 8th I went 8 miles to Lord Penmure's:[2] The first half of the way through an exceeding fine Country, the latter a mixture of Heath and Corn: We came to Hynde Castle on an eminence which is only an old tower, the walls of which were six feet thick & twelve feet square within; there was a door on one side, and a Window on the three other sides. I observed that great stones were laid on the sod without any other foundation, as in most of the Antient Castles.

Lord Penmure's is a fine situation commanding a view of the Sea, the Firth of Tay, and of a fine Country everyway.

[1] Engraved in Pennant's *Tour*, 1772, part 2, Pl. xviii., p. 166.
[2] Panmure House, Panbride, near Carnoustie. See Warden's *Angus or Forfarshire*, 1885, vol. v. p. 57.

There is a grand avenue to the house, to the right and East is a mount, and a Plantation of firr Trees with winding Walks through it: There is a Lawn before the house, which was built at the latter end of the last Century: A building to the West side of the Lawn seemed to be a greenhouse: One Vista to the West is adorned with a ruin through which a pillar appears, and to the North of it is a star of Eight Walks with a pillar in the Centre: There is also a pretty Mount to the west of the house with a Statue on it, and one to the North East on which another is to be placed. The rest of the demesne consists of fields finely planted, and hills at a little distance covered with firrs.

I came two miles and a half to the north east to the Shoar, and travelled as much further to Aberbrothick; commonly called Arbrooth, a flourishing town on the North side of the bay, on the river Brothock or Brothe, it consists of about 1000 houses built of red freestone which make one street half a mile long, and two other Small Streets: They have a great trade in linnen yarn, Sail Cloths, Osnaburgs[1] and other linnens, and have formed a very pretty basen by the help of three or 4 piers into which a vessel of 100 Tons can come: They have a Congregation of Seceders about 50 of them, and of the Congregation of Four (as they call it which are Nonjurors) there is a very small number: It is a royal Borough under Lord Penmure.

There are ruins here of a famous Abbey[2] founded by William the Lyon in 1178 to Thomas a Becket: It is called Monasterium Baiounse and by Demster Aberbredock-Knidel: King John made the inhabitants free of all places in England except London: They had a Mitred Abbot who gave the inferior orders: The Church and especially the West End was Exceeding Grand, they are all high Gothic Windows, three of them at

---

[1] Osnaburghs, or Oznaburgs. 'The name given to a coarse linen cloth manufactured in Angus, from its resemblance to that made at Osnaburgh in Germany.'—Jamieson's *Scot. Dict.* 'The first manufacturer of the cloth called Osnaburghs . . . was John Wallace, merchant, and some time provost of Arbroath, who began that business in 1740.'—*Old Stat. Ac. Scot.*, vol xii. p. 177.

[2] See Pennant's *Tour*, 1772, Part 2, pl. xiv.; *Arbroath and its Abbey—Aberbrothock*, by D. Miller, 1860.

the East End: In the Cross isle are two stories of flat Gothic arched Niches, and a passage over them in the Wall, & over that there is a large round window: There were eight Windows in the body, and probably as many Arches: The grand front consisted of two high towers supported by buttresses, on which and the Walls in front an octangular solid building is raised, which is crowned with a round kind of pedestal probably designed for Statues. Over the door are three single windows, and over them again a round window of great size (if I mistake not) taking the window frame in, thirty feet in diameter. The North side of the Church is entirely destroyed: to the East of the South transept was the Chapter house overarched, and a story over it probably destined to the keeping their Archives: In the Chapter house are six flat Niches on three sides with pillars supporting the Arches, under which the Members doubtless sat: Adjoyning to that transept was a grand building, and a door from it to the Gallery in the Church; this might be the Abbot's Lodgings. A large Building joyns on to the South West Angle of the Church, which might be the Appartment for Strangers, and to the west of this is a grand gateway consisting of four flat arches, within which is a great door, and a small one Contiguous to it. This seems to have been the grand Entrance to the Abbey; and in the town I saw a fine wall which I suppose was the Enclosure of this religious house. John Hamilton second Son of the Duke of Chatelherault, was the last Commendatory Abbot, afterwards made Marquis of Hamilton: In favour of James Marquis of Hamilton son to John it was made a temporal Lordship in 1608, and then belonged to Lord Dysart who sold it to Patrick Maule, Lord Panmure, Gentleman of the bedchamber to James the VIth, with Advowsons of 34 parish Churches.

I proceeded from Arbroth all the way by the Sea side: passing several little fishing villages, most of them near rivulets, which form coves for their boats. We saw the light house at Buttonesshead which appears like a pillar: The prospect that way is not very agreeable, as there is a range of sandy Hillocks towards this point. Further on the small villages are thick, and the hanging ground to the North is beautifull.

Within three miles of Dundee, I saw Broughty Castle on a point to the South, as soon as we had turned to the West from Buttuness;[1] and a little beyond it to the North is Fort Hill,[2] where there seemed to be remains of a Modern fortification. We had also a plain view of St. Andrews to the South West of us as soon as we turned Westward, the land of Fife extending a considerable way to the East of it towards the Frith of Forth.

There was much Smoak over Dundee, and dark clouds to the West, and an appearance of a large segment of a circle beyond the tower which we took for a mountain, but going on, & the appearance being very near an entire circle, it looked something like the Moon in Eclypse: & seeing light through it, I conjectured it might be some kind of Ventilator; it afterwards proved to be a new invented windmill of which I shall have occasion to say something more.

We came to Dundee: The bay is called the Frith of Tay. This Town is rather above it on Tay River, well situated on a head of land where they have made what they call a Harbour or rather a Bason with two great piers, one to the East, the other to the west, and a pier in front with an entrance on each side: here a ship of 500 tons can lye.

The town consists of one street that runs paralel with the river, which widens in two places and forms two sort of oblong squares: in one of them is the town house, a handsome Fabric of freestone built by Adam the Architect. It is in the whole about half a mile long, another street stretches westward from the Quay, and another extends from the Square westward for a quarter of a mile; the two squares are handsome and so is the last Street; but the other parts of the town are narrow and not kept in the best manner: It was walled round, and there is a small hill to the North West called Windmill hill, which might be formerly the site of a Castle.

They say Edward longshanks as they always call Edward the 1st of England, burnt the town; and Monk in the last Civil War cut a regiment to pieces here, who broke their parole, put many of the inhabitants to the sword, and set fire to some parts of the town, having taken it by storm; & this fright'n'd all Scotland:

[1] Buddon Ness.   [2] Drumsturdy-moor-law.

The Parish Church must have been very large. The square tower[1] is now standing, which is very handsome, & rises about 100 feet high to a Gothic Balcony, the building is carried about 50 feet higher, with battlements in the same style, I believe it is 50 feet square at bottom, exclusive of the Buttresses: The Cross Isle and East End of the Church consist of plain low single Gothic windows. There is a singular cornice all round: The transcept is divided into two modern Kirks, and the East End into a third. They have a Library in their Vestry which consists of a good number of books: In this town are Seceders, and Glassites[2] so called from one Glass of the town, who being deprived, on what occasion I did not learn, set up this Congregation, which is very strict & holds some different tenets from the other Seceders. The Congregation of the English Church consists of about 450 in and about the town. They have a neat Chapel and Organ of which Dr. Heyington a very eminent Musitian (who took his degree in Musick at Oxford and Cambridge and is about 80) is the Organist. Most of the Gentlemen in the Country are of this Congregation. There are about the same number of Nonjurors, but the greater part of them are women.

The black friars or Dominicans were to the North where the burial place now is. They were founded by And^w. Abercromby a Burgess of the town. Jno. Grierson much esteemed for his learning, and many years Provincial of the order professed here. To the west of the harbour are ruins, where the hospital now is which place is called Monkshill, and probably belonged to the Conventuals of St. Francis founded by Dervorgilla Daughter of Lord Galloway, and mother of John Baliol, King of Scotland: There is no tradition where the Friars of the Trinity were founded by James Lindsay about 1392; no more than of a Nunnery of Clares.

They have a great trade here in Sail Cloth, Osnaburgs and other linnens, which is much Encreased of late, as that trade in Germany has been obstructed by the war: The houses here are 4 or 5 stories high.

[1] The tower of St. Mary's Church forms the frontispiece to Maxwell's *History of Old Dundee*, 1884.
[2] Formed originally by the Rev. John Glass on his being deposed from the charge of Tealing.

To the west of the town Mr. Robertson of Fife has in conjunction with a Company, built a most extraordinary Windmill of his own invention, the appearance of which I observed was so extraordinary under those particular circumstances which may rarely happen. The Diameter of the room is 30 feet, the wall is six feet thick and I believe about twenty high, on this by triangular Machinery is fixed a Wheel with three radii 56 feet and 8 inches in Diameter. There are 24 radii more which are strengthened by a piece of timber fixed at one end and to the axle of the Wheel; to Each of which a Vane of wood is fixed of half its length, and another between them, forty-eight in all, according as the Wind requires; so that if the wind is high they are fixed more upright to the wind, that they may take less of it: The grand wheel is moved round properly to the wind by a cogwheel, which turns in a hoop of iron fixed horizontally all round the top of the tower: on which the whole machinery belonging to the wheel turns and moves the wheel with it: The Machinery of the wheel itself is most like the wheel of a Ventilator: It turns four Mills, for barley, oats, wheat, and is of power to move a much greater number: As the Machine must be turned to the wind that it may pass through the vanes, set with the edges opposite to the wind; the question is how it will stand stormy nights when the wind often veers about, and may take it every way in a very short time.—I am, &c.

LETTER XLIV.

DUNKELD, *August* 14*th* 1760.

DEAR SISTER,—I set out on the 9th and a quarter of a mile from the town passed by Dudop an old house of the Duke of Douglas's, built about a Court with a round tower at each corner. We went on and instead of crossing over to the North side of the hill, we continued on the South side by Lord Gray's and by Fowlis Church which is a very fine piece of Masonry of hewn freestone: There is a small round window at the East End and on the north side a small high window practiced with three segments of a circle at the top, and I suppose the same on the South Side; we then came over some heathy hills, the south end of which is called Dulsinan[1] on which was Macbeth's habitation :

We Descended into the fine plain and came to Couper which is a poor small town, in which they have a little Manufactory of linnen : There was an Abbey of Cistercians founded by Malcolm 4th in 1164, only a small part of what I take to be the east end of the Church is standing.

We went on and forded the large river which falls into the Tay a little lower and had a prospect of most beautifull hills a very little way to the north, and travelled in view of the Tay going to the North west, and passed near the Seat of Delvin[2] a most charming situation on the high ground over the river, and commanding a fine view of these hills : The old name of this place is Inchstrathill[3] which is said to be the ancient city of Cullen, that consisted of many strong Castles belonging to the Picts, who burnt it, that the Romans might not make a fortification of it :

We crossed a low hill, came in between rocky mountains, and passed by a very pleasant place Gairn Tully[4] belonging to Sir John Stuart finely planted with firrs. Here the hills appear in such a manner, that a traveller can hardly imagine that there is anything beyond them but rocky mountains : But as we entered in between them, we found ourselves in a narrow Valley with high Mountains on each side ; and a little before we came to Dunkeld had a view of it situated in between these Grampian Mountains which open for some way and form a kind of Amphitheatre through which the Tay runs.

The Duke of Athol has a Seat here and I did myself the honour to wait on his grace and the Dutchess, and staid at their house meeting with a most polite reception.

The town is small but the buildings are improving ; we had come from Angus into Perthshire where we crossed the river . . .[5] after leaving Couper.

This Shire is divided into Athol, Glenshie, Broadalbin, Stormont, Strathern, Gourie, & Monteith.

---

[1] Dunsinan.   [2] Delvine, the seat of Sir Alex. Muir-Mackenzie, Bart.
[3] Inchtuthil, *Old Stat. Ac.*, vol. ix. pp. 504-7.
[4] Should be Murthly, belonging to Sir —— Stewart, Bart., of Grandtully.
[5] River Isla.

Dunkeld was a Bishop's See: Constantine the IIId King of the Picts at the instance of Adamnanus founded a monastery here in 729 of Kildies or Culdees or Colentes Deum who had wives, and only abstained, when they ministered. David King of Scots expelled the Culdees and founded a Bishop's See here about 1127; The Diocese of Argyle was at first in this See, but Bishop John Scot[1] got that Diocese to be separated from it about 1201.

Bishop Lauder of 1452 built a bridge over Tay, near his house, & part of an arch of it is seen; his lands on the north side of Tay he got erected into the barony of Dunkeld, and those on the south into the barony of Aberlady, and purchased See houses or Lodgings for the See, in Edinburgh, and in Perth. Bp. Douglas of 1516 translated Virgil's Æneid, and writ several poems which are much admired.

The walls of the Cathedral remain entire; a tower is built to it on the south[2] side of the west door, as if the design was to build another answering to that. The body of the Church consists of seven Arches on each side and over them are seven circular windows above the roof of the isles, with Gothic ornaments like those at Westminster Abbey, except that the bottom of them is in a straight line whereas those at Westminster are a segment of a circle: In the Quire all the windows are different which was the taste of one age;[3] This part is fitted up for the Kirk; to the North of it, is the small Chapter house which is the burial place of the Duke's family, over which there is a room that might serve for the Archives: The Bishop's house they say was to the South of the Church by the river close to the site of the old bridge:

A little to the North of the Church is the Duke of Athol's house, which is not large. But as there is a warm winter situation, the Duke has built very extensive offices and the finest Kitchen I believe in Britain; Behind them is a very handsome Kitchen Garden; on the east side of which is a long narrow hill beautifully shaped into walks, and at the end of it over the avenue to the house is a Statue of the Gladiator; on the South and West side of the house is a Lawn, from which

---

[1] See p. 90. [2] Should be north side.
[3] See Billing's *Baronial and Eccles. Antiq. of Scot.*

the road is crossed to the wood and fields, that are divided by a high road which comes round by the End of the Church, and there is a communication made between them by a bridge over the road; this wood consists of two walks, one above terminated to the East by a view of the Church, the other is close to the river, and both end to the East in a lawn which is before the green house; and to the West at a bowling green: There are two ways to the upper part which chiefly consists of Corn fields, one to the right leads up to the farmhouse, in which there is a handsome room with a fine bow window in it, the other directly behind the house; from the latter, one way, leads to a fine piece of water on this Eminence, on the further side of which are houses for poultry, and a room to dine in: another way to the left, by an upper and lower walk, leads to a turret called the fort, below which are cross walks, as to fortify the hill, and at the bottom a beautifull Chinese house, with the Pheasantry and Dovery near it for Turtles: This is opposite to the bowling green on the river: From the fort there is a walk round to the water, and another from that down to the road by the Chinese house: To the West of the water ends a chain of high rocky hills, which run from the North East, and there is one single hill to the south of it with a remarkable summit, and a stone on it called the King's Table; beyond this in the side of these hills is a natural Cave in the rock, and whoever sits in it sees only the river and the beautifull fields and woods over it, no part of the hills appearing, which has a fine effect.

A small mile to the South West on the other side of the river and just over a Cascade of the river Brand,[1] Mr. Murray[2] the Duke's Son in Law, has made a hermitage[3] on the rocks which hang over the water, commanding a view of the Cascade which is near and falls about twenty feet: A very handsome room is built with a window towards the fall, the Garden is

---

[1] The Braan.

[2] Captain John Murray, M.P. for Perthshire, son of Lord George Murray (who commanded in the '45). He succeeded his uncle as third Duke in 1764, and was the great-grandfather of the present Duke.

[3] 'Johnson [Innkeeper at Inver, the Boat of Dunkeld] told me yt the Bp. of Ossory spent several Hours in this delightful Hermitage, and wrote a good deal in it.'—Bishop Forbes's *Journals*, ed. by Rev. J. B. Craven, 1886, p. 241.

made within the precincts of the hermitage, with flower beds and borders about the rocks, which appear in different altitudes, and there are also two little basins of water. Just over the river towards the Cascade is a Seat formed in the rock with some grotesque work in it, and water works, which with the basins are supplied from a reservoir above where there is a mineral water, and another towards the river, of Steel and Sulphur, if I do not mistake, which has been lately used Medicinally. About half a mile higher up is a greater fall of water:

In returning we went on half a mile to the North West descending through the wood to the Tay, having a beautifull small hill to the right covered with oats; and turning to the right before you come to this is a way leading to Belville, a hill which commands the finest prospect of all, with a winding way to the top of it. We returned down by the river to the ferry. They have a fine freestone here, but no limestone nearer than Fife and Blair: They use the former brought by sea to Perth.

A little below Dunkeld is Burnham[1] hill mentioned in Shakespeare's Tragedy of Macbeth, there are ruins on the top of it said to be the house of Malcolm. They find curious pebbles in these hills, and also a sort of Asbestus, & a sparr mixed with a black mica, which when pounded, serves for sand. They found a head of a spear in brass about a foot long in the ground within a circular foundation of a building supposed to be a burial place.

I saw here the wood of the shrub broom which is a most beautifull mixture of browne and white, much like the rose wood when it is worked and polished. I here also saw a room wainscoted with Larch boards from trees of the Duke's own planting,[2] it is white and full of knots which add to the beauty of it: 'twas cut green and does not warp: and being put on the fire green it extinguishes the fire and does not easily burn as they say, even when it is dry.—I am, &c.

[1] 'Till Birnam wood remove to Dunsinane.'—*Macbeth*.
[2] Larch, first imported from the Tyrol in 1737.

LETTER XLV.

BLAIR OF ATHOL, *August* 18, 1760.

DEAR SISTER,—On the 15th I set out with the Duke for the Blair of Athol 16 computed and 20 measured miles, with milestones all the way. We travelled eight miles by the river Tay to the place where the Tumel falls into it. Here there is a road by crossing both rivers to go from Blair to Tay Mouth 12 miles: the road from Dunkeld to Tay Mouth being on the other side of the Tay:

We travelled about six miles further to the place where the Garry falls into the Tumel, by which river we went a mile, and came to the famous pass of Gillicranky,[1] which is a road made on the side of the hill over the river, there being no passage on the other side: the road is a mile long and then the Country opens again: King William's Army under General Mackay[1] marched through this pass, and just after they had entered the plain engaged on an eminence to the North, at a house to the right, where they were defeated by the Highlanders under Lord Dundee who was killed: the King's troops fled up the hills to the South and the Highlanders came down to the Baggage in the plain which they plundered and returned home, which happened in July 1689.

In this road are several small Druid temples: In about three miles more passing over the Tilt we came to Blair situated between an Amphitheatre of hills beyond which the tops of mountains appear to the North-west and East, the ground is rather uneven, but there are fine meadows on the flat ground to the South and South West towards the river: On an Eminence to the West is a summer house wainscoted with Larch, and on a little hill beyond it there is a small Obelisk, and a grove of firr trees on another beyond that: all round the house is lawn; and the offices of the house and stables are so disposed

---

[1] Killiecrankie. See *Life of Lieut.-Gen. Hugh Mackay of Scourie*, by John Mackay.

to the South East in separate compartments as to appear very well from the house and from every other part.

To the North of the house runs a small stream over which are 3 or four bridges that appear in view at once and between them a Chinese rail, and close to this a square tower is built for a Clock: Higher up to the North West this stream passes through a Vale, which is most beautifully planted with many sorts of American trees; This is called Diana's Grove, from a Statue of her with a Stag on a rising ground, from which there are eight walks; below in the wood is the temple of Fame, and on an Eminence in another part are the statues of three boys supporting a basket of flowers and fruit: and there is a walk all round the grove, and a great plantation for near a mile on each side of the gully, which may be made very fine: In this grove there is a walk of tall Larch trees cut up within like a hedge.

To the North and North East are three little hills, on that to the West is a pleasant summer house that commands a fine view of the whole, which consists of about 1200 Acres. On the middle hill is an Urn; on the other to the East is an Obelisk with a gilt ball on the top of it, round this is a building with seats in it which I believe will be removed: This enclosure with several fields continues on to the Tilt which runs in a deep rocky Gully called a Den, with several Cascades [1] in it, and a rivulet tumbles down from the East, over which, at a hamlet on the top of the hill is a bridge, from which there is a waterfall between rocks in a bed rather deep, and adorned with wood; it falls from several rocks in many breaks, and the whole may be 300 perpendicular feet; but is not seen altogether, except perhaps after great rains. All this rock is a blewish limestone:

There is a riding to drive round this part, the three hills and the Kitchen garden which is to the North East between the middle hill and Eastern hill, situated in a valley; in the whole length of which Kitchen garden, the Duke has made a fine piece of water, with six or seven islands and peninsulas in it, two of which are for the swans to breed on, having thatched houses built on them for that purpose, and the wild ducks

[1] Pennant's *Tours Scot.*, 1769, p. 118; 1772, pt. 2, p. 59.

breed on the islands: The Garden is formed on a gentle declivity on each side all walled round. There is a pidgeon house at one Angle and a Gardeners house at another, and at the south end is a semicircular Summerhouse which is all glass in the front; In the walk leading to this and on each side of the Cross Walk, are about twenty grotesque figures in lead, and painted, which have a very pretty effect in that situation, at each end is a parterre of many sorts of perennial flowers; the garden is about 1200 feet long, the breadth is not the same but may be from 4 to 500 feet. This is the most beautifull Kitchen garden I believe in the world:

To the East of it is a fine walk with a Colossal Statue of Hercules in it, the walk extends a good way round, most of the fields are fenced with very broad double ditches, and plantations on them, and there are some plantations made in the fields to break the view, being planted in manner of Clumps. The most beautifull prospect is to Kily Cranky, near which there is a grove, and beyond that a hill adorned with Corn fields and groves, or broad divisions planted with trees, which has altogether a most striking effect.

The house consists of a large high pile of building with dairy offices and a farm house to the west of it, and a long chain of building of two floors to the East extending about two hundred feet in length with a return that stretches on to the East end of the house near the whole breadth of it; in this latter is a fine Dining room, within it a Drawing room which belongs to a bed chamber; To this you enter from the ground, the other consists of a common drawing room, and five bed chambers, with a smaller room to each of them in which is a bed for a servant. But under both these which form an L the ground falls so, that there are offices for servants to which there are entrances from without at the lower end. And yet the ground rises in such a manner that from the upper floor of these, there is a flight of stairs of several steps to the ground rooms of the grand house, most part of which consists of four floors; The ground floor is arched for offices of Different kinds, & the Duke has a Dining room in it and one room designed for his Study, but never used. This house consists of three parts. The old tower of the Cummins, of one room and three

Closets on a floor, one of which is in a turret, built at the back of it, and probably served as a staircase; There are two floors built with a bedchamber in each: it did consist of four more stories, which the Duke took down. To this an Ancestor of the Duke about the time of James the 5th built a room 52 feet long and twenty seven broad, and only began a fabric for two very fine rooms on a floor which was raised but one story; these are now finished with Closets to them. Up one pair of steps is a most beautifull large dining room, adjoyning to it a Drawing room, and beyond that a bed Chamber; over this the room is 27 feet high, and is a most magnificent Saloon, with two grand bed chambers in the fabric which was left unfinished: To this a part consisting of the grand room there was a round tower that was three stories high, but part of it was taken down, and what remains serves for a back stair case; and an addition is also made to this part for a grand stair case which is of Mohogny, but wainscoated all the way up, in compartments for pictures, and with a fine freeze at each landing place of Pomeranian red deal which looks like Cedar. Over the two end buildings are rooms for servants, mostly in the roof, which do not appear on the outside: All the rooms in general are finished in the highest manner with Carvings and Stucco Ceilings; But those of the great fabric are exceeding grand and adorned with costly Chimney pieces of Marble & Exquisite Carvings, some with hangings of tapestry, others with Genoa Damask, beautifull Marble tables, fine beds and the richest furniture: Here is one particular piece, a bureau[1] made of the wood of broom fineered, the folding doors of which are glass in Gothic figures, and the frames are most beautifull in this wood, and particularly an Urn of Carved work at the top of it has a fine effect: This wood is brown in the middle and white on each side, and is much like rosewood. They have limestone here in several parts.—I am, &c.

[1] Pennant's *Tour Scot.*, 1769, p. 118. The bureau is still (1887) in very good preservation.

Letter XLVI.

TAYMOUTH, 18*th August* 1760.

DEAR SISTER,—On the 18th I left Blair highly satisfied with what I had seen, and with the politeness of the noble possessors which cannot be exceeded.

I went in the high road, ten measured miles north west to Dalnarnick [1] near to the river Garry into which the Tilt falls a little below Blair; we went over the foot only of one hill; About the place where we passed the Bruar Water,[2] I saw a village [3] to the South, at which there is an old Celtic Mount: We then turned to the South where this great road from the North divides and goes south to Sterling:

We went over one hill, and going along the side of another we came down to the river Ranack, which is a water that rises in the North out of a Loch called Loch Eruch,[4] it then falls by a river [5] into Loch Ranack, which runs to the east and empties itself by this river into Lough Tomel [6] that falls by a river of that name into the Tay, near which we travelled to Blair: Above it is a narrow Country improved, and a road made by art to Lough Rannack, where they have large firr trees which are felled, and cut into boards: Lower down the country is wider, and most beautifull contrasted with fields and woods about Loch Tomel, and 'tis said all the way down: so far we had a coarse whin or firestone; having passed the river, I saw a spot which I took to be limestone, and I was informed that all the way to Taymouth there is limestone, mostly a blew marble mixed with veins of sparr, which continues for about five miles on each side of Lough Tay.

We came over a hill and then crossed a Gully [7] in which a Stream runs; above it is a heathy country, below the water runns between rocks, all highly adorned with Birch trees, and a Corn Country for some way on each side of it: Two streams

---

[1] Dalnacardoch.
[2] See Burns's poem, 'The Humble Petition of the Bruar Water to the Noble Duke of Athol;' part now beautifully planted.
[3] Struan.   [4] Loch Ericht.   [5] River Ericht into Loch Rannoch.
[6] Loch Tummel and River Tummel.   [7] Glengowlay.

unite and between them stands the Castle of Garth, the stream[1] there falls down the rocks some feet into a basin worn by the water, and from that about 15 or 20 feet into the above mentioned river, which soon falls into the Lyon, and that into the Tay to the East of Taymouth: We crossed the Lyon and the Tay to Taymouth.

The Tay by its winding forms a peninsula, in which stands the Earl of Broadalbin's house. The way to it is either to cross the Lyon and Tay where they meet, or to cross the Lyon and keep on South, & to cross the river Tay where it runs east again; or to go two miles lower and cross over at Tay bridge which must be done when there are floods: The vale to the East is exceedingly beautifull in fields and plantations, and so they say it is for twelve miles to the place I must have come to, which is twelve miles also from Blair, in case I had taken that way: Nothing can be imagined finer than this peninsula and the hills on each side, especially to the south, which are exceeding beautifull in fields and plantations, as I shall more particularly describe.

Several rivulets rise to the west, north, and south & form Loch Tay, which is near 20 miles long, & about a mile broad, appearing like a large river. It empties itself by the Tay, over which four miles lower is a bridge with these inscriptions on it.[2]

MIRARE.

Viam hanc Militarem
Ultra Romanos Terminos
M. Passuum C C L hâc illac Extensam
Tesquis et paludibus . . . insultantem
Per montes rupes patefactum
Et indignanti Tavo
ut Cernis instratam.
Opus hoc arduum Suâ Solertiâ
et Decennali Militum Operâ
An Ær X^{ue} 1733 Posuit G. Wade

[1] Keltney Burn.
[2] 'The middle arch is 60 feet diameter, and it bears the above inscription, made Latin from English, as I have been told, by Dr. Friend, master of Westminster-school.'—Captain Burt's *Letters from the North of Scotland*, 1728-1736, vol. ii. Letter 26. Also Pennant's *Tour Scot.*, 1769, p. 99.

Copiarum in Scotia præfectus,
Ecce quantum Valeant
Regis Georgii 2ᵈⁱ Auspicia

" At the command of his Majesty King George the 2d this bridge was erected in the year 1733. This with the roads and other military works for securing a safe and easy communication between the highlands and trading towns in the low Country, was by his Majesty committed to the care of Lieutenant General George Wade commander in chief of the forces in Scotland, who laid the first stone of this bridge on the 23d of April and finished the work in the same year."

At the place where the Lough empties itself by the river is a promontory to the south of it, on which stands the Church, and a small village called Kenmore, and on the side of the hill to the south is the Minister's house: This is a mile from Lord Broadalbin's house; his plantations extending to within a quarter of a mile of it: The river winds and forms the shape of a Swan's neck, so that the house stands in a peninsula, the Isthmus of which is about half a mile broad:

The house is near the East side of it, and behind it and the offices is a fine lawn of uneven ground adorned with single trees; to the west of it by the river is a broad walk finely planted which extends to within a quarter of a mile of the mouth of it, and where it makes the greatest bow, a fine walk of lime trees of great size and meeting at top forms the string; towards the end of the walk on an eminence is a pleasant summer house commanding a view of the rich country to the east and of the Lake to the west, with the hills to the south of it highly cultivated, and at the end of the walk is a triangular mount for a turning Seat: on a mount to the South is an arched summer house; and on a long mount nearer the village a fortification is designed as an object for prospect. On the other side upon a terrace is a beautifull broad walk, with a fine summer house at the west end and an open Cross house at the other just over the river at the south end of the Isthmus: This walk is 2800 yards long, the other taking in the string of the bow is 1900 yards in length. To the south of the lawn at the foot of the hill a road passes to the village, and to a short way up the hill leading to the South: From this road there is a walk up the hill which leads to the west to the end of a broad walk with trees planted on each side and leading to the East, at the end of it is an open building with Seats; This walk has the most retired and quiet look that I ever saw. From this there is a walk up the hill to a lawn in which there is a very large beech tree with a seat round it, that commands a fine view to the west; From this lawn there is a narrow winding walk with several seats at proper distances leading to the round tower, the walls of which are about three feet thick, and the room 18 in Diameter, and there is a way up to the leads, the top being finished with Battlements; from which there is a very fine prospect to the West and North: From this height we descended to the North East to a seat called Æolus which affords the most pleasing prospect every way, and has itself a most beautifull effect in prospect especially from the North: It is built with two square pillars of hewn stone supporting an angular pediment in front, and it is open on both sides, except a little part which is closed for shelter to the Seat: and the trees are high behind it: From this we descended half a mile, passing mostly through fields to the Octagon Summer house on an Eminence, near which is a small Druid Temple, and to the west of it on the plain, a Kitchen Garden walled in of above four Scotch acres.

Another day we went to the Island in which there was a Priory (belonging to Scone) of Canons Regular of St. Augustine founded by Alex[r] 1st about the beginning of the 13th Century. It is called Loch Tay,[1] and Sybilla his Queen, daughter to Henry 1st of England dyed here, and was buried in the Church. What is supposed to be the Chapel is still standing, a stone for holy water having been found in the wall and a Cross like that of Malta; but there have been buildings erected at each end of it; which whether they were part of the Convent or not I cannot say; but this is certain, that the Campbell[2] family in the last Civil War, then Baronets, did live in it, and defended that part against Montrose, who on that account destroyed this Country.

We crossed over to the other side, & rid two miles by the Lake, and turned into Glyn Lyon, going Eastward, and pro-

---

[1] The Isle of Lochtay.   [2] See *The Black Book of Taymouth*, 1855.

ceeded thro' that vale for about a Mile, we came to a small entrenchment called Fortnegall[1] (The Stranger's Fort) it measures on the south side forty four yards, and on the west 35. The Rampart is about fifteen feet high, there was an opening on one side in the middle, and a causeway made over to it near the corner on the south side, which if it be a work of

An Antient Vase.

the Romans, this bridge was made since their time; there is an appearance from it of what looks like irregular lines, but it seemed rather to be Channels made by the running of the water, the ground being as high within as round the edge of the bank : exactly opposite to the middle of one of these lines which is 200 yards in length, is a stone set up on end, in the middle of a hollowed ring, which doubtless is a tomb: Lord Broadalbine has a Copper Vase[2] with three feet, which is said to have been found near this place. A drawing of it is here given.

[1] Fortingall. The etymology very doubtful.
[2] 'An urn or vase (a tripod) of a mixed metal, something like a coffee-pot, with a handle and spout. It was found, about the year 1733, in the prætorium of a Roman camp in Fortingall.'—*New Stat. Ac. Scot.*, Perth, vol x. p. 468.

The Lyon which rises to the west runs through the vale; part of which was Mr. Robertson's Estate [1] that is forfeited, to whom the woods about Lough Rannack did belong, in which there are large firr trees. The boards cut out of them sell for 8d each on the spot: we fell into the road I came into Taymouth within two miles of Lord Broadalbine's house, and turned up the east end of the high ridge of hills which we had encompassed, on which is a rocky summit, that is very stony, and where it is not a precipice, 'tis strengthened by a Wall without Mortar 8 feet thick; and there are many outworks of walls below to strengthen the weak parts, most of which have been destroyed, we descended down to Taymouth. The Lough consists of three reaches, the two first which we saw are each three miles long, the other 4 miles, in all fifteen measured miles, and a mile broad. There are Salmon in it in season all the year round, Pikes, Perch, Eels, and large Lough trout rarely caught which weigh 30 or 40lb. This family and that of the Argyle about 400 years ago branched out from a Common Ancestor, and inhabited the isles in Lough Awe as mentioned before.[2]—I am, &c.

Letter XLVII.

Drummond Castle, *August the 22d* 1760.

Dear Sister,—On the 22nd I set out and went 3 miles to Tay bridge which consists of five arches, and is adorned with 4 obelisks. A little above it is Sir Robert Menges,[3] an old Castle [4] with a fine plantation, and some walks made through them, we had a fine view of the vale in which the Tay runs: & ascending the hill to the south, passed by a large stone set up on end, came over a high hill, and went along the side of another hill having a rivulet to the East, which falls into the Brand [5] water

---

[1] Strowan or Struan. [2] See p. 68.
[3] Sir Robert Menzies of that Ilk. [4] Built in 1571.
[5] Braan river.

that empties itself into the Tay by the Hermitage at Dunkeld; in which vale we saw a very pretty improved Country, as well as about Lough Eruechy[1] of which we had a prospect at a distance. Here is a good public house[2] eleven measured miles from Creif and above nine from Tay bridge. Four miles more brought us to a little hamlet called Newtown on the river; Here the high rocky mountains make a dreadfull appearance projecting over the valley, which by the winding of the river, appears like two distinct valleys and is called the Mouth of the highlands.[3]

We went on in one of these Vales with the hills on each side, which make it a difficult pass, we ascended over the foot of the mountain, and came to a little house called Creif, where the late Duke of Perth endeavoured to establish a linnen Manufacture which did not succeed: It is finely situated on an eminence about a furlong from the bridge over the river Erne, which rises out of Lough Erne falls into the Tay below Perth, and gives the name of Strathern to all this fine vale: before we reached this place, we had passed a fine situation[4] in the vale belonging to the late Mr. Campbell,[5] who had built a large room for a library of choice books which he and his two immediate predecessors had collected, and has been since bought by booksellers in Edinburgh. There are small hills to the North covered with trees which have a most beautifull effect.

I came on two miles in the Sterling road, turned to the right, and went a mile to Mr. Drummonds—married to Lady Catherine Paulet the late Duke of Bolton's daughter; who is of the house of the late Duke of Perth. This is a very fine situation on an eminence commanding a view of the windings of the Erne which are very remarkable, of a fine flat country abounding in woods for near two miles round, and of the hills covered with woods to the North and West. The Earl of Perth who was Chancellor of Scotland to James the 2d and transacted the Scotch affairs, made these great plantations of several kinds of firrs, also of beech, sycamore and many other sorts of trees, some of the spruce firrs are three feet in Diameter. This Estate has paid off £70,000 debts, and the Rent

[1] Loch Freuchie or Fraochie.   [2] Amulree.
[3] Glenalmond.   [4] Monzie.   [5] See p. 244.

of this as of the other forfeited Estates, is now applied for publick uses and collected by the receiver general of Scotland. There is a remarkable thing here, a vein of rocks about 50 feet broad, and in some places more, runs through the Country and rises above ground: On a part of it Drummond Castle,[1] now entirely ruined, was built; it is said it runs from Dunbarton to Stonehive near Aberdeen, in Different Directions.

There are very large woods to the North and west which are cut down once in 25 years, and are most beautifull in prospect.

We went five miles to Ardoch, in the way to Sterling, to Sir William Sterlings, who showed me the Camp of Ardoch[2] on the river; for this is one of the Camps made by Julius Agricola; It consists within the Entrenchment of about two Acres of ground, on the side to the river were only two fosses, one of which has been destroyed by the road; on the other side are five fosses, and a rampart: within which there is a broad way all round; In the Prætorium is a very small fossee for the General's Tent nearer to one side than the other, the outer rampart cannot be less than 20 feet high, to the North of this fort is a large Camp extending about 500 yards in length 200 in breadth having a Morass to the West; from about the North East corner of it a line is Drawn, and there is a Roman road near it; which latter they say goes to Perth, and from that town to Cowper in Angus, but I doubt whether it goes further than Perth; The line extends to the Camp at Strageth; and about two measured miles from the Camp, is a small fort called the Castle Camp with one fossee and a kind of terrace round the Camp. We saw the Roman road plainly; it is overgrown with heath, and the soil is become black by the rotting of the Vegetables, I observed about two or three yards from it on both sides small holes, not deep enough to be dangerous, which doubtless were made to supply gravel for the road:

In the way to Sir William Sterling's house is a break in the bank near the village, where he found stones that formed three

---

[1] Drummond Castle was destroyed by fire during the Rebellion of 1745, but was partly rebuilt in 1822. The estates descended through a daughter of the Earl of Perth to the family now represented by the Baroness Willoughby d'Eresby.

[2] See Stuart's *Caledonia Romana*, p. 60.

little caves which he opened, and in each there was a Skeleton, and probably there were more. If Julius Agricola's forces were worsted in this place by the attack of the Caledonians according to Tacitus, the Caledonians might have hurried their dead here: Sir William showed us a small Urn[1] of Earth found in a Camp with the usual ornaments of lines, it contained pieces of a burnt Skull which I saw, he said also that a pipe of Lead about 8 inches in Diameter with a bore of six inches but not long, was found in the camp. And to the North of the Camp is a small Mount, from which the General might harrangue the soldiers.

Six miles from this place is Dumblane on this river, and on this side of it we saw Sheriff Muir where the Duke of Argyle beat the rebels under Lord Marr on the 13 of Nov. 1715.

S^r —— Sterling father of S^r W^m on some Disgust in the beginning of this Century went into the Russian Service & lived in that Country for 40 years, marrying the Daughter of General Gordon. He returned & died at home: His Son showed me the Statue of a Urus about 4 inches long in silver weighing about a pound; it was found in Siberia, there were rivets in the horns, so that probably it was a sort of pedestal for something fixed on it: He showed me also a piece of Amber 2 inches and a half long, and about half of a small fish like a young herring was enclosed in it; the head and eyes being most perfect. I saw also a small dish about a foot in Diameter, on the outside there is embossed work, enamelled & likewise on the inside in several compartments, are enamelled figures which seemed to be scripture history with russian inscriptions round them.

To the West in the Country of Monteith lives Mr. Erskine[2] who has writ the best abridgement of the Scotch laws.—I am, &c.

[1] 'An urn, filled with ashes, a fragment of the unburnt skull, and a piece of money. The last had, in all probability, been put into the mouth of the deceased as the fare of Charon, for wafting him over Styx.'—Pennant's *Tour Scot.*, 1772, pt. 3, p. 103. See *Old Stat. Ac. Scot.*, vol. viii. p. 495.

[2] John Erskine of Carnock, afterwards of Cardross in Menteith, author of the *Institutes of the Law of Scotland.*

Letter XLVIII.

DRUMMOND CASTLE, 23*d August* 1760.

D SISTER,—From the Castle Camp near Ardock we went to the East, and crossed the road which leads to Queensferry opposite to Edinburgh and soon came to the park wall, and then to the Church of Tullibarden,[1] to which there is a Saxon door, old narrow windows, and some that are Gothic : It is in form of a Cross, and at the East End is the burial place of the Tullibarden family who married the heiress of Athol that brought them the Dunkeld and Blair Estate to which they removed : Their names were Stewart, but on this marriage, they took the name of Murray of the Athol family. Sir David Murray Ancestor of the Duke founded here in 1446 a Collegiate Church in honour of our blessed Saviour with a Provost and some Prebendaries. Here is a sort of a small wooden Catafalch placed over the tomb (as one informed us) of Patrick Earl of Tulibarden. The old Castle is standing and was inhabited by Lord George Murray :

We came back to the Edinburgh road, and so again through Muthil where I saw a soldier 98 years old, who had been under Charles 12th at the battle of Pultowa :[2] Here is a Nonjuring Congregation of about 100. And there are a few papists about the Castle. They have no Limestone in this Country except a little which is very bad and is found in the Roadway from the Castle to the Camp near Comery.[3]

The Texati seem to have inhabited Aberdeenshire ; the Vacomagi Moray Bamfshire and part of Perthshire to the Erne, the Caledonii and Silva Caledonia seem to have included the rest of Perthshire and the East parts of Inverness Shire and Ross Shire, the western parts of those Shires being inhabited by the Cerones. The Venicontes, the Vecturones of the New Map, inhabitted Fife, among whom Banatia is thought to be Orrock by which I take to be meant the Camp or town on Lough Or.

---

[1] Which now gives the title of Marquis of Tullibardine to the Duke of Athole's eldest son.   [2] Fought July 8, 1709.   [3] Comrie.

But of this I have spoken more fully above,[1] from the light I have since had from the New Map.

At Tallibarden we were very near Kilcarden an old Castle of the Duke of Montroses. Strathern, or rather the river Erne is thought to be Terne of the Classical writers: The Earl of Perth was Hereditary Stewart of Stratherne: as the Athol family were of Athol and Stormont two other parts of Perthshire.

I made an excursion from Drummond Castle to the West, and descended the hill near to Balluck,[2] an old ruined house on a lake which was an Apenage to the family of Perth: We went near the hill of the Beacon,[3] and over the fort of it, and came into a beautifull Valley, through which the river Erne runs: This plain is encompassed with an Amphitheatre of hills; we went along the South Side of it, and in four computed miles from Drummond Castle came to the rivulet called Urghill[4] where it falls into the Erne from the South:

A little above this confluence on the old bed of the former, is that Camp which is supposed to be the Camp of Julius Agricola immediately before he engaged and defeated Galgacus. It is called Galgan Ross: Here it is supposed Julius came to Attack the Caledonians, and as he was determined to fight he probably made only this slight entrenchment to his Camp: The Caledonians were on the hills and seem to have come to them; there is an entrenchment on three sides, the Banks to the old bed of the river making the South Side; about fifty yards within this is another which I judge to be a sort of Prætorium: about 100 yards to the South of it is a Camp with a very slight fossee, on three sides of which about the middle at the Entrances is a Semicircular fossee; from the Eastern Entrance is a road made to the Northern way into it, which is continued to the Entrance into the other Camp on the North Side of it. I looked attentively to see if any line was drawn from each Angle of the inner Camp to the large one, but could observe none. The fosses are all single, those of the inner Camp are strongest; near the South Entrance of the great Camp within it is a great stone set up on end, and a little further another with three small ones near it, which might be placed over Aulus Atticus Commander of a Cohort who fell in

[1] See p. 180.   [2] Balloch.   [3] The Eagle's Craig.   [4] The Ruchill.

this action. This Camp indeed seems only to have been begun; the Caledonians probably giving them an opportunity of Engaging immediately after the Romans came here and began this Entrenchment. According to the opinion among the learned, the Caledonians might attack the 9th Legion at Ardock and the Camp might afterwards be strengthened by stronger ramparts: or it might have been at the Camp at Strageth.

The river Urghill comes out of a valley to the South West, and the Erne from another to the North West, and about six miles higher is Lough Erne which is a mile broad and five miles long, and at the end of it is the road from Sterling and Fort William, which is joyned by the road from Glasgow at some Distance to the North of Loughlowmon: To this place, where there are two bridges one over the Erne and another over a rivulet which falls into it from the North, the Country has made a fine road from Crief, and purpose to continue it on to the road which leads to Fort William:

In this road we returned on the North side of the river and passed by a fine place and house called Laws[1] belonging to the late General Campbell, and now to his son, the heir and Cousin German to Lord Loudon; It is under the hill, on the side of which are fine plantations. About two miles further we came to Auchtertyr[2] Sr Patrick Murray's: Before we got to it, we entered in between the hills which extend to the East about two miles near to Crief, they are uneven at top and covered with wood, mostly firr, and afford that beautifull prospect I mentioned in the road to Drummond Castle. Sr Patrick's house is situated on the side of a hill covered with wood & over a lake in which there is an old castle on a peninsula. The plantations of this hill are seen over the other hills.

At the East End of them we had seen in going a very pretty place of Mr. Campbells, who has another Seat[3] which I saw in the vale, before I came to Crief, where there is a fine room built for a library as mentioned before. We went under Crief, crossed the Erne over a bridge, and turned to the West round the hill and near the wood to Drummond Castle, instead of going, as I did at first along the high road to Sterling: having had an extream pleasant ride round these beautiful romantick vales.—I am, &c.

[1] Lawers.   [2] Ochtertyre.   [3] See p. 239.

Letter XLIX.

Methuen, *August the 25th*, 1760.

Dear Sister,—On the 25th I set out and travelled three miles west to Strageth, and saw the remains of the Roman Camp there which are very inconsiderable: The river Erne was plainly to the East, and probably was to the North, & there is a small brook to the South, along which there is an Outwork; The fossee of the Camp being carried in a strait line: There are the remains of two deep fossess to the west at the South West Corner, but to the North they have been destroyed, tho there are remains of some irregular works as within the supposed ramparts. From this place it is said there was a line to the Camp Castle[1] mentioned before, and I suppose a sight of the Castle from some place near:

Here is a ford over the river, and a ferry boat also to Inverpeffery[2] where from an Eminence in the Church yard that commands both the reaches of the river which here makes a turn, is a Church divided into three parts, to the East is the burial place of the Perth Branch of the Drummond family, to the West of the Maderty branch, and in the middle Lord Strathallens, who forfeited in the Rebellion of 1715: The last Lord Maderty left the Estate to the Second Son of the Duplin family (Hay) the issue of a Niece, in case the descendants of another Niece should be extinct, which event happening, the Estate, about £1000 a year, is by that Disposition come to the Bishop of St. Asaph, who upon coming into possession took the name of Drummond.

The same Lord Maderty[3] left an income to build and found a library, with a Salary for a librarian, on a spot where there was a small building in which he had his Library to the West of the Church, & where he lived entirely abstracted from the World; here they have built a handsome room, over some con-

---

[1] See p. 240. Kemp or Camp Castle. Pennant's *Tour*, 1772, pt. II, p. 100.
[2] Innerpeffary.   [3] David, Lord Madderty.

venient apartments for a Librarian, who, with the books, is to be fixed there:

Here was an enclosure with a round tower at each Corner, and from it there is a fine avenue to an indifferent house, where that Lord had formerly lived: we passed the house and going a little North, we soon came to the Roman Road from Strageth to Perth which is seen across the heath, and enters into Garth wood which is a plantation of Firrs, and afterwards passed by the wood of Duplin; and I was told goes to Couper in Angus, which I doubt, and should rather think that it went to the Fort or Camp at Lough Or & so to the Wall:

We turned to the North down to Inchaffray Abbey in a Valley, through which the river Pou[1] runs, which rises a little to the East; another rivulet of same name rising very near it, and runs to the East: It is probable that the place was made an island by a fossee. The Etymology of Inchaffray being the Isle of Masses (Insula Missarum) for it was an Abbey founded by Gilbert, Earl of Strathern in 1200 for Canons regular of St. Augustine brought from Scone James Drummond having obtained it of Alexander Gordon Bishop of Galloway, it was erected by James 6th in 1607 into a Lordship under the title of Maderty from the Parish Church of that name which we passed & is a little to the South of it: The family lived here until within these 70 or 80 years. There is nothing remaining but a little part of the North East pillar of the tower of the Church which was in the middle of it as appears by the great ruins; to the South of the Church is an Enclosure and a Gable End with a Chimney to it, called the Fraters house, with an arched vault made of hewn stone, this might be the Dormitory, as the Enclosure probably was the Cloyster.

Crossing the rivulet on a bridge, I saw above and below it a large dike made to Drain the ground, which is an exceeding rich soil: And tho it certainly would produce very fine wheat flax and hemp, yet we saw it under Oats and barley, As they have a notion that they have no manure for Wheat: For in these parts there is no Wheat except what is eat in the Gentlemen's houses: They plough without intermission, one year barley manured, the other year Oats without manure: and

---

[1] River Pow or Powaffray.

so to the Gates of Perth they have indeed some Wheat close to that town, where they might turn their flat ground to much better account in Meadowing, being the finest soil for it, but all is under Corn, which, 'tis said, is owing to the little expence they have in tilling the ground, which brings very fine Crops:

We saw to the west Mr. Murray's[1] of Abercarney, and going on, passed by Balgouan[2] Mr Graham's, married to Lord Hopton's Sister. It is a fine house and situation, and highly improved by plantations, there being a riding all round his Demesne. About Inchafferay we came into the fine road made by the Country from Crief to Perth, which goes a little Distance from the Eastern Port, and passes through the Village of Methuen.

The Parish Church here was Collegiate for a Provost and Prebendaries, founded by Walter Stewart Earl of Athol, one of the sons of Robt IId, the Church is entirely altered, but there is one Gothic window at the South End of the transcept. Margaret of England, Dowager of James 4th purchased this place for her third husband Henry Stewart who was of the Royal family, whom she got to be made a Baron by James the 5th.

The Road passes by the Garden of Mr. Smith of Methuen half a mile beyond the Village: We went to this gentleman's house, which is a good building with a round Turret at each Corner, in a most delightfull situation, there being a fine Terrace which commands a view of the beautifull Vale, of the hills, and mountains (which are at a due distance) of the Firr woods of Duplin and Perth and of Huntingtore, which afford alltogether a most rich scene; and all the Country is under Corn.

Here I saw the picture[3] of the great uncle of this gentleman by the great grandmother, whose name was Creightoun, who for his great capacity and learning was called the Admirable Creightoun. He was Tutor to the Prince of Mantoua, who (for a cause not known, but is intimated to be some affair of Gallantry) with the Russians that were present, as 'tis supposed, undertook to murder him, attacked Creighton: He

---

[1] The Morays of Abercairny.   [2] Balgonie.
[3] Engraved in Pennant's *Tour*, 1769, Pl. xl.; also a Memoir of James Crighton, *ibid.* pp. 313-328.

defended himself with great courage and was just dispatching the prince, who presently dropped his Mask, on which Creighton presented the handle of his sword to the prince, who instantly murdered him: on which acc^t it is said, the Duke his father refused a great while to see him. Another Sister of Creighton married Bishop Graham of Orkney. There is an acc^t of this Creighton in Mackenzie's Scotch Worthies.

From this place I was shown Longcartie, where in 980 there was a battle with the Danes called Hay's battle:[1] for the Scotch giving way, one Hay who was at plough with his two sons, took up the beam of the plough to which the oxen were yoked, and went with his two Sons, armed with a plough share and yoke, reproached them for flying, made them rally and led them on, doing execution with the plough Tackle; by which they gained the victory; and the King ordering the man to be brought to him, directed that as much ground should be given to him as a hawk could fly over; which was all the way to the parish of Errol, where they say the hawk's stone remains, showing the flight about two miles to the west of Mr. Crawford's of Errol. & this person was the founder of the Kinoul family, which have the action represented at Duplin in two or three paintings, and small statues in wood of this old Man and his Sons, with their weapons in their hands, which are the supporters of their Arms.

I saw also the Mountain called Dunsinan[2] which is the Southern Summit of that hill which I passed from Dundee to Couper. On this Mountain Macbeth had his house, of which the foundations are still seen, and it is mentioned in the tragedy of Macbeth.—I am, &c.

[1] Battle of Luncarty. See *Hist. Scottish Wars*, second edition, 1825, p. 25.
[2] 'On the hill of Dunsinane was fought the renowned battle between Macbeth, the Thane of Glammis, and Seward, Earl of Northumberland. Edward the Confessor had sent Seward on behalf of Malcolm III., whose father, Duncan, the thane and usurper had murdered. Macbeth, who was signally defeated, was pursued, it is said, to Lumphanan in Aberdeenshire, and there slain, 1057. The history of Macbeth is the subject of Shakespeare's incomparable drama.'

LETTER L.

PERTH, *August the* 27*th*, 1760.

DEAR SISTER,—On the 26th Mr. Smith accompanied me: this gentleman has planted the road on each side, in so much that the Country looks like that which is between Chantilly and Paris. A battle[1] was fought here on the 19th of June 1300.

We soon came to Tibbermoor a small village and church; on the heath to the North East near the North End of Duplin Woods, The Earl of Montrose had an engagement on the 11th of September 1644. We went on to the west of Duplin Wood, where the Roman Road enters it, and the ridge of rocks comes to it which is broader, and covered much with heath: we came to Duplin house to which there is a handsome Front to the North and large offices. There is a narrow Gully to the East, and a terrace to the South, which as well as the house commands a most glorious view of the windings of the Erne, of a most beautifull vale, of the hills to the East and South, and of the Mountains of Fife beyond them: The place is on all sides adorned with plantations, and there are some very good pictures[2] in the house, particularly a Titian with three figures, one of which is much like Raphael, when he was very young. Lord Kinoul is fitting up this charming place for his residence.

We descended from Duplin, took leave of Mr. Drummond and came across the hills to the East to Elcho which gives title to Lord Wems's eldest son:[3] We came to the part called Elchow Wester, Elchow Easter where Lord Wems has a larger house being a mile lower on the Tay:

I came to see what remained of a Nunnery[4] of Cistercians

[1] Battle of Methven, 19th July 1306. See *Hist. Scottish Wars*, second edition, 1825, p. 60.
[2] For a catalogue of the pictures in Dupplin House, see Pennant's *Tours*, 1769, p. 85; *ibid.* 1772, pt. II, pp. 80-88. Bulloch's *George Jamesone, The Scottish Vandyck*, 1885, p. 150, and for portraits of the first Earl of Kinnoull, see Dixon's *Gairloch, Its Records, Traditions, etc.*, 1886, pp. 75 and 82.
[3] Lord Elcho, eldest son of the Earl of Wemyss and March.
[4] Nunnery founded by David Lyndsay of Glenesk, at Grange of Elcho, parish of Rhynd.

founded by David Lindsay of Glenert and his mother: Nothing is to be seen of it but the tower of the Church and the foundations of buildings: Nearly opposite to this, on the other side of the river is Kinfauns the Estate of Miss Blair, now Lady Gray, by whom that Lord is entitled to £2400 a year a large estate.

We turned to the North, towards Perth, and passed under Magdalenes on the side of the hill, and then by Leonard in the plain, a Priory of Cistercian Nuns founded before 1296: But James 1st suppressed it, and annexed it to the Charterhouse of Perth, together with the Magdalene lands:

We came to Perth by the finest turnpike road in Britain, which leads from Edinburgh. It is said that a small City called Berth was with all the inhabitants, and a child of a King of Scotland destroyed by a great inundation; The Tradition is that this City was on the North side of the Almond, which falls into the Tay, two miles to the North of the town:

King William the Lyon built Perth in a better position: It was afterwards called St. Johnstoun of Perth, from the Parish Church: But it has recovered its ancient name of Perth: It is said that the English, in the war between the Bruces and Baliols, fortified it, but that afterwards these fortifications were destroyed; it was however walled round; for three of the gates remain, that to the North was called Castle Gavel,[1] where probably in ancient times there was a Castle: Cromwell took this town and built a fortress at the South End of it, the ramparts of which remain. This place is most delightfully situated in a most beautifull country, there are small hills to the South and west, the fine river Tay and a rising ground beyond it to the East: it is open to the North on which side is adorned with noble plantations, among which are those of Bussy, belonging to Lord Kinoul, a furlong from the town: and what adds greatly to the Picture the water of the Almond, 2 miles distant, is brought round the town: and in summer is entirely carried off this way; at each end of the town is a large Green belonging to the Community, which are let by the town at so much a head for Cattle; and the North Green is much

---

[1] The castle of Perth was demolished by King Robert Bruce. The Castle Gable—the street on the east of it, was the only entrance to the town from the north in 1760.

used for bleaching and washing: The Town consists chiefly of two streets, from East to West, near half a measured mile long, and two streets which extend one to the South, and the other to the North from the great street.

The Parish Church of St. John is a large handsome building which has been adorned with Gothic Windows, for on the South side over the Quire are narrow windows of three arches with a sort of a plain frieze round them in the old Saxon Style; with a Spire on the tower covered with lead: There are five arches in the body and in the Quire which form two separate Churches, in one of them is the Seat in which the King used to sit. There is a fine doorcase with many members in the Saxon Style which was brought from the Carthusians, and so probably were some of the windows. The Franciscan Observantines had a Monastery here where the burial place is to the South, founded by Lord Oliphant in 1461. To the North of the Walls of the town was the Monastery of the Dominicans opposite to the gate, where there are now houses and Gardens. James the 1st was murdered in this house, and buried at the Carthusians here, which he had founded in 1429 after his return from his Imprisonment in England. The Carthusians was a fine Monastery; where the hospital now stands for decayed housekeepers: The Water brought from the Almond, runs to the East of it, on which they probably had their Cells, Chapels and Gardens; and in a garden beyond that of the hospital, they had their fish ponds, of which there are still some marks; It was called Monasterium Vallis Virtutis, and was the only Monastery of Carthusians in Scotland.

James the 6th granted to George Hay a Peerage under the title of Lord of the Charterhouse of Perth, and the rents being too small to support the Peerage he resigned it to the King, who accepted it; which practice of Resigning Peerages has been common in Scotland, but as matter of favour to some particular persons:

The Hospital is a grand fabric built out of the Estates that were in the hands of the Corporation for the use of the poor:

When the Duke of Cumberland passed through Perth after the battle of Culloden, the town made him a present of Earl Gowrie's house, in which the famous conspiracy is said to have

been carried on. It is built something like a Castle, what is
standing of the old fabrick is an L. I saw the room in which
the Conspirators dined; and the room to which the King was
led, the window out of which he called, and the Cupboard where
the armed man was placed. There was another Stair Case by
a turret, as I suppose, from abroad, which is now taken down:
on the whole I find the story of the Conspiracy is generally
disbelieved in Scotland: Some suspect there was a design to
carry the King to England, others to intimidate him for certain
purposes, and the exceeding good character of the Persons concerned induce others to cast reflections on the King himself.[1]

Two miles from the town beyond the hills to the North
West, was Ruthven Earl Gowrie's Seat, which from that time
changed its name by Act of Parliament, and that apellation
was for ever after to be entirely disused. It is now called
Huntingtore[2] and is the Dower house at present of the Dutchess
of Athol who lives in it.

They have a town house & Jayl at the end of the great
Street by the upper Quay, and two Quays lower down, and to
that which is most distant, a ship of near a hundred tons can
come up. There was a bridge here over the Tay, but it was
carried away by the floods: They export from the river at this
place and Dundee to the value of £10,000 in Salmon, the
pickled to London, and Salt Salmon to Holland to be sent to
Spain, of £10,000 in Wheat and Barley, of £150,000 in Linnen:
they have also a great trade in Skins of all sorts from the
North of Scotland: And they are famous for weaving Damask
Table linnen.

A quarter of a mile to the West was Tullilum where a Convent of Carmelites was founded by Richard Bishop of Dunkeld
in 1262, where the Synods for the Diocese were held untill they
were removed to Dunkeld. For more particulars of the history
of this town I refer to the annexed paper containing Extracts
relating the history & state of Perth. Soon after I arrived
the Provost[3] and another of the Corporation came to see me

---

[1] The Gowrie conspiracy is clearly proved in Tytler's *Hist. of Scot.*, vol. iv. pp. 276-296.

[2] Ruthven Castle, or Huntingtower. For plans and views see MacGibbon and Ross's *Castellated Arch. of Scot.*, 1887, vol. i. pp. 395-401.

[3] Lord Provost William Stuart.

PERTH.

and with great politeness showed me everything about the town, and in the evening pres.nted me with the freedom[1] of the place.—I am, &c.

SUMMARY FROM THE PRINCIPAL WRITS[2] IN RELATION TO PERTH.

1. King William the Founders Charter granting many Liberties priveledges and immunities Dated Anno 1210.
2. King Robert the 2d Charter of Confirmation granting all fines specified to uphold the bridge of Tay. Dated May the 5th the 10th year of his reign.
3. King Robert the 2d Charter of fewfarms for rent of £80 Sterling dated 9th October the Eleventh year of his reign.
4. King David the Second's Charter ratifying all former Charters, and erecting a Guild dated the 10th of April, the 36 year of his reign.
5. King Robert 3d Charter of Confirmation dated the 6th of May 10th year of his reign.
6. King Robert 3d Charter Conferring the . . . of Sheriffship within the Borough on the said Borough dated 10th of April 4th of his reign.
7. A transumpt of a Charter granted by . . . . Containing the offices of Sheriffship and Crownership conferring the fines of the same on the Borough for upholding the bridge of Tay.
8. Two Exemptions for passing upon assizes if the Deed be not done within a mile of the town.
9. King Robert 3d 2 Charters disposing the fines raised upon Forestallers and a part of the Common Muir for upholding the bridge of Tay.
10. A part of the Borough Mach on Burgage farms disposed to the Chartrouse, black & white friers, &c.
11. King Robert the 2d grants power by a Charter dated the 15th day of March the 16th year of his reign for the Borough to make Statutes and laws to be observed within themselves.

---

[1] Mr. William MacLeish, City-Clerk, writes: 'Can find no reference to the freedom of the City being presented to Bishop Pococke in or about 1760.' See notes, pp. 3, 47, 168, 182, 183, 210.

[2] An MS. Index of the Perth Charters, etc., is in the City Chambers: it consists of forty-eight numbers.

12. James the 2d by Charter Exempts Perth of the Custom of Salt and Skins &c. dated the 5th of March 1451.
13. James the 5th ratifies the Charter of James the 2d.
14. The 24th of Decemb^r 1458 Lord Ruthven Dispons to Perth, that part of the Common Muir called Catside.
15. Perth dispons certain lands to Robert King for upholding the Causeys without the town dated the 8th of May 1459.
16. An Indenture betwixt Perth and Richd Joiat concerning the boot[1] of Ballhoupe dated the 10th of June 1464.
17. Three indentures betwixt Perth, Lord Ruthven and the Laird of Ballhoupe anent the Miln lead and Laws work,[1] &c.
18. Two Decreets obtained by Perth against Dundee one discharging the Toist the other Confirming the Priority of place to Perth, & a Warrant to the Earl Marshall to place Perth in Parliament next to Edinburgh.
19. A Charter of Confirmation granted by King James the Sixth by which the Bridge of Earn and the Customs thereof are disponed to Perth, the said Charter also Contains a Confirmation of all the liberties Priviledges and immunities of the Burgh of Perth dated Novemb^r 15th 1600 with a seasin following thereupon.
20. A Liberty granted by the Abbot of Dumfermling to Perth of burying within the Quire of the Parish Church dated the 9th of June 1540 Confirmed by the Arch Bishop of St. Andrews.

Queen Ann Consort to King Jam^s the 6th by her Charter grants to Perth the parsonage and Vicarage (reud) tends of the parish, which Charter is confirmed by parliament.

Perth is infeft and seised in the Colledge yard and patronage thereof by virtue of a Charter granted it by King James the 6th and his Queen.

A Charter Dated the 10th year of Robert the third is the first I can find wherein anything is granted for the support of the bridge of Tay.

Charters granted by the King to the town of Perth,

---

[1] See *New Stat. Ac. of Scot.*, 1845, vol. x., Article Perth, p. 73.

and by King William the Lyon 1210. One by King
Robert Bruce ; reign 12th.

Two by King Robert the 2d reign 4. Four by King
Robert the third, one by James 2d, one by James 5th
a Charter of Confirmation of all the above by James
the 6th 1600.

21. A Charge direct by the Kings Majesty to possess Perth in
the fishing of Laughlan all being submitted by the town
and Lord Oliphant and Directed in favour of Perth.

22. Two remissions granted the town of Perth for the Down
Casting at one and Down pulling at another the house
of Duplin dated 1461. A remission for burning the
house of Clackmannan and a Discharge from the Comptroller for £2000 ster. imposed upon the town anent
Clackmanans affair. Those which are mark^d [in italics]
are unknown. *Laughlaw. Inshcrrat*, Inshyr & Inch.
Kings Inch. Pynorce:[1] *Great Customs. Carnacks
Strength. St. Johnstons Hunts up.*[2] Dragon's hole, a
cave high in the rock of the hill of Kinoul.

Windy Fowle the hollow betwixt its two tops, Earn
side wood Eastward of Newburgh, Wallace town betwixt
Moncrief & Kilmonth, St. Cohells Well by Ruthven
now Huntingtower, Macbeth's Castle on Dunsinan hill.

Wallace's Cave at Kilspindice. Lawtey the top of
Kinoul hill. More down the hill above Montrief.

From Hollingshead.[3] Cunsdag King of Britain built three
temples one at Bangor to Mercury, one in Cornwall to Apollo,
and one at Perth to Mars which was repaired by Julius
Agricola in the reign of Domitian, and the first bridge thrown
over the Tay at Perth and a Castle built, the ruins of which
are still called the Castle Gavell.[4] After Bertha was swept
away by an inundation of the river Tay, & Almond, King
Willm the Lyon founded the present town of Perth richly
endowed the Community, laying the foundations of the walls
which were afterwards greatly strengthened by Edward the 1st
of England whose garrison was expelled by Wallace, after his

---

[1] See *The Pyneurs (i.e.* Shore Porters), by John Bulloch, 1887.

[2] 'St. Johnstoun's Hunt's up!' a spirited local band. See Adamson's *Muses Threnodie*, edited by Cant (1774), p. 133.

[3] Holinshed's *Chronicles.*   [4] See Note 2, p. 250.

abdication it was retaken and repaired by the English who kept possession till King Robert Bruce besieged, took it and raized its walls to the ground. The town continued open till after the Battle of Duplin, when the Earls of March and Mar the Gover^{rs} of Scotland were overthrown. Baliol refortified it, and leaves a garrison which was besieged by the Earl of March and after 3 months taken, & razed again. King Edward the 3d takes Perth and rebuilds its walls, upon it charge the six abbacies, viz. Couper, Lindores, Balmerinock, Dunfermling, St. Andrews and Arbroath, & kept a garrison there till it was besieged by Robert the Second, & the Eng^{sh} expelled, the walls being in a great measure demolished. Thus it continued till a Burgess was killed by some highlandmen who were pursued by the Townsmen to a place called Hoghmanstains where many were killed and wounded, on which occasion to Defend themselves it was refortified by the inhabitants, the old walls serving for the foundations, the ruins of which are still standing. On King William the Lyon's founding Perth the Temple of Mars the Castle, the lines of a Camp and the ruins of the Bridge all Roman works were extant. On the spot where he founded the new town he built a bridge on the old foundation of eleven arches which was frequently impaired by the great floods in the river particularly on 23d Nov. 1567 when the bridge of Almond was carried away. On the 20 Decr 1573, 3 arches next the town and Lowswork carried away but soon repaired in 1582 Jany 14 five arches carried away, and likewise soon rebuilt. Decr 23d 1589 2 piers were carried away and afterwards repaired, but on the 14th of October 1621 the bridge was entirely carryed away, and never yet rebuilt, in 1544 on St. Magdalen's day was fought a battle on the bridge of Tay on Cardinal Bethun's endeavouring to intrude Kinstans upon the town for Provost, wherein many were slain, a number of the inhabitants zealous for the reformation of religion took arms in order to appease the Cardinals Cruel usage of the Protestants, fell under his power, all agreeing in testimony of their resolution to put a hempen cord about their necks, wherewith they should be strangled if they either turned their backs or denied their faith, from whence a rope is yet called a St. Johnston's ribband.

Before the reformation there were in Perth 5 Monasteries

viz., Charterhouse founded by James 1st and richly endowed, he was burried there. The white fryers, the black fryars or Augustines, The grey fryers, the Carmelites : without the Town was St. Leonards, Tullilum and St. Magdalenes, St. John's Church yet extant, St. Mary's by the North Shore : where the jayl now is St. Catherines, and by the theatre St. Paul's, besides the Chapel of the holy Cross, St. Annes and our Ladys of Lorretto.

A Royal palace by the black fryars, from the garden from which King Robert was a witness of the Battle[1] fought in the north inch betwixt the Clans Chatan and Kay, and the Victory obtained by the valour of Henry Winder a sadler of Perth who undertook for a french ½ Crown to supply the place of one who had fled.

Another royal palace opposite to the grammar school in the South Street. Spey tower where the Spey gate is now, Monks tower towards South gate port.

King Malcolm Kenmores Castle at Fort Eveot.

The Picts entirely routed on the Moor of Scoon having rallied seven times in one day.

The Tower of Abernethy, built by the Picts on the Grave of one of their Kings, that no Scot might walk or ride over his belly. Æneas Julvius was legate in Scotland when James the 1st was murdered ; his house was in the Meeting house Close north side of the High Street.—I am, &c.

Letter LI.

Cowper in Fife, *August* 29*th* 1760.

Dear Sister,—On the 27th Mr. Smith of Methuen took leave of me, and two Gentlemen accompanied me, one into whose hands he put me, and Mr. Wood Ld Kinoul's Agent, we crossed the river in a boat, but the horses forded. We rid two measured miles to the side of the Abbey of Scoone founded

---

[1] Combat, A.D. 1396, between 30 of the Clan Quhele (or Clan Chattan) and 30 of the Clan Kay (or Clan Dhai—the Davidsons, a sept of the M'Phersons). One of the combatants having retired, or deserted, his place was filled by Henry Wynd, called *An Gobhcrom*, The Crooked Smith, or Bandy-legged Smith. The various stories of this brutal encounter are somewhat conflicting: *Winton*, vol. ii. p. 373, and notes, p. 518; Fordun a Goodal, vol. ii. p. 420; *Hist. Scottish Wars*, second edition, 1825, p. 144; Browne's *Hist. of the Highlands and Clans* ; Sir Walter Scott's *Fair Maid of Perth*.

by Alexander 1st in 1114 for Canons Regular of St. Augustine.
The Kings were crowned here formerly in the Fatal Chair[1]
which Edward the 1st Carried to England and is now in Westminster Abbey with the stone under it which is granite, and
they say was brought from Egypt, but seems to be some of the
Common Granite[1] of Scotland; and it is most probable that
the Kings of Scotland were crowned on this stone, for the
Chair itself is of Gothic workmanship. The Kings of England
are now crowned in this Chair, and another is made like it for
the Coronation of the Queen: This Abbey was by James VI.
erected into a Lordship in favor of Sir David Murray a Cadet
of the family of Tullibarden under the title of Lord Stormont,
from the Country on the other side the Water, which is
called by that name. There are buildings on three sides of
two courts, A long gallery almost the whole length, being one
side of both of them: The coved cieling of wood is adorned
with History paintings relating to James 6th, if I mistake not,
in twelve compartments: There are rooms in the other parts
for lodgings &c. and in one is a bed of Queen Mary's working,
in which she lay in the Castle of Loch Leven when she was
confined by her own Nobility. There are also some tapestry
hangings of Needlework: over the windows in front are reliefs
of persons on horseback with these inscriptions round them—
over one Godfridus Bullonius. Another Carolus Magnus. A
third ——— Rex, A fourth Machabæus, and in one court over
the windows are these reliefs of the Heathen gods with their
proper emblems Cybell, Mars, Venus, I observed everywhere
that the Initial letters of D. L. S. for David Ld Stormont were
let in after the wall was built. I take this to have been the
gallery of the Abbot's Lodgings: over the gateway one
Unicorn supports the Arms of Scotland with its feet. There
is a small Church which seems to have been erected after the
reformation. In it is a Magnificent tomb, as 'tis said made in
Italy, over David Lord Stormont, and in the Church they say
Charles the 2d was crowned by the Kirk. The Church yard is
encompassed with a wall and the surface is 5 or 6 feet above
the ground on the outside; They have a Tradition that earth

[1] See Dr. Skene's *Coronation Stone*, 1869. Dr. Geikie, in App. p. 50, says:
"The stone is almost certainly of Scottish origin; that it has been quarried out
of one of the sandstone districts between the coast of Argyle and the mouths of
the Tay and Forth."

was brought here from every Barony in the Kingdom that held of the King, and that here, on the death of the Predecessor, every Tenant in Fee took livery & seisin as of the King. There is a tradition that on the Moor of Scone the Picts were entirely defeated by the Caledonians. I saw a little higher the inlet of the Almond.

We returned back opposite to the town, which lies in the parish of Kinoul, from which Lord Kinoul has his title. We went on and came to the hills of Kinoul, that abound in Agates and Chrystall, the latter enclosed in hollow stones which fall from these fine high rocks that are opposite to Elchow. We saw Elchow house on the other side, built high in the Castle manner: we proceeded near the river & saw the mouth of the Erne, which they say formerly (as appears by old writings) fell in at Inver Gaury, The Tay having run further to the North through the Carse of Gaury,[1] which was all a Morassy soil till it was drained some years agoe and is called the Mire of Gaury, before which time, the Erne run in the present bed of the Tay:

In three computed miles we turned the point of the hill to the South, going nearer to the river, and here opened a most beautifull view of the finest part of Gaurie, consisting of beautifull Eminencies planted with trees: Three miles more brought us to one of these, on which Mr. Crawford's house of Errol stands near the village of that name: The principal front of the house is to the East with a lawn before it, wood at a distance, single trees and clumps nearer, there is a handsome front to the South commanding a view of the river with a lawn before it, and a Wood on each side, there is a Lawn also and wood before the Eastern front; all along to the South is a terrace which commands a view of the river beyond Dundee; and from it a walk round the Wood that extends ¾ of a mile to the west from the house. In the garden are two or three trees of Thuya or Arbor Vitæ and as many of Cypress, which are above two feet in Diameter at the Bottom: The views every way are very fine: There is a prospect of the house of Cragy the late Lord Presidents, on an Eminence under the hills to the North west of Macbeth's Dunsinan hill, of the fine Vale of Gaurie in which is the Castle of Maginen[2] of the Drummonds, the present Dutchess of Athol's family: a flat extending

---

[1] The Carse of Gowrie.   [2] Castle of Megginch.

about six miles to the East, with wood enough to adorn it, but not so much as to intercept the view of the beautifull fields, and there is a fine prospect of the bay, called Inver Gaury into which the Tay formerly run; near the bottom of this bay is Castle Lyons, belonging to the Earl of Strathmore, a house to the East of the bay from Inver Gaury, which is a fine situation; and we had a view of Lord Grays and Foulis, which I passed from Dundee to Couper, the Church of Foulis I then took notice of, it was Collegiate and endowed with a provost and prebendaries by Sir Andrew Gray the Ancestor of Lord Gray in the time of James IId of Scotland; I must add, the view of the hills to the North covered with Corn, the Mountains appearing over them; and on the other side of the water a fine narrow flat from Abernethy to the West, to Bambrick Castle & Balmerino and the bottom of the hills above it covered with Corn and in some parts with Wood even to the summits of them, with Mountains appearing over them, altogether render it one of the most delightfull inland situations in the world.

I walked to Maginch and was assured that the land would bear a succession of the following Crops without lying fallow (viz) flax, wheat, pease, barley, oats, Clover two years and the same round again. The land here is worth twenty shillings an Acre, in the Mire not above seven, it having been a heathy common, & constantly peeled by the Common people to mix up for Manure.

On the 29th in the afternoon I crossed the Tay in a boat to Newbrugh & came where Mr. Crawford took leave of me, and Mrs. Haies of Mugrum, having sent her postchaise for me, a Gentleman he recommended me to, went with me in it two miles to Abernethy a place of great Antiquity, finely situated a small mile from the river Erne, and the same from the Tay, opposite to the influx of the Erne. It was the place of residence of the Kings of the Picts; and here the Metropolitan of their Kingdom resided, It was first a place of retirement for St. Bridget and a number of Virgins: she died here about 518.

It was then made a Bishop's See and was possessed by the Culdees who seem to have chosen the Bishop. But when Kenneth the third King of the Scots defeated the Picts, he removed the See to St. Andrews in the 9th Century: It was afterwards a Priory of Canons Regular of St. Augustine who were taken from Inchaffray in 1273. The present Church is small and probably the first Church built here. The Door is of the plainest Saxon Architecture.

They say the great Church was to the North East of it, and is entirely destroyed; a few yards from the North East corner is the round tower,[1] in the street below, a step appears round it, probably there were more. The wall is three feet six inches thick at the Door, and within it is eight feet three inches in Diameter, in all eleven feet nine inches, it may be twelve feet at bottom, it is said to be seventy feet high, but taking in the top and steps it might be 84 feet high; as I have commonly found these towers to be seven Diameters in height: There are about seventy tiers of stone to the top, nine of which are from the step to the door, so if there were three steps, that makes twelve. The door is finished with a projecting door case round it and a true arch, the four windows at top in the same style with an Architrave at the spring of the arch. There are three very small windows between that and the door, each of them lighting two stories, 7 stories in all. The floors extend to rather more than three quarters of the circle, the rope of the bell coming down by the open space, and they ascend by ladders. There is an Architrave round the top but there is no sign of any pointed pyramidal top: It is of fine hewn stone and excellent workmanship: I think there is

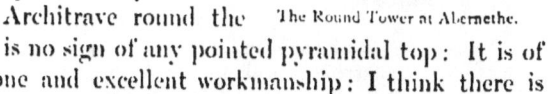

The Round Tower at Abernethe.

---

[1] Figured in Gordon's *Itinerarium Sept.*, 1727, Pl. 62, p. 164; Muir's *Notes on Remains of Eccles. Arch.*, 1855; Anderson's *Scotland in Early Christian Times*, 1881, p. 42.

no manner of Doubt but this tower was built in honour of St. Bridget, notwithstanding the tradition mentioned under the records of Perth. A drawing of it is seen on page 261.

One of the name of Moncrieff[1] was some years ago Minister here, deprived on account of his Doctrine, Heterodox Tenets, and became with four more the Heads of the Seceders; he lives at a Village to the North near the river and has formed a sort of university for educating young men for their Congregation, I was told there were about twenty who boarded here and at that Village with the farmers, for two shillings a week and attend his lectures: It is a very poor Village at present: there is a Seceding Meeting house here. I came to Mrs. Haies's house at Mugrum near the west end of Newbrough.—I am, &c.

Letter LII.

St. Andrews, *August the 30th,* 1760.

Dear Sister,—On the 29th I went to see near Mugrum a large stone set up on end about twelve feet high three broad and near a foot thick, on the North edge are the remains of some lines, cut by way of ornament; the west side is entirely defaced, but in the East side are some marks of a figure[2] which seemed to be better drawing than usual on such Monuments: The stone is set into a socket in the base, after the manner of the Egyptian Obelisks.

From this place we went half a mile up the hill to Macduff's Cross,[3] of which nothing remains but the square rough pedestal,[3] with the socket in which the Cross was probably fixed, and there are some holes in the sides of it, in which they say Iron hooks were fixed to tye the nine heifers to which were brought

---

[1] Rev. Alexander Moncrieff, one of the four founders of the Secession Church.
[2] Mugdrum Cross figured in *New Stat. Ac.* vol. ix. p. 68.
[3] 'Macduff's Cross,' by Sir Walter Scott.

> ' 'Twas the pedestal
> On which, in ancient times, a cross was reared,
> Carved o'er with words which foiled philologists ;
> And the events it did commemorate
> Were dark, remote, and undistinguishable,
> As were the mystic characters it bore ! '

by those who fled to it as an asylum, to be protected by Macduffs.

From this place I went to Newbrough which is on the bounds of Fife, it is a town of one street, and there being many trees in their gardens on each side, it appears very beautifull from the river like a little town in a wood. They are all here either linnen weavers, or farmers; and both here and at Abernethy they have two or three Bailies, who are the Magistrates, and fifteen Council; this place was anciently infamous for their notion of Witches: And when the poor old women were judged to be such, they sent what they called a pricker, to run a needle into them, and if they were so old as to Discover no sense of pain, they were condemned by the Bailies to be burnt; and I was assured that three were burnt on the hill towards Macduffs Cross in 1669.

Very near the East End of Newbrough are the ruins of the Abbey of Lindores: It was first founded in this forrest of Ernside by David Earl of Huntingtore brother of King William when he returned from the holy land in the year 1178. He brought to it the Tyronenses of Kelso of the rule of St. Bernard and St. Bennet first established at Tyronium in the Diocese of Chartres in France: The Church was dedicated to the Virgin Mary and St. Andrew: The site of it is seen but it is entirely ruined. David Duke of Rothsay eldest son of Robert the third is said to be burried in this Church who was starved at Falkland by his uncle: It was erected into a Lordship by James VIth in 1600 in favor of Patrick Lesly son of the Earl of Rothes, and his Descendant Lord Lindores is now Colonel of a regiment of invalides, the family formerly lived here, but the Estate is now in Mrs. Haies's son of Mugrum.

In the garden is a dead holy tree standing with its boughs even since the great frost of 1740, it is above three feet in Diameter. There was a gallery round it within the lower boughs, and a room on the upper boughs in which they say James 6th dined: They had a shady walk for about a quarter of a mile to an elevated ground near the river called Mount Holy, which was a place for the Monks to retire to for Exercise and amusement. A rivulet runs by the Convent which rises out of a Lough half a mile long and a quarter broad between the hills: A little further, I was informed, Wallace was defeated and hid himself in a gully covered with Shrubs, which to this day is called Wallace's den.

We came about two miles to Bambrick[1] anciently the Estate of the Lords of Abernethie, which came about 200 years agoe into the Rothes family by marrying the heiress; It is an L; the old Castle forms the angle to the south west to which they have joyned some modern buildings to the East, and there are remains of a fine gallery with a grand Chimney piece leading to a building northward over the river; This gallery seems to have been built to the old enclosure, the wall being very thick:

I went on near the Sea about four miles to Balmerinach. It was an Abbey of Cistercians, founded by Alexander IId and his mother Emergald[2] a Daughter of the Earl of Beaumont. It is called Balmurerim, and Habitaculum ad Mare: It is said to have been a stately building, and the Kitchen shows it, which consisted of four fine Arches supported by two rows of Octagon pillars, the Capitals of which are short and adorned with foliage. The fireplace was between the two Eastern pillars, which were larger than the others, and there is no building between them, but there seems to have been an isolated double grate, so as to dress the victuals on both sides, and from the middle of the arch between them to the West, the space between the Mullions of the groyn'd arches are not filled up, but were left open to receive the smoak: The foundations of the Church are quite destroyed; a house having been built out of all these ruins. The monks were Cistertians brought from Melross, and it was dedicated to the Virgin Mary & St. Edward: King James 6th made Sr James Elphinston Lord of Balmerinach whose descendant was beheaded in 1746, and this part of the Estate, about £200 a year, loaded with Debts was sold to the Earl of Murray.[3] This was the Seat of the family.

We crossed the hill to the South, and had a view to the North East of Newtown, a house built to a Castle on a rising

---

[1] Ballanbreich, usually pronounced Bambreich.
[2] Abbey of Balmerino, founded by Queen Emergarde.
[3] After the forfeiture of the estates to the Crown they were sold to the Yorks Building Co., who subsequently sold them to the Earl of Moray.

ground between the hills, which is seen at a great distance from the North west and commands a view up the Tay and of the Country of the river and the Sea towards St. Andrews. We came into a beautifull Amphitheatre between the hills out of which rise several streams and fall into the Eden, and crossing over a hill came in four long miles to Couper, finely situated on the river Eden, which is formed by several streams rising to the West and Northwest beyond Falkland: And from the hill I saw a most glorious prospect of a very rich vale to the West, in which we had a view of the Earl of Leven's Seat with fine plantations about four miles distant. Couper is a small town in which there are about 2000 Souls, who chiefly subsist by shops and Marketts for Cattle Corn &c. and it is the high road from Dundee to Edinburgh: They have a handsome Market house and Cross,[1] and a good parish Church with a gallery at the top of the tower, and another about half-way up the Spire: The Castle hill is at the South East side of the town: At the foot of this hill was the Dominican Convent founded by the Macduffs Earls of Fife; But it was annexed to St. Monan the fine Chapel being first much Destroyed: There are no remains of anything belonging to this Monastery: There is a Nonjuring Congregation here which is pretty large.

Tower on the Angle of the Church Wall at Darisy.[2]

[1] Subsequently removed to the top of the hill of Wemyss Hall.
[2] See Billing's *Baronial and Eccles. Antiq. Scot.*, 1845-52, vol. i.

I took leave of Mr. Lang who had accompanied me, and came on towards St. Andrews, & travelling near the Eden I came in two miles to Darisy, where there is a Castle and a fine Chapel near it, which they told me belonged to Cardinal Bethune who built the Chapel. It is a most delightfull situation on a hanging ground which commands a view of the windings of the river, of two bridges over it, and of three or four Gentlemen's Seats to the South. The Chapel is built with ornamental buttresses between the modern Gothic windows, and with battlements at the top; at the South West Corner an Octagon tower is built on the Wall, and the two battlements with stones between the angles to support it. They end in a point, every stone widening up to the foundation of the tower. There is a very short Octagon spire on it, with four upright windows in it. I suppose it must rest on a pillar in the Church, a drawing of it is seen on page 265.

We crossed the Eden on a bridge and going from it to the South East, we had a fine view of some Gentlemen's Seats to the North of it delightfully situated in the plain, and of the bridge of six arches built near its mouth, being the high road from Dundee.—I am, &c.

Letter LIII.

Elly House, near Elly in Fife, *Sepr. 1st*, 1760.

Dear Sister,—We came to St. Andrews in four miles from Darisy. This City is most pleasantly situated on the high ground to the Sea, two miles to the South of Eden, and on a hanging ground over a small brook to the South of the town which might be of great use in carrying on any manufacture. The City is finely laid out in three broad streets near a Mile long which run East and West, and there was a row of houses built to the South and called . . .[1] which faced to the North Sea, and must have been very pleasant, this City being situated on a head of ground formed by the Sea to the North and the

---

[1] Probably the Scores.

rivulet to the South; three narrow Streets cross these at right angles. The original of Devotion to this place was owing to some relicks of St. Andrew, concerning which there is this extraordinary Legend. Regulus, a greek monk of Patræ in Achaia, who was in possession of the relicks of St. Andrew, was admonished in a vision in 370 (three days before the Emperor Constantine came to Patræ to remove those relicks) to take the armbone, three fingers of the right hand, a tooth, and a lid of the knee, and to carry them to a Western region; He embarked with them in company of Damianus a Presbyter, Gelasius, and Cabaculus deacons, and three virgins. The vessel split on the rock at St. Andrews, and they came ashore with the relicks to this place, then a forrest called Muchross (The land of Boars). Hengustus King of the Picts and of all the low Country of Scotland visited the relicts, called the place Rarimont[1] (The King's Mount), gave them the whole forrest, built a church now called St. Rules or Regulus, and by the Highlanders in Eirshe (at this time) Kilreule.

This Church is supposed to be standing at this day, and consists of a very fine square tower about 100 feet high with a door in the south side of it, and small buildings to the East, It seems to have had at three different times three different roofs: and to the East of that was a smaller building now entirely destroyed, in which the relicks might be kept; to the west was another building probably of the same dimensions as the first, to which by the marks on the tower it appears that there had only been one roof; to the south there seemed to have been a shed extending as far west as to the door, by the marks in the wall. The building is about two feet wider than the tower, and so far a Buttress comes out at each of the western Angles that it might be on all sides equally supported, which seems to be very judicious: A very ancient Cornice with modilions runs round the tower in a line from the building; the windows on each side at the top of the tower are very narrow with a true arch supported by Saxon pillars, and over them are very small holes to let in light, the two windows on each side

---

[1] Kilrymont (Cil-righ-monaidh), *i.e.* 'Cella regis in monte,' or The Chapel of the King on the Mount. See legends of the See in Gordon's *Scotichronicon*, 1867, vol. i. p. 72.

of the building are narrow and not long, covered with one
stone cut into a flat Arch: There is a window in the tower to
the East which looked into the Church, in which the inner
stones are cut in true arches, but the outter stone has been
worked in a different shape from them with an arch somewhat
inclining towards the Gothick, but I am persuaded it was so
formed since it was put up: The Arches at both ends of the
building are supported by round slender pillars, the long
Capitals of which are quite plain; as they are of the windows
in the tower: There is much adjectitious work within the tower
to form a stone staircase some way up, and on it rests a frame
of wood of several floors, now going to Decay; I apprehend it
consisted originally of several floors with ladders up to them like
the round towers; The whole is built of a fine white freestone
which was got near the tower, is of excellent masonry, and
resembles much the most ancient buildings about Rome and
Venice, and may be of the 5th Century, it may be before the
Romans left Britain; There is a small window above the larger
windows, and two below, both at such a distance from the
windows and the Door as that it may be supposed that the
large window lighted two floors, as well as the door below, so
that the ground floor excepted, there seemed to have been in
the whole six stories. As mentioned before Keneth the 3d
King of the Scots, when he defeated the Picts, removed the See
to St. Andrews.

The Cathedral[1] a few yards to the North west of this building was a very grand fabrick: It was begun by Bishop Arnold,
who had been Abbot of Kelso, about the year 1160. This
Cathedral seems to have been entirely Saxon, there appearing
no sign of the Gothick style except in a narrow arch in the
upper gallery on each side of the Altar, and it seems also to
have been a greek Cross, for there are four windows in this
style in the western part, which might have extended somewhat
further: For the west end of the Cathedral was blown down
in a storm, and was rebuilt and probably enlarged by Bishop
William Wishart about 1274, there having been about six

---

[1] For views of West Front of Cathedral, St. Regulus, and College Church, see
Billing's *Baronial and Eccles. Antiq. of Scot.*, 1845-52, vol. i.; Pennant's *Tour*,
1772, Pl. xxii. p. 191.

Gothic windows added, besides two arches, that seem to have been the Vestible of the Church : The west end is very grand, the towers on each side of the door are part of an octagon towards the west, and crowned with round pyramids, having windows in them to the four Cardinal points. In the half pediment at the end of the isle is a Gothick window being a quarter of a circle, or a triangle, one side of which is the segment of a circle ; the Triangle being the Emblem of the Trinity ; There seems to have been a building on each side under it, probably a Chapel ; All the windows of the old Church were built with true Arches, they were long windows and not very narrow. In the Transcept were eight arches some of which are not pierced through for windows and under them as many intersecting circles, there were two galleries in the walls all round the Church : In the west end were three tiers of windows each consisting of three ; those at the top were short, and two of them were destroyed to make room for a Gothic window which might be done when the west end was built, there are round pilasters to the Angles on the outside, which are formed at the corners of the towers, and at the corners they goe all the way up and are crowned with Capitals. These two towers are finished at top with pyramids on bases, both of an octagon form : The North side of the Church is entirely destroyed. The West end of the Cathedral was not finished till 1318 by Bishop Lamberton.

Adjoyning to the Church a priory was founded with a prior and Canons for the Cathedral by Alexander 1st, this is also said to be founded by Bishop Robert who had been Prior of Scone under King David the 1st, that is he brought the Canons to it from Scone in the year 1140. The Culdees seem to have continued as part of the Chapter and were permitted to live with them on condition that they would live regularly & peaceably, otherwise they were to be expelled. K. David granted this Prior and the Canons Regular of St. Austin, the Culdean Priory of Loch leven : The Priory is a large Enclosure with round towers, in most of which are niches for statues and on many, the arms of Priors who built them : There is a grand gateway of four arches from the town, and within it, is a large gate and a small one ; There was also a gateway to the south.

Everything is destroyed within this Enclosure: They pretend to show where their Chapel stood. The prior was invested with Episcopal Ornaments, and took place of all the Abbots of Scotland in Parliament.

Bishop Roger first built the Castle of St. Andrews in 1200 in which two Bishops lived: Bishop Lambert is also said to have built a house for the Bishop which might be in the country. The House of the Archdeacon and of some others belonging to the Cathedral are still shown, & a protestant Bishop lived in a house near the Cathedral.

The Castle of the Arch Bishops is built round a Court to the Northwest of the Cathedral on a head of land washed on three sides by the Sea; The front of the Gateway, and if I mistake not was built by Cardinal Bethune. On other parts are the arms of those who are supposed to have built them. In this Castle, Cardinal Betoun was murdered not long after he had seen some persons burnt for heresy, and especially the famous Wishart; and from that very window his body was thrown to satisfy the populace, from which he had seen these miserable objects.

The Parish Church here is a handsome building; In it Arch Bishop Sharp was buried, and over him is erected a stately Monument of the Corinthian order with his statue, and a Relief representing his murder, the Statuary work which is very indifferent was executed in Holland.

In the west end of the street called Shoegate or Southgate, are remains of the north part of the transept of the Church of the Observantines; it is of fine light Gothic Architecture and covered with a beautifull Arch. The Latin School is on the site of the Convent, it was founded by Bishop Kennedy and finished by Bishop Graham in 1478. Jno Walbrook a famous Mathematician in the time of James Vth was provincial of this order and resided here:

Between the north gate and middle gate is the Site of the Dominicans now the bowling Green and a field, without the least remains of it, it was founded by Bishop Wishart in 1274. James Vth annexed Couper and St. Monans to it. On the plain to the South of the Priory are some houses, called the Noude, which they speak of as a Convent, & might be the Carmelites mentioned in St. Andrews of which they have no knowledge.

There is a University here, which did consist of two Colleges for Philosophy, Law and Physick, and the College of Divinity: Bishop Wardlaw is said in 1411 to have first laid the foundation of a University for teaching Arts and Sciences: And yet if I mistake not, Prior Heberden[1] founded the College of St. Leonard. The next Bishop, Kennedy, in 1456 founded St. Salvator College and was buried under a very beautifull Gothic monument of freestone which he himself erected: and there seems to have been a Couchant Statue on it: His Successor Graham obtained that this See should be erected into an Arch Bishoprick: Arch Bishop James Betoun began to found the divinity College which he left to be finished by his Nephew and Successor the Cardinal, one part of it for the library, and a room under it for Exercises; This building is of hewn stone, and the parliament was held in it, when the plague was in Edinburgh: A Court adjoyns to it which is the Divinity College: Here are lodgings and a large room in which they eat with one of the Professors who always attend in turns. There are about eight on the foundation and as many Exhibitioners, the former have their Lodgings and diet, and the latter their Diet only, and they have a large room for their Lectures: They have a principal and four other professors: beyond this College is a building erected for an Observatory under the famous Gregory, who not agreeing with the Professors here went to Oxford. In the Library is a Manuscript of one or two of the Classicks not very old, one is a poem, the other a part of Cicero's Works, and some Church books.

Leonards College was by Act of Parliament united to St. Salvators and is now let for houses and lodgings: There is a Tower to it as well as to St. Salvator, and the parish Church: And the two principals and sixteen other professors were reduced to thirteen. They are repairing their Chapel at St. Salvators in which is a very fine Gothick tomb in freestone of the founder Kennedy, erected by himself; A Couchant Statue of him seems to have laid on it. They have a room for Exercises and a Library: In which I was shown a very fine Gothick Mace or Verge of Silver gilt. On it is the name of

---

[1] Prior John Hepburn of the Augustinian Monastery, 1512.

the maker Paris: It was given by Bishop Kennedy. They have also a number of large pieces of silver with the Arms Embossed and many engraved, of the best annual shooters with a bow and arrow, which being made too large, they are now reduced to the size of a large Medal with Engravings on them. Here they have about sixteen on the foundation and twenty-four Exhibitioners. The Students live in the College and must attend the hall, the price of their diet fixed. They are four years in Phylosophy, and six in divinity for all parts, Except the Highlands, for which four is sufficient, but since Presbytery has been established, They don't take the Degree of Doctor of Divinity. They are kept strict to their Studies, and do not attend any diversions that will take them off. They remain in the University from November to June, the students in Divinity only till Aprill, and then they all go away in the long vacation and the Colleges are shut up. The Professors having all families and houses in the town. They have a rector over the University who is Vice Chancellor; The two principals and two divinity professors commonly are chosen in their turn, the Duke of Cumberland is their Chancellor: The Duke of Chandos's two Sons travelling in Scotland the beginning of this Century, the Duke gave a £1000 to found a Professorship here for Physic and Anatomy. Dr. Thomas Simpson a brother[1] to the Professor at Glasgow was the first Professor. He has made very curious observations in Physick and published a book in 1752 (viz) *An inquiry how far the vital and animal actions can be accounted for, independent of the brain.* He has also made some very curious observations and drawings in relation to the wonderful Structure of the *Echinus* which he is now about to publish. In the other book there is a curious acct. of the ossified brain of a Cow which I saw: The Cow did not appear different from other Cattle when alive, but by frequent snorting. I had a letter to one of the professors who carried me to the library, where the Rector and all who were in town met me, showed me everything about the town, dined with me, and invited me to the divinity hall to sit with them and take some refreshments.

They say there are only between three and **4000** Souls in

[1] See note 4, p. 3.

the town. They are mostly farmers and shopkeepers, & a few merchants, and people that subsist by the University. They have a pier for small vessels and boats, but the weather must be good, when they enter, the Coast being mostly rocky, and there is a bay before the mouth of the Eden.

There is a little promontory to the North of the enclosure of the Cathedral, and just over the pier, on which was the Collegiate Church called Kirkheugh; They show the place a little beyond the pier where it was first built, and was called the Lady's Craig; but the Sea encroaching on it, 'twas built on the heights; It consisted of a Provost and ten prebendaries and belonged to the Culdees till the fourteenth Century: In it was the Statue of King Constantine who retired and professed himself a Culdee: It was called Præpositura Sanctæ Mariæ de rupe, also Capella Regia & Capella Domini Regis Scotorum.— I am, &c.

LETTER LIV.

LESLY IN FIFE, *September 2d*, 1760.

DEAR SISTER,—On the first of September I left St. Andrews accompanied by Dr. Simpson. We went by the sea side and passing over the bridge the Dr. showed me a plant growing out of the joints of the stones, which we could not come at. It is I think peculiar to this place and is called *Secale Scoticum Imperatoriæ affine*. The lands round about the town which were in the Church now belong to the Colleges: There is a ridge of low hills called Barnymount (in the Map Byre hills) which seems a corruption from Boar hills, there being a tradition that when they hunted the boar here, he always ran along this hill to Boar hill: There are several stones about this road, set up on end, & they have a tradition that there was a battle here with the Danes. We passed by Kings Barns where they say the Kings of the Picts lived, which might be their hunting Seat as well as their Farm.

We came on six miles in all from St. Andrews to Crail a small town about a mile from the South East point of the

Coast of Fife, called Fifeness: Here was a Collegiate Church founded at the desire of the Prioress of Haddington, for a Provost, a sacristan, and two Prebendaries in 1517. The Choir part seems to be old, but the body of the Church is a modern Gothic building. There has been an attempt here to establish a Manufactory of bone lace: but the people have not so much application as they ought to make it turn to account. They have here as in all the other little towns on the Frith of Forth in Fife, piers built for the Securing of Vessels; and they most of them carry on some fishing trade; there being very good fish at the isle of May opposite to this place, in the mouth of the Frith of Forth: where there was a Cell of Canons Regular of St. Augustine which belonged to the Monks of Reading in Yorkshire founded by K. David to All the Saints, and afterwards was dedicated to St. Hadrian: Bp: Lamberton of St. Andrews purchased it from the Abbott of Reading and gave it to the Canons Regular, tho' Edward the IIId. protested against it. Barren Women used to go to this Cell in Pilgrimage.[1]

In two small Miles we passed through another town called Kilreny, and then through the two Anstruthers, Easter and Wester, where is the ancient seat of the Anstruthers, which is not now inhabited: Another mile brought us to Pittenweem: Here was a Church of Canons Regular of St. Austin dedicated to the Virgin Mary. The old tower remains, but the Church has been almost entirely destroyed, and what remains of the old building is inhabited by a nonjuring minister, who has a few followers mostly women. Here they have a port that will receive a ship of between 2 & 300 tons, and they have two ships that belong to the Whale fishery which is declining. They have in its infancy a Manufacture of Carpets like the Turkey. This town, the two Anstruthers and Pittenweem send a Member to Parliament:

In a mile more we came to St. Monan[2] an industrious fishing Village. At the West end of the town is the Church of St. Monan. This Chapel was founded by David the IId. and was served by a Hermit; King James the IIId. of Scotland gave it to the Dominicans and it was erected into a Priory, when this order was made a distinct province from that in England. It

---

[1] See Sibbald's *Hist. of Fife*.   [2] St. Monance.

is built on an Eminence very near the Sea, and appears to have been in the shape of a Cross, but the west part is destroyed: It is a very solid antient building with an old plain Cornice, the Cavetto of which is adorned with heads of beasts: The Windows of the Transcept are like those of a Castle splaying outward and turned with true arches, if I do not mistake: The south side seems to have been the model for the Chapel of Derisy [1] with three windows and ornamental buttresses, but where the door is in the place of the next but one to the transept, there is only a narrow window to the east of it, there are two windows at the east end divided by a buttress: To the north there was a building joyned on to it, now destroyed, which took up almost the whole side of the Cross. It is built of the freestone which in some parts is beautifully honey combed by the weather; The East part serves for the Parish Church of Abercromby; the rest is without roof.

Another mile brought us to Elly [2] where there is a harbour for large Ships, and on the East side of it is a rock of freestone in which they find Garnites; and being set with a foil they look like rubies, and are so called. From this place I went to Elly house close to it, and visited Sr Jno Anstruther. It is a good house built to an old castle, there are some good pictures in it, particularly Copies of some of the Luxemburgh Gallery. Sr John has a good Collection of books also of the Roman Coins, with some greek, and several Modern Medals collected by his father, who laid out this place in very good taste; and made Plantations on each side of the lawn before the house; and there are 4 terraces round the woods: In the front is the Frith of Forth, and to the west the bay of Largo appears like a great river; There are several Mounts about this Country, which are called Laws, as they say from making their Laws on them. This is the common opinion as I was told: But Low or Hleaw [3] in Saxon signifies a Tumulus, & in Staffordshire & Worcestershire they call a Barrow a Low, as you may see in *Plots* Staffordshire under Clent, in his Chapter of Antiquities. There is such a one near the House which is called Elly Law, near it they found a passage under ground, going first straight

---

[1] Dairsie.   [2] Elie.
[3] Sax. *hlaw*, a hill, heap, or barrow; Goth. *hlaiw*.

forward then as a segment of a circle, and again in a line leading to an oval apartment like one of the Picts houses, and such I am inclined to think this was, and so might some of the others. What is very extraordinary they found the whole full of a rich black earth. There were no bones in it or any other thing.—I am, &c.

Letter LV.

Kinross, *September 3d*, 1760.

Dear Sister,—On the 2nd Dr. Simpson took leave and Sr. John Anstruther rid with me near to Balgoun.[1] I set out to the west & saw Kelly[2] Lord Kelly's under the hill to the North East; going on we passed in sight of Balcarras belonging to the Earl of that name, and a rock near it is called Cumerland which gives title to his eldest son: We came at the bottom of the bay to Lunden; Here lives the next Heir to the Perth family Mr. Drummond; near it are three stones set up on end from 4 to six feet broad and about fifteen feet high, there seem to have been two or three more so as to form rather an oblong square than a Circle, and was doubtless an Antient Druid temple.[3]

We passed near Leven at the mouth of the Leven where there are salt works and a harbour for ships of between 2 or 300 tons; we passed by some great Coal pitts and the waggon roads from them to the Sea; There is plenty of Coal in these parts but none to the North of the Eden.

We went near Balgoun belonging to the Earl of Leven & gives title to his eldest Son; there are fine plantations about it, we crossed the high road from Perth and Falkland to Kinghorn ferry for Edinborough, and came to Lesly where I waited on the Earl of Rothes Commander of the forces in Ireland. It is a large house built round a Court in King Charles the 2d's time by the first Earl of Rothes; for Lord Hadington marrying the Duke of Rothes's only Daughter, he procured an Act of Parliament, that his second son should enjoy the title of the

---

[1] Balgonie Castle.   [2] Kellie Castle.   [3] Near Lundin House.

Earl of Rothes: The ascent to the first floor was to have been by stairs on the outside, the rooms of it are grand, the ceilings of fretwork, and there is much good old Tapestry in the Apartments: In the Gallery, which is a very good one, are the family pictures, and in one room is a very fine portrait of Rembrant by himself: The house[1] is situated on an Eminence over the Leven to the south of it with hanging gardens, and there is a rivulet to the north, the hills to the south are finely planted, and so is the ground to the west: To the east and north are beautifull fields enclosed with plantations.

On the 3d I came a mile into the high road to Falkland which leads to Perth and southward to Kinghorn, after travelling three miles to the north we came to Falkland, having a view of the Vale of Eden as far as Couper, and of Melvil, Ld. Levens I had seen before, which is a very fine large house built by Sr. John Bruce's Ancestor the famous Architect. Falkland is a poor small town remarkable for a hunting palace[2] of the Kings of Scotland: It is built on two sides of a Court: The front to the Street is a Chapel over two Stories of rooms: The Ceiling seemed to be in good taste, formed in Compartments made of Wainscoat, and painted, but I could not get into the room. There are six windows, with ornamental buttresses between them, in each of which are two Niches for Statues, & some of the Statues remain: There is a grand Gateway with a round tower on each side; the east part also consists of six windows; there are arched offices under the whole, and the same number of windows in the Chapel part, and between them, double pilasters below: To the upper stories are irregular Corinthian pillars on a single pilaster, which supports an entablature, on each side of which is a statue on the east side, and a console on the south, on which there might be also a statue. These fronts also are adorned with heads in Medalions: The Kitchen and house offices were to the north, but are in ruins; and the east part is without roof or floor.

---

[1] Leslie House, a magnificent seat built by the Duke of Rothes, round a court like Holyrood Palace. It contained numerous portraits. On the 28th Dec. 1763 it was burnt to the ground.—*Old Stat. Ac. Scot.*, vol. vi. p. 53.

[2] Figured in Pennant's *Tour Scot.* 1772, pt. ii. Pl. xx. p. 185. For plans and view, see MacGibbon and Ross's *Castel. Arch. of Scot.*, 1887, vol. i. pp. 497-504.

Ressey[1] lake near this place, has been lately drained by making a deep fossee from it to the Eden: We were here at the foot of the Eastern Mountains called the Lomonds, by which we went three miles; They principally consist of a fine freestone for building: We crossed a rivulet to the North, and turning West again, we came in two miles to Burleigh Castle, an Estate belonging to Colonel Irwin; near Lough Leven, and close to it is Melonothart,[2] where there is a large seceding Meeting house, that Sect abounding in these parts; one of the preachers of them having been Minister of this Parish, and Deprived:[3]

We had passed near Port Mallock[4] where there was a Church of Augustinian Canons, said to be situated in St. Servanus's isle on the north side of Loch Leven: had its name from St. Moack and was founded by Eogarch[5] King of the Picts, and formerly inhabited by Culdees; it was sacred to the Virgin Mary, and in 1570 was united to St. Leonards College in St. Andrews, nothing remaining of it but the Parish Church.

At these Villages above mentioned, we came into the road from Perth to Queensferry, and in a mile more to Kinross, a small town where they have a Manufactory of Cutlery ware, it is very near Loch Leven: Close to it Sir John Bruce has a large house with an avenue; it was built by his grandfather, the Architect of Leslie and Melvile's houses, as well as of the front of Holyrood in Edinbro' in Charles the 2d's time. This house has four fronts of Eleven windows, with Corinthian pilasters at the Angles: A sort of Attick window is above the Entablature which together with a roof rather of a high pitch has a bad effect as well as the Disposition of the offices on each side, which appear as dead walls paralel with the house, and there is an ornament of Carving or Stucco on each side of the door, which being white, appears at a distance as if there had been a portico to the door that had been taken away, and has a bad effect; he has practiced over the gates, two Cornu Copiæ in a segment of a Circle, which does not look well; it may be notwithstanding a very good house within.

The garden extends to the lake where we took boat to go

[1] Rossie Loch. [2] Milnathort. [3] Rev. Mr. Mair.
[4] Portmoak.   [5] Rogasch.—*Old Stat. Ac.*, vol v. 171.

about half a mile to the island of the Castle of Loch Leven,
which is about a quarter of a mile in circumference, and large
ash trees grow in it. The Castle[1] consists of five floors, the two
lowest are arched over; there was an ascent up to a door in
the second floor, and a narrow staircase by another way. The
walls are seven feet thick and closets are practiced in them to
the south: To the south also was the Kitchen and they say
adjoyning to it the Chapel, there were round towers at two of
the Corners of the Enclosure: Here they kept Queen Mary
a year, and she escaped when they were at morning Mass: a
boat was ready, and horses to the south west. She went to the
Abbey of Dundrenan, and there embarked, as mentioned before,[2]
for England.—I am, &c.

LETTER LVI.

DYSERT, *September 4th*, 1760.

DEAR SISTER,—On the 4th we crossed a bridge over a rivulet
which falls into Loch Leven very near the town, from which
running water is brought through the town: Two miles further
the road comes in at Glandevin, in which road we were when we
went to Tullibarden, leads from Creif to the Queens ferry for
Edinborough, here I saw limestone, which is brought four miles
from the Mountains to the Southwest. I think the place is
called Restenet. We left this road, and going along the South
Side of the Lough, we came out of Kinross-shire (which we had
entered about half way from Falkland) into Fife again; Towards the east end of the Lake we had the island about half a
mile from the Shoar, which is called Inch Lough Leven. In it
was a priory dedicated to St. Cerf[3] by Brudens a Pictish King,
who gave it to the Culdees, David the first granted it to St.
Andrews, and so it was vested in the Augustinian Canons:
Robert Winters[4] was Prior of this place who writ in old Scotch

---

[1] For plan and views, see MacGibbon and Ross's *Castel. Arch. of Scot.*, 1887, vol. i. pp. 146-149.

[2] See page 25.   [3] St. Serf or Servanus.

[4] *The Lochleven Chronicle; or, A History of the World, from its Creation to the Captivity of James I.*, in Scotch metre, by Andrew Wintan.

Metre, a history from the beginning of the World to the time of James 1st when he lived; which is in the Advocates Library: They have pike, perch, & Eel in this water.

Leaving the lake we turned to the South and came to Kirkness, and from that by Sir Michael Markams, two miles to Lough Or, where I saw what is called a Roman Camp on the north side of the Lake, encompassed by the lake, and a Morass, it is small and irregular towards the Lough, the fossee that way being carried circular as the ground happened to lye, for it appears that the Lough has forsaken the Dyke. There is a stone causeway to it, and they say it was defended by a rampart to the east, where there is a Drain now made. This Camp is near 300 yards long from east to west and about 100 broad at the west end. On the heighth to the south over the circular part are ruins of a chapel. This lake[1] must be about a mile long and near half a mile broad, it affords perch, pike and Eels: Towards the east end and near the north side, is a round island with a square Castle in it encompassed with a Circular wall, to which on the west and north side two offices were built. There seems to have been a Causeway with a Drawbridge to it, and now people can walk to it, the water being about four feet deep, there are foundations of walls all along the Edge of the lake near it, and foundations of a circular building appear: This Castle belonged to Workelaws[2] of Tory, who were masters of the greatest part of Fife.

Going on I soon crossed this stream and then another which I believe is that which comes from Lough Fitty: About a mile to the west of Lough Or, I saw a fine plantation with house and offices which belongs to Adams the Architect. We ascended the hill, came into the Coal Country, and passed by a place called Lough Galley,[3] over the Lough of that name, which place belongs to Mr. Elliot a Lord of the Admiralty, whose brother, Captain Elliot, destroyed Thurots fleet: From this, another stream runs which we passed: This beautifull country is diversified by little ridges of rocks extending from east to west, which cause an agreeable variety.

---

[1] Loch Ore, now drained and added to the estate of Lochore.

[2] The Wardlaws of Torry; the name of *Robertus Wardlaw* is inscribed on the tower.

[3] Lochgelly.

We passed by a Quarry of limestone about a mile from Lough Galley, & came to Kirkaldy six miles from Lough Or, passing at the west end of the town by a large house called Abbottshall, which was the Country house of the Abbott of Dunfermling: We passed to the East the long town of Kirkcaldy and came in a mile to Dysart to General Sinclairs at the west end of the town: where he has a house nicely finished, and there are gravel walks and a lawn down to the Sea, this gentleman is brother and heir to Lord Sinclair who forfeited in 1715. He has here great Collieries. The wells down to them are eight feet in Diameter, cut through the rocks and there are wooden stairs down to the bottom. They have worked 150 feet deep, raise the water by fire engines, and are making one piston about 50 inches in diameter: They find two or three Seams one after another, divided by rock. Here is a pier for the boats to come and load with Coal and Salt, For the General has large Salt pans.—I am, &c.

Letter LVII.

Dumfermline, *Sber 5th*, 1760.

Dear Sister,—On the 5th I went towards Kirkaldy, where there are three or four contiguous towns. The first is Sinclair, which is only a small Village with an old Castle situated on the seashore, where the Sinclairs formerly resided; The principal tower is Semicircular, with an addition of part of the square, and there are two or three round towers, the next town is Pethhead, and then there is a little space between it and Kirkaldy, and last of all is . . . .[1] They have in these towns a considerable linnen trade, mostly of sailors cheques, and 'tis probable there are about 1000 houses in them.

From thence we went up to the north half a mile to Enderteel[2] to the Quarry which is of the nature of the Derbyshire Marble, but so hard that they make Millstones chiefly of one bed of it, and it is very difficult to polish; there is also a bad

---

[1] Linktown. [2] Inverteil Quarry.

yellow cast in some parts of it: It is full of Trochi, and Entrochi, of the Conchæ Amoniæ, some Mycetitæ, Coral, and other Shells, and I saw in an adjacent rock a mass of Coral: The Belemnites are in the Marble, but I could find none loose. I took specimens of all these.

We came in two miles to Kinghorn, where there is a ferry seven miles over to Edinburgh, which passage, together with letting houses, is the support of this small town; which is situated on a head of land: We passed by a Lough, a mile round, from which a stream flows constantly to the town. At the Sea Cliffs there is petrified moss formed by the dropping of the water from the rocks. We came to a Quarry, the top of which is a fine white freestone, and below it is limestone, and so are the quarries on to the west, but in some places the limestone is below the level of the Sea, and then it is difficult to raise it by reason that the water comes up on them; and I was told that below the level of the Sea it is all limestone. From this quarry they take the finest freestone for building.

In about a mile more we came to Brunt Island,[1] where they have a square Church with a Cupola at top. They have a fine harbour which will hold a ship of 300 tons, & into this place ships come in bad weather; and this is the chief support of the place, the people not applying to any Manufacture. There is an old Parish Church[2] near the town with three Arches in it, supported by Pillars: over this flat Country there is a high perpendicular rocky hill, and it is called the King's Craig;[3] less than two miles brought us to Aberdour which gives title to the Earl of Moreton's Eldest Son, here the Earl has a small seat and an Obelisk built on an Eminence towards the Sea. Here also is an old Castle and a round building adjoyning to it near the Church; here was a Nunnery of Clares, but no remains or any particular acc^t of it. They have a little harbour, and carry on some linnen trade:

Going on I observed the high ground extending to the west, and a quarter of a mile south of it a high narrow hill with a sharp top about a mile long, the north side being covered with wood, as is the south side of the other, and between them is Sir Robert Henderson's house situated in the delightfull Glyn of

---

[1] Burntisland.   [2] The Kirkton.   [3] The Bin.

.... [1] We turned out of that road to the south and passed by Dalgaty[2] an old house and well built small Church which belonged formerly to the Marquis of Tweedale, and now to the Earl of Murray:[3]

We came by a strand to Dunibrizel[4] the Earl of Murray's, a good house tho' of no great outward appearance ; There are some fine tapestry and pictures in it, particularly one of King Charles the 1st after the battle of Naseby with a melancholy determin'd countenance, and two boys holding his horse: near the house a very elegant Chapel is built of freestone in chisell'd work, for the service of the Church of England, and a burial vault under it. The Earl who was uncle to the present, married an aunt of the Duke of Argyle, who loved building: The situation is most delightful, and commands a distinct view of Edinburgh, to which it is almost directly opposite ;

We came in a mile to Inverkeathing, where there is a natural basin, which if it were cleansed would be a most beautiful harbour : The town is situated on the side of a hill, there are many inhabitants in it who are contented with the products of a few acres of ground and apply to no kind of business ; Here was a Convent of Franciscans ; I could not be informed of any remains, and suppose it was at the parish Church ; the ruined East End of which is old, and so is the tower. A little below it at a head of land is the Queens ferry where horses and carriages ferry over two miles, and have after seven miles to go to Edinburgh : And here is the best freestone in this Country : I went a little way in the road and turned to the west to Lord Moreton's lead mines at Casern Hill :[5] They have been worked but a little time by the mine adventurers, who pay to the Lord the 7th dish ; I took a specimen of the steel and soft ore.

Came in three miles through fine vales to Dumfermling, which is a town most beautifully situated on a hill made by the winding of a brook that forms deep glyns or Gulleys on the south and west sides of it, and before that, running from the east, makes another not so deep, a quarter of a mile to the north of the town, where it turns at the south west angle is a natural steep ground which extends from east to west in a

[1] Fordel.   [2] Dalgety.   [3] Earl of Moray.
[4] Donibristle.   [5] Castland Hill; the mine was soon wrought out.

promontory on which there are ruins of a small Castle;[1] These glyns are finely adorned with wood on one side, and gardens behind the houses on the other to the west; but on the south, both sides are covered with wood for a considerable way; and on that side towards the confluence of the two streams (having only the Castle between) was situated the famous Abbey of Dunfermling, it was in some degree begun by Malcolm IIId and finished by Alexander the 1st before the year 1120, was governed by a Prior, and might then be an hospital, for it is called Monasterium de monte infirmorum: But Malcolm's son David 1st made it an Abbey. They were Benedictines. Burntisland, called formerly Wester Kinghorn, was the Castle and harbour of this Abbey: Kinghorn and Kirkaldy also belonged to them. The first Abbot Gosfrid died in 1154. It was dedicated to the Trinity and St. Margaret Queen of Scotland, & was vested in the Crown by Parliament in the time of James VIth. After the Reformation it was given to Secretary Pitcairn, afterwards to the Master of Grey and then to Alexander Seton first made Lord Urquhart, and then Earl of Dunfermling in 1605: The Conventual Brethern of it who reformed, had their portion reserved to them: The Church[2] has been a noble Saxon building, consisting in the body of eight arches. The door is fine, and there are seven narrow arches turned over it: A more modern porch, cut in Saxon taste, has been added to it: Originally there were no windows over the great windows, but on the north side they seem to have been broke out; the upper windows towards the east were made with angular tops and round pillars on each side, but both sides seem to have failed and are supported by large buttresses; and the three windows towards the west part of the north side are Gothick, with small narrow Gothick windows over them: There were two galleries over the isles with large single Saxon arches in front of them: The pillars are large, and the pair to the East are adorned with lines that twist round, and the next with half lozenges with lines on each in shape of the head of a spear. The walls of the towers and of the Church are crowned with projecting battlements like a Castle; The tower

---

[1] Dunfermline Palace. See MacGibbon and Ross's *Castel. Arch. of Scot.*, vol. i. pp. 514-519.

[2] See Henderson's *History of Dunfermline*, 1879, pp. 14-244.

was built with a spire that has windows in it: The south tower seems to have been taken down to the height of the walls of the Church on account of a great crack in the west end, which might be made by their opening a Gothick window: There is a round window over the door divided into four compartments by a Cross. The windows consist of three members, the grand door to the west of five, the cornice all round is adorned with heads; There were two Towers on each side of the middle of the Transept, one of them fell down about six years agoe and I suppose the other was pulled down. The stone of the Shrine of St. Margaret, seems to have been about ten feet long five broad and a foot thick of a grey kind of Marble, and there seem to have been five pillars on each side to support the Shrine, it is in the Middle of the Church near the East end; so that if the high altar was to the west, it must have been very close upon it. The Transept of the Church is destroyed, & one side of a new Gothick Quire is standing; which appears to have been the whole width of the transept and consisted of five fine Gothic windows; but there are no signs of the Quire on the south side; It seems to have been widened to take in the six tombs of plain flat stones over the Kings of Scotland who were doubtless buryed in the Church yard, as they lye near the north side of the new quire: There is a ceiling of boards made to the Church about as high as the top of the large arches, rising gradually towards the west end; and when it approaches the gallery, it rises higher so as to be above it, and has an exceeding bad effect to the eye, but was contrived to throw the sound of the voice upon the Audience:

To the south of the Church was the Refectory; Between the windows are ornamental buttresses, in each of which is a nich for a statue. One window towards the east end is built with an Arch setting out, and an arch of communication within a bow window, from which I suppose there was some portion of Scripture read at the time of eating, and it is called the library, where the Bible or Legends might be kept, out of which they read: There were six windows to the west, and one larger than the others to the East, where the great table might be. It is called the Frair Hall. It was about 30 feet wide in the Clear by 120: If I do not mistake, under it were two arched Vaults; & adjoyning to it are buildings which extend further to the south with single narrow Gothic windows and this was probably the Dormitory :

From the Refectory to the south side of the tower of the Church was a building called the Skaipell, of the meaning of which I could not be informed ; But have since met with that word as signifying a Tennis Court : To the west of the Church are some buildings which were erected after the Reformation by James VIth with an inscription on them, and adjoyning to the southwest corner of the Refectory is a grand gateway : To the west of this seems to have been the Abbot's appartments and those for strangers consisting of two floors, to each of which was a grand room and a smaller at the end of it ; the principal great room is below : There were arched Vaults under it ; Here the Kings of Scotland resided after the Reformation, when they came into these parts, the royal bed being now to be seen which was sent from Denmark by the Queen of James 6th who was received here as it is said, and that it was the marriage bed ; and Charles 1st they say was born here. These grand appartments are built on the side of the hill, with spaces for either windows or chimneys to the number of twelve and buttresses between them, and is a very grand work ; there having been arched vaults under them ; and the building, as seen from the side of the hill below, appears of a stupendous height, each compartment for the windows is about ten feet and the buttress 5 feet in all 160 feet in length.

The Royal bed[1] is partly preserved in the Inn. The feet were large and adorned with carved work, the upper part being a lyon's head ; there is a beautifull carved Cornice to the lower

---

[1] 'Within these 30 years, there was to be seen in the bed-chamber of an inn at Dunfermline, the nuptial bed of Queen Anne, which she is said to have brought along with her from Denmark. For this piece of royal furniture, the innkeeper, Mrs. Walker, a zealous Jacobite, entertained a very high veneration. Bishop Pocock of Ireland, happening to be in her house, and having seen the bed, offered her 50 guineas for it, which she refused, telling him, "That she still retained so great reverence for the two royal personages whose property it was, and who slept in it when they resided here, and to their posterity, all the gold and silver in Ireland was not fit to buy it." Some time before her death, Mrs. Walker made a present of the Queen's bed to the Earl of Elgin, an heritor in this parish. The bed is of walnut-tree, of curious workmanship, and ornamented with several very antique figures neatly carved.'—*Parish of Dunfermline*, by Revs. A. Maclean and J. Fernie, 1794. *Old Stat. Acc. of Scot.*, vol. xiii. p. 448. The Earl of Elgin writes (1887) : 'The pieces which agree with the description

part, and it is divided into four compartments by Modillions adorned with heads, all the parts between being finely carved: The pillars at the head consist of a figure of a Woman, on carved pedestals, they hold up the garment with one hand, and in the other is a Violin hanging down, those at the feet are men with beards; a Cornu Copiæ of flowers covers them in part behind, and Clothes on the head to which they hold up, one hand hangs down also behind, the other holds the garment before, on the head is a pot of flowers, on that a beautifull Vase with a long neck the belly of which is adorned with four heads, the whole being carved, & this supports a Corinthian Capital, the women are the same, except that the clothes on the head come down narrow below the breasts, and they have not the hand lifted up to the head. The Vase and capitals seem to be walnut and the lower part of the bed: but the rest is a deep red wood well polished, and so is the cornice of the bedstead below, for there is nothing rests on the Capitals: The head piece remains, which is a woman lying in repose, a dog at her head and a stag approaching towards her; on each side is a sphinx. These seem to have been emblems of fidelity in the woman; of benevolence in the man, and of wisdom and prudence in both; The top, if there was any is lost, and there seems to be something wanting to the head.

They have Seceders here; and likewise Mr. Glasside's[1] Church who was deprived for not executing the orders of the assembly, but they do not differ from the Established Kirk. There is a lough[2] about a mile to the west of the town, from which they have brought water almost sufficient to supply the inhabitants. This Town thrives in Manufacturers; they make much table linnen of all kinds, ticking, carpets, and striped woolen stuffs for womens ware. It consists chiefly of a long Street, a back street which is shorter, and a cross street at the west end; and must have in it above a thousand families. They compute within the parish there are towards 8000 people, taking in those in the Country as well as the Town.—I am, &c.

given by Bishop Pococke were so much decayed, that it would have been scarcely possible to have used them for this purpose [bedstead]. They have therefore been set up as a chimney-piece [at Broomhall], in which form they are more likely to be preserved.'

[1] Glassites, followers of Mr. Glass.   [2] Cairncubie.

Letter LVIII.

DUNPLANE IN PERTHSHIRE, Sepr. 7th, 1760.

DEAR SISTER.—On the 6th I left Dunfermling and saw two or three Laws not far from it, some of them are planted round with trees: we soon had a view of the Forth, which upwards is extremely beautifull, there being a distant prospect of the fine country on the other side: In three miles we came to a place called Torbyburn, and then to Torby itself where there are Salt works: This place they pronounced Torry, and up higher on one side of the Burne, they told me were the remains of Workdaws[1] Castle, who as mentioned before, commanded almost all Fife.

Going a mile further we came to Cullros or Kyllenros. This is just within the Shire of Perth, into which we entered again: it is a small town and was erected into a Burg of Barony in 1484. The present parish Church, was the Abbey Church of the Cistercians founded here by Malcolm Earl of Fife in 1217, the Monks being brought from Kinloss. Alexander Colvill was the last Abbot, and his brother Sr James of Ochiltry Bart. was in 1604 made Lord Colvil of Culros, to whom the Abbey was granted. The tower is in the Saxon style, and so is a door to the south of it which was the Entrance of the Convent: some Gothic doors are built near it: in a Chapel to the North is a fine Monument to Mr George Bruce and his Lady with their Couchant statues, and their three sons and five daughters kneeling below. Going on, I saw the old small parish Church of Culros, which is patched up with several kinds of buildings, and over the doors are tombstones with Crosses on them: over the west door is an oblong square window separated from the door only by a single stone: this west end seems to be of great antiquity.

We proceeded and crossed a stony heath about two measured miles, passing by Tullyallan Church and a large old ruinous house on the river. We then crossed a rivulet, and came into

[1] Wardlaws. See note p. 250.

Clackmanan Shire about that place. This is a small shire, consisting only of five parishes. The river appeared very much like the Thames towards Gravesend; and when we came near Clackmanan, the river was most delightfull: we ascended to Clackmanan, a poor small town situated on a single hill, with the Castle of Sir Henry Bruce, at the west end of it, whose family produced five Kings and Queens of Scotland: And in it we saw the Sword and Helmet [1] of K. Robert Bruce: the Castle consists of five floors two of which are arched, there being a large room and a smaller on each floor. From the top of it is a most charming view of the windings of the Forth, especially of two islands a little higher, and of Sterling with its Castle on a single long hill, as well as of all the Country round and of the river below.

From this place we went two measured miles to the North to . . .[2] Lord Cathcarts, on a rising ground about a mile from the mountains. The approach to it is round three sides of the plantations, and by a Village partly new built, where the present Lord has settled a Manufacture of Osnaburgs. Half a mile further stands the House[3] of a very singular form, which consists of an oblong square pile of buildings to which a Fabric is added at each end with a bow or recess of three sides at each end, and to the Western building a large semicircular bow is joyned, which with the additional building, forms a very fine room, a lobby being taken off it at one end & a staircase &c. at the other. That below is the dining room, and both command a most delightfull view towards Sterling; as the Leads at the top doe of the whole country. The house is crowned all round with battlements, and with pediments in the middle, a Cornice with plain Modilions ranging round. The pediments at each end are adorned at the bottom with a plain Architrave but not in the fronts. In the middle of the entrance is a balcony, and in the back part a Gallery between the two bows, which is supported by wooden pillars below. The offices are hid by walls built with battlements and square towers at the corners, & sheds are built against the wall for several uses.

[1] Bequeathed by Mrs. Bruce in 1791 to the Earl of Elgin.
[2] Sauchie, now the property of the Earl of Mansfield.
[3] Schaw Park House.

The whole is made as white as possible and the walls at a distance make it appear like a very grand house. The other rooms of the house are very convenient. The two grand rooms are highly adorned with pictures: The ground is laid out in lawn near the house, and the hills to the east are planted with Clumps and groves; in front of the house the top of the garden wall appears, which is built to humour the ground, the wall is only on one side and lined with brick, it is a fine exposition to the south and south west, and will be very beautifull when it is finished. This estate came by his Mother, heiress of Sir John Shaw.

Close to the foot of the Mountain is the seat of Charles Areskine[1] Lord Justice Clerk, called Alva, he is one of the Lords of the Session; There are fine woods about it, and up the side of the hills; and to the North east up the Mountain, on the same rivulet is Castle Campbell, said to be the first residence of the Campbell family. From this place I came two miles to Alloa a very disagreeable Coal town. Here is the seat of the late Earl of Mar (who forfeited Anno 1715) now of Lord Erskine his eldest son, much admired for its situation: it is on a flat, half a mile from the river: The gardens are laid out in the old way, with four Vistaes, the one is to the East; another to the south takes in Lord Dunmore's house, and there is a fine avenue that way to the river: It has a view of Sterling Castle to the west; To the East it is finely planted in triangles after the taste of King Charles the Second's time. But in reality the place is finer in prospect than on the spot; There is a tolerable house built to the Castle.

I came on from Alloa having all the way for four miles the Castle of Sterling in view, till I came within two miles of it, when after passing two rivulets on bridges we turned to the north west, and went by the side of the Abbey Craig on which I observed a square fortification at top; one of the rivers was the Alan, called above Glin Knig water on which Dunblane stands; and going directly north, after travelling seven computed miles we arrived at Dunblane; we had passed a fine place adorned with wood up the side of the hills to the right which is very beautifull.—I am, &c.

[1] Lord Alva—C. Erskine of Aberdona.

Letter LIX.

Stirling, *Sepr. 8th* 1760.

Dear Sister,—Dunblane, though a poor town as to buildings, is very pleasantly situated on the river Alan, consisting chiefly of one street built paralel with the river, and the Cathedral is at the end of it. There was anciently a Convent of Culdees here, which continued after it was made a Bishop's See by David the IId. St. Blaan was head of the Convent in the reign of Keneth the IIId from whom it has its name, Dunblane, (Blane's hill or fort). The first Bishop whose name is met with is about 1150; Bishop Finlay called Dermoch built the bridge before 1419, which is a fine Arch 42 feet wide, and twelve broad: it appears to have been pulled down and new built, and the tradition is that the Bishop thinking it weak built another arch over a new one to make it stronger. The tower is at the side of the present building of the Cathedral and appears to have been at the west end of a Fabric which joyned on to it, and might have been the first Church, perhaps of the Culdees: two Gothic stories of a light coloured stone appear to have been built on five Saxon stories of red freestone, the same as the rest of the present buildings. The body of the Church consists of eight light Gothic arches, over each of them are two Gothic windows, and in the isles a Gothic window to each division into four parts. The west window is very fine and lofty, & built double, so as there is room to go between the inner and outer window. The door is beautifull and consists of about a hundred members, computing every minute member. The Quire only is the present Church, and consists of six windows on the south side, that which is farthest to the East and to the west being narrower than the others and consist of two parts, the others of four: There is only one on the north side answering to the most eastern window on the South side. The East window is extremely beautifull ending in four parts at top, adorned with circles between the Gothic Arches, and there are as many Gothic arches in the middle; on each side of it is a long Gothic window, and all of them rise to the top of the Church. The isle continues the whole length on the north side, but is now divided to the north of the Quire into a School and Vestry; the four Stalls on each side at the west end of the Choir remain with the fine ornaments over them of carved Gothic pilasters, and there are 13 Stalls on each side, a division being made at the sixth as for the Chantor and Treasurer. There is a Sepulchral nich on the south side of the Quire. The church yard is over the river, which is to the west of it. To the south was the Bishop's house, the ruins of which are seen, which were demolished by undermining, it extended all down to the end of the library: opposite to it were the Canons houses which are standing. In a street to the east of the Church are remains of the small house in which Bishop Leighton and the reformed Bishops lived. The See of Dumblane at the Reformation was computed to be worth £313 one of the least whose Rents were paid in wheat, beare, meal and oats. At the west end of the spot on which the Bishop's house stood, is a library founded by Bishop Leighton who sent his books to it; but gave some to the library at Glasgow: There is a good Collection of Books in Divinity, and they lend them to every one who enters his name and gives half a guinea for the use of the library.

They have a small Manufactory of linnen, and thread, and Shoes, which they send to Glasgow:

There is a Seceding house set up here on their displeasure being taken that the patron of the living would not accept of their recommendation, but they do not differ in Doctrine; The Tenants of the Patron and some others set up the person they would have put in as a lecturer in the Kirk and raise a subscription of £50 a year.

There is a pleasant walk a measured mile long over the river to the south east, terminating at a Gentleman's house, called Kippenross, where there is a Sycamore which measures at the root and branches 34 feet round, and eighteen at the smallest part, four great branches grow out of it: There are plantations on each side of the walk, it is mostly hanging ground to the river, and on the whole very beautifull.

I rid a mile and a half to Sheriff Muir, to see the place of battle between the Duke of Argyle and the Rebels under Lord Mar in 1715. The King's forces were encamped four days on

an eminence defended by a vale, and extended half a mile down
to Dunblane ; The Rebels on a moor to the north west of the
Alan : They met on the height of the hill, and the right wing
of the enemy broke the left of the King's forces, and pursued
them to the lines, but finding that Argyle had broke their left
wing, they returned and were cut to pieces, about 1000 of the
enemy falling : We saw several little risings where 'tis supposed
the dead were buried : They pursued them even through the
Alan and up the Mountains, and several of the Enemy were
drowned in the Alan.

We had here a pleasing view of the Neighbouring Country,
which includes Strathallen, the Strath on the Forth, and extends almost to Monteith and Lough Loumond, all very fine,
though much intermixed with Heath. Most of the Gentlemen
of this County are of the Church of England, but some of
their ladies go to the Kirk.—I am, &c.

LETTER LX.

EDINBURGH, *Sepr.* 10*th*, 1760.

DEAR SISTER,—On the 8th I came from Dunblane to Sterling
and passed near Kier to the west a large house and fine plantations
of Mr. Sterling who has a considerable Estate there. We crossed
the Alan again, and going by the banks of it, went near the long
rocky hill called Abbey Craig on which I thought I saw some
fortifications : And we had to the west Craig Fort, a small
rocky hill covered with wood to the east, with the house at the
foot of it belonging to another gentleman of the name of Sterling. I remarked in the fosses on each side of the road a bed
of Oysters and other Shells about two feet from the surface and
a foot thick, which they are digging out for manure. This
convinced me of what I had imagined as I came to Dunblane
(viz) that the flat grounds beyond Alloa and on this side of it
were formerly part of the bay.

We went near the tower of Cambus Keneth in a peninsula
made by the winding of the river in the Shire of Clackmanan ;

which belonged to the Canons Regular of St. Augustine founded by David 1st in 1147, nothing remained but the tower and the plain monuments of some of the Kings. Abbot Alexander Miller was the first president of Session on the institution of the College of Justice by James Vth and was employed by him in many embassies. We crossed over the Forth to Sterling on a fine bridge of four arches. From the Castle I saw, up the river, Blair, a large seat of the Drummonds.

Sterling is finely situated on the side of a hill, on the west end of which is the Castle, commanding a most extensive prospect of a beautifull Country, and the windings of the Forth which runs 24 miles to Clackmanan, that is but five miles distant by land: There is a broad short street which leads up to the Castle; the rest of the town is not well laid out: There are not the least remains of the Franciscan Fryers; it is now a garden and called the Friary: it was founded by James 4th in 1494 who often dined with the Monks here, assisted at Mass, and passed his Lent at the Convent, and on good friday dined with the Community on bread and water and upon his bare knees. I could get no acc^t of the Dominican Monastery founded by Alexander the 2d near the walls. Richard the 2d is said to have died in this Castle, and to have been buried in the Church at the high altar: At the upper end of the broad street is a magnificent building, though in the bad taste of the time of James Vth, Entering it by a gateway to the left is the fine Gothic building of the Collegiate Church of the Royal Chapel of Sterling erected into a Collegiate Church by Pope Alexander 6th at the desire of James 4th with all the officers of a Royal Quire; The Dean being the Queen's Confessor, with Episcopal Jurisdiction. The Deanry was first in the provost of Kirkheugh, then in the Bishop of Galloway, and was by James 6th anexed to the Bishoprick of Dunblane: This is the only Church in the town; from this place we returned into the Street, and passing by the Duke of Argyle's ruinous house we ascended to the Castle: The site is a high rock, which appears in some of the back streets of the town below. I observed it was that black granite in small grains which is so common in Scotland. We first came to the outer part, which was built in Queen Anne's time, and was shewn opposite to it, the battery which the Rebels planted in 1745, that was soon silenced by the Cannon from above: I saw here the brass Cannons with the name of Sidney on them which were taken by the Rebels at Falkirk, and afterwards retaken here, with many other Canon, if I mistake not, after the Defeat at Culloden. We then came within another fortification and from that went into the part where the palace[1] stands which is built round a court: To the west is the old part, to the north the Chapel which is new, and to the east the parliament house,[1] which is a long room with thick walls and built like a Castle. The grand body of the building is to the south, with five windows every way, being itself a pile of building round a small court of the most extraordinary architecture of James Vth with strange kinds of pillars one over another, and as strange figures resembling Careatides at a time when architecture in Italy was in its highest perfection. I went into this part, into the grand room, destined for the Queen's Ladies; also State Apartment, then the King's and another grand room I suppose leading to his which was locked: in the small court the Lyons were kept. To the rooms of State, there are ceilings of wood adorned with carvings of heads &c. The prospect from the Castle is extremely fine. There is always a Comp^y of 100 invalids here. This town chiefly subsists by shops, and the great through fare to the North especially from Glasgow.

I proceeded on my journey, and came in a mile to St. Ninians where there is an old Church tower, and a modern Kirk. We passed Bannock Burn, famous for the entire defeat of the English by the Scots under Robert Bruce, where Robert the 2d saved himself in a boat: And the Scots were quiet for a year or two after: We turned out of the high road to avoid the droves of Cattle going to Falkirk fair, and travelled two miles to the East having a fine view of the river, and a little beyond Bruce Castle, we turned to the South and were within a mile of Airth; in the road I saw some petrifications of Bellemnites, Trochi, Entrochi, and Conchae Anomiae, which were very sparry, but I do not know from what place they were brought.

We came to the river Carron; just to the north of it was

---

[1] For plans and views, see MacGibbon and Ross's *Castel. Arch. of Scot.*, 1887, vol. i. pp. 464-478.

Arthur's own or oven,[1] near a mill for the building of which, to the eternal reproach of the owner, this noble Remain of antiquity was destroyed. They are making great buildings here for Iron smelting houses. There is a harbour near it on the river Avon.

We came on to Falkirk, a long town of one street. But the country near it is infamous for the scandalous defeat of our army by the rebels in 1746, which in 1747 was related to me[2] in this manner by a person I met with on the spot and showed me the whole scene of the battle. The General had been informed the day before that the Enemy were making round on the hill, and despised them : This intelligence was repeated to no purpose. It was on the 17th of Jany 1746, and in the morning not very early, They were told the Enemy was on the hill near them ; The officers were most of them in bed : our people were called to arms and despising the enemy, marched up the hill ; the weather was not good ; the Enemy fired on them from the height ; and the horse were flanked by their fire from a defile, which I saw. The regiment in which a certain Lieutenant Col. commanded, fled under pretence of misunderstanding the word of command, he endeavoured to rally them, but to no purpose, and all flying, he went and fought at the head of another regiment. Thus ended this day of reproach.

We went on six miles to Linlithgow commonly called Lithgow, which consists of a street ; it may be three quarters of a measured mile long : Here is the very handsome modern Gothic Church formerly belonging to the Palace which stands just before it ; it is hewn freestone inside and out, and remains much in the same way as it was fitted up at the Reformation, with the King's Semicircular Seat against a pillar opposite to the pulpit : There is a Chapel to the South, in which they say James 4th was attending Vespers, and an old man came to him and desired him not to go to the battle against the English at Flodden Field, for that he would not return ; immediate search being made the old man could not be found, and 'tis supposed to have been a contrivance of the Queen's. I had no information of a Monastery founded for Carmelites in 1290 by the

---

[1] See Gordon's *Itin. Sep.*, Pl. 4, pp. 24-32.
[2] See p. 3. This also confirms note 3, p. 1.

Citizens. The palace[1] is built round a court, the south and west sides by James 5th, the north by James 6th. The parliament house is a fine room, the south end is all chimney, but divided into three below, by two pillars with Gothic Capitals adorned with foliage and above by two walls, at the north end is a musick gallery, & in the west side a gallery is practiced in the walls for the hearers, to the East are windows; on the west side Mary Queen of Scots was born: In the middle was a fine fountain adorned with Statuary and Sculpture, but they say our Soldiers after the battle of Culloden destroyed it to get the lead; and when they left it, burnt the palace as by accident; it is situated in an Island on a Lough, a mile long, and a quarter of a mile broad. There are perch, jack and Eels in this water. This seems to have been a place for the Kings to retire to as a Villa to Edinburgh.

We came on 5 miles to Hopetown[2] house about a mile to the north of the road. It is a very fine situation, a promontory which stretches to the north into the Frith, so that the sea or river is to the west of it, and is seen in front to the east, which is the way the house stands: It is a very grand house of 21 windows, a Colonade of a quarter of a Circle of 12 flat arches of the Doric order joyn it to the fine Stables on one side, and to the library on the other. To the Stable and library is a tower built with a Cupola: The library is about 100 feet long. You see through the rooms of the house to a window at each end about 300 feet. The house in front is adorned with Corinthian pilasters all the way up: There is an attick story above the Entablature, and a banister all round at top divided by pedestals over the solid parts on which there are vases. To the offices between the windows are Couplets of Doric pilasters all executed with fine freestone. The house was originally designed by Sr ... Bruce but many alterations since made. The approach to it is grand; and Lord Hopton has lately enlarged the hall and finished a grand apartment with plain wainscoating and plain paper, the pictures are all in white frames and scrued on to the wainscot, and it is to be hung with

[1] For plans and views, see MacGibbon and Ross's *Castel. Arch. of Scot.*, 1887, vol. i. pp. 478-497.
[2] See p. 3 for Bishop Pococke's visit in 1747.

crimson damask ; there are several good pictures : Behind the house is a large lawn adorned with Statues ; a walk through the middle of the plantations and all round them and some across, but it is all in the Wilderness still with clipped hedges of holly and yew round the quarters ; to the south is a bowling green and an open summer house ; beyond the plantations is the mount which was the site of the Castle of Abercorn : The ground about it is a grove of Elm trees ; and here the garden terminates with a Deer park adjoining : beyond this is the Sea, and also to the north ; and from this spot the Bass Island is seen and the mountains about Lough Loughman, altogether not much less than 100 measured miles: The sheep keep down the great quantity of grass that must otherwise be mowed, and the manure is swept up by those who attend them, and notwithstanding this nine men are constantly employed in the garden.

About a mile to the west is Blackness Castle, and a little west of that is Caeridden[1] where Antoninus's Wall is supposed to have ended. To this Castle there is a governor and a Serjeant's Command, and opposite, on the South side, is Rosaith[2] Castle an Estate belonging to Lord Hopton.

I went on to Queensferry a small town, chiefly supported by the passage into Fife: Here was a Monastery of Carmelites founded by the Laird of Dundas in 1290. The Church in shape of a Cross seems to have been built to an old Castle in the middle which is as broad as the Church: Opposite to Queensferry is the island of Garvey[3] on which there is an old Castle : Opposite to Aberdour, to the East is Inchcolm[4] an island in which there was an Abbey of Canons Regular of St. Austin, the ruins of which I saw in 1747. It was founded by King Alexander in 1123 and dedicated to St. Columba Abbot of Hye. Abbott Walter Bowmaker continued Fordon's *Scoti Chronicon* in the 15th Century. Henry 2d. son of James Stuart Lord of Ochiltree was made a Peer by the Title of Lord Inch Colme in 1611, his father having been made Commendator of the Abbey. I took in the way to Edinburgh Mr. Hope's

[1] Carriden. See *Caledona Romana*, pp. 263, 361.
[2] Rosyth Castle in ruins.
[3] Its past history will be overshadowed in its present use, that of giving a central support to the greatest engineering work of modern times—the Forth Bridge. [4] See p. 2.

5 miles from the town, brother to Lord Hopeton; it is a very handsome house, and a fine improvement of fields and plantations about it on the river Almond.

I crossed the Almond on a bridge; at the mouth of this river is Cramond, a Roman Station the old Alaterva,[1] where the Cohors prima Tungrorum was garrisoned and where they built an Altar to the Matres Alaterva, as may be seen in a curious inscription found here which is in Horsley the 29th under Scotland; and on the side of the river an eagle is cut on the rock.

Near the bridge I have been informed is a water fall of five and twenty feet, which is called a Lin; 3 m. S.W. of Cramond and 4½ west from Edinburgh near the road to Lithgow in a field to the north of it near Lennerbridge and a farm house called Catstean,[2] is a stone of that name 4 ft. 6 in. high 3 broad and three feet thick with this inscription on it, In hoc tumulo Jacet Veta. F. Vecti, a battle is supposed to have been fought here in which Vota the son of Vectus was killed. On the north side of the Pentland hills, the Roman Roads from Teviotdale and Tweedale unite and come to Cramond.

I came by Barnton Ld. Marchmounts at present inhabited by Lady Cassils and on the 9th arrived at Edinburgh leaving Crostorphin[3] to the South where there was a Collegiate Church founded by Sr. Jn⁰ Forrester ancestor to Lord Forrester in 1429.—I am, &c.

Letter LXI.

Edinburgh, *Sepr.* 15*th*, 1760.

Dear Sister,—Edinburgh is most pleasantly situated, and consists chiefly of two streets, one up the ridge of a hill about a measured mile long finely built and paved, many of the houses being of hewn stone, and all with stone window Coins, and six or seven stories high to the Street, and some of them more backward, even to 14 stories. It terminates at one end

---

[1] See Gordon's *Itin. Sep.*, pp. 116, 117.
[2] Catstone, 'In this tumulus lies Vetta, son of Victus.' Figured in Anderson's *Early Christian Times in Scot.*, p. 248.
[3] Corstorphine.

with the Esplanade before the Castle on the highest ground, which is a fine walk, commanding a view of the Frith and Leith and of the Country to the South. The other street, the Cowgate, is about half as long; at the end of which about the middle of the other, St. Mary's Wynd and Leith Wynd cross it at right angles. And there are several small streets to the south of the Cowgate.

Charles the 1st in 1633 made Edinburgh a Bishop's See and appointed for the Diocese all the parts of the Arch Bishoprick of St. Andrews to the South of the Frith of Forth in the Shires of Edinburgh, Haddington, Linlithgow, Sterling, Berwick and Lauderdale, and made St. Giles's Church the Cathedral; to have precedence of all Suffragans and to be Suffragan to St. Andrews: But in 1639 Episcopacy was abolished in Scotland, restored at the Restoration, & was again altered to Presbytery under K. William on account of the adherence, though a weak one, of the Bishops to the Interest of James the 7th for they would not take the Oath of Abjuration, but in other respects were willing to submit to the Government: The interest of the Kirk was thought the stronger by the Court; and it is plain they were not favoured by the Bishops in England, probably under the notion that they were zealous Jacobites. The Church of St. Giles's is divided into four parts[1] serving for so many parishes. The Choir is called the New Church, in which are the seats of the King, the Magistrates, and the Lords of Session. In the south isle the General Assembly of the Church hold their annual Convention, in which is a Throne for the King's Commissioner. It is a handsome modern Gothic Church. The Dominican Convent stood where the infirmary and the high school are at present, and was called *Mansio Regis* where the King might probably have had a house; It was founded by Alexander IId in 1230, Cardinal Bagimont convened the Clergy here to value their livings, by which they were taxed at Rome. The Observantines or Grey Friars stood where the City burial place now is, called the Grey Friers. It was founded by the Citizens for a School of Divinity and Philosophy, and

---

[1] Now restored (by the removal of the partitions) into one church. The restoration was due to the public spirit and munificence of the late Dr. William Chambers of *Chambers's Journal* celebrity.

James 1st sent to Cologn for the monks in 1446. This Church being destroyed at the Reformation the City of Edinburgh built a Gothic parish Church on the same spot in 1612, and in 1721 they built to it the new Church of the Grey Friars for another parish; St. Mary's Nunnery stood near the garden wall of the Marquis of Tweedale's house; from it the street St. Mary's Wynd has its name. There was an hospital called Maison Dieu in Bell's Wynd in this part.

Holy-Rood House or *Domus Sanctor Crucis* was an Abbey of Canons Regular of St. Augustine founded by David the 1st in 1128. John Bothwell son of Adalis Bishop of Orkney Commendator of it, was in 1607 made Lord of Holy Rood house. James 2d laid out £10,000 on it. And the Mob tore all the inside to pieces at the revolution. The roof of the fine Abbey Church was gone to ruin but it is now repaired.[1]

In 1584 the City of Edinburgh was divided into four parishes. St. Giles's for the South West, Magdalen Chapel for the South East, New Church for the North West, Trinity Church for the North East. At different times they added other parishes till they amounted to Eleven, the present number. To the north east is Canongate Church built out of a publick fund when James the 2d converted the Abbey Church into a popish chapel: This parish is on the spot of the old town of Herbergate.[2] The windows are singular consisting of three parts crowned with a circle.

Christ Church built in 1641 is now called the Trone Church from the Trone or public Scales; This Church is in the High Street, and is a handsome Modern Gothick building with a tower and a small steeple built by the City as 'tis said on the plan of Inigo Jones.

St. Mary's Chapel in this parish was founded by Eliza[th] Countess of Ross in 1504. The lower part is now the hall of

---

[1] The roof had been repaired with such heavy flagstones, that it soon gave way, and falling inwards, completed the ruin of the Chapel.

[2] Town of 'Herbergare,' probably from the Saxon *Herberg*, an inn or house for the entertainment of travellers. *Vide* Maitland's *Hist. of Edinburgh*, 1753, p. 148. 'Burgh callit the burgh of Harbargarie, now callit the Cannogait.'— *Holyrood Charters*, Bannatyne Club, 1840. The exact site, or even the existence of Herbargarie, is a much disputed point.

the Wrights and Masons, and the upper part is a Music room;
it has been new fitted up with a Venetian Window, and is a
handsome building.

In this parish also is a Chapel for service according to the
Church of England built by Ld. Chief Baron Smith in 1722
with one Chaplain at £60 a year, and another at £50. It was
built on the ground he purchased for that purpose. At the
South East Corner of black friars Wind, part of the Archiepiscopal palace of St. Andrews is now standing.

St. Cuthbert's, now called the West Church, dedicated to an
English Bishop, is supposed to have been built by the English
when they recovered Lothian from the Picts, and gave it up to
K. Ingulphus[1] in 956, and is said to have contained the whole
town of Edinburgh. The present Church does not appear to
have been any part of the old fabric. This parish is so large
that a new Church is built to the East of the Walk called the
Meadows, and they give it the name of the New Church.
Another parish is Haddows or new North Church parish, they
meet in the north west part of St. Giles's Church. Lady
Yester's Church is a mean building near the Infirmary. The
high School and Surgeons' hall is also near it which latter is a
neat building.

The old Church is in the middle of St. Giles's: The Parlia-
ment Close and down to the Cowgate was the Church yard of
St. Giles's. In a back alley I saw a fine Saxon door case to a
Church, but omitted to see it again, and after I left Edinburgh,
I was informed it was the door to St. Giles's, on which I can-
not depend.

The Tolbooth Church is the South West part of St.
Giles's.

Trinity College Church[2] and hospital was founded by Mary
of Guelden Wife of James 2d, it is commonly called the College
Church and is a Gothick building. The foundress is buried
in it.

The City of Edinburgh bought of Lord Balmerinach the

---

[1] Indulfus.

[2] This church had to be removed for railway improvements, but was subsequently rebuilt, largely with the same stones, a little to the south of the
original site.

Superiority of the District of the Western Lestalrig called the
Caldton; And in 1715 got it erected into a Burgh of Barony
being situated to the North East of Edinburgh, it is to be
looked on as a suburb of Edinburgh, and is governed by a
Bailiff with proper officers.

Abbey Hill though in the parish of South Leith is judged
to be a suburb of Edinburgh.

Besides twelve Churches there were four Chapels belonging
to Hospitals or Charity Houses, eleven meeting houses 3 of
the Established Church of England and 3 nonjuring, an independent, a Seceders, Quakers, French and popish, and 329
Streets wynds or lanes and Squares or closes or Courts, and
other openings, and ten Market places; and the inhabitants
are computed at 50,000. The Hospitals and Charity Houses
in Edinburgh are very considerable.

The Charity Work house was finished in 1743 by Collections;
There are about 600 in it, all kept to work in their several
ways, are allowed 2d out of every shilling they earn; and it is
supported by Contributions & some taxes. It is a plain handsome building being a half H: An infarmary, a place for
lunatics, and a weaving house, have been built near it.

Heriots Hospital is another founded by George Heriot son
of a Goldsmith and bred in that buissiness, and Steward to
James 6th; he left the money to the City of Edinburgh, and
it was finished in 1650. There are 100 boys Clothed and
taught in it; They wear brown Cloaths and leathern caps;
& are kept very neat. It is a very magnificent building
on a hill to the south of the green market, is adorned with
a tower in front crowned with a Cupola, and turrets at the
Angles.

The infirmary is a fine building of Stone and begun in 1738
by Contributions and is an half H. The front is adorned with
pillars, & stuccoe, and the window frames of the whole are of
hewn stone. There are six wards in it, and separate rooms
for Patients labouring under Fevers & other acute disorders,
particularly under infectious distempers; the Small Pox indeed
is rare among Adults, most people here have it commonly
when they are young.

The Merchants and Mrs. Erskin founded an hospital in

1695 called the Merchants' Maiden hospital[1] for 50 girls; it is in the part of the town called Bristo, and receives only the Daughters of Decayed Merchants.

The tradesmen and the same Mrs. Erskin, founded in the Horse Wynd, the Tradesmen's maiden hospital[1] for decayed Tradesmens daughters.

Watson's Hospital, in Heriot's field, was founded with money left by him, for the Education of Children and grand children of deceased Merchants: They allow here ten pounds a year for five years to a certain number to follow their Studies in the College, and £30 when they leave the University. Twenty pounds with apprentices, and £50 to set up, being all kept and maintained in a very handsome manner. I took a view of Holy-rood palace. In the front are two round towers at each angle which were built by James the 5th. Out of the window between the northern towers David Ritzio's Body was thrown after he had been dragged from the Queen and murdered: Four sides of a Court were built to these in the front, of only one story above the ground floor, which belongs to Duke Hamilton: on the other three sides up one pair of stairs are the state appartments which are never inhabited: Over the side, opposite to the entrance, the Duke of Argyle has his appartments to the north, Lord Broadalbin to the South, and Lord Summervile to the West:

Adjoyning to it I saw the Church of the Abbey with six Gothic Arches on each side. In the north wall of the isle are arches intersecting each other, on the opposite side Gothic arches, by way of ornament, and about seven feet from the ground: There was a door to the west, now built up, and King James VIIth came from the palace to a Gallery in the body of the Church: part of which still remains. The Royal Vault which I saw in 1747 is now closed; In it were buried James 5th and his queen Magdalene, his son and a natural daughter, and King Henry murdered by Bothwell. The Duke of Roxborough's Vault is shewn, and the bodies appearing like Mummies are in coffins without lids: In the Church are

---

[1] These hospitals or boarding-schools, after one or two removals to more eligible houses, have been recently reconstituted under the Educational Endowments Acts.

the Monuments of Bishop Wishart and Lord Sutherland of 1713, and in a Chapel or Vestry is a Monument of Lord Belhaven of 1639.

I went to see the Physic Garden which was part of the Royal Garden; To the South East was the King's Park taking in what is called Sailsbury Craig, & the rock called King Arthur's Chair upon it: A large lump of brown and white Jasper has been found in this rock; this part lets for £500 a year, is mortgaged to Ld. Haddington, and is the Jointure of the Dowager.—I am, &c.

Letter LXII.

Sepr. 17*th*, 1760.

Dear Sister,—I went to see the Castle at Edinburgh which contains six English acres. It is said that the Kingdom of Northumberland did extend to the Frith of Forth, and as Simon of Durham in the 9th Century calls it Edwinesburgh or Castle, and David the 1st in 1128 calls it Edwines burg, so he supposed it was built by K. Edwin about 626, it is on a rock of black whinstone, a sort of granite composed of small grains: The Esplanade before it is 274 feet above the Sea, about 90 feet above the Grass market, and 120 above the north Lough. To the East is a half Moon; and there are remains of three sides of the old palace; That to the East was built by James 6th. The Southern part seems to be old. At the south east corner of these buildings, Queen Mary (being rather afraid to come out, and being suspected also in conjunction with Bothwell to have had an intent to destroy the Child she was then big with, which I think does not seem probable) was delivered of James VIth in a very small room, rather a Closet, with a window opening to the East, through which they suspected that the design was to let him down in a basket: But if there was any such design, it is most probable that it was to secrete him, and pretend an abortion, in order to enjoy a greater power, and it may be to send him to France and educate him a papist. On one side is the date 1566, on the other the day of the Month June 19th. And on the West side were these verses—

> Lord Jesu Chryst, that Crounit was with Thornse
> Preserve the Birth quhais Badgie[1] heir is borne,
> And send Hir Sonee Successione to reign still,
> Lang in this Realme, if that it be Thy will.
> Als Grant O Lord quat ever of Hir proceed
> Be to Thy Glorie Honor and Prais sobeid.

In the East part near this room, the regalia[2] are kept, which are not shown : The south side of it, which is the oldest part, was the parliament house, and is now the officers lodgings : A Barrack is built on the north side, where there was a large Church that was turned into a Magazine. Most of the other parts of the Castle are new for the use of the Governor and other officers, for Magazines, and store houses of all kinds, in which they have everything in great order. The great Cannon was sent not long ago to London to be new cast : They have always a Company of invalides here, and generally three or four Companies of other Soldiers. The Castle is supplyed with water by a well 120 feet deep which must have been made with immense Expence as the rock is very hard. There is a fine prospect every way from this Castle which is a most singular situation.

In the high Street is a relief of the Emperor Severus and his Empress Julia of exquisite workmanship, and though only busts show the hand to be very masterly. And not far distant is an old house with a round tower in front in which there are niches and broken Statues. They call it Keneth's house, but it is supposed to have been Arch Bishop Kennedy's house of St. Andrew's & the Gothic work about the niches somewhat resembles the Sculpture on his tomb, the back part of it being much in the same taste.

The Exchange newly built opposite to the Parliament Close is a half H. The front of the Porticos, the pilasters, Cornices, Windows & door frames and other ornaments are of hewn

---

[1] Arms—Armorial bearings.

[2] The Scottish regalia were, with much formality, supposed to have been stored in an apartment called the Crown Room on the 26th March 1707, but the suspicion was that they had been secretly carried to London. They were, however, discovered there on 5th February 1818, carefully secured in a large oak chest, and are now exhibited in the room.

stone, the rest of Ashler being all freestone. The Portico in front is closed up for shops, and that opposite to it was made for the merchants to meet in wet weather; for when it is fair they always assemble in the street before the Exchange. The City purchased the houses, and undertakers built the whole, who let the Custom House for £300 a year, and the rest in lodgings and shops.

The Streets of Edinburgh are finely paved like St. James's Square, with a gutter on each side near the walking place, which is cut in a Semicircular form in hewn stone about 8 inches broad, through which the water runs that overflows the reservoir towards the Castle, which is supplyed by water brought from the Pentland hills by pipes; and is kept full for use in case of fire. There are flag stones for foot people on each side of the street, with stones set up to keep off the carriages which is a late improvement.

The first hill I mentioned to the north is to be divided into three streets from East to West, and the houses to be only three stories high, which will make it a most noble City. The Parliament House takes in the west side of Parliament Close; At the end of it the Ordinary Judge of the Court of Sessions sits on the south side of the treasury; and in a room near sit the President and Lords of Session, to whom there is an appeal from the Ordinary Judge: Upstairs, the Court of Exchequer sits on business relating to the Revenue: There is a fine Marble Statue of President Forbes in an attitude of sitting and speaking, with an elegant latin inscription, erected by the Advocates; It is the work of Roubillac.

We went down under the Treasury, to the Advocates Library which is a choice collection of books in all kinds, but more especially in the Civil Canon, and all other branches of the Law. They have a Folio Bible in large paper with all the Scriptural prints bound up with it that could be collected by a gentleman in England. They have several valuable MSS. as Martial 800 years old, Juvenal 600, Persius and Statius near that age.

The Vulgate Bible in two small octavo Volumns in two Columns; And several curious books of the first printing. They have also a large Collection of Medals, several curious Greek Medals, though no series, A pretty good Collection of the Silver Roman, and of large and middle brass mixed, Several modern medals and some Coin of different Countries: The Keeper of it is Mr. Goodall,[1] who has writ much in defence of Mary Queen of Scots and affirms that some letters referred to in Robertson's history of Scotland are spurious but this remains to be proved.

Edinburgh is governed by a Lord Provost and Corporation; he may continue two years, and when any person is found of superior merit in that high office, they put in another the third year, and bring him in again the year after.

A gentleman here who is a Chymist, has found out a Method to make Sal Ammoniac: It is more white and Transparent than the Egyptian, and it is thought that Soot goes into the Composition, There being an Alcaline Salt in the Coal.—I am, &c.

LETTER LXIII.

ARNISTOWN, *Sepr. 18th*, 1760.

DEAR SISTER,—I made some excursions round Edinburgh. From the Castle one sees two Eminences extending from East to West: The North Lough is to the south of them, and they are divided by the river Leith, upon this Lough there is a Sulphurous water lately found, to which the people are resorting all the day, it consists of Sulphur and an alcaline Salt, and is good in Scorbutic disorders. I rid to it, and then across the other hill to Newhaven. A street along the top of each of these hills with hanging gardens on each side, and a street at the east end of them extending to the West end of Leith would make it a most glorious City. They purpose, as before mentioned, to build three streets along the Southern hills.

New haven is now only a poor fishing village; The Edin-Burghers having bought the place, not chusing that trade should take a turn that way; Though James 4th made a harbour and Dock at this place; From it we saw Royston now called Caroline Park the seat of Lady Dalkeith & Barnbugal Lord Roseberry's.

We came half a mile to Leith harbour, passing first by the

[1] Walter Goodall, author of *Examination of Letters said to have been written by Mary Queen of Scots to Earl of Bothwell*, 1754, 2 vols.

Cittadel, which consists of two Bastions to the land: It was, when in repair, a Pentagon: It now belongs to the City of Edinburgh, and the Sea is gaining on it; it was formerly a burial place and there is a stone gateway to it. The Harbour is formed by stone and wooden piers, & small vessels come up to the bridge; it is said it will hold 100 vessels, being the harbour of Edinburgh. The Leith is crossed on a stone bridge from which one enters from North Leith to South Leith. The only Convent of the Canons of the order of St. Anthony in all Scotland was at Leith: it is said to be called the South Kirk, and to be situated at the south west corner of St. Anthony's Wind, near the Kirkgate, but I did not see any remains of it. On their Seal was this legend, *Sigillum commune capituli Sancti Anthonii prope Leith*:[1] Their houses were called hospitals, and their governors Preceptores, which I suppose is the reason why this Monastery has by mistake been called, A Preceptory and Hospital of the Knights Templars of St. Anthony. The Canons were brought from St. Anthony of Vienne in France.

A Chapel was built in Leith about the 15th Century which was then in the parish of Lestalrig: It is a plain Gothic building: And near it is King James 6th's Hospital with his Arms over the door. They build ships at the harbour and there is a great rope yard at the east end of the town: As the people of this trade cannot work in wet weather, so they must keep an exact account of the weather, and 'tis said at Glasgow they work 40 days less in a year than here, and at Greenock 56, which is but 16 miles west of Glasgow.

Leith was fortified by the French in the 16th Century, and the Eng^{sh} being called to the relief of the Scotch, anno 1560, it was agreed that the French should evacuate Leith, after having been in possession of the fortress from the time they built it in 1596. Leith belongs to Edinburgh and one of its Magistrates is Baron Bailiff and Judge Admiral of the town, whose Deputy resides here constantly: North Leith was in the parish of holy Rood house, and the Abbot built a Chapel here, which by Act of Parliament is made a parish Church, and North Leith a distinct parish by itself. It is computed that there are 7,000 souls in Leith.

[1] See Roger's *Hist. Notices of St. Anthony's Monastery, Leith*, 1877. p. 13.

From this place I went a small mile to Lestalrig or Restalrig a very small village. Here was a Collegiate Church begun to be founded by James 3d and was finished by James 5th. The Gothic Church is in ruins, and there are large buildings near it, probably the Lodgings of the Members of the Church. It was the Parish Church of South Leith till it was removed by Act of Parliament to Leith.

I saw a little way up the hill the ruined Chapel [1] in the park; and going South about a mile I came to West Dudiston,[2] to the South of the Park hill, with a fine lake to the west of it, about half a mile long, and a quarter broad; it rises from the springs issuing out of the hill called Arthur's Seat in the Park: Here is a very old Church with Modillions on the Entablature adorned with Grotesque heads in the Saxon style.

I passed to the East of the Lake and went a mile to Craig Miller, a Castle finely situated on a rock; There are several additions to the old Castle; it belongs to the Prestons and under their arms is a Rebus, a press and a ton: From the Quarry here the town is supplied with rough stones, and between the beds is a stratum of a sort of Red Marle about a foot thick. A little to the south of this place, is Drum, Lord Somervilles Seat finely situated and planted. It is in the forrest where the King used to hunt, called Drumselch.[3]

I passed near Sheens,[4] where there was the only Dominican Nunnery in Scotland, as reformed by St. Catherine of Sienna, from which it has its name; it was founded by Lady Roslin Countess of Cathness. I came to Edinburgh in the road which is to the west of Salisbury Craig, in the King's Park.— I am, &c.

LETTER LXIV.

HADDINGTON, *Sepr.* 19*th*, 1760.

DEAR SISTER,—On the 16th of Sepr. I left Edinburgh, went eastward to the Strand, and beyond the saltwork towards Musselborough & turned up to the right, to Sr. David Dal-

---

[1] See Roger's *St. Anthony's Chapel*, 1877, p. 16.
[2] Duddingston.
[3] Drumsheugh.
[4] Sciennes.

rymple's[1] where I dined by invitation. It is an exceeding good house, highly finished, and most elegantly furnished. The library is an excellent room 40 feet long. There is a most noble Collection of Books, and many fine editions, and some of the first printed Classicks. The lawn and plantations behind the house are fine. Here I saw chairs made of the wood of the Laburnum tree, which is much like the Virginia Wallnut, a deep brown. Sir James, Father to Sir David made a great Collection of Scotch pebbles on this Shoar, and some towards Dundee; employing the children in the hard winter to pick them up: and Sir David was so kind as to make me a present of several of them. I came through Musselborough where they have a harbour made by piers, and a linnen manufacture: There is a good bridge here over the Esk; on the other side of it is Inveresk: Here is a curious subterraneus passage under a hill to convey water to a Mill to the north. It was the work of the late Mr. Adams, the Architect, he brought the water from the Esk, and proposed to carry it on a level under the hill, but coming to sand, in order to avoid that, he sank down fifty feet, and carried the canal through the rock 800 feet; it is four feet wide and six high, and then sunk a shaft or well by which the water rises and runs in a canal northward towards the Mill; it is 100 feet below the top of the hill, and they were a year and a half about it.

A little to the north of the mill is Pinkie, a large house belonging to the Marquis of Tweedale now let to a private person. Here the Scotch beat the English on the 10th of September 1547; and twenty years afterwards, Q. Mary encamped here, advised Bothwell to provide for his own security, disbanded her troops, and became a prisoner to her subjects.

A little beyond it is Preston,[2] the field of the infamous battle between the K. Forces and the Rebels in 1745. They had laid on their Arms all night, and General Cope who commanded the K. Forces was in his coach, and yet they were surprised, & the enemy came suddenly upon them at break of day, & took some of their picket guards: The horse first

[1] New Hailes.
[2] Prestonpans, September 21, 1745. The doughty General is immortalised in the favourite Scottish ballad 'Johnnie Cope.'

gave way, and a panic seems to have seized our army ; Many of the horse did not stop, till they got to Berwick, and brought the first news of their own defeat.

We came three miles to Dalkeith great part of the way by the Park wall : This small town is pleasantly situated over the fine hanging ground on North Esk. They have some linnen Manufactury here, and they are about to settle some trade in the Iron ware. The Duke of Buccleugh has a house at this end of the Park, and another at the other end a mile off, which latter was a purchase ; The late Duke used to sleep there, as the wholesomer air, and receive his Company here. The house is a half H with a pavillion built at each end in front, and is situated just over a beautifull glyn ; the sides of which are covered with wood, and the water is kept up so as to appear like a considerable river and form a cascade. The house is all wainscoated with Dantzick Oak, and is adorned with a profusion of Marble in Chimney pieces, tables, sideboards, and Seats. There are several good family pieces ; and a fine one of the Duke of Monmouth, when 14 years of age, as a John Baptist, with very little drapery on it ; I believe it is of Sir Peter Lelly : There is also some of Gibbons's carving in wood : The furniture and particularly the Tapestry hangings are very rich. The other house is furnished as richly as this, and is a very pleasant place. The parish Church was Collegiate, founded in the time of James the 5th by James Douglas Earl of Moreton, the west part is in repair ; The east part is fine & in ruins ending in three sides in the modern Gothic taste, and seems to have been built when it was made Collegiate.—I am, &c.

Letter LXV.

Dunbar, *Sept. 20th*, 1760.

Dear Sister,—On the 17th I set forward and crossed from North Esk to South Esk and came to Newbattle, where the Marquis of Lothian has a house on the site of the Abbey filled with Pictures, of which nothing but some arches remain under the house. They were Cistercians, and founded by David 1st in 1140. Their Charters were writ into a Chartulary which is in the Advocates Library. It was erected into a Lordship in 1591 in favor of Mark Ker son of Sir Walter Ker of Cessford Ancestor to the Marquis of Lothian; it is a fine enclosed well improved Country.

I came to the Castle of . . .[1] where we crossed the Esk over a bridge, and travelling southward passed by Coal Mines and crossing a rivulet which falls into the Esk, came in a mile to Armiston the seat of the Lord President Dundass, whose Father succeeded President Forbes, who was succeeded by this Gentleman's immediate Predecessor President Craigie. His father built here a fine house, the ornamental parts of hewn freestone, and a pediment in the middle, supported by four Ionic pillars. The offices are very large, & convenient and joyned to the house by a closed Colonade. The park fields &c. are between that rivulet I passed, and South Esk, which form beautifull glyns on each side covered with wood; Before the house is a fine lawn adorned with single trees and Clumps; behind it is the farm—it consists of eleven hundred Scotch Acres, and there are ridings round the whole, which wind in such a manner round the glyns as to make the circuit thirteen miles: Near the house are beautifull winding walks round some uneven grounds over glyns beautified by the prospect of Chinese and other bridges that make it a most delightfull place. The park also glories in many large timber trees. There is an ash tree near the house which is about 25 feet in circumference, the branches shooting out a very little way above the ground: There is an old ruin in the circuit, called the Temple and a small Gothic Church a little below it. These were Templars founded by King David, in whose time they first came into Scotland. At the north end of this Demesne we saw the old house of Shank where Sr. George Mackenzie lived who writ the Institutes of the Laws of Scotland. And from one part we saw the famous Castle of Brothwick to the East. Armiston house is very well finished and furnished, and there is a large room up two pair of Stairs for a Library, taking up one half of the house; In it are some rare books of the first printing; and here I saw an Original of the Solemn League and Covenant

[1] Dalhousie.

which was signed by the Nobility and Gentry. When I was in Scotland in 1747 I went to see several places on North Esk.

At about three miles south of Dalketh is Hawthorn den or glyn with a Castle built close to it, where Drummond the poet lived in K. James 6th time. The Grottoes are cut in a perpendicular rock several rooms one within another, and no other passage to them, but by boards laid from a shelf of the rock to the entrance of the cave; Here they searched for the young Pretender in 1746. Near it is the fine and entire Gothic Chapel of Roslyn, as it is commonly called, which is very beautifull; it was a Collegiate Church founded in 1446 by Will[m] Earl of Orkney and Cathness for a Provost six Prebendaries and two singing boys. Over the door in Gothic characters is this inscription, Fortœ est vinum, Fortior est Rex, Fortiores sunt Mulieres, super omnia vincet Veritas. Near this place three battles were fought in one day, with three columns of the army of Edw[d] the 1st under John de Segrave K. Edward's Regent of Scotland, but the Eng[sh] historians say under Ralph Confray; in which they were all entirely and separately defeated on the 24th of Feby. 1302 under the command of Cumin and Frazier.

Near this place I dined with the late Baron Clark a great antiquarian, at his seat of Pennyline[1] situated in a bottom on this river, a sweet spot, and here he had many valuable antiquities, among them a statue of the Goddess Brigantiæ, a deity of the Brigantes, supposed to be the Picts. It is four feet high in a kind of Toga with a Mural Crown, a head in relief on the breast, with a spear in the right hand and a globe in the left; it has this inscription[2]

BRIGANTIAE S AMANDVS
ARCITECTVSIMPERII
IMP. I.

Two miles to the west on Pentland hills, at Rullion Green,

[1] Penicuik.
[2] See *Dissertio de Monumentis quidusdam Romanis*, by Baron Clerk, 1731, p. 7.

Dalzel on the 24 of Novr. 1663 routed the Covenanters who, as Burnet says, were a harmless people, become mad by oppression. A mile east of Pentland hills I was at St. Catherines or the Kaimes, where is what they call *The oily well*,[1] it is mixt with an Unctuous Bituminous Substance, which forms a Coat on the top of the water, and is in taste and smell exactly like the Bitumen of the Dead Sea. They say it is good for Scorbutic disorders.

To the north of St. Catherines before mentioned, is an old Camp,[2] of which Oliver Cromwell took possession just before the battle of Dunbar.—I am, &c.

LETTER LXVI.

DUNGLAS IN EAST LOTHIAN, *Sepr.* 21, 1760.

DEAR SISTER,—On the 18th I left Armiston, crossed the high road that leads from Edinburgh the furthest way to London, called the Eastern road, and passed over a rivulet called Gore, to the east of which the Country consists of a limestone: For we soon came to Loughend limestone quarry, in which the slates rise thin, but are full of small shells and some asteriæ and astroitæ; and soon after came to a Hamlet of that name. We saw at some distance to the south, a fine plantation and good house belonging to Mr Nicholson.

We came to the rise of the Tine which falls into the sea near Dunbar: And crossing it passed by Creichton Castle a large building, and near it a small Chapel built with very plain buttresses, which I suppose was the Collegiate Church founded in 1449 by Sir William Crichton Chancellor of Scotland for a Provost nine Prebendaries and two singing boys.

A little further we went near the Parish Church of West Crichton, built to a tower like a Castle as broad as the Church; The Western building has been taken away, we came to a Village of Crichton which I suppose is East Crichton, at the west end of which is a small hill, and the top of it has been

---

[1] The Balm Well.
[2] Galachlaw, where Cromwell encamped in 1650 with 16,000 men.

fortified: We saw to the north Cranston the seat of the Duke of Gordon, where his Grandmother lives, about a mile to the west of Saltoun:

We came to a small Camp which has been much destroyed, but seemed to have had four fossees round it; it is partly of an oblong square figure with the angles taken off, about 100 yards long from east to west and eighty wide: we then passed by a quarry in which I observed some small Coral in the limestone: and came to Salton on a rivlet which falls into the Tyne, and near it is Milton, the seat of a Fletcher Lord Milton one of the Lords of Session: on the other side I saw a wall of blew limestone, in which there are the Conchæ anomiæ.

In about two miles came to the Village of Gifford, and then half a mile by the avenue to Yester the Marquis of Tweedale's pleasantly situated between rising grounds on the rivlet called Yester, which passes before the house under an arch, and is not seen there. The house is the architecture of old Adams, it is all hewnstone, and a pediment in front supported by four Corinthian palasters; There is a pavilion built on each side: and the offices are large and handsome. The rooms of the house are spacious and lofty, especially the hall and grand room looking to the park; and a room above which is thirty feet high, 40 long and 28 wide, and is to be stuccoed and finished in a grand manner. The rest are well finished, and there are several good pictures of Sir Peter Lely's painting, and a fine one of Henderson[1] by Vandike. There is also some good Tapestry: The lawn behind the house is fine, with large trees interspersed, where the sheep feed, and there is a terrace round it; on one side is a hermitage and on another a summer house in a little island; beyond this is the park, and then the farm, in which the fields are very beautifull: The whole within the wall is Eleven hundred Scotch acres.

A little beyond to the south east are the ruins of the old Castle[2] of Yester, on a sort of a high head of land formed by two rivulets, and well defended by a fossee at the entrance, it

---

[1] May this not be the portrait of the 'Unknown Gentleman' in Yester House, by Jamesone, painted in 1644, and described as one of his finest? See *George Jamesone, the Scottish Vandyck*, by John Bulloch, 1885, p. 182.

[2] Famed for its 'Hobgoblin Hall.'

seems to have consisted of two grand buildings of strong fine masonry; In the back of the great Chimney is a window; Under the other part is a fine vault, turned with a ribbed Gothic Arch, it is about 15 by 40 and from it was an arched passage down to the Water: It was the ancient seat of the family, was taken and destroyed by the Duke of Somerset in the time of Edward 6th.

From several parts of the park are fine views of the country, and especially towards the north: In the lawn behind the house on the East side of it is the old Collegiate Church of Yester, the middle part of which being destroyed, The Marquis has rebuilt it in very good Gothic taste; and it is the family burial place: Here was a Collegiate Church to St. Cuthbert for a Provost six prebendaries and two Choiristors founded in 1420 by Sr William Hayes of Locher Wood and Yester.—I am, &c.

Letter LXVII.

Berwick on Tweed, *Sepr. 22d*, 1760.

Dear Sister,—On the 19th I left Yester and came in three miles to Hadington, which is a town well situated on the Tine. And they have a large Woollen Manufacture of Clothes; There was a Monastery of Grey Friers here, where William first Lord Seton was buried; Edward the 1st defaced it; The Quire was so beautifull that it was called *Lucerna Laudoniæ*, and as it appears plainly that the Church here has been much altered; it might be the Church of these Franciscans as well as the parish Church. For I ommitted to enquire if for the Monastery. To the tower of the Church are Saxon windows, not of the greatest antiquity; There was a kind of a Gothic division in them across each window: The West door also is Saxon and divided into two parts. The whole Church seems to have been originally in that taste, and built of a white freestone, but the new Gothic windows, and the buttresses are of red stone, and so is the tower in the middle.

I am inclined to think that the Church was originally an oblong square and without isles, for on the side of the body of the Church it appears plainly that there were large windows coming down lower than the roof of the isle. There are 4 windows on each side of both parts of the Church. This place was fortified by the English and defended for them by Sir George Wilford against the French General Monsr De Frie[1] with 10,000 men;—but the plague breaking out, the Earl of Rutland raised the Siege, leveled the works, and brought the Eng^{sh} home. Sir John Ramsay, who did execution on the Gowrie Conspiracy, was made Viscount Hadington, and since that, it is an Earldom in a family of the Hamiltons. Near it is Athelstan,[2] so called from Athelstan an English Commander slain there about the year 815.

I went a quarter of a mile to New Mills, Mr. Charters's, who has built a large house of the red freestone, with a Paladian Ionick Logis on the first floor of the grand front, and a bow window in the middle of each side. There is a fine galery on the second floor in which room and in another are several very good paintings: The avenues are planted with a wood on each side, and the lawns with Clumps and single trees. There is a bowling green and Summer house, and a fine walk by the river, and a most beautifull Kitchen garden that way. A little on this side of Salton the freestone begins, and I believe ends at the Tine; to the north of which the Country seems to be all a firestone.

A very short ride brought us to the Abbey, which seems to have been the Cistercian Nunnery mentioned to have been at this place, Governed by a Prioress and her Chapter, founded in 1178 by Ada Countess of Northumberland Mother to Malcolm 4th and K. William. There are no remains of the Abbey except a few arches of vaults. To the East of Haddington is a place called Nungate, and about it is St. Martin's Chapel the walls of which are standing. We went on northward, and came to that ridge of rocks which extends to North Berwick law, having crossed the road from Berwick on Tweed to Edinburgh in which I traveled in 1747.[3]

We came to that remarkable high Conical rock, called North Berwick Law, which I believe is wholly composed of Granite,

---

[1] General Andrew de Montalembert Sieur D'Esse.
[2] Athelstaneford.   [3] See p. 2.

of a bad red Colour: We descended to North Berwick a small illbuilt town situated on a strand: A promontory stretches out from it which seems to have been an island, from the north end of which a pier is built that extends to the west, within which, vessels of 200 ton can come at spring tydes, but commonly those of about 100 tons: On this promontory is a small ruined Chapel, arched over, and a tower a little to the northwest of it: They told me it was called St. Elan and was a Monastery: I suppose it must have been the Cistercian nunnery built to the honour of the Virgin Mary in 1266[1] by Malcolm son of Duncan Earl of Fife.

This Town has a trade from their distilleries and Manufacture of Starch: They also have large Granaries here, & export a great quantity of Malt and of several kinds of Grain. It is said that King Edward 1st after the battle of Banock Burne gave up this Castle, and retired to the Castle of Dunbar.

I proceeded two miles to Tantallon Castle, at the mouth of the great bay, called the Frith of Forth: it is situated on a promontory, and the sea washes its high cliffs on three sides: There is a deep fossee before it, over which there was a wall, and there seems to have been a drawbridge; There are marks of a modern Bastion before it, and from a little Gully, a line is drawn to the north cliff at a little distance, which is joyned to the grand fossee by a line on each side: The walls I believe are sixty feet high, and so are the towers in which there are six stories, besides the Vault under them; It appears that the Southern tower has fallen down, and has been rebuilt with hewn stone. For part of the old tower remains, the basement is divided into three parts by two double tiers of hewn stone, at proper distances, and above into eleven parts, but towards the top there are only single tiers of hewn stone.

The gateway is divided in the same manner upwards from about twenty feet from the bottom; the top part, where it projects for the battlements is of hewn stone, The Northern tower seems to have been built in a rougher manner: To this stupendous wall, there were appartments built on the inside, but all is destroyed and carried away, and there is a passage to the

---

[1] Founded by Duncan, Earl of Fife, in 1154. The Earl of Carrick, in 1266, confirmed to the nuns the grants of his fathers.

top through the wall. On the north side is a building which seems to have consisted of two large rooms, and vaults under them, which were probably the State apartments: There is no wall to the East or South. From this Castle Archibald Douglas Earl of Angus gave James 5th a great deal of Trouble.

From hence they generally go to the Bass from which there is a fine prospect in fair weather, but bad weather prevented me going to it. The Solan Goose, called in Ireland the Gannet, breeds here: There are three or four rocks in the sea near Berwick. I went on three miles to Tyningham The Earl of Hadington's. Here is an old Church and the finest clipt holly hedges, as a fence to the fields, I ever saw. The plantations of firr trees also and the ridings are very fine. I came into the high road from Edinburgh to Dunbar, and in three miles more to that town, which is eleven measured miles from Haddington and 27 from Edinburgh.—I am, &c.

Letter LXVIII.

Cornwall in Northumberland, *Sept.* 23*d*, 1760.

Dear Sister,—Dunbar is pleasantly situated on an eminence —over a bay near the mouth of the Tyne:[1] It chiefly consists of one broad street and another at right angles with it, which leads to the harbour:

They have a large Church here:[2] The old part of the Quire consists of small narrow Gothic windows: There are three of them at the east end, The body seems to be an addition of four arches and a transept, There is a large Chapel built to the south; The east end is now separated from it, under which there is a Vault, for the family of Hume[3] Earls of Dunbar, The first being Sir George Hume, who was made by King James 6th Baron Hume of Berwick and afterwards in

[1] The river Tyne separates the parish of Dunbar from that of Tynninghame.
[2] Demolished in 1818, and the present church built on the site.
[3] Home—pronounced Hume—created Earl of Dunbar in 1605.

1515 Earl of Dunbar, as some say for clearing the country of Robbers:[1] And at the east end is a magnificent monument covering the three windows, with this inscription on it. Here lyeth the body of the reight hon^{le} George Earl of Dvnbar Baron Howme of Barwick, Lord heigh Tressr. of Scotland, Knight of the most noble order of the Garter, And one of his Mat^{to} most ho^{ble} privie Covnsell whoe depted this life the xxix day of Jannvary MDCXI.

He is represented in the mantle of the order as Kneeling (at a Desk with a book on it) on a Cushion placed on a Sarcophagus, on each side of him are Cariatides of men in Coats of Mail, holding with one hand the Arms on a shield; They support an Entablature upon which on each side are the Statues of Justice & Charity with a Corinthian pilaster on each of them, between them is the inscription, and above on the Entablature on each side is a Coat of Arms, between these is a Sarcophagus and on the middle of it seems to have been a Coat of Arms; The Execution and Design is very fine and it is said to be Italian, on it is this Motto, Homo ditat, Deus beat.

They had here a Monastery of red friars founded by Patrick Earl of Dunbar & March 1218. There was also a Convent[2] of white friars or Carmelites founded in 1263 by Patrick Earl of March. There is a place they call the grey friers which I suppose was the Carmelites, a plain tower is standing but no other part, and some sheds seem to have been built against it.

I went to see the harbour which is cut out of the Rock, a pier is formed to the East, and there is an opening to the north, but rather difficult to enter, and it is not practicable when the wind blows a little hard from the north east. It will hold a ship of 300 tons, and they can enter here when they cannot sail into the Frith of Forth. The Castle was built on a rock, which is a peninsula; on the south side is a gateway leading to a ruined building, which seems to have consisted of two grand appartments in the Castle way; over it in the middle are the Arms of Scotland, and on each side of it a Coat

---

[1] The achievement of Patrick Cospatrick or Dunbar; created for the valorous act Earl of March.

[2] Monastery:—no vestige now remains.

of Arms: From this apartment a high wall extended to an island near the shoar, but it is every way a perpendicular Cliff: There is a covered way to it through this wall; The Castle was the seat of the Earls of March who for this reason were commonly called Earls of Dunbar.

[1]The passage into the harbour as observed before is very narrow between two rocks, one of them is the east side of the harbour, The other is a promontory stretching out about 100 yards to the north, and 50 feet wide, having the sea on each side of it when the tyde is in: And this head is a most extraordinary natural curiosity: It is of a red stone which is not a limestone, but looks rather like a very hard freestone. This appears on both sides like the Giant's Causeway in Ireland: The stones on the west side are from a foot to two foot over, they are larger on the east side, from two feet to four feet. I saw them from three to eight sides, but only one or two of the first and last: They may be said to be in Joynts, but differ from that in Ireland as both the pillars and the Joynts in each

[1] The following was communicated by Dr. Pococke to the Royal Society;—it is very nearly the *ipsissima verba* of the text:—' An account of a Production of Nature at Dunbar in Scotland, like that of the Giants-Causeway in Ireland; by the Right Reverend Richard Lord Bishop of Ossory, F.R.S., read before the Royal Society, Feb. 26, 1761. The passage into the harbour of Dunbar is very narrow, between two rocks: one of them is the east side of the harbour; the other is a promontory, stretching out about a hundred yards to the north, and is about twenty yards wide, having the sea on each side of it, when the tide is in. This head is a most extraordinary natural curiosity: it is of a red stone, which is not a lime-stone, but appears rather like a very hard free stone. It looks on both sides like the Giant's-Causeway in Ireland: the stones on the west side are from a foot to two feet over; on the east side they are larger, from two feet to four feet. I observed the pillars from three to eight sides; but only one or two of the first and last; they may be said to be in joints, but are strongly cemented together by a red and white sparry substance, which is formed in lamina round the pillars, and between the joints, two or three inches in thickness. The interstices between the large pillars, which are but few, are filled with small pillars, without joints. The pillars consist of horizontal laminæ: the joints are not concave and convex when separated, but uneven and irregular: they lie sloping from east to west: on the west side, towards the end, the pillars become very large & confused, as I saw them to the east of the Giant's-Causeway, and in the isle of Mull; except that these are divided by such a sparry substance into a great number of small figures, which seem to go down through them. There are spots and veins of a whitish stone in the pillars. There is no sign of anything of the kind in any of the rocks near, that I could observe or hear of.'
—*Philosophical Transactions, Royal Society, London*, vol. lii. p. 98.

pillar are strongly cemented together by a red and white sparry substance, which is formed in lamina round the pillars, and between the Joynts for two or three inches in thickness. The interstices between the large pillars which rarely happen are filled with small pillars without Joynts. The pillars consist of horrizontal Lamina, the Joynts are not concave and convex when separated, but uneven and irregular. They lye sloping from East to west: on the west side towards the end the pillars become very large and confused as I saw them to the east of the Giant's Causeway, and in the isle of Mull, but these are divided by a sparry substance into a great number of small figures, which seem to go down through them: There are spots & veins of a whitish stone in the pillars. They have taken these stones to make up some of the south part of the pier, and have drove in pieces of wood to fasten them. There is no sign of anything of this kind in any other of the rocks.

About a mile to the south are Trochi and Entrochi in a brown Earth in the Cliff as I was told; They are found on the Shoar and some of them which I procured, are in a red stone.

They have here some linnen Manufacture, and Export of Corn and an import of boards, timber, hemp, flax, iron, &c. They have very little fishing trade, the Fish they say has failed, particularly the herrings; some supposed for want of the proper food, which they are supposed to suck out of the ground, as they are seen with their mouths fixed into the ground; and their tails up. I here was assured that the Skait are found in those bags I have formerly mentioned in this shape one in each, and the fishermen assured me that they sometimes find three or four in the Skaits belly;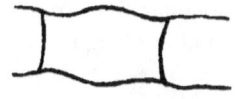
These are Skeats Eggs. I have opened one with a young Skeat in it. As well as I could be informed the black belong to the black thorn back Skait: The long white ones to the other kind of Skaits.

In the town house I saw the ancient Militia pikes which are very large and a sort of bill on a handle with a hook to the back of it to draw a man from his horse. When Cromwell went against the Scotch, who took up Arms in favour of Charl^s the 2^d he was encamped where the Duke of Roxborough's Park now is, within a small mile of Dunbar, and was so encompassed by the enemy on the hills all round, that he was in such great want of Provisions, as to think of embarking his foot, and of forcing his way through with the horse. In the morning he went up to a little eminence to prayer in sight of his Army, and seeing the enemy coming down the hill to engage, he rose up, and said the Lord hath delivered them into our hands. They came down with their Bibles under their arms, and it being windy and beginning to rain, their matchlocks would not fire, so they turned their backs, and were entirely defeated.—I am, &c.

LETTER LXIX.

MILERSTONE., *Sepr.* 24*th* 1760.

DEAR SISTER,—I went on a mile to Broxmouth, where the Duke of Roxborough has a house and park, encompassed with a high Wall. I came to the Bay beyond Broxburn, where I found in the rocks what I took to be a small Kind of Coral, but am not certain. I then came to a bed of the Mycetitæ Coral, and something like the Spawn of fish, and then to the same Kind of Coral and Vermiculi. And I observed that lines run straight from north to south in the Freestone, and that by irregular lines from east to west, they were divided into a great number of figures; and in some parts, the Joynts form a Circle five or six feet in diameter, within which, the stones were divided into many irregular parts.

At the old ruined Chapel[1] of Skitraw is a soft blew slate: Towards the rivulet which comes down from Dunglass Glyn, are the petrifying Springs; They form a sort of figure like Moss, and also a Yellow Alabaster, especially on the outside:

[1] There stood, at one time, on the Skateraw shore a chapel, dedicated to St. Dennys. The remains have now yielded to the sea.—*New Stat. Ac.*, vol. ii. *Innerwick*, p. 243.

DUNGLASS.

I saw a vast mass of it which has fallen down from the cliff, it is about 30 feet long 12 broad & six or seven thick. The water passes through the freestone, & forms what they call a petrified Moss, and when it happens to pass through a harder bed of it, the fine parts adhering to one another, may form the Alabaster. From Skitraw it is mostly freestone.

A little beyond this, is a large head of land extending four or 5 miles to the east, as one side of it is Fast Castle. Half way between the angle of the bay and the head the rock projects to the north, here the whin or fire stone begins, but the freestone breaks out underneath it in one place. A little beyond Skitraw at the foot of the hills on each side of a rivulet and Glyn is a Castle, one is called Inverwick[1] place; The other Thornton Castle.

I came on to Dunglass Sr John Hall's, very pleasantly situated, the sea appears at the end of the lawn, which is before the house, on each side of which is a wood, & a rivulet runs towards the end of the lawn under a small arch over which the ground is raised; in the Glyn, it runs up on a quarry of freestone in which between the stones the West Indian plant called Opuntia marked like the Echinus is found petrified. I saw one near three feet long, and have several specimens of them, they are the same as are found in the Winter torrents at Castle Comer in the County of Kilkenny in Ireland: on the east side of the avenue hid by trees is the Collegiate Church founded in 1450 for a Provost and Prebendaries by Sir Alexander Hume, Ancestor to the present Earl. It is kept in repair but not in service, and is well covered with stone slates; the doors though not Saxon are true Arches; and it is a good building:

To the back of the house is a beautifull Glyn[2] covered with Wood of 40 years growth, it is about 120 feet deep to the north and 90 to the south, in which the perpendicular cliffs of freestone add to the Picture; above the house is a Coal pit,[3] the Coal of which rises small, and is full of sulphur, so that it is used only for burning lime, and by the poor people; a most

---

[1] Innerwick Castle.
[2] Dunglass Dean—a picturesque ravine.
[3] Not been worked for a century.

extraordinary road is cut through this perpendicular rock by
Sr John Hall being like the road of Penmen Maur in North
Wales in Miniature: They have found in the coals a sort of
Iron Mendik, and between the rocks a kind of light brown
Pipe Clay: They have also here an uncommon red earth. He
is about to make a bridge from the south side to the north for
the greater convenience of the Carriage. There is a little hill
to the west of the house which was fortified with bastions of
earth, as 'tis said, by the Queen Regent during Queen Mary's
minority: The late owner built a Summer house on it, and
made a bowling green within the fortress. At Inver Andrew
place is a mount, at the foot of which they have found several
caves made with four stones, and covered with a single stone,
in each of which was a Skeleton, that fell to pieces on being
touched.

It is observed that if Firr trees are cut down, when the roots
rot, they destroy all trees whose roots adjoin, except Oak, even
firr themselves, which is supposed to be owing to Vitriotic
Acid in the roots. Land here, near the Sea, lets for 30 and 35
shillings an acre. It is observed that the land which inclines
to the north, produces better and fuller Corn, than that which
is in a Southern exposition. Sir John Hall has a good house,
being part of a large one built round a Court. There is a
gallery in it 90 feet long. This Gentleman is also making a
harbour to the South of the rivulet near the old Salt house.
—I am, &c.

Letter LXX.

Melross on the Tweed, *Sepr. 26th* 1760.

Dear Sister,—I Departed from Dunglass on the 22d and
leaving East Lothian came into Mers, or Berwickshire, then
going about two miles in the road that leads to Berwick, we
turned out of it to the east, to go to Coldingham, and passed
by an old Chapel in ruins, and then by a Quarry of stones which
are used instead of Slates for Covering, and not far from Fast

Castle at the south east head of this bay. We then had St. Ebb's head[1] to the east a little before we came to Coldingham, (so called from St. Ebbes landing there, after she had embarked in a boat on the Humber on her father Edelfred King of Northumberland his being made a prisoner.

Coldingham is famous for its Nunnery, situated in a Valley on a rivulet, with a gentle descent to it, on three sides, and in view of the Sea: It was founded by St. Ebbe and had a very tragical end: for the Abbess and the Nuns cut off their upper lips and noses to avoid the lust of the Danes in 870 who set fire to the Monastery and burnt them in it.

In 1098 K. Edgar founded a Benedictine Monastery here to St. Cuthbert and gave it to the Monks of Durham with great privileges; little remains of it except part of the Church which is of later date than the foundation of the Second Priory, and the Architecture is singular, the east part is rather low: The whole is built with single Gothic windows, except as described; The transept was high and grand, with four tiers of windows in the gable, the highest a narrow window, then a round window, and a double window on each side of it, then two tiers of three windows each: between these two last tiers within are two arches: on each side were two galleries formed in front by a long arch and two short arches divided by pillars only: There does not seem to have been any building to the West of the middle part of the transept for the great door is in it, opposite to the east end; and a building comes against it to the south of the door which might have been the refectory; to the north of these is a Churchyard where the Cloyster might have been; what is most singular in the South Gable on one side is a work like a projecting chimney with a short pillar on it: This they told me was to let down a picture of our Saviour, and they have a particular name for it.

Buchanan, it is said, calls this place Collidum, and Cambden thought it to be Colania[2] of Ptolemy, which has been fixed to Carnwath near Lanerk.

We went on six computed and nine measured miles to Berwick; in three miles we passed a pleasant village called Eden[3] on the

---

[1] St. Abb's, from Ebba the daughter of Ethelfrith.
[2] See p. 45.   [3] Ayton.

Hy,[1] about two miles from it is a little seaport town called Hymouth:[1] We passed by Lamurtin[2] and Lamurtin hill on which there is a Camp, and near Hollydown[3] hill to the west, famous for many battles between the Scotch and English.

We left Scotland and came into the government of England to Berwick, on the 24th from Cornhill we went into Scotland again: Here in one spot three Countys and two Kingdoms meet.—I am, &c.

Letter LXXI.

Selkirk, *Sepr. 27th* 1760.

Dear Sister,—On the 23d I went, from Cornhill in Northumberland, a mile to the ferry over the Tweed (within half a mile of Coldstream), which I crossed and stopt at that poor town, there are no remains of the old Cistertian Nunnery here except a part of the Gateway; it was founded by Patrick Earl of March, and Derder his Lady about 1166, near it is Abbey Leys,[4] doubtless the dairy of the Abbey, where Mr. Pringle has built a handsome house, and made a beautifull plantation. Half a mile below the ferry is old Coldstream, where I observed a ruined Chapel: About a quarter of a mile from Cornhill The river seems to have left its Chanel and to have encroached on the Scotch side and left a piece of Scotland on the east side, for there is one field there in Scotland, so that in this place two Kingdoms meet and three Counties, that is Mers in Scotland, Northumberland in which Cornhill parish is situated, and a part of the Bishoprick of Durham.

I left Cornhill on the 24th and having passed Wark and Carram[5] crossed a stream into the Shire of Roxborough, Tiviotdale in Scotland: & going over a hill came towards Kelso, passing near Hampside Ford, where there is a tradition[6] that James IV. was seen to pass the morning after the battle of Flodden field: The Country appears exceeding beautifull about

[1] River Eye, Eyemouth.
[2] Lamberton.
[3] Halidon.
[4] Lees, the seat of Sir Wm. Marjoribanks.
[5] Carham.
[6] See p. 350.

Kelso. The hanging ground is covered with wood to the south, there is also wood to the west and a very rich country every way: They have lately built by subscription and a tax on ale in Kelso a fine bridge of six arches, the largest of which is 63 feet wide.

Kelso would be a very disagreeable town if it were not for a large square, in which there is a handsome Town house: But it is famous for its Abbey of Tyronenses first founded in Selkirk by David 1st when Earl of Northumberland, it was then removed by him to Roxborough, first under the Castle, where there were some buildings not long agoe, and it is to this day called the Freres, and part of the old wall round it remains; It was removed again by the King to Kelso: The lands belong now to the Duke of Roxborough, being given by James 6th to Sir Robert Ker of Cessford his Ancestor; Very little remains of it except part of the Church which appears from the style to have been built at the time of the first foundation, being entirely of Saxon Architecture; and it is very singular: To the South is a small building with a Saxon door to the west, the north side is adorned with the like arches, and they say that it was part of the Cloyster, but unless it were a building within the Cloyster, it must have been too near to the Church.

I went to a place which is over the river on the west side of the town, and commands a view of the windings of the Tweed, and the Tiviot falling into it which makes the Freres and the Castle of Roxborough a peninsula. The Castle itself, situated on an eminence, is of an irregular figure, the old wall that encompassed it remains in part, and within there is a Clump of trees; and Sir James Douglas has built a house which appears as on the same side, though it is to the south of the Teviot. There is an additional beauty from the terrace before the Duke of Roxborough's house, which is a rampart to the west covered with wood: The Teviot could be brought in so as to water a fossee round the Castle.

The Duke's house was on the spot of the Freres now called Fleurs,[1] but the late Duke removed it to the place where it now stands, on an eminence to the North of the Castle: The

[1] Floors Castle.

house is about 200 feet long, on each side are offices in a half H which appear square to the grand front. They are joyned to the house by an angular Corridore: The whole is built of rough stone, with window cases of hewn stone: It is strange so large a house should not afford one grand room: There is a fine Lawn to the front, and the fields are beautifully divided and planted, so that every way it is a charming place and situation; and the adjacent country is beyond all dispute, the flower of Scotland. From the Duke of Roxborough's house, I went two miles to the river Eden to see a waterfall of that river down a rock near 40 feet high, which they say is very fine in a flood:

I was shewn a small ridge which extends from the Tweed towards the town of Dunse,[1] and is called the Caym[2] or Comb, and is imagined by some people to be, without appearance of truth, a roman work, but it is certainly natural.

We went to Stichhill Sir Robert Pringles, where I dined. It is a good old house with a long avenue before it formed by wood on each side & a large plantation on the Demesne; above is a rock which has been fortified, and commands a fine view of the Country, particularly of Hume Castle a little to the north east, where Lord Hume's Ancestors resided, it is situated on a high hill: I here saw a great Curiosity made of a Composition like princes metal, it appeared at first like a large bracelet[3] for a Warrior (a drawing of it is here seen) but the objection to that is that it is much worn towards the broad part at one end and a little on the other part on the same side. Half of another also found with it is worn on the same sides: They are of fine workmanship, and ornamented in very good taste. There are holes at each end which are not in the least worn, otherwise it was conjectured that they might have served for stirrups. I have thought they might be bracelets, to go over the arms and clothes of a man, and that it might be worn by

---

[1] Recently resumed the ancient name—Duns.

[2] Kames.

[3] 'A massive collar of cast bronze was found in digging a well at Stitchell, in Roxburghshire, in 1747, and is now in the National Museum.' Probably this bronze armlet was part of the same find. It closely resembles the *unknown* armlet in the National Museum, Fig. 126, in Anderson's *Scotland in Pagan Times*, 1883, p. 149. For collar, *ibid.* Fig. 112, p. 136.

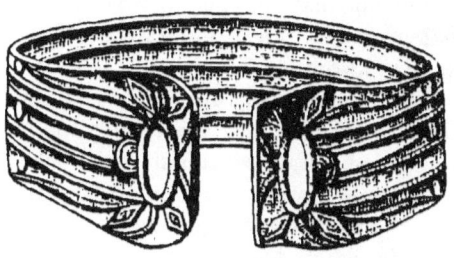

[Front.]

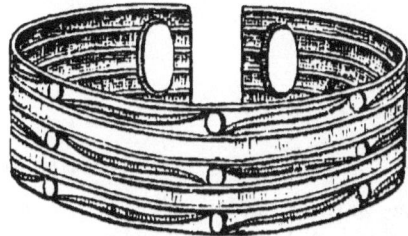

[Back.]

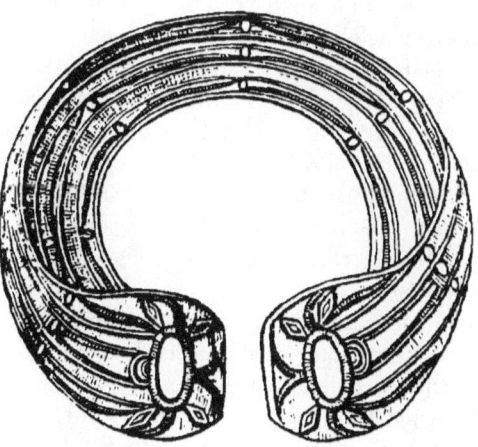

Representation of Ancient Bracelet (Bronze Armlet).

resting either the bow or spear on it: But by viewing them more exactly any one may consider by what use they could be worn in that manner. They were found three feet under ground in digging a well here.

In the way to Mellerstane, Mr. Bayleys,[1] I saw two stones laying in the ground, about six feet long, in shape like the stones of the Giant's Causeway, and it is said there was a third: Whether these were brought from Dunbar or elsewhere, or worked by art I cannot take upon me to determine. I came to Millerstane Mr. Baily's.[1]—I am, &c.

Letter LXXII.

Wooler in Northumberland, *Sepr.* 28*th* 1760.

Dear Sister,—Mellerstain is well situated on an eminence with a hill behind it to the west, adorned with Plantations formed into Ridings and Stars. The offices are finished, and there is a fine lawn and wood both to the Front and back of the intended house; below to the east is a fine piece of water; There are Woods on each side, and on a hill to the north of the Water is a Star. The rest is divided into very fine large fields with hedge rows of firr and other trees and quicks round them: the late plantations consist of double hedge rows and a walk between them: and Mr. Bailey[1] is every year carrying on these improvements. His Aunt Lady Murray, sister to his mother Lady Binny[2] was a great heiress which she left to his Mother, and remainder to him.

At the end of a cross walk, called the Grove, is a building which appears like a temple, and on each side of the door is an English inscription, and likewise a very elegant latin inscription writ by Dr. King, Principal of St. Mary Hall Oxford. To the honour of the Father and Mother of Lady Muray, and Lady Binny,[2] mother to Ld. Hadington[3] and Mr. Bailie[3] which are here inserted.

[1] Baillie.   [2] Binning.   [3] See p. lxiii.

INSCRIPTIONS ON THE MONUMENT
OF THE RIGHT HONOURABLE
GEORGE BAILLIE, of Jerviswood, Esqr;
AND
LADY GRISELL BAILLIE; at Millerstain.

(on the front)
Built by George Baillie, of Jerviswood, Esq., and Lady Grisell Baillie
A.D. 1736
The Pious PARENTS reard this Hallowed Place,
A Monument for them and for their race.
Descendants make it your successive cares,
That no Degenerate Dust e're mix with Theirs.

(on the right side)
H. S. E
Georgius Baillie,
De *Jerviswood* Armiger:
Ex antiquâ et honestâ familiâ oriundus.
Vir
probus, gravis, sanctus,
Civis optimus, et libertatis publicæ vindex;
Nec minùs in Angliâ, quam in Scotiâ nostrâ,
Notus et celebratus
Ob pietatem in suos, liberalitatem in egenos,
Munificentiam in hospites, fidem in amicos,
Justitiam in omnes.
Qui
In studiis, in negotiis, in quotidiano sermone
Suavitatem morum, severitatemque
Ita feliciter miscuit;
Ut neque in acerbitatem,
Neque in mollitiem
Procederet.
Tanta erat illi humanitas,
Atque animi Candor,
Ut nemini malediceret;

Nemini, ne quidem inimicissimis, injurias faceret:
Si quas acceperat
Obliviscerctur.
Tanta illi oris dignitas,
Ac vis orationis et ingenii
Propè singularis ;
Ut facilé sibi conciliaret
Principes Reipublicæ viros ;
Quibus cum vixit familiarissimè.
Neque unquam aut amicorum conviviis,
Aut regum consiliis interfuit ;
Quin maximâ,
Dum sibi minimam sumebat,
Gratiâ valeret et authoritate.
Uxorem duxerat GRISELDAM,
Patricii Comitis de *Marchmont* filiam
Natu maximam ;
Ex quâ suscepit filias duas
Griseldam et *Rachaelem.*
Sub regno GULIELMI immortalis Viri,
Nec non sub felicissimo ANNÆ imperio,
Amplissimis functus est procurationibus
Prosperè, integerrimè,
Regnante GEORGIO primo,
In eorum ordinem cooptatus,
Qui adminstrandis rebus maritimis præsidebant :
Deinde unus ex aerarii prefectis constitutus.
In utroque consessu,
Munus suum curavit diligenter,
Explevit, ornavit.
Quum valetudine paullo infirmiore impeditus,
A negotiis publius se removisset ;
Eadem magnitudine animi,
Qua laboribus suffecerat,
Otium usurpavit.
Cùm ætatis annum
Quartum & septuagesimum impleverat,
Ex vitâ discessit
Inter lachymas & amplexus suorum,
VIII. Id. August. MDCCXXXVIII.

(*On the left side*)
Here lieth
The right Honourable Lady Grisel Baillie,
Wife of GEORGE BAILLIE of *Jerriswood*, Esquire,
Eldest Daughter of the right honourable Patrick Earl of *Marchmont*,
A Pattern to her Sex, an Honour to her Country.
She excelled in the Characters of a Daughter, a Wife, a Mother.
While an infant,
At the Hazard of her own, She preserved her Father's life;
Who under rigorous Prosecution of Arbitrary Power,
Sought Refuge in the close Confinement of a Tomb,
Where he was Nightly Supplyed with Necessaries conveyed by her
With a Caution far above her Years,
A Courage almost above her Sex;
A Real Instance of the so much celebrated Roman Charity.

She was a shining Example of Conjugal Affection,
That knew no Dissention, felt no Decline,
During almost a Fifty Years Union,
The Dissolution of which She survived, from Duty not Choice:

Her Conduct as a Parent
Was Amiable, Exemplary, Successfull,
To a Degree not well to be exprest,
Without mixing the Praises of the Dead with those of the Living,
Who desire that all Praise, but of Her, should be silent.

At Different Times She managed the Affairs
Of her Father, her Husband, her Family, her Relations,
With unwearied Application, with happy Oeconomy,
As distant from Avarice as from Prodigality.
Christian Piety, Love of her Country,
Zeal for her Friends, Compassion for her Enemies,
Cheerfulness of Spirit, Pleasantness of Conversation,
Dignity of Mind,
Good Breeding, Good Humour, Good Sense,
Were the Daily Ornaments of an usefull Life,
Protracted by Providence to an uncommon Length,
For the Benefit of all, who fell within the Sphere of her Benevolence.
Full of Years, and of Good Works,

She dyed on the Sixth Day of December, MDCCXLVI.
Near the End of her Eighty first year,
And was Buried on her Birth Day, the 25th of that month.

About 5 miles to the north lives Mr. Spotswood, of Spotswood,[1] descended lineally from Arch Bishop Spotswood ; who is a great antiquarian ; And in the same Tract are the two Gordons and Huntly, formerly the Estates of the Gordon family from which they have their Titles.

From Mellerstein I went to the Abbey of Dryburgh on the Tweed, about 3 miles below Melross ; They were Prœmonstratenses founded by Hugh Moreville Constable of Scotland and his wife Beatrix de Beau Camp, in the time of David the 1st. James the 6th made Henry Erskin younger son of the Earl of Mar Lord of Dryburgh afterwards Lord Cardross and Ancestor of the Earl of Buchan. It is Gothic Architecture of the single narrow windows ; There were five in the east end, the front of the galleries consists of single arches and two lower on each side ; some of them are adorned with Carvings of Stars : under the Galleries are windows turned with an Arch that is a very small segment of a Circle, in which are round windows in six compartments. The arched Chapterhouse[2] remains, and a fine kitchen, with the arched roof supported by two Octagon pillars, the sides of which are divided by angular members, and there is a curious Chimney piece, the Chimney being built within the room, all of hewn stone : The site of the hall remains on one side of it, and the Abbott's grand room and appartments at one end.

There are many beautifull Glyns in this part, from which several streams empty themselves into the Tweed.

On the 26th I left Mellerstain and came four miles to Melross, pleasantly situated on the Tweed. Here St. David founded an Abbey of Cistercians in 1136. It was much destroyed by Richard the 2d and by Edward the 2d. James Douglas was Commendator at the Reformation, who preserved the Archives now in possession of the Earl of Moreton. Thomas Lord Binning was made Earl of Melross in 1619. Nothing remains of this Abbey but the magnificent Church. No part of which is of the time of King David. The arch of the northern isle is very narrow and pointed, the south isle is in the same taste but wider, This body consists only of four

[1] Spottiswode.
[2] See Morton's *Monastic Annals of Terriotdale*, p. 323.

arches, it seems to have been a design for a small Church after it was first destroyed, and the Design altered between the building of the North and South isles, and to these isles, it appears, there were walls on each side so as to enclose the Choir, and what was to have been the Entrance seems to have been small with a Gallery over it to this which seems to have been afterwards designed to be the Quire ; and doubtless there were arches to the West to form a body corresponding to this ; and the Skreen might be rebuilt afterwards as it is in a more delicate design.

This Church I suppose to have been ruined when the Abbey was a second time destroyed : For nothing appears so old as the time of King David. The windows over the Arches in the body were small in a new Gothic style, and within the opening, between the Gallery and the body, it is now as a window with a flat arch, but seems to have been divided into two by a pillar: They afterwards probably designed a transept, The north part of which is built with single Gothic windows, and seems to have been finished before the south part of the transept was executed : when another design was probably conceived, which was to build Chapels to the south side of the old isle, with very fine Gothic windows. Nine of which are standing, and it is supposed that there were three more to the West, to make the south transept in the same style, with a most beautiful Gothic window and two chapels to the east of it, one with the window to the east, the other to the south if I do not mistake, for another Chapel is added to the east of the northern Chapel, with a fine Gothic window to the east, so that in the east part of the Church, beyond it there is only one extreme fine Gothic window facing to the south as there is on the other side to the north, in which style is the most Magnificent Gothic east window, of a very light architecture and in the highest Gothic taste of Henry 6th the north side beyond the transept corresponding to the south side. As to the particular architecture of this last addition, beginning with the Chapels to the South of the old isles, they were divided by low walls of hewn stone, with windows or openings in each, that people through those windows might see the Elevation of the host: There are ornamental buttresses between the windows from which half arches are turned which rest against pillars built on the wall of the old isles from which such another arch is turned to the body, of the Church, these buttresses have Niches in them, one, if I mistake not, in each ; in all which were Statues, and these buttresses are finely adorned with carved work and with Statues of men and women on each side ; among those remaining are St. Andrew, and next to it the Virgin with our Saviour in her arms ; The Drapery is very fine, and it is highly ornamented with Sculpture, on the lowest buttress. are the Arms of Scotland supported by two Unicorns, the bottom of the escutcheon resting on their knees, above it is I. Q. and under the arms 1505. It is supposed to have been set up on the Marriage of James IV. which was settled here by Bishop Fox.

In one part are the Arms of the Abbey a Mail or hammer and a Rose, which is a poor rebus, the place seeming to have its name from the hill over it Mul (*bare*) Ross (*a head or hill*). There are also many arms about the Windows : There is a fine door and window at the south end of the transept, over the door is a Lyon Rampant, and above is St. John with three disciples on each side as Ornaments of Sculpture to the arch of the door. To St. John's Statue is this inscription, the Statue being represented as looking up. Ecce filius Dei : For over the window and on each side of the arch are our Saviour and his disciples likewise in alto relievo. There are angular buttresses on each side, in each of which if I mistake not are two Niches. In one a Monk is in relief at the bottom with this inscription Passus e. q. ipse voluit. To another in the same situation is this inscription. Cū venit Jes. Seq. Cessabit umbra. About the windows of the Chapels which face to the south and east are reliefs of Musitians with all kinds of instruments, and women with their Veils probably to represent Vocal Music.

On each side of the east end is a fine window divided into three parts, very beautifull, and exactly in the same style as the east window, which seemed to me to be in a lighter and finer style than those of Henry the 6th's Chapels at Cambridge &c. : It is divided into four parts. On the top of it is cut in relief a man with a beard, and a globe on his left hand resting on his knee, and a young man on his right hand, both with Crowns on their heads. It is supposed there was a Dove and that it is a representation of the Trinity: on each side of the window in angular pilasters are several niches the tops of which are adorned with reliefs of animals, and the bottoms with two grotesque figures of men. This window is 31 feet high 15½ broad, the south window 24 high & 16 broad.

As to the inside of the Church, in the new Chapels to the south are niches for placing the Elements for the service of the Altar, which are beautifully adorned with Sculpture. The arch of the South end of the Transept is entire; and in a round tower are geometrical stairs; in which the angles are taken off under the steps so that it is a smooth surface all round of which they make great account; though only done by taking off the Angles of the stairs which form the steps.

Over the door is this inscription

> So gages the Compass even about
> So Truth and Laute do but doubt
> Behold to the End John Murdo

On the south side of the door the following lines [1]

> John Murdo sumtym callit was I,
> And born in Parysse certainly;
> And had in keeping all Mason Work,
> Of Santandroys the hye Kirk,
> Of Glasgu, Melros, and Pasloy,
> Of Niddisdayl and of Galway.
> Pray to God and Mari baith,
> And sweet St. John keep this holy Kirk from Skaith.

At the north end of the transept is a door from the Abbot's lodgings, and to the east of it another, to an arched place called the Wax Cellar where 'tis supposed they kept the tapers for the Church. Above this a private Vault was discovered to which the only entrance was by taking up the first step of the Stairs leading to the Abbot's house, where without doubt they deposited their valuable effects in time of Danger. On the west side of the transept is the Statue of St. Peter, with a

[1] See note 1, p. 50.

book in his right hand, and two keys in his left, and on the south side St. Paul with the sword.

Over the middle of the transept was the grand tower, one side of which only remains with three or four single windows in it. The tradition is that the high altar was isolated and just to the east of the tower: and it seems as if there was another altar at the east end, if so be there was such an altar as they suppose where the ground is certainly higher, but may be occasioned by some ruins. What remains of the Church is 258 feet long. The Transept is 137 feet 6 in. long. The Tower from its foundation is 75 feet high. It is computed that there are now 68 niches remaining for Statues.

The ornamental trestle arches of the Cloyster in the wall of the Church are remaining, next to the door is one beautifully adorned with a gothic arch and ornaments in very high taste over the Stone for holy water: and another at the other end answering to it, and wrought with a beautifull simplicity; The Masonry of these and of the Transept and east end is exceeding good in hewn stone. On the north wall of the Church are visible marks of fire, the stones having cracked and flown: The Capitals of all the pillars are of a running single foliage.

Many great persons were buried here. As Alexander the 2d at the high altar. S. Waldeons Abbott of the Monastery and son of King David. Many of the Douglass family, and particularly James who was General & died in the battle which he gained on the 9th August 1388 at Otterburn agst Sir Henry Piercy Sirnamed Hotspur who was afterwards Earl of Northumberland. David Fletcher several years Minister here, and at the restoration made Bishop of Argyle.

Great part of the Abbey is said to have been demolished in the time of Henry the 8th (and probably was never repaired) by Ralph Ivers[1] and Sir Bryan Laton[1] who had got a grant of the Mers and Tiviotdale to be held of England. But Archibald Earl of Angus defeated them on Ancrum Muir. Since the Reformation the materials have been taken away for several buildings; and in the body of the Church now used for service, an arch has been turned on the inner South wall, and

---

[1] Sir Ralph Evers and Sir Bryan Latoun, 1544.

on a new well built wall to the north within the northern pillars, and makes a most miserable appearance.

The Chronicle of Melross from 735 to 1270 published by Dr. Gale in 1684 is thought to have been begun by the English when they had possession of the Monastery and is a sort of a Continuation of Bede's history: Many buildings belonged to the Convent, the enclosure of which was they say a mile round, and they have a strange story that a bakehouse with ovens one over another as high as the tower of the Church and of hewn stone was destroyed about sixty years agoe. It is said several Gentlemen in order to retire from the world in the times of Popery built themselves little houses near the Abbey.

A mile and a half to the East, at old Melross, was a Monastery of the Culdees supposed to be founded in the 6th century by Columbus or Aidan, according to Bede St. Cuthbert in 643 was the 3d Abbot, and went afterwards to Lendisfarne: It is also mentioned by Nennius in the 9th Century: Foundations of the enclosure have been found: Where the Church was situated is called Chapel Know or Knole. But 'tis supposed that there were not much buildings about it, as Bede acquaints us that the Churches were of oak and thatched with reeds: Backer's Cross near adjoining is supposed to be Becket's Cross.

A mile to the west of Melross is Newstead famous for Masons, probably the descendants of those who built the Abbey. Here they mention Red Abbey Steed, and suppose it was an Abbey: and they have found there foundations of houses, a great deal of lead, and several seals I suppose of the Middle ages: There was a bridge over the Tweed at this place, the ruins of which are seen, Gordon[1] mentions curious octagon pillars of it hollow in the middle, which are now entirely destroyed, as I was informed. Many Roman coins have been found there.

To the south of Melross are three remarkable summits of Eildon Hill: It is said that on the top of the north east hill is a Roman Camp with two fossees a mile and a half in Circumference 4 entrances and a prætorium, on the north side of the middle summit is a place called Bourjo, of which there is a tradition that the Druids sacrificed in the Grove of Oaks which

---

[1] See Gordon's *Itinerarium Sept.* 1727, Plate 64, p. 166.

is encompassed with a fossee, and there is a wall to it from the east & west. From the Camp a line is drawn two miles to the west to another Camp on the top of Cold street hill fortified in the same manner, and with several outworks. These, with that in Darnwick Ground, called Castle Steed, form a triangle, and the two last might be Castra Exploratum. To the south west of Eildon Hill is a Military way, and it is said there was a military Station at Kippilaw,[1] it goes through Halidon[2] park and in some places through marshes; it had a communication with Coldshields, and with a Camp on the other side of Tweed called the Rink. Towards Darnwick at Skinner or Skirmish hill was a battle fought the 18th July 1520 between the parties who wanted either to keep or get possession of James 5th.

Taking the north side of the river on a hill to the west of Drygrange is a british Camp; on a hill near Gattonside another, as well as opposite to Newstead which is called Chertes Know. Near Easter Loughe is a fine place called the nameless Den, where on the side of the bray are some petrifications which are washed down to the river by the rains, they are of the substance of fine Marle: near Leeder there has been a Camp; and near Clackmae is another with three fossees—called ridge walls—and near it another with a single fossee called Cherterlie, from this there is a military road to the south, another to the north going to Chapel Muir and Blainslie to Cheildhelles Chapel. A mile south of ridge wall is another small camp called Brownhill. All which camps plainly show that this has been a great scene of action between the English & Scotch when thus invaded each other by crossing the great natural Barriers the Tweed, & the Teviot.—I am, &c.

LETTER LXXIII.

ALNEWICK, NORTHUMBERLAND, *Sepr. 29th* 1760.

DEAR SISTER,—At Melross I took leave of Mr. Baillie, and went on for Selkirk four miles, I saw up the small river Gala,

[1] Kiplaw.   [2] Haliedean.

a place which has its name from it, called Galashiels. This is a famous place for weaving of linnen. I came on a little eminence near a mile from Melross to the remains of a Camp called Castle Hed; in some parts a double fossee is seen: From it, it is said there is a military road leading to Tweed at the Nether Barnfoord with a deep ditch on each side: It is also said that a mile to the south of it near Huntley wood is another large camp.

I turned soon to the south and travelled near the river . . . [1] which falls into the Tweed a little lower, to the east of which stands Selkirk a poor small town: About three miles above it two rivers unite, the north part[2] rises out of Lough of Low[3] and St. Mary's Lough: The other called the Etterick rises to the south of it which gives name to the forrest of Etterick, and both of them rise towards Moffat.

On the other side of those mountains we passed by, out of which the river Anan rises. K. David when Earl of Northumberland began to found an Abbey here, but the place not being convenient for an Abbey he removed it to Roxburgh, as mentioned before, and afterwards when he was King to Kelso. The tradition is, that they could not get stones, and being too cold, they removed or sold the materials, and from this say the vulgar, it was called Selkirk, though I imagined it was rather from being the Kirk of the Cell. They pretend to show some old foundations of it about the present parish Church.

I had designed to have gone ten miles further across the mountains to Peebles in order to find the Coria or Caria Damniorum placed 22 miles from Coria Ottadenorum supposed to be near Jedburgh, The first it is conjectured was between Lyne kirk north west of Peebles and Kirkurd; and at Lyne a Roman Camp is placed in Dorrets map of Scotland; but the weather was so bad that I proceeded in my way to England.

At Peebles there was a Monastery of Red friers called the Ministry or Cross Church founded by Alexander 3d in 1257.

On the 27th I set out eastward and going over disagreeable hills, came in seven miles to the great road like a turnpike from Jedburgh by Melross to Edingburgh. We came to it at Ancrum the seat of Sir . . . Scot. To the east of it near the

---

[1] Ettrick. [2] Yarrow. [3] Loch of the Lowes.

road, are some remains of a fortification : A little below it the river . . . [1] falls into the Tiviot, I passed the first river and near the confluence on a rising ground are some remains of walls, which are called the Mantle Waes. It may be about 100 yards broad from east to west and two hundred long, the present walls (of which a good part remains to the east and north) are built with buttresses, and I do not take them to be very old :

A mile from it on the Tiviot is a place called Chester where there might be a Camp, though I could not hear of any remains. This Mantle Waies or Walls I take to be Coria Ottadenorum or Gadenorum. And there is a wood near called the Wheel Causeway, and they say there are signs of a Roman Road in three several places. Having crossed the Teviot on a bridge, I came in two miles to Jedburgh, seeing on the other side . . . [2] Mr. Scots a fine situation with beautifull fields and plantations.

Jedburgh is prettily situated between the hills on the river Jed ; There are two tolerable streets in it, but though they had formerly some of the linnen and woollen manufactures, they are now quite decayed. Here was an Abbey of Cannons Regular of St. Austin founded by K. David. There are great remains of the Church, and in the west end of the Quire, and the isles of each side are remains of two arches, as well as of two more to the transept, they are built on pillars six feet in diameter with the rude Saxon Capitals, and over them is a gallery with an arch divided into two parts by small pillars of the same kind, which show how very low architecture was in those times ; To the east of these are single Gothic windows, with an arch on each side of them in the Gallery, and the same over them.

There are nine arches in the body of the Church with a light arch over each divided into two by a light pillar which supports the two inner arches, over each of them is a window with a small arch and a false arch on each side of it. The west door is very fine Saxon work, consisting of five large and five smaller pillars ; and to the south leading to the Cloyster is a Saxon door with five pillars to it. There is a tower in the middle with 3 windows of trestle arches on each side. The Groyn

[1] Ale Water.   [2] Blank in the MS.

JEDBURGH.

Arch in the middle lately fell in: The pillars consist of eight pilasters which are a segment of a circle, with a fillet down the middle of them: The upper pillars are composed only of four: It is one of the most compleat and grand Churches[1] in Scotland: the site of the Cloyster remains; and to the south of the west end of the Church were the Abbots lodgings built on the water.

This Abbey was made a temporal Lordship in favour of Sir And^w Kerr Ancestor[2] of the Marquis of Lothian. One would imagine that there had been a Nunnery here, for some very old orchards to the east of the Church are called the Ladies yards as some fields to the south of the west end of the Town are called the friars yards, where part of the old Enclosures are seen. It was a Monastery of Observantines founded by the Town in 1513 Adam Abel was a monk here who writ the Scotch history to 1536 in Latin, part of which was printed at Rome.

Jedburgh is a Royal Borough, here are Independents, Cameronians, & Nonjurors, who have their several Meetings: and as they could not have their own choice on a vacancy, they built a Church, brought the Minister they would have chosen, who was fixed in a parish and allow him £160 a year; so that the Established Minister has but 150 hearers, out of near 5000 Souls belonging to the parish in the town and Country: This is a fine place for Fruit particularly apples and pears, of which they send to neighbouring towns to the value of £300 a year.

I left Jedburgh in the afternoon, and came in two miles to Creiling hall on a rivulet which falls into the Jed, and in two more to Setford[3] Castle, near such another rivlet; This building consists of a grand apartment on each floor and a smaller in a return adjoyning to it: In another mile we came to Merbo hill on a larger rivulet and in an open plain, and going on we passed by the rise of the River Bowman, and ascended to Yetham the last village in Scotland: And about a mile from it came into England having that river to the right, being I believe not above three miles from that place, where we had entered Scotland to the west of Carram and so took leave of Scotland, this being the Shire of Roxborough which includes Tiviotdale and also Liddesdale in which I had been, and extends very near to

---

[1] See Jeffrey's *Hist and Antiq. of Roxburghshire*, 1864.
[2] See p. 329.   [3] Cessford.   [4] Yetholm.   [5] Carham.

Netherby (at which place I was) in Cumberland: Jedburgh being the town for the Sheriff's Deputy to attend in, and hold his Courts for that Shire.—I am, &c.

Letter LXXIV.

Rothbury in Northumberland, *Sept. 30th 1760.*

Dear Sister,—On the 22d of September I came to Berwick near the mouth of the Tweede which is a town and County extending on the north side of Tweed about three miles, and as I apprehend every way as far as the parish of Berwick. It stands on the north side of the Tweed the Frieda of the New Map. It is near the mouth of the Tweed and is very finely situated, it was first given in ransom for K. William of Scotland to Henry 2d, and was afterwards often taken and retaken. It formerly stood on an eminence within the present rampart, which is now called the Castle; The old Castle as the Citadel without the walls being doubtless joyned to it, which was very strong in its natural situation. There were two waies to it, and a wall down to the river, which seems to have been built with steps down the top of it like the walls of Antioch.

The town is now a modern fortification, with two Bastions to the north, and Queen Elizth built a fine bridge here of fifteen arches: I could get no acc^t of any of the Mousteries of this place, which were the red friars founded by a Scotch King. The Dominicans at the mouth of the Tweed founded by Alex^r 2d in 1230: A parliament was held in this Convent by Edward the first to determine the right of the crown between Bruce and Baliol.

There were also Franciscans, and Bernardine Nuns founded by David 1st, but Robert 3d gave their possessions in Scotland to the Abbey of Dryburgh on acc^t of their attachment to the English: The Parish Church is a handsome Gothic fabric, though somewhat singular and seems to have been built so late as the time of Queen Elizabeth or James 1st. Opposite to it is a handsome barrack and Store houses built round a Court.

They have erected in the middle of the chief street a very beautifull town house and Market house of free stone. The lower part is in the rustic Channel style, over which there is a first floor and an Attick story; a Tuscan portico in front, and a tower over it crowned with a spire: The two stories of the tower are of the Doric, and Ionic orders, all exceeding good architecture: They have a good quay, and build small ships here. The export is chiefly Salmon and Corn; They have plenty of Coal about four miles from the town.

I came to the other side commonly reckoned in Northumberland, but for about two miles south is within the Bishoprick and County of Durham, which extends to the west, and not observed in Maps.

I shall here give some acc^t of the Kingdom of Northumberland. It was subjected to the Saxons by Osca brother of Hengist, was under the Danes who did homage to the Kings of Kent. The Kingdom of Bernicia between Trent and the Frith of Forth was subject to the Kings of Northumberland, and when this Kingdom came to an end, all to the South of Tweed became subject to Scotland: But Northumberland was given to Egbert King of the North Cumbrians, and Eanred their King paid him tribute: The Danes had it under Alfred, who were dispossessed by Athelstane. Though the people made Eitric the Dane their King: From this time they were Earls; and the Peircies came to be the Earls of Northumberland, They were descended from the Earls of Brabant, the true offspring of Charlemagne who were called Percies when Jocelyne the younger son of Godfrey Duke of Brabant married Agnes sole heir of William Percie, whose great grandfather came into England with William the Conqueror.

I went on the 23d three miles in the turnpike road to the west, and leaving it came two miles to the west north west to Norham or Northam, of old, called Ubbanford; it belongs to the See of Durham, Egfrid Bishop of Lindisfarne built the town and Church; the next Bishop Ralph built the Castle a little to the east of the town on an eminence over the river. The wall round it takes in a pretty large compass: Over the river is a ruined building, which they say was the Church. The old castle part is to the east, it is an oblong square building, in which there are two rooms sixty feet long, one is fifteen wide the other about twenty with vaults under them, there

were four stories, and the walls seem to be about seventy feet
high, and are twelve feet thick, over a door are remains of
three Coats of Arms. This Castle is built of hewn free stone.

The Church is at the west end of the town. The east end
is very old, on the north side are small arched windows with
members over the arches, and from them a Water table is
carried along the whole length of the building; on the south
side the Arches of the windows are supported by a Corinthian
pillar on each side with a base and plinth, and only four single
leaves round them and seem to be very old. The entablature is
adorned with four heads in the lower member and four less in
the member over each window. The south side of the body
consists of five or six arches supported by round pillars with
octagon capitals, and four single leaves on each side with the
top of a leaf appearing between them above, and betwixt the
bottom of the leaves is a Circle formed from the outer line and
another within them. The former seems to be the old Church
built by Egfrid, in which Ceolwolph King of Northumberland
who became a Monk at Lindisfarne, was buried, to whom Bede
dedicates his Ecclesiastical history. And when the Danes had
destroyed the holy island, the body of St. Cuthbert Bishop of
that place was deposited here. And where on this Account
and St. Ceolwolph's great devotion was paid to the place, it is
probable the body of the Church was built, which has been in
part destroyed. Over the door is this inscription. This Church
was repaired by the Parichinaris of Norham Maister Patrick
Wait being preacher there Anno 1617.

We went on in this turnpike road which comes within half
a mile of this town. At Ribby near about 200 years agoe
were found the Shedds of a Knights belt and the hilt of a
sword, which were given to Bishop . . .[1]

We came in two miles to Wesel[2] bridge over the Till, which
has its name from Wesel[2] house on an eminence over it; a little
below which it falls into the Tweed: The bridge here consists
of one arch 90 feet and eight inches wide.

From Flodden I saw at a small distance Etal, of old the seat
of the Manners's from whom the Duke of Rutland's family is
descended; Here is a wooden bridge on stone piers, near Etal

---

[1] Blank in the MS.   [2] Twizell.

is Ford Castle, Mr. Carrs where there is a stone bridge over the Till, both fine situations. Two miles more brought us to Cornhill, a considerable village very near the Tweed:

They have here a water like that of Epsom Wells, from which they extract a Salt; it is esteemed good in Nopinlick and Scorbutic disorders: Near it is a cold bath, which they use much when they drink the water. This parish is in Northumberland.

From this place I went three miles by Brankeston where there is a thatched Church, to Flodden Field, famous for the battle with James the 4th (who being drawn in by the French, that made use of two or three of his own subjects as tools, to invade England, when Henry the 8th lay before Tournay); The Earl of Surry was sent against them as the Scotch historians say with 26,000 men, the Scotch not above 7000. Thomas Lord Howard led the van, Sir Edward his brother one of the wings, Lord Dacres, and Clifford, and Sir Edward Stanley the rear: The van and one of the wings came over by Wesel bridge, the rear by Mylfield ford above Ford Castle: The Scotch were divided into four parts, one of which was a Corps of reserve.

The King engaged in the middle: They were drawn up first on a hill near the King's Seat, but seeing the English coming towards Brankeston and apprehending they wanted to cut off the rear from the Camp, they moved to the hill nearer to the village, and came down to them in the valley at the well. In the first onset, 'tis said the English were broke, but the Highlanders coming on without order they began to rally were supported and the battle was very bloody; there was a gentle rising ground with a little hollow to the south of this. The rear of the English who passed at Mylfield, it is supposed, either crossed over the hill to the north or came round the end of it, which drew the battle more towards that part; the Scotch still fighting most bravely, though the Corps of reserve under Lord Hume it is said could get no word of command from him to engage. They fought till the night separated them, 5000 were killed on each side, but of the Scotch a great number of the flower of their Nobility.

The English did not know they were Conquerors, till Lord Dacres went next morning on the field of Battle, saw their artillery, and the Dead bodies not stripped.

It is thought that the Earl of Surry made use of a Lady and her Daughter at Ford Castle to cause delays, and that the King was amused at that house. The Earl of Surry sent to the King to leave England or come down and fight fairly, and appointed a day, which he did not keep, that those who were at first against this enterprise, advised him to take all advantages of situation, but to no purpose, and when he did not keep the day to retire:

They show a rock where the King sat, doubtless before the battle, in which he was certainly present. This is called the King's Seat. Many were dressed like him to prevent their aiming at the King, and one was taken up dead and buried for him, but he had not the iron chain,[1] about him, which the King wore for pennance. And it is at this day reported in the Country, that he was seen passing the next morning Hampsideford already mentioned;[2] and the Scotch believe he was conducted to Hume Castle, and murdered there; Lord Hume being in such circumstances as to give reason for this suspicion. And I was told that lately a silver chain was found not far from Hume Castle, and that it is in possession of Lord Marchmont: in which case, if it was the Chain about the King, it must have been a silver chain he wore and not a chain of iron, I saw some little risings in the ground, which seemed to be places where the bodies had been buried.

On the 24th I left Cornhill and soon came to Wark, where I had seen at a distance the remains of a Castle which is on the decline of the hill, and seems to have been encompassed with a circular wall; at some distance from the Castle, a deep fossee is cut through the Hill, so as to make the east end of the hill serve for a Camp. Here is a ford which the Scotch commonly passed when they came into England in time of war.

We came to the last parish or rather Chapelry in England called Carham, The minister of which goes often to Kelso, and performs divine Service to a few of the Episcopal Church settled there, under a legal license. We passed the bounds of this parish which is also the bounds of Scotland.—I am, &c.

[1] 'James bound an iron chain round his body, to which he added a link every year during his life.'—Buchanan's *Hist.* B. XIII. civ. ix.
[2] See p. 328.

ITINERARY.

A Route in computed miles, and English measured miles, reckoning that two computed make three measured, taken by one of the company, and not compared with the miles in this account. The miles in Ireland are computed as 11 make 14 English.

Date	Place	C.	M.	Date	Place	C.	M.
April 12.	1760. Left Kilkenny.						
	To Queen's County, Mr. Vicars's,	20	...	May 6.	To Kirk Gunnion,	10	15
	To Dublin,	64	...		To New Abbey,	6	9
24.	To Drogheda,	22	...		To Dumfries,	5	8
	To Dunlear,	8	...		To Stank of Ruthvel,	8	12
25.	To Dundalk,	12	...	7.	To Hoddam Castle,	4	6
	To Newry,	8	...		To Annan,	4	6
26.	To Bannonbridge,	8	...		To Gretna Green,	6	9
	To Hilsborough,	13	...	8.	To Carlisle,	6	10
	To Lisburn,	2	...		To Penrith,	14	20
	To Dean Fletcher's and back,	4	...	9.	To Brougham Castle,	1½	2
					To Lowther Hall,	1½	2
					To Shap,	4½	7
	Total,	161	204	10.	To Orton,	4	6
					To Pendragon Castle,	8	12
					To Kerby Stephens,	3	4½
					To Brough,	3	4½
28.	To Donaghadee	13	19				
30.	To Portpatrick by Sea,	17	25		Total,	103½	156
	To Stranraer,	3½	5				
May 1.	To Glanluce,	6	9				
	To Whitehern,	14	21	12.	To Lead mines,	2	3
2.	To Whitehern Island and back,	4	6		To Greta Bridge,	10	15
	To Wigtown,	8	12		To Richmond,	7	10
	To Newtown Stuart,	6	9	13.	To Easby Abbey,	1	1
3.	To Garliss Castle and back,	3	5		To Burton on Swale,	2	2
					To Cattarick Bridge,	1	1
	To Ferrytown	6	9		To Appleton,	2	2
	To Gatehouse,	6	9		To Cattarick Bridge,	2	2
					To Darlington,	8	13
				14.	To Gunflis,	3	4
	Total,	86½	129		To Raby Castle,	6	9
				15.	To West Aukland,	4	6
					To Bishop's Aukland,	2	3
5.	To Tongland,	6	9		To Woolsingham,	7	10
	To Dundrennan, Abbey,	6	9		To Stanhope,	4	6
				16.	To Isop Burne,	7	10
	To Aughan Keran,	3	5		To Alston,	10	15

[The orthography of many of these place-names has already been annotated throughout the text.]

TOUR THROUGH SCOTLAND, 1760.

		C.	M.			C.	M.
May 17.	To Featherstone Castle,	8	11½	June 6. To Dun Staffnage,		4	4
	To Haltwesel,	3	4½	To Isle of Mull,		9	9
	To Brampton,	8	12	To Aughan Crage,		4	5
				7. To Benissan,		18	27
	Total,	97	140	Total,		118	140
19.	To Naworth Castle,	3	3	8. To Craig,		4	6
	To Bew Castle,	6	9	To I Colm Kill,		2	2
	To Neatherby,	7	10	To Porticurrich and back,		4	4
	To Long Toun,	2	2	To Cromarty in Mull,		2	2
20.	To Gratna Green,	4	6	9. To Aughan Craig,		21	31
	To Eaglefeckin,	6	9	10. To Island of Lismore,		8	8
	To Lockerby,	4	6	To Airds,		6	6
	To Moffett,	12	18	13. To Fort William,		16	24
21.	To Old Wells,	2	2	14. To Fort Augustus,		18	28
	To New Wells,	3	5				
	To Leadhills,	9	13½	Total,		81	111
22.	To Carmichael,	12	18				
	To Lanerk,	4	6	16. To Inverness,		21	33
23.	To Carstairs,	3	5	17. To Culloden and back,		6	10
	To Bonny Town,	5	7	To Fort George and back,		14	26
	To Lanerk,	2	2	20. To Dingwell,		10	14
	To Hamilton,	10	15	To Sir Harry Monro's,		3	4
24.	To Glasgow,	8	12	To New Town,		2	2
				21. To Ardmore,		10	15
	Total,	102	148½	To Rose Hall,		16	24
28.	To Renfrew,	4	6	Total,		82	128
	To Paisley,	2	3				
	To Baith,	8	12				
	To Kilwinin Abbey,	6	9				
	To Irwin,	2	3				
29.	To Kilmarnock,	6	8				
	To Glasgow,	16	24				
30.	To Dunbarton,	8	13	23. To Clane Hall,		6	8
	To Bonhill Ferry,	2	3	24. To Mowdel,		24	36
	To Luss,	8	12	25. To Durness,		24	36
	Total,	62	93	Total,		54	80
June 1.	To Torbut,	8	8	... To Cape Wrath and back,		24	32
	To end of lake and back,	18	18	... To Smoo and back,		4	6
2.	To Ackinloss,	12	12	... To the Kyle and back,		4	6
	To Inverary,	10	10	... To the Glebe and back,		1	1
	To top of hill and back,	4	4	30. To Kintail,		18	28
	To valley and back,	6	6	July 1. To Tongue,		2	3
	To the woods and back,	4	4	To Strathy,		18	18
4.	To Sir Duncan Campbell's,	21	33	2. To Bighouse,		5	7
				To Sanside,		3	5

ITINERARY.

		C.	M.
July 3.	To Thyrso,	10	14
	To Orkneys,	18	18
4.	To Dwarfie Stone and Stromness,	28	28
5.	To Kirkwall,	16	24
	Total, two weeks,	151	190
7.	To Capt. Moodie's,	20	30
11.	To Ratter,	9	9
	To Pict's House and back,	2	2
	To Johnny Grott's House and back,	8	12
12.	To Lord Cathness at Myrtle,	7	10
	To Sir Patrick Dunbar's,	4	6
	Total,	50	69
14.	To Sir William Dunbar's,	8	12
15.	To Wick,	2	2
	To Dunbeath,	16	24
16.	To Dunrobin,	20	30
17.	To Dornock,	6	9
	To Skibo,	3	4
18.	To Innerchasley,	4	6
19.	To Taine,	2	3
	To Guines,	4	6
	To Catbol,	2	2
	To Cromarty,	6	8
20.	To Fowles,	16	24
22.	To Lord Lovat's seat, Beaulieu,	7	10
	To Inverness,	6	8
23.	To Fort George,	7	13
	To Kilbrack,	3	5
24.	To Nairn,	6	8
	To Lord Murray's,	6	8
	To Forres,	2	3
25.	To Broughsea,	6	8
	To Duffus,	4	6
	To Spiney Castle,	3	4
	To Elgin,	1	1
26.	To Pluscardine Abbey,	3	4
	To Elgin,	3	4
	Total, two weeks,	146	212
28.	To Gordon Castle,	6	9
	To Cullen,	7	10

		C.	M.
July 29.	To Barrife,	8	12
	To Forge land,	5	7
30.	To New Deer,	10	15
	To Old Deer,	4	6
	To Peterhead,	8	12
31.	To Slanes Castle,	6	9
Aug. 1.	To Ellon,	8	12
	To Old Meldrum,	6	8
	To Money Musk,	6	8
	To Paradin and back,	4	6
2.	To Aberdeen,	12	18
	To Seaton and back,	3	4
	Total,	93	136
5.	To Stonehive,	10	14
	To Bervey,	6	10
6.	To Montrose,	8	12
	To Brechan,	6	8
7.	To Forfar,	8	12
	To Glaimes,	3	5
8.	To Lord Penmure's,	8	12
	To Arbroath,	7	10
	To Dundee,	12	18
9.	To Coupar in Angus,	10	15
	To Dunkeld,	10	15
	To the hill and back twice,	4	6
	To the Hermitage and back twice,	3	5
		95	142
15.	To Blair,	15	20
	About the place at several times,	6	9
	Total,	21	29
18.	To Taymouth,	20	30
22.	About the place several times,	10	15
	To Glyn Lyon and back,	6	9
	To Crief,	18	27
	To Drummond Castle,	2	3
	Total,	56	84
25.	To Ardock,	4	6
	To Tullibarden,	4	6
	To Drummond Castle,	4	6

		C.	M.			C.	M.
Aug. 25.	To Galgacan and back by Crieff,	10	15	Sept. 9. 13.	To Newhaven and To Leith,	2	2
	To Methuen,	8	12		To Craig Miller Castle,	2	2
26.	To Duplin,	3	4		To Edinburgh,	2	2
	To Elcho,	3½	5				
	To Perth,	2	3		Total,	48	63
27.	To Schoon,	2	2				
	To Erroll,	10	14	16.	To Musselburgh,	3	4
	To Maginch and back,	2	2		To Dalkeith,	3	4
28.	To Mugdrum,	3	4	17.	To Armistown.	6	8
	To Abernathie,	2	2		About the place,	10	10
29.	To Newbrough,	2	2	18.	To Gifford and Yester,	11	16
	To Lindores,	1	1		About the place,	6	6
	To Balmerinack,	6	8	19.	To Haddington,	3	4
	To Coupar in Fife,	4	6		To North Berwick,	6	8
	To St. Andrews,	6	8		To Dunbar,	7	10
				20.	To Broxburn,	1	1
	Total,	76½	106	21.	To Dunglass,	4	6
					About the place,	4	4
Sept. 1.	To Crail,	6	9				
	To Kilwenny,	3	4		Total,	64	81
	To Anstrather,	2	2				
	To Pettin Weme,	2	2	22.	To Coldingham,	7	10
	To St. Monan,	1	1		To Berwick upon Tweed,	7	10
	To Ellie,	1	1				
2.	To Leven,	6	8	23.	To Northam,	6	9
	To Leisley,	6	8		To Cornhill,	4	5
3.	To Faulkland,	4	6		To Coldstream and back,	3	4
	To Kinross,	7	10				
	To the isle and back,	2	2		To the Spaw and back,	2	2
4.	To Lough Orr,	4	7		To Flodden field and back,	6	9
	To Kirkaldy,	6	8				
	To Dysert,	2	2	24.	To Kelso,	7	10
5.	To Kirkaldy,	2	2		To Stitchall,	3	4
	To Kingshorn,	2	2		To Mailerstanes,	3	4
	To Inverkeithing,	4	6		About the place,	6	9
	To Dunibrical,	2	3		To Dryburgh Abbey and back,	6	9
	To Inverkeithing,	2	2½				
	To Dumfermling,	3½	5	26.	To Mellross,	4	6
6.	To Culross,	6	8		To Selkirk,	4	6
	To Clackmannan,	6	8	27.	To Jedburgh,	10	14
	To Lord Cathcart's,	2	3		To Wooller,	18	26
	To Aloa,	2	2				
	To Dumblaine,	7	10		Total,	96	137
	Total,	90½	121½	29.	To Whitingham,	107	151
	To Sheriff Muir and back,	6	6	Oct. 3.	To Newcastle,		
				7.	To Jarrow,	90	128
8.	To Sterling,	4	6	11.	To Scarborough,		
	To Falkirk,	8	12	13.	To Bridlington,	98	140
	To Linlithgow,	6	9	18.	To Godmanhan,		
	To Hopton,	6	8	20.	To Landborough,	83	111½
	To Queensferry,	2	2	24.	To Chatsworth,		
9.	To Hopton,	2	2	27.	To Chesterfield,	...	160¾
	To Edinburgh,	8	12	29.	To London.		

ITINERARY.

SUMMARY OF THE NUMBER OF MILES TRAVELLED IN THE THIRTY WEEKS.

		Miles Travelled.	
IRELAND.			
First and second weeks—Total,	.	204	
			204
SCOTLAND.			
4th week—Total,	. . . . .	129	
5th week ,,	. . . . .	156	
6th week ,,	. . . . .	140	
7th week ,,	. . . . .	148¼	
8th week ,,	. . . . .	93	
9th week ,,	. . . . .	140	
10th week ,,	. . . . .	111	
11th week ,,	. . . . .	128	
12th week ,,	. . . . .	80	
13th week ,,	. . . . .	190	
14th week ,,	. . . . .	69	
15th and 16th weeks—Total,	. . . .	212	
17th week—Total,	. . . . .	136	
18th and 19th weeks—Total,	. . . .	171	
20th week—Total,	. . . .	84	
21st week ,,	. . . . .	106	
22d week ,,	. . . . .	121½	
23d week ,,	. . . . .	63	
24th week ,,	. . . . .	81	
25th week ,,	. . . . .	137	
			2496
ENGLAND.			
26th week—Total,	. . . .	151	
27th week ,,	. . . .	128	
28th week ,,	. . . .	140	
29th week ,,	. . . .	111½	
30th week ,,	. . . .	160¾	
			691¼
Total in all,	. . . .		3391¼

LIST OF STAGES TWIXT LONDON AND EDINBURGH.

East Road.	Miles.		West Road.	Miles.	
Haddington,	16	...	Lintoun,	12	...
Dunbar,	11	27	Beild,	12	24
Old Cambus,	10	37	Moffat,	12	36
Berwick,	16	53	Lockerbie,	11	47
Belford,	15	68	Alison bank,	10	57
Alnwick,	14	82	Carlisle,	9	66
Morpeth,	19	101	Penrith,	14	80
Newcastle,	14	115	Kendal,	18	98
Durham,	15	130	Burton,	7	107
Darlington,	18	148	Lancaster,	9	116
Northallerton,	15	163	Garstang,	10	126
Borrowbridge,	19	182	Preston,	10	136
York,	17	199	Wiggan,	14	150
Tadcaster,	9	208	Newton,	7	157
Ferrybridge,	13	221	Lastock,	12	169
Doncaster,	15	236	Brereton Green,	5	174
Bawtry,	8	244	Newcastle-under-Line,	10	184
Tuxford,	16	260	Stone,	7	191
Newark,	13	273	Litchfield,	16	207
Grantham,	14	287	Coleshill,	12	219
Colesforth,	7	294	Coventry,	8	227
Stamford,	13	307	Dunchurch,	8	235
Stilton,	14	321	Daventry,	6	241
Bugden,	14	335	Towcester,	10	251
Bigilsward,	16	351	Fenny Stratford,	12	263
Stephenage,	14	365	Dunstable,	9	272
Hatfield,	12	377	St. Albans,	10	282
Barnet,	9	386	Barnet,	10	292
London,	11	397	London,	10	302

The whole of the East road is measured, and mile stones erected, but the West road is all computed miles.

York is for ordinary made a Stage, tho' it lyes about 8 miles off the road; so that by the East road the distance betwixt Edinburgh and London is about 389.

INDEX.

Abbey of Luce, 12, 13.
—— of Sweetheart, 27.
—— Craig, 290, 293.
Abbotshall, 281.
Aberbrothock Abbey, 220, 221.
Abercairney, 247.
Abercorn, Earl of, 56.
Abercromby, Andrew, 223.
Abercromby Church, 275.
Aberdeen, 186, 201-210; Carmelite Convent, 203; charters, 204; Library and MSS., 207; Cross, 203; inscriptions, Cathedral, 205; King's College, 207; Marischal College, 208; Monuments, Cathedral, 206; Provost of, 210; students, 204; Trades' Hall, 202, 203.
—— Lord, 199.
—— William, Earl of, 199.
Aberdour Castle, 282; Nunnery, 228; Obelisk, 282.
Aberlady, 226.
Aberlemno Crosses, 217.
Abernethy, 260, 262; church, 260, 261; Round Tower, 257, 261.
—— Lord, 264.
—— iron forges, 184.
Able, Adam, 345.
Achany, 115.
Achnacary, 98, 99.
Achness, Rosehall, 114.
Ackergill Tower, 160.
Acre, English, 113; Scotch, 113.
Adams, the architect, 48, 222, 280, 311, 316.
Adders, 126.
Advocates' Library, 2, 307.
Agate, 87, 154.
Aiden, King, 78.
Aird, Rev. Dr. Gustavus, 131.
Airds, Argyleshire, 91, 95.
—— Ross-shire, 108, 115.
Airth, 295.
Alabaster, 198.
Albany, Duchess of, 61.
Alcluith, 61.

Aldourie, 102.
Alexander III., 81.
Allanfearn, 104.
All Angels' Day, 86.
Allan river, 290, 291.
Alloa, 290.
Allt Granda, 177.
Almond, river, 251, 255.
Alness, 111.
Alstonmoor, 36.
Altar, Iona, 82; Roman, 33, 34; St. Andrew's, Glasgow, 82.
Altrie, Lord, 197.
Alva, Lord, 290.
Amber, 93, 241.
Amulree, 239.
Anack, river, 57.
Ancrum, 343.
—— Muir, 340.
Andrew, Bishop, 188.
Andrew, St., 263, 265, 266, 267.
Angel's Hill, 86.
Angus, 225.
—— Archibald Douglas, Earl of, 320.
—— Earl of, 340.
Ankerville, 174.
Annan, 34.
Annan, river, 7, 37, 40.
—— William, 47.
Annandale, 7, 33.
—— Marquis of, 38, 40.
Anne, Queen, 151; nuptial bed of, 286.
Anstruther, 274.
—— Sir John, 275, 276.
—— Sir W. C., 44.
Anthony, St., 309.
Antrim, 5.
Appleby, 1.
Apples, 130, 151, 345.
Appin, 95.
Aray, river, 65, 66.
Arbroath, 220, 221; Chapel, 220.
Archdall, Rev. M., lviii, lix, lxiv.
Archibald, Bishop, 186.
Ardbrecknish, 68.

INDEX.

Ardchattan, 69, 70.
Ardchonal Castle, 68.
Ardmaddy, 71.
Ardmagh, 5.
Ardmore, 111.
Ardmucknish, 71.
Ardoch, 240, 242, 244.
Ardschrinish, 77.
Argyle, Bishop of, 69, 72, 78.
—— Earl of, 51, 99.
—— Duke of, 65, 84, 87, 241, 283, 292, 294, 304.
—— Family, 68, 238.
Argyleshire, 115.
Aria Theophrasti dicta, 72.
Arkaig, Loch, 99.
Armadale, 131.
Armlet, ancient bronze, 330.
Arniston, 313, 315.
Arnold, Bishop, 268.
Aros Castle, 76, 77.
Arsbrook, 114.
Arthur's Oven, 296.
Asbestos, 228.
Ash, 130.
Athelstaneford, 318.
Athole, 225.
—— Duchess of, 252, 259.
—— Duke of, liv, 68, 199, 225, 228, 229, 232, 242.
—— Walter, Earl of, 247.
Auchencraig, 74, 77.
Auchencairn, 25.
Auchencat, 39.
Auchindoun Castle, 185.
Augustine, St., 236, 246, 258, 274, 294.
Austin, St., 269, 274, 298, 344.
Avona, 92.
Avon, river, 296.
Awe, Loch, 238; river, 68.
Ayr, 4.

BAGIMONT, CARDINAL, 300.
Baile-Mhoadain, 69.
Baillie, George, 333.
—— Lady Grisell, 333.
—— Mr., of Ardmore and Rosehall, 111, 113.
Balcarres Castle, 276.
Balfour, Mr., 2.
Balgonie Castle, 276; Mr. Graham's, 247.
Baliol, John, 18, 27.
Ballanbreich Castle, 264.
Ballantrae, 4.
Ballintory, 77.
Balloch, 243.
Balmerino Abbey, 294; Castle, 260.

Balmerino, Lord, 302.
Balm Well, 315.
Balnagown Castle, 175.
Balreny Castle, 185.
Banco, the Thane, 98.
Bannatyne, Christopher, 47.
Banff, 194; Convent, 195; Cliff Caves, 195.
—— Lord, 195.
Bannockburn, 295, 319.
Barber, Dr., 5.
Barclay (Quaker), 211.
Barklay, Andrew, 212.
Barley, 17; cake, 88; mode of preserving, 159.
Barnard Castle, 27.
Barnbogle, 308.
Barra, 93; battle of, 186, 200.
Barren women's pilgrimage, 274.
Barrel's Regiment, 3, 105, 107.
Bass Rock, 298, 320.
Beaches, white, Iona, 87.
Beaton, Bishop James, 16, 50, 271.
—— Cardinal, 256, 270, 271.
Bean bread, 178.
Beattock, 10.
Beau Castle, 36.
Beaufort Castle, 178.
Beaumont, Earl of, 264.
Beauly, 103, 110; Loch, 108, 180; Priory, 178; river, 108, 178.
Beckett, Thomas à, 220.
Beckett's Cross, 341.
Bede, 14, 24, 61, 78, 81, 341.
Bedstead, royal, 286.
Beef salted in skins, 93; stand, Marquis of Annandale's, 40.
Beech Tree Avenue, 66.
Beith, 56.
Belfast, 5.
Belhaven, Lord, 305.
Belleville, 228.
Bell, Robert, 47.
Beltonford, 2.
Benbecula, 93.
Ben Clibrec, 118.
—— Cruachan, 68.
—— Hope, 123, 129, 130.
—— Lomond, 68.
—— Loyal, 130.
—— Maddy, 131.
—— Nevis, 68, 99.
Bennett, Saint, 263.
Bennochie, 200, 212.
Benvheir, 97.
Beregonium, 69.
Bernard, Saint, 263.
Bernera, 93, 113.
Bernie, 186; church, 191.

INDEX. 359

Berridale, 163.
Berwick, 1, 320, 328, 346, 347.
Beaver skins, 138.
Binning, Lady, 332.
—— Lord, 336.
Birchfield, 113.
Birnam, 228.
Birnock Clooves, 39.
Birrens, 6.
Birsay, 142.
Bishop Auckland, 36.
—— of Caithness, 134.
—— Forbes, 97.
—— John of Dunkeld, 90.
—— of the Isles, 81.
—— of Argyle, 90.
—— of Orkney, 137.
—— of Ross, 110.
—— of Sodor and Man, 81.
Bishoptown Castle, 16.
Bituminous fossil, 154.
Blaan, St., 291.
Blackbourn, Mr., 1.
Black game, 26.
Blackness Castle, 298.
Bladenoch, river, 18.
Blainslie, 342.
Blair Athole, 68, 229, 230, 231, 232, 233.
—— Drummond, 294.
Blankets, 11.
Blantyre, Lord, 56.
Boat, 11, 37, 87.
Boarhill, 273.
Boddom Head, 197.
Boleskine, 101.
Bolton, Duke of, 239.
Bonnets, Scotch, 59.
Bonnington Fall, Clyde, 46.
—— House, 46.
Borve Castle, 131.
Bos Primigenius, 72, 91.
Bothwell Castle, 4; Church, 48.
—— Earl, 150.
Bowmaker, Abbot Walter, 298.
Bowness, 199.
Boys in boat driven out to sea, 210.
Braan, river, 227, 238.
Bracelet, British, lxvii.
Brahan Castle, 178.
Brampton, 32, 36.
Brankston, 349.
Brass cannon, 295.
Breadalbane, Earl of, 64, 68, 71, 225, 234, 304.
Bread baked in pot, 133; of pease and oats or barley, 178.
Breakfast at Hopetoun, 3.

Brechin, 213, 215; Cathedral, 215; chapels, 216; Cross, 216; Round Tower, 215.
Bride's Close Quarry, 44.
Bridget, St., 262.
Bridius, King, 78.
Brigantia, Goddess, 314.
Bristow, Mr., 5.
Brochs, 93, 111, 116, 118, 166, 185, 228.
Brockley Mills, 193.
Brodie Castle, 182.
—— Dr., 192.
—— Mr., of Elgin, 192.
Brody, Rev. Mr., 181.
Brooch, oval, 91.
Broom, 228.
—— Loch, 101, 113, 114, 115.
—— Spinning School, 114.
Brora, 165.
Brothock, river, 220.
Brough, 36.
Brougham Castle, 36.
Broughty Castle, 222.
Brounhill, 342.
Broxmouth, 324.
Bruar, river, 233.
Bruce, Baron of Kinloss, 184.
—— Bishop, 186.
—— Castle, 38, 295.
—— George, monument, 288.
—— Marjory, 54.
—— Mrs., 289.
—— Robert the, 30, 289.
—— Sir Henry, 289.
—— Sir John, 277, 278.
—— sword and helmet, 289.
—— the architect, 277, 278, 297.
Brudens, King, 279.
Buccleuch, Duke of, 2, 312.
Buchanan Castle, 3.
Buchan, 193, 195, 196; like Northamptonshire, 196.
—— Earl of, 80, 188, 196.
Bullers of Buchan, 198.
Bunchrew, 180.
Bunessan, 77.
Bunting, snow, 140.
Bureau made of broom-wood, 232.
Burghead, 185.
Burgh Mills, 5.
Burleigh Castle, 278.
Burnett of Leys, 200.
—— Professor Alexander, 218.
Burnswork, 6, 34, 37.
Burntisland Church, 282; Bin Hill. 282; Kirkton, 282.
Butter, 88, 94.
Buttonesshead, 221, 222.

Burial, ancient, 326.
Burial-place, 89.
Burra, 151, 153.
Buy, Loch, 131.

CADZOW CASTLE, 47.
Caer Gunnian, 26.
Caerlaverock Castle, 31.
Cail, 127.
Cake and wine entertainments, 118, 130.
Cairn, 130, 177, 211; chambered, 165; near Farr, 131.
Cairndow, 65.
Cairnbulg Castle, 198.
Cairngorm, 201.
Cairnsmuir, 20.
Cairn William, 200.
Caithness, 159, 160.
—— Bishop of, 167.
—— Countess of, 310.
—— Earl of, 158, 160, 163, 195.
Caledonia, Sylva, 115.
Callernish, 94.
Cambuskenneth, 293.
Cambus, Old, 2.
Campbell, General, 71, 244.
—— Lady, 71.
—— Mr., 69, 89.
—— Mr., of Levenside, 61.
—— Mr., of Monzie, 239, 244.
—— of Airds, 91.
—— of Dunstaffnage, 74, 76.
—— of Tiree, 78.
—— Principal, 208, 209.
—— Prior John, 69.
—— Sir Duncan, 71.
Campbells of Taymouth, 236, 238.
Campbelltown, 66; Cross, 85.
Camp Castle, 240, 242, 245.
Camstraddan, 62.
Camus Cross, 217.
Candida Casa, 14, 18.
Canisby, 155.
Canna, 93.
Cantæ, 115.
Cantie, 132.
Cantire, 92.
Caolchurn Castle, 68.
Capercaillie, 110.
Cape Wrath, 124, 125, 126, 131.
Caprington, 58.
Cardonald, 56.
Cardonness Castle, 20.
Carham, 328, 350.
Caristown, 217.
Carlisle, 1, 9, 33, 36.
—— Lord, 195.
Carmichael Burn, 44.

Carmichael, Sir James, 46.
Carnabii, 163.
Carn ban, 95.
Carnegy, Sir D., 214.
Carnonacæ, 115.
Caroni, 132.
Caroline Park, 318.
Carpenter, John, 22.
Carpets, 44, 59, 274, 287.
Carr, Mr., 349.
Carrick, Earl of, 30.
Carriden, 298.
Carron ferry-boat, 113.
—— Iron-works, 296.
—— Loch, 101.
—— —— Spinning School, 114.
Carstairs village, 45.
—— Roman antiquities, 45.
Cart, river, 53, 60.
Carter, W. Allan, lx.
Cartigo, river, 114.
Carts, 36.
Cassley, river, 113; falls, 114.
Castland Hill, 283.
Castle Campbell, 290.
—— Craig, 110, 176.
—— Grant, 68.
—— Kennedy, 12.
—— Leod, 109.
—— Stewart, 104.
Castledykes, 45.
Castlemilk, 33, 37, 57.
Catanach, Professor James, 208.
Caterthun, 217.
Cathcarte, Earl of, 60, 289.
Catherine, St., 310.
Catholics, Roman, 93.
Catina, 115.
Cats, wild, 26, 120.
Catstone, The, 299.
Cattle, black, 18; to be blessed, 86.
Cautie Loch, 10.
Cava Isle, 134.
Cawdor Castle, 181; tradition, 182.
Celnius, 195.
Celtic mount, 233.
Cessford, 313; Castle, 345.
Chac, 140.
Chalmers, Principal John, 208.
Chamler, Mr., 92.
Chandos, Duke of, 272.
Chanonry of Ross, 110.
Charles I., portrait, 283.
Charmale, 189.
Charterhouse, Lord, 251.
Charteris, Mr., New Mill, 318.
Chatelherault, 47.
—— Duke of, 56, 57, 221.
Cheese, 88, 94.

INDEX.

Cherries, 130.
Chertes Knowe, 342.
Chester, 344.
Cheyne, Bishop Henry, 204.
Chinevix, Mrs., 5.
Christ Church, Hampshire, 24.
—— —— Orkney, 142.
Chronicles of Melrose, 24, 341.
—— Saxon, 79.
Church, circular, 137; thatched, 349.
Churn, 116.
Clackmae, 342.
Clackmannan, 289.
Cladh an Diesart, 85.
Clans Chattan and Kay combat, 257.
Clary, 19.
Cleres, Rev. Mr., 5.
Clerk, Baron, 2, 314.
Clet, 133.
Clifton, 64.
Clochmaben stone, 35.
Clock timed by stars, 67.
Cluniac monks, 53.
Cluny Hill, 183.
—— Loch, 101.
Clyde, river, 20, 40, 41, 43, 47, 61.
Clydesdale, 41.
Clyde's Nop, or Nape, 40.
Clyne House, 165.
Cnoc a Choire, 115.
Cnoc nan Aingeal, 86.
Coal, 17, 25, 57, 60, 110, 276, 280, 290, 313, 325, 347.
Coble, 164, 214.
Cockburnspath, 2.
Cockles, 25, 152.
Cod, 25, 88, 145, 153.
Coins, collection of, 173, 200, 208, 275, 307.
Coir nan eas, 121.
Coldingham Nunnery, 327; Priory, 327.
Coldstream, 328.
Colefish, 145.
Coleman, Mr., 5.
Collection plates, 148.
Collieries, 281.
Cologne, 30.
Colonia, 45.
Colonsay, 71, 93.
Colquhouns, 61, 62.
Columba, 78.
Colville, Alexander, 288.
—— Lord, 288.
Comlongon Castle, 31.
Comor Castle, 325.
Compass Hill, 93.
Compost, manure, 149.
Comrie, 242.

Comyn, John, 7, 30.
—— Sir Robert, 30.
Conavii, 132.
Cope, General, 311.
Copper, 41, 42, 100.
Cora linn, 40, 46.
Corbie Hall Farm, 45.
Corehouse, Lanark, 46.
Cormac Ulfhadda, 84.
Cornhill, 328, 350.
Coronation Chair, ivory figure, 72, 74, 75; Chair and Stone, 258.
Corsincon, 30.
Corstorphine, 299.
Corryburgh, 180.
Coryvreckan, 71.
Coulside Loch, 120.
Coupar Angus, 225.
Court of Session, first President, 294.
Covenanters, Rullion Green, 315.
Cowie, 211.
Cows, 94.
Crabs, 14.
Craig Fort, 293.
Craigmillar Castle, 310.
Craig Nuke, 69.
Craig, The Eagle's, 243.
Craigie House, 259.
—— Lord President, 313.
Crail Church, 273, 274.
Crailing Hall, 345.
Cramond, 3, 299.
Cranston, 316.
Crawford, Mr., of Errol, 248, 259, 260.
Crawfordjohn, 43.
Crawfurdland Castle, 60.
Creag Chailliun, 114.
Cream, piggin of, 118; whiskel, 116.
Creones, 115.
Creran, Loch, 91.
Cree, river, 18.
Creetown, 19.
Crichton, Admirable, 247.
—— Castle, 315; Church, 315.
Crieff, 239, 244, 247.
Criffel, 27, 30.
Crimond, Lord, 200.
Crimson dye, 92.
Cromarty, 110, 176, 180.
—— Earl of, 109, 175.
—— Firth, 108.
—— Obelisk, 109.
Cromwell's map, 19; fort, 104, 184; camp, 315.
Cromwellian soldiers, 69.
Crosses, Aberlemno, 217; Camus, 217; Farr Church, 131; High, 66; Market, 17, 18, 66, 265.

Crottle Corkir, 92.
Cruachan, 68.
Crudin, 186.
Cudins, 124, 145.
Cuithes, 145.
Culcairn, 110, 176.
Cullen, 193, 225.
Culloden, 101, 104, 105; battle of, 106, 129, 295; plan of battlefield, 105; Wood, 107.
Culrain, 114.
Culross Church, 288.
Cumberland, Duke of, 98, 101, 105, 107, 108, 251, 272.
—— Stone, 105.
Cumin, Mr., Inverary, 67.
Cumins, The, 101.
—— Tower, 99.
Cummerland, 276.
Cumming, Provost, of Altyre, 183.
Cumnock Castle, 31.
Cunningham, Sir John, 58.
Cupar, Fife, 265, 277; Cross, 265.
Curds, 88.
Curicle, or boat, 87.
Custom-house officer, 37.
Cuthbert, Mr., 111.
Cuthbert, St., 302, 317.
Cutlery ware, Kinross, 278.
Cyderhall, 168.

DA COSTA, E. M., xliii, xlv.
Dacres, Lord, 349, 350.
Dalgety, 283.
Dalhousie Castle, 313.
—— Earl of, 215.
Dalkeith, 2, 314; Church, 312; Palace, 312.
Dalnacardoch, 233.
Dalrymple, Sir David, 310.
—— Sir James, 13, 311.
—— Sir John, 13.
Dalrymples, 12.
Dalziel, General, 315.
Damsa, 144.
Dancing, round corpse, 88.
Danish Kings' tombs, Iona, 84.
Dairmagh (Darmach), 78.
Dairsie Church, 265, 266.
Darnaway Castle, 183.
Darnick, 342.
David, King, 44.
Dean Castle, 60.
Dee, river, 20, 199, 201; Bridge, 211.
Deer, Abbey of, 196.
—— Old, Chapel, 197.
Deer destroying trees, 68; drive, 121; mouse, 138; Gaelic names, 119; red, 89, 117, 119, 120, 121, 126;

red, fawn, killed by eagle, 124; red, kill adders, 126; roe, 68, 117, 119.
Delvine, 225.
Dennys, St., 324.
Denoon Castle, 218.
Dermoch, Bishop, 291.
Dervorgilla, 8, 18, 27, 30, 223.
Deskford, Lord, 194.
Detersunt, 95.
Deveron, river, 194, 195, 196.
Dingwall, 108, 109, 176, 178.
Dionard, river, 124.
Dish, with embossed work, 241.
Diver, black-throated, 117.
Dog, sheep, 140.
Doll of Brora, 165.
Donaghadee, 4, 11.
Donald's Island, 116.
Donaldson, Professor Alexander, 208.
Donibristle House, 283.
Doir-a-Chata, 115.
Don, river, 199, 200, 209, 210.
Dornoch. 129, 134, 167; Cathedral, 168; Palace, 168; Firth, 111, 115, 117, 168, 219.
Doune, 114.
Douglas, Bishop, 226.
—— Archibald, Earl of, 48.
—— Duke of, 22, 43, 224.
—— Sir James, 329.
Douglas coal, 41; mill, 43.
Drinking healths, 88, 116, 118.
Drogheda, 5.
Druid remains, 70, 77, 85, 86, 93, 94, 102, 104, 141, 143, 211, 229, 236, 276.
Druids, Isle of, 85.
Druid's temples, 341.
Drum, 310.
Drumcondra, 5.
Drumlanrig, 9.
Drummond Castle, 240, 243, 244.
—— Lord Provost, 2.
—— Mr., 239, 249.
—— —— of Lundin, 276.
—— of Hawthornden, 314.
Drummuir, Lady, 107.
Drumsheugh, 310.
Drumsturdy Moor Law, 222.
Dryburgh, Abbey of, 330, 346.
Drygrange, 342.
Dry-stone buildings, 185.
Duart Castle, 74.
Dublin, 5.
Ducarel, Dr., xli, xlv.
Ducks, wild, 116.
Duddingston, 310.
Dudhope, 224.
Duffus Castle, 186.

INDEX. 363

Duffus, Lord, 186.
Dumbarton, 3, 23, 61, 240.
Dumfries, 7, 8, 20, 27, 30.
Dumna, 115, 131.
Dun Ach'-an-Eas, 114.
—— Alishaig, 111, 112, 114.
—— Bar Castle, 130.
Dunbar, 2, 320; battle of, 315, 324; Castle, 319, 321; Church, 320; Harbour, 322.
—— Bishop Gavin, 204, 206.
—— Earl of, 320, 321.
—— —— tomb, 321.
—— Mr. William, 162.
—— Sir Patrick, 158, 159.
—— Sir William, 160, 183.
Dunbeath, 134, 163, 166.
Dun bhail an righ, 69.
Dunblane, 241, 290, 291, 292, 293; Bishopric, 201; Cathedral, 291, 292; Library, 292.
Duncan, Provost, of Mosstown, 210.
—— Rev. Mr., 3.
Duncansbay Head, 140, 155.
Dun Core, 115.
Dundaff Linn, 46.
Dundalk, 5.
Dundas, Dr., 3.
—— Lord President, 46, 313.
Dundee, 222, 223; large windmill, 222, 224.
—— Lord, 229.
Dundonald, Lord, 54, 56.
Dun Dornadilla, 121, 122, 123.
Dundrennan Abbey, 22, 23, 24, 279.
Dunfermline, 191, 192, 283-288; Abbey, 284, 285, 286.
—— Abbot of, 281.
—— Earl of, 284.
Dungavel Hill, 43.
Dunglass, 326; Castle, 61; Dean, 325.
Dunhead, 218.
Duniquaich, 65.
Dunkeld, 225, 226, 228, 229, 239; Cathedral, 226; Duke of Athole's house, 226.
Dun-mac-Sniachan, 70.
Dunmore, Lord, 290.
Dunnottar, 209, 211, 212.
Dunolly Castle, 74.
Dunoon, 90.
Dun Quarry, 214.
Dunrobin, 166.
Duns, 330.
—— John Scotus, 30.
Dunsinane, 225, 248, 259.

Dunstaffnage, 72, 73, 74, 99; chess-man, 75; Echo rock, 74; Scots kings' vault, 74.
Dun Varrich, 130.
Dupplin, 246, 247, 248, 249; battle of, 256.
Durcha, 115.
Durham, 1.
Durness, 124, 127.
Duror, 96.
Durrow, 78.
Durward, Sir Alan, 213.
Dwarfie Stone, 135.
Dyes, Highland, 92.
Dykehead, 37.
Dysart, 281.
—— Lord, 221.

EAGLES, 27, 125, 135.
Earl's Cross, 167.
Earn Loch, 239; river, 239, 243, 244.
Earnside Forest, 263.
Earthenwares, 52.
Easdale, Isle of, 71.
Ecclefechan, 7, 10, 37.
Eck, Loch, 90.
Edderachylis Bay, 113.
Eden, river, 265, 266, 278.
—— Vale of, 277.
Edinburgh, 2, 299-307; Advocates' Library, 307; Arthur's Seat, 305; Barony of Calton, 303; Herbergare, 301; Holyrood, 301, 304; Restalrig, 303; Silversmith, 210; Sciennes Nunnery, 310.
—— Castle, 305; regalia in, 306.
Edward, St., 264.
Eels, 131.
Egfrid, Bishop, 347.
Eggs, 88, 94.
Eglinton, Earl of, 57, 58.
Eigg, Isle of, 93.
Eildon Hills, 342.
Eilean an Stalcair, 95.
—— Donuil, 116.
—— Vhou, 63.
Eil, Loch, 98.
Eirke, l.
Elan, St., 319.
Elcho, 249, 259.
Elderslie, 53.
Elgin, 188, 190, 191; Cathedral, 188, 189.
—— Earl of, lv, 184, 286, 289.
Elie, 275.
—— Law, ancient burial, 275, 276.
Elliot, Captain, 280.
—— Mr., of Lochgelly, 280.

364   INDEX.

Ellon, 199.
Elphinston, Bishop, 205, 207.
—— Sir James, 264.
Elvanfoot, 10, 40.
Engelwood Forest, 36.
Engines, large pumping, 281.
Ennard, Loch, 115.
Episcopi Lismorenses, 90, 205.
Ereska Isle, 91.
Ericht Loch, 233.
Erribol Bay, 129; Loch, 124, 128.
Errickstane, 10, 40.
Errig, 65.
Errol, 259.
—— Earl of, 198, 199.
Erskine, Charles, of Alva, 290.
—— John, of Cardross, 241.
—— Lord, 290.
—— Mr., of Dun, 214.
—— Mrs., 304.
Esk, North, 212; South, 212, 217; river guide, 20, 36, 313.
Esquimaux, 138.
Essex, 18.
Etal, 349.
Ettrick, river, 343.
Evicting tenants, 97.
Evie, 142.
Ewe, Loch, 115.
Ewin, King, 74.
Experiment, the war-ship, 129.
Eyemouth, 328.

Factor shot, 97.
Fairbairn House, 178.
Fair Isle, 153.
Fairs, 18.
Falkirk, 3; battle of, 176, 295, 296; Tryst, 295.
Falkland, 265, 277.
Fara, Isle of, 134, 151.
Farmer, Captain, 129.
Faroe, 155.
Farout Head, 124.
Farquhard, Earl of Ross, 170.
Farr, Bay of, 119, 130; Church, 131.
Fast Castle, 325, 327.
Fast Day, 59.
Fearn Abbey, 170, 171, 175.
Feldice, Thomas, 2.
Ferguson, Mr., of Pitfour, 197.
Ferrytown, 18, 19.
Ferryport, Mull, 77.
Fife, Earls of, 194, 265, 288, 319.
Findhorn, river, 183, 185.
Findlater, Earl of, 3, 193.
Finlaggan Loch, 93.
Finlay, Bishop, 291.
Fir boards, price of, 238.

Fisher families, 166.
Fitty Loch, 280.
Flannel, 11.
Flax, 101.
Fleet, His Majesty's, 107.
—— river, 20, 167.
Flemming, Prior, 15.
Fletcher, Mr., 5.
—— Lord Milton, 316.
—— Rev. David, 340.
Flodden, battle of, 328, 349, 350.
Flood, F. W., l.
Floors Castle, 329.
Flota Isle, 134, 150, 151.
Fochabers, 192, 193.
Font Church, 17.
Food in Durness, 127.
Forbes, Bishop Patrick, 205.
—— —— Robert, 97, 109.
—— Lord President, 105, 180, 313.
—— Master of, 192.
—— Mr., 129, 130.
Ford Castle, 349, 350.
Fordel, Glen, 283.
Fordyce, Mr., 2.
Forest, Earl of Sutherland's, 118.
Forfar, 217.
Forglen, 195.
Forres, 183; Pillar, 184.
Forrester, Lord, 299.
Forsyth, Rector Thomas, 51.
Fort Augustus, 99, 100, 101, 110.
Forteviot Castle, 257.
Fort George, 104, 110, 180.
Fortingall, 237; ancient ewer, 237.
Fortrose, 104, 180.
Fort William, 62, 63, 64, 68, 71, 72, 91, 98, 99.
Fossils, 165, 241, 282, 295, 316, 323, 324.
Foulis, 109, 176.
Fowlis Church, 224, 260.
Foxes, 26, 116.
Foyers, Fall of, 101.
Foyle, 64.
France, King of, 100; tomb of, 84.
Fraser of Foyers, 101.
—— of Gorthleg, 107.
—— of Reelick, 180.
—— Dr., of Achnagairn, 178, 180.
—— —— picture of, 207.
—— Provost, W. S., 168.
Fraserburgh, 198.
Frau, Fro, or Froth, 116.
Frazer, Dr. W., xlix.
Freedom of burghs, liii; Aberdeen, 210; Dornoch, 168; Forres, 183; Glasgow, 3; Kirkwall, 150; Lanark, 47; Nairn, 182; Perth, 253; Tain, 169.

INDEX.   365

French privateer, 129.
Freuchie Loch, 239.
Friend, Dr., 234.
Frieze, 11.
Fruit, when ripe, 169.
Furze, 32.
Fyne, Loch, 90.

GALACH LAW, 315.
Galashiels, 342.
Galley, 100
Galloway, S, 11, 12.
—— Earls of, 12, 16, 18, 19, 20, 23, 24, 27, 150, 151, 223.
Gannet, 126, 320.
Garlais Castle, 19.
Garmouth, 184.
Garnock, river, 57.
Garry, Loch, 100.
—— River, 229, 233.
Garth Castle, 234.
Garvie Island, 298.
Gatehouse of Fleet, 20.
Gattonside, 342.
Geanies, 172.
Geese, wild, 116, 126, 320.
Gerard, Professor Alexander, 208.
Giant's Causeway, 5, 77.
Gibb, architect, 202.
Giese, 133.
Gifford, 316.
Gigha, 92.
Giles, St., 300.
Girnigoe Castle, 160, 161.
Girvan, 4.
Glamis, 217, 218, 219.
—— Lords of, 218.
Glasgow, 3, 4, 47, 48, 49, 50, 51, 52, 60; College, 52, 209.
Glass bottles, 52.
Glass, Rev. John, 223.
Glasserton, 14.
Glean Beallach na Meirlach, 121.
Glenbeg, 93, 113.
Glencairn, Earl of, 60.
Glencaple, 30.
Glencoe, 97.
Glencoul, Loch, 113.
Glencroe, 64.
Glendevon, 279.
Glenelg, 93.
Glen Finnan, 98.
—— Fyne, 64.
—— Garry, 100, 101.
Glengonar, river, 43.
Glengowlay, 233.
Glenluce, 11, 12.
—— Lord, 13.
Glenlyon, 236.

Glenmoriston, 100.
—— Laird of, 101.
—— Spinning School, 114.
Glenmuick, 114.
Glenshee, 225.
Glenteyral, 30.
Glimsholm, 151.
Gloves, 139, 197.
Goats eating adders, 126.
Gold, 43, 100; ornament, 213.
Goodall, Mr., of Advocates' Library, 308.
Gooseberries, 151.
Gordon, Abbot, 12.
—— Bishop, 12, 204, 246.
—— Castle, 184, 193.
—— Dean John, 12.
—— Dukes of, 193, 199, 316.
—— General, daughter of, 241.
—— Louisa, 12.
—— Mr., 130, 176.
—— Professor George, 208.
—— —— Thomas, 208.
—— Sir John, 176.
—— Sir Robert, 12, 185, 186.
Gordonstoun, 186.
Gosfrid, Abbot, 284.
Gottenburgh, 17.
Govan, 53.
Gowrie, 225.
—— Carse of, 259.
—— Earl, 251.
Graham, Bishop, 248, 270.
—— Mr., of Græmeshall, 151, 153.
—— —— of Balgonie, 247.
Grampton, Mr., 40.
Grandtully, 225.
Grant Castle, 68, 184.
—— Rev. Dr., 2.
—— Sir Archibald, 200, 201.
Granton, Moffat, 40.
Graves, Rev. James, xlix, lvii.
Gray, Lord, 224, 260.
—— Lady, 250.
—— Master of, 284.
Græmsay, 137, 140.
Gregory, Professor John, 208, 271.
Greenland fishery, 155.
Gretna Green, 6, 35, 36, 37.
Grierson, John, 223.
Grim, Ben, 132.
Grimbister Holm, 144.
Grouse, 26, 89.
Gulls, 158, 198.

HADDINGTON, 317, 318.
—— Earls of, lxiii, 276, 305, 318, 320.
Hadrian, St., 274.
Hakon, Earl, 137.

Halladale, 132.
Haltwhistle, 36.
Hamilton, 4, 47, 48.
—— Abbot, 170, 221.
—— Dr., 2.
—— Dukes of, 22, 47, 48, 304.
—— Lord Claud, 56.
—— Mr., 4.
Hampshire, 24.
Hares, 68, 116.
Harlaw, battle of, 199.
Harris, 91, 92, 94.
Hartfell Spa, 39.
Harvey, Alexander, 52.
Hawkhead, 56.
Hawks, 193.
Haworth Castle, 36.
Hawthornden, 2, 314.
Hay, Sir Thomas, 13.
—— Sir William, 317.
Hay's battle, Luncarty, 248.
Hays of Mugdrum, 260, 262, 263.
Hazard sloop, 129.
Hazlewood, 60.
Hedderwick House, 214.
Heddle, Mr., 151.
Helmet, 88, 289.
Helmsdale, 164.
Henderson, a painting, 316.
—— Sir Robert, 282.
Hepburn, Prior John, 271.
Herbergare, 301.
Hermit's cell, 136, 209.
Herring, 11, 71, 214.
Hexham, 1.
Heyington, Dr., 223.
Highland cabins, 116, 127; dyes, 92; hospitality, 118; manners, 116.
Hobgoblin Hall, 316.
Hoddam, 7, 33, 34.
Hoghmanstains, 256.
Hogs, small, 139.
Holborn Head, 134.
Holly-tree, large, 263.
Holy Island, 1.
Holyrood, 2, 8, 71, 78, 278, 301, 304.
Holy Sepulchre, 81.
Home, Earls of, 43, 320.
—— Sir George, 320.
Honeyman, Archdeacon, 137.
Hope, Loch, 124, 129.
—— Mr., 298.
Hopetoun, 3, 51, 297.
—— Earls of, 3, 10, 38, 41, 247, 297, 298.
—— Lady, 3.
Horses, 4, 11, 68, 76, 86, 88, 129, 154.
Horsley, 109, 115.

Houten Head, 135.
Howard Castle, 195.
Howgate Pass, 43.
Hoy Island, 135, 137.
Hoys, 4.
Hudson's Bay, 138.
Hunda, 151.
Huntingtower, 247, 252.
—— Earl of, 263.
Huntly, Lord, 187.
Hut, General Wade's, 101.
Hyde, Mrs., 5.
Hynd Castle, 219.
Hyndford, Lord, 44.

ICELAND, 154, 155.
Inchaffray Abbey, 246, 247.
Inchcolm, 2, 298.
Inchcoulter, 177.
Inchkeith, 2.
Inchmurrin, 62.
Inchtuthil, 225.
Indians, 138.
Indies, East, 103.
Indigo, 51, 57.
Inisch Drunish, 85.
Inischonel, 68.
Inkle wares, 52.
Innerpeffary, 245.
Innerwick Castle, 325.
Innes House, 192.
—— John, Elgin, 190.
—— Mr., of Sandside, 133.
—— Sir Harry, 192.
Inveraray, 63, 64, 65, 132, 177; cross, 85.
Inverawe, 68.
Inverbervie, 212.
Invercarron, 169.
Inveresk, 2, 311.
Invergarry Castle, 100.
Invergordon, 175.
Inverhope, 129.
Inverkeithing, 283.
Inverlochy, 72, 99.
Invermoriston, 101.
Inverness, 93, 101, 102, 103, 104, 107, 110, 115, 180, 219.
Inversaddell, 98.
Inversnaid Fort, 63.
Inverteil Quarry, 281.
Inveruglass, 63.
Inverury, 200.
Iona, 66, 77-89, 93; last Abbess of, 86; monuments, 82-86.
Ireland, students from, 52.
Irish kings' tombs, 84.
Iron, 17, 25, 70, 74, 76, 77, 93, 137, 153, 200, 326; wares, 52.

INDEX.

Irvine, 56, 57.
Irwin, Colonel, 278.
Isla, river, 225.
Islay, 77, 93.
Isle of Man, 79, 81.
—— Druids, 85.
Isles, Bishops of the, 69, 79.
—— Lord of the, 71.
Islesburgh, 154.
Itinerary, 351-357.
Ivers, Ralph, 340.
Ivory, 138.

JAMES IV., penance chain, 350.
—— V., 95.
—— VI., picture of, 193.
Jasper, 198, 305.
Jedburgh, 343; Abbey, 217, 344.
Jocelyn, Bishop, 49.
John-o'-Groat's House, 155.
Johnson, Dunkeld, 227.
Johnston, Lord, 38.
—— Mr. James, 39.
—— Picture of, 207.
—— Sir Theodore, 38.
Joiat, Richard, 254.
Jorfiara, Castle of, 138.
Jura, 71, 93.
Justices of Peace, 88, 89, 97.

KAIL, 127.
Keating, Dr., 84.
Keith, 184.
—— Family of, 197, 209.
—— Hall, 200.
—— Sir William, 212.
Keith's collection of coins, 208.
Kellie Castle, 276.
Kelp, 93, 139.
Kelso Abbey, 57, 326, 343.
Keltney Burn, 234.
Kenmay, 200.
Kenmore, 235.
Kennedy, Bishop, 270, 271, 272.
—— Castle, 4, 12.
—— Mr., of Montrose, 213.
—— Professor William, 208.
Kentick Hill, 43, 44.
Ker, Sir Andrew, 345.
—— Sir Mark, 313.
—— Sir Robert, 329.
—— Sir Walter, 313.
Kerian, St., his staff, lxvii.
Kerrara Island, 71.
Kerwick Bay, 125, 126.
Kiel, 70.
Kier, river, 31.
Kilchurn Castle, 68.
Kilcolmkill, 70, 96.

Kilkenny, 11.
Killiecrankie, 229, 231.
Killin, 64.
Kilmacalmuag, 113.
Kilmare, 114.
Kilmarnock, 4, 57, 58, 60.
—— Lady, 4.
—— Earl of, 4, 198.
Kilmaronock, 3.
Kilpatrick, New, 60.
—— —— Old, 60.
—— —— Roger, 30.
Kilravock, 181, 193.
Kilrenny, 274.
Kilrule, 167.
Kilrymont, 297.
Kilwinning Abbey, 56, 57.
Kincardine Church, 113 ; Castle, 243.
Kindeace, 175, 180.
Kinfauns, 250.
King, Dr., 332.
Kinghorn, 282, 284.
—— Wester, 284.
Kinglass, 65.
Kingsbarns, 273.
King's Inch, 25.
Kinloss Abbey, 184, 196.
Kinnaird, 198, 214.
Kinneder, 186.
Kinnoull, 259.
—— Lord, 249.
Kinross, 278.
Kinsale, 138.
Kintore, 200.
—— Earl of, 200.
Kippenross, 292.
Kippilaw, 342.
Kirkby Stephen, 36.
Kirkcaldy, 281, 284.
Kirkcudbright, 20, 22.
Kirkgunzeon, 26.
Kirkheugh, 273, 294.
Kirkhill Church, 178.
Kirkintilloch, 52.
Kirkness, 280.
Kirkpatrick-Fleming Church, 37.
Kirkpatrick, Sir Roger, 7.
Kirkurd, 343.
Kirkwall, 134, 137, 144-153.
—— Provost of, 150.
Kirtle, river, 10, 37.
Kismul, 93.
Knitting in Orkney, 138.
Knock, 77.
Kol, Norwegian, 145.
Konlikan, author of, 180.

LAIRG, 118.
Laing, Bishop John, 51.

Lamberton, Bishop, 269, 274.
—— Hill, 328.
Lambholm, 151.
Lanark, 43-47.
—— Monastery, 44.
Lanercost Abbey, 36.
Lang, Mr., 266.
Langside, 56.
Larch, 42, 228, 230.
Largo Bay, 275.
Lascelles, Colonel, 62.
Laton, Sir Bryan, 340.
Lauder, Bishop, 226.
Lawers House, 244.
Laws, Mr., 89.
Leadhills, 41.
Lead-mines, 10, 19, 41, 42, 64, 93, 283, 341; pipe, 241; smelting, 41; white, 42.
Lees Abbey, 328.
Le Hazard, privateer, 129.
Leighton, Bishop, 188, 206, 292.
Leith, 2, 308, 309; St Anthony's Monastery, 309.
Lely, Sir Peter, 312, 316.
Lennox, Countess of, 61.
Leslie, 276, 277.
—— Professor John, 208.
Lettersuna, 95.
Leucopibia, city of, 14.
Leven, 276.
—— Earl of, 265, 276, 277.
—— Loch, Argyle, 97.
—— Loch, Kinross, 278, 279.
Levenside, 61.
Lewis Island, 94, 125.
Lincluden, 8.
Lindores Abbey, 263.
—— Lord, 263.
Lindsay, David, of Glenesk, 250.
—— James, 30.
—— Lord of Byres, 212.
Linen, 17, 37, 52, 53, 101, 144, 193, 194, 197, 212, 214, 218, 220, 223, 239, 281, 282, 287, 311, 312, 323.
Ling, 88, 145, 153.
Lingay Island, 91, 92, 93.
Linnhe, Loch, 91.
Linlithgow, 3, 47, 296, 297.
Lismore Island, 72, 90, 91.
—— Dean of, 88.
Littlegill, 43.
Loadstone, 93.
Loaghal, Loch, 120, 130.
Lobsters, 14, 152.
Lochaber, 98.
Loch Awe, 68.
—— Cautie, 10.
—— Cure, 31.

Lochend Quarry, 315.
Lochendwood, 317.
Loch Etive, 68, 69.
—— Fyne, 65.
Lochgelly, 280, 281.
Lochiel's house, 98, 99.
Lochleven Castle, 25, 258.
—— Priory, 269.
Loch Lomond, 3, 65.
—— Long, 64.
—— Loyal, 130.
Lochmaben, 38.
—— Stone, 35.
Loch Nadir, 24.
Lochnell House, 71.
Loch of the Lowes, 343.
Lochrutton, 9.
Loch Ryan, 11.
—— Scriden, 76.
—— Shiel, 98.
—— Spelvie, 76.
—— Urr, 31.
Lochwood Castle, 38.
Loch Lochy, 91.
Lockerbie, 10, 38.
Loinid (a whisk), 116.
Lomond, Ben, 63.
Lomonds, the, 278.
Longevity, 93, 177, 242.
Long Hope, 151.
Longormes, Lord of, 12.
Longtown, 36, 37.
Lorn, Lords of, 69.
Lossie, river, 188, 190.
Loth, 164.
Lothbeg, 164.
Lothmore, 164.
Lothian, Marquis of, 312, 313, 345.
Loudon Castle, 59.
—— Lord, 244.
Lovatt, Lord, 101, 107, 108, 178, 179.
—— Monument, 179.
Lowther Hall, 36.
—— Hills, 40.
Luce Abbey, 12.
Lumsden, Professor John, 208.
Luncarty, battle of, 248.
Lundin House, 276.
Luss Castle, 62.
Lussa, river, 76.
Lyar, 140.
Lychtoun, Bishop, 206.
Lyon, Mr., 2.
—— River, 234, 238.
Lyons Castle, 260.
Lyttelton, Rev. Dr. Charles, lviii, lxi.

MACBETH, 98, 225, 248.
MacCoull, Duncan, 69.

INDEX. 369

MacCulloch, Rev. Robert, 164.
MacCullochs, The, 20.
MacDonalds of Glengarry, 100.
Macdonald, Rev. Murdo, 128, 129.
—— of the Isles, 82, 93.
—— of Clanranald, 85.
MacDougalls of Lorn, 69.
MacDowal, Ronald, 12.
—— Uchtred, 12.
Macduff's Cross, 262, 263.
Macduff, Lord, 195.
Macfarlanes, Laird of, 63, 64.
MacFingone's tombs, 82.
MacKail, Dr., 135.
MacKay, Captain, 130, 132.
—— Colonel Hugh, 113.
—— Elizabeth, 113.
—— General, 229.
—— George, of Bighouse, 113.
—— Janet, 113.
—— Lieutenant James, 132.
—— Mr., 129, 169, 175.
—— Rev. Thomas, 118.
Mackays, a loyal clan, 128.
Mackenzie, Bishop, 149.
—— Catherine, 118.
—— George, 109.
—— Sir George, 313.
Mackerel, 14, 25.
MacLean (aged 180), 93.
MacLean's tomb, 83.
MacLeod, Duncan, 69.
—— of Assynt, 114.
—— of Cadboll, 172.
—— of Geanies, 172, 175.
—— of Hamir, lvii.
—— Laird of, 94.
—— Professor Roderick, 208.
—— Rev. Neil, 77.
MacPherson, Rev. John, 89.
—— Rev. Martin, lviii.
Madderty church, 245.
—— Lord, 245, 246.
Maelpatrick Stone, 84.
Magdalene, New, 214.
Maid's fillet, 117.
Mair, Rev. Mr., 278.
Malcomson, Robert, 19.
Malt, 103.
Man, Bishop of, 81.
—— Isle of, 79, 81.
Mansfield, 289.
Map, Cromwell's, 19, 26; Dorret's, 137, 199, 343; New, 26, 31, 34, 35, 53, 58, 69, 101, 103, 110, 115, 131, 163, 164, 172, 175, 180, 192, 195, 196, 198, 199, 219; Quartermasters', 19; Richards', 26.
Mar, Earl of, 201, 241, 256, 290, 292.

Marble, 71, 82, 98, 124, 194, 199, 282.
March, Earl of, 256, 321, 328.
Margaret, Queen, 284, 285.
Mariæ de Trayl, 23.
Marischal, Earl, 196, 197, 200, 203, 211.
—— College, 203.
Markland, 9.
Markham, Sir Michael, 280.
Massacre of Glencoe, 97.
Marten's skins, 138.
Martin's voyages, 94.
Martin, St., 318.
Maxwell, Bishop, 148.
—— John, 25.
—— Sir H. E., 14.
—— Sir Thomas, 26.
—— Sir William, 14.
Maxwells, the, 20, 31, 34.
Mary, Queen, 25, 34, 56, 258, 279, 311.
May Island, 274.
Meadie, Loch, 120.
Megginch Castle, 259, 260.
Mein, river, 37.
Meldrum, Old, 199.
Mellerstain, 332.
Melrose, 49.
—— Abbey, 336-340.
—— chronicle of, 24, 341.
—— Earl of, 336.
Melsetter, 151.
Melville, 277.
Member of Parliament, 47, 108.
Memnon, statue of, 74, 125.
Menteith, 225, 241.
Menzies, Sir Robert, 238.
Methven, 247; battle of, 249.
Middleby, 6, 33, 37.
Middleton, Mr., of Seaton, 209.
Miles, English, 113, 121; Highland, 113.
Millcraig, 111.
Miller, Abbot, 294.
—— George, 169.
Milles, Dean, xxxvi, lx, lxvi.
—— Rev. Isaac, xxxi, xxxii, xxxiii.
Milligan, Dr., 39.
Milnathort, 278.
Milton, Lord Fletcher, 316.
Mineral wells, 66, 76, 93, 228, 349
Mitchell, Mr., 3.
Moak, St., 278.
Modan, Bishop, 69.
Moffat, 9, 34, 38, 39, 40.
—— Round Forts, 39, 40.
Moine, the, 124, 126, 129, 132.
Molendinar Burn, 49.

2 A

Monan, St., 274.
Monance, St., 265.
Monar, Loch, 114.
Moncrieff, Rev. Alexander, 262.
Monk, General, 222.
Monkshill, 223.
Montrose, 212, 213, 214.
—— Duke of, 243.
—— Marquis of, 99, 114, 163, 249.
—— Muir, 213.
Monymusk, 200, 201.
Moodie, Captain, 134, 151, 153.
—— Commodore, 151.
—— Mr., 151.
Moray, Earl of, 104, 183, 264, 282, 283.
Morays of Abercairney, 247.
More, Elizabeth, 54.
—— Sir Adam, 54.
Moreville, Hugh, 56.
Moriston, river, 101.
Morpeth, 1.
Morton, Earl of, 150, 283, 312, 336.
Morven, 89.
Mount Tabor, 97.
Mudale, 120, 130, 164.
Mugdrum Cross, 262.
—— House, 262.
Muir of Ord, 110.
Mull, 74, 76, 87, 88, 89, 90, 115.
—— Funerals, 88.
Munches, 25.
Mundik, 41, 326.
Munro, Alexander, 13.
—— Bailie Donald, 169.
———— Mr., Achany, 115, 117.
———— Mr., of Culcairn, 110, 176.
—— Rev. George, 131.
———— Rev. James, 185.
—— Sir Harry, 109, 176, 177, 178, 180.
—— Sir Robert, 176, 179.
Murdo, John, Architect, 49, 50, 339.
Murkle, 158.
Murray, Bishop Gilbert, 167.
—— Captain John, M.P., 227.
—— Lady, 332.
—— Lord George, 227, 242.
—— Mr. James, 133.
—— — Sir David, 242, 258.
—— Sir Patrick, 244.
Murthlach, 204.
Murthly, 225.
Musselburgh, 2, 310, 311.
Muthill, 242.

NAIRN, 109, 182.
—— river, 107, 182, 193.
Naver, Loch, 119, 130, 131.

Navidale, 164.
Nectanus, Bishop, 204.
New Deer, 196.
Ness, Loch, 100, 103.
—— river, 103.
Netherby, 36.
Nevin, Rev. Mr., 5.
New Abbey, 8, 28, 29.
—— —— Lord of, 28.
Newbattle Abbey, 312.
Newburgh, 260, 262, 263.
—— Witches, 263.
New Hailes, 310.
Newhaven, 308.
Newry, 5.
Newstead Abbey, 341.
Newtown, 41.
—— Fifeshire, 264.
—— Perthshire, 239.
Newtown Stewart, 12, 19.
Nicholson, Mr., 315.
Nigg, 173.
Nith, river, 7, 9, 20, 30.
Nithsdale, 7, 30, 31.
Norden, Mr., xxxvii.
Norfolk, 18.
Norham Castle, 347; Church, 348.
North Berwick Law, 318; Nunnery, 319.
Northumberland, Countess of, 318.
Norwegian Kings' Tombs, 84.
—— ancient oval brooch, 91.
Norwegians, 99.
Norwich, 18.
Noth Hill, 201.
Nottingham yarn, 194.

OBAN, 71, 74.
Obelisk, 109, 282.
O'Brien, Captain, 129.
Ochtertyre, 244.
Ogilvy, Lady Anne, 178.
—— Sir Alexander, 195.
Oich, Loch, 99.
Old Cambus, 2.
—— Deer, 196.
Oliphant, Lord, 251, 255.
Omhan, whisked cream, 169.
O'Phelan, John, xlix.
Oransay Island, 93.
Ord, the, 163.
Ore, Loch, 246, 280.
Orkney, 126, 131, 134, 151.
—— Bishop of, 148.
—— Earls of, 137, 142, 148, 149, 150.
Orphir, 137.
Orton, 19, 32, 36.
Osnaburg cloths, 220, 223, 289.
Ossory, Bishop of, xlvii, lxiii.

INDEX.

Otterburn, 340.
Oxen, 18.
Oykel, river, 113.
Oysters, 25, 77, 152.

PAISLEY, 53.
—— Abbey, 55.
—— Bailie of, 56.
—— Lord, 56.
Panmure, Lord, 215, 216, 217, 219, 220, 221.
—— House, 219.
Panter, Patrick, 213.
Papa Westray, 149.
Paul, Earl, 137.
Paulet, Lady Catherine, 239.
Pease bread, 178.
Pebbles, 87, 311.
Peebles, 47, 343.
Pendragon Castle, 36.
Penicuik, 314.
Pennyland, 133.
Penrith, 1, 32, 36.
Pentland Firth, 140, 153.
—— Hills, 314.
Percy, Sir Henry, 340.
Perth, 250, 257; battle of, 257; trade, 252; writs and charters, 253-255.
—— Earl of, 239, 243.
Peterhead, 197, 198, 211.
Peterkin, Rev. William, 42.
Philamorte dye, 92.
Picts' house, 95, 111, 133, 135, 137, 156, 157, 158, 163, 164, 166, 276.
Picture of James VI., 193.
Pigeon's egg, petrified, 198.
—— house, 136.
Piggin of cream, 116.
Pikes, ancient, 323.
Pinkie House, 311.
Pitcairn, Secretary, 284.
Pitfour, 197.
Pitmedden, 199.
Pittenweem, 274.
Plomp, 35.
Plummer, Professor, 39.
Pluscardine Priory, 187, 190, 191.
Pococke on the Flood, lvii.
Polecat, 26.
Pomona Isle, 134, 135.
Poole, General, 102, 104.
—— Lady, 102.
Portland, Duke of, 36.
Portmoag, 278.
Port na Churiach, 87.
Port na Crois, 95.
Portpatrick, 4, 11.
Portsoy, 194.

Port Sonachan, 68.
Portus Salutis, 175.
Port-Yerrock, 14.
Postman, speed of, 127, 128.
Potatoes, introduction of, 128.
Pow, river, 146.
Powan, 63.
Powton, 18.
Prestonpans, 2 ; battle of, 177, 311.
Pretender, the, 98, 100, 105, 107, 129, 314.
Prett's Mill, 44.
Pringle, Mr., of Stitchell, 328.
—— Sir Robert, 330.
Pultney's Regiment, 105, 107.
Pynoree, 255.
Pyrus Aria, 72.

QUARRYWOOD, 191.
Queensberry, Duke of, 9, 10, 39, 41.
Queensferry, 283, 298.

RABY CASTLE, 36.
Radcliffe Library, lxvi, 180.
Ralph, Bishop, 347.
Rannoch, Loch, 233, 238.
Ramsay, Sir John, 318.
Raths in Ireland, 118.
Rats, none in Sutherland, 120.
Ratter, 153, 155.
Ravenstruther, 45.
Raymore, 104.
Reay, 131, 133.
—— Lord, 113, 121, 124, 128, 129, 130, 131, 169.
—— Master of, 130.
Regalia of Scotland, 306.
Regulus, St., 267.
Reid, Bishop, 148, 178.
—— John, 169.
—— Professor Thomas, 208.
Reilig Orain, 84.
Renfrew, 53.
Rents paid in cattle, 128.
Repentance Tower, 34.
Reregonium, 11.
Restalrig, 303, 310.
'Rest and be Thankful,' 64.
Restenet Church, 216, 217.
—— Kinross, 279.
Reuda, 61.
Reynell, Mrs., 5.
—— Rev. W., xliv.
Ribton, Sir George, 5.
Richard, Bishop, 252.
—— of Cirencester, 26, 110.
Richmond, 1.
—— Duke of, 193.
Risa Isle, 134, 151.

Rivaulx, 23.
Rizzio, murder of. 304.
Road, proposed, 121.
Rob Donn, 126.
Robert the Bruce, 35, 44, 83.
Roberton, 43.
Robertson, J. G., lix.
—— of Struan, 238.
—— Mr., 224.
Robinson, Dr., 181.
—— Mr., 1.
Rock of Lamentation, 114.
Roderick the Impostor, 94.
Rogasch, King, 278.
Rognvald, Earl, 137, 145.
Roman works, 6, 33, 34, 35, 38, 45, 46, 52, 53, 57, 60, 240, 246, 249, 280, 298, 299, 314, 344.
Rossie, Loch, 278.
Rona Island, 125.
Ronaldshaw, 134, 149, 153.
Rooing wool, 139.
Ropes, 57.
Roscorriel, 25.
Rose of Kilravock, 181.
Rosebery, Lord, 308.
Rosehall, 113-115, 168.
Rosemarkie, 110.
Roslin, battles of, 314.
—— Chapel, 2, 314.
—— Lady, 310.
Ross, Commissary, 174.
—— Countess of, 301.
—— Duncan of Kindeace, 175, 180.
—— Bailie, 169.
—— Earl of, 56, 170.
—— Euphemia, 54.
—— General, 175.
—— Provost David, 169.
—— Rev. Mr., 130.
—— Sir John C., 46.
Ross-dhu, 62.
Rossal, 76, 77.
Rosyth Castle, 298.
Rothes, Earl of, 263, 276, 277.
Rothesay, Duke of, 263.
Rotundo Chapel, 137.
Round Towers, 215, 261.
Roxburgh, Duke of, 304, 324, 329.
Roy Castle, 184.
Royston, 308.
Rubies, Elie, 275.
Ruchill, river, 243, 244.
Rusane, Major, 3, 4.
Rules, St., 267.
Rullion Green, 314.
Russel, Jerome, 51.
Rutland, Duke of, 349.
—— Earl of, 318.

Ruthven Castle, 252.
—— —— Lord, 254.
Ruthwell Cross, 32.

St. Ann's, 327.
St. Andrews, 222; 267-271; 273; Archery medals, 272; Library MSS., 271; Muchross, 267; Priory, 269; Relics of St. Andrew, 267; Colleges, 271, 278; St. Regulus, 267, 268, 269.
St Andrew's Episcopal Church, Glasgow, 50.
—— Anthony's Chapel, Arthur's Seat, 310.
—— Austin, 86.
—— Bernard, 57.
—— Catherine's Cross, 217.
—— —— (the Kaimes), 315.
—— —— Spring, 2.
—— —— Stone, 66, 67.
—— Columba, 78, 82, 85, 87, 96.
—— Duthus' Church, 170.
—— Fergus, Wick, 160.
—— Francis, 223.
—— Giles, 188.
—— Johnstoun's Hunt's up, 255.
—— Kentigern's cell, 49; Church, 44.
—— Kilda, 94.
—— Leonard's Hill, 195.
—— Machars, 205.
—— Magnus, 137.
—— —— Cathedral, 145.
—— Martin, 14.
—— Martin's Cross, 85.
—— Mary's Island, 22, 23.
—— —— Loch, 343.
—— Michael's Day, 86.
—— Molocus or Moluag, 90.
—— Monance Church, 274, 275.
—— Mungo, 49.
—— Niniair, 14.
—— Ninian's Church, 295.
—— Oran, 86.
—— Oran's burial-ground, 83.
—— —— Chapel, 85.
—— Patrick, 60, 61.
—— Regulus Chapel, 176.
—— Winning, 57.
Sal-ammoniac, 308.
Salmon, 23, 65, 103, 114, 119, 129, 134, 144, 192, 194, 204, 211, 212, 213, 228.
Shee, Dr. Peter, xlix.
Shells, 25, 26, 114, 119, 156.
Shell-beds, 111, 174, 193.
—— Fossils, 174.

INDEX. 373

Sheriffmuir, 241; Battle of, 292.
Shetland, 153.
Shetlanders, German manners of, 153.
Shin, Loch, 115, 118, 121, 167.
Sillacks, 145.
Silver-mines, 10.
Silver out of lead, 42.
—— Statue of an Urus, 241.
Simon, Mr., of Dublin, xlvii, xlix.
Simson, Professor, 3, 273, 276.
—— Prof. Thomas, 272.
Sinclair Castle, 160, 162.
—— Dr. Thurso, 177.
—— General, 281.
—— Lord, 281.
—— Lord Henry, 149.
—— Mr., 155.
—— Mr., of Lybster, 162.
—— Provost, 160.
—— Sheriff, 163.
—— Sir James, 155.
Sinclairtown, 281.
Skateraw Chapel, 324.
Skate's eggs, 323.
Skeletons, Ardoch, 241.
Skene, Loch, 201.
—— Mr., of Skene, 217.
—— Professor Francis, 208.
Skerry, 132.
Skibo, 169.
Skinner, Colonel, 104.
Skins of foxes and hares, 116.
Skirmish Hill, 342.
Skye, 93, 101, 107, 115.
—— Poets, 89.
Slains Castle, 198.
—— Caves near, 198.
Slate, 36, 65, 71, 98.
Slowie or Sloy Loch, 64.
Smeaton, 2.
Smelt-mills, lead, 41.
Smith, Lord Chief Baron, 302.
—— Mr., of Methven, 247, 249, 257.
Sinoo Cave, 126.
Snaid, river, 63.
Snowbird, 140.
Sodor and Man, Bishops of, 81.
Solemn League and Covenant, 313.
Somerset, Duke of, 317.
Somerville, Lord, 304, 310.
Sonachan Ferry, 68.
Sorbus Sylvestris, 72.
Soulisgeir Island, 125, 126.
Southesk, Earl of, 214.
Southwark Jail, 152.
Spean, river, 99.
Spear-head, brass, 228.
—— in urn, 110.
Spey, river, 192, 193, 195, 201.

Spinage, 91.
Spinning School, 114.
Sponges, 119, 120.
Spotiswood, Sir Robert, 27.
Spottiswoode, Archbishop, 336.
—— Mr., 336.
Spynie Church, 187; Loch, 187, 192; Palace, 187.
Stair, Earl of, 4, 12, 13.
Stalker Island, 95.
Standard of Pretender, 98.
Standing Stones, 149, 177, 193, 219, 273, 276.
Stanhope, 36.
Stank, 31.
Stennis Church, 144; Loch, 140; Stone-circles, 142, 144.
Stewart, Bishop David, 187.
—— of Appin, 95, 96.
—— of Burray, 151.
—— Robert, 150.
—— Sir James, 152.
—— Sir John, 225.
Stiel, George, 129.
Stirling, 3, 64, 99, 294, 295.
—— Castle, 289, 290, 294.
—— Chapel, 24.
—— Palace, 295.
—— Archibald, of Garden, 42.
—— Mr., of Kier, 293.
—— Sir William, 240, 241.
Stitchell, 330.
Stockings, 139, 197, 211, 212; prices, 199, 204.
Stone-circles, 102, 104, 142, 165, 193.
Stone from Firth of Forth, 195, 202.
Stonehaven, 211, 240.
Stone of Odin, 144.
Stonyfield, 104.
Stormont, 225.
Stormonth, Lord, 31, 32, 258.
Strageth, Camp of, 240, 244, 245, 246.
Strahan, Colonel, 114.
Strathallan, 293.
—— Lord, 245.
Strathcarron, river, 113.
Strathearn, 225, 239, 243.
—— Earl of, 246.
Strathkyle, 113.
Strathmore, 120, 123, 130.
—— Earl of, 218, 219, 260.
—— river, 121, 124.
Strathnaver, 133.
Strathpeffer, 109.
Strath Spey, 184.
Strathy Bay, 131, 132.
—— Lady, 132.
—— Loch, 131.
Strawberries, 42.

Stroma, 156.
Stromness, 138, 140, 153.
Struan, 233, 238.
Struthers in Fife, 212.
Stuart, Lord Provost of Perth, 252.
—— Professor John, 208.
Students from Ireland, 52.
Stukeley, Dr., xl, xli, xlvii, 26.
Sugar, 51.
Sundial, Tongue House, 130.
Susannah Mine, Leadhills, 41.
Sutherland, 93, 115.
—— David, Cambusavie, 168.
—— Earl of, 12, 166, 168; his forest, 118; his regiment, 192.
—— Ensign Kenneth, 169.
—— Fencibles, 164.
—— Gentlewoman, 117.
—— Kenneth, jun., 168.
—— Lord, 304.
—— Regiment, 132.
—— Rev. John, 169.
—— William, of Sciberscross, 168.
—— —— of Wester, 162.
Suffolk, 18.
Surrey, Earl of, 349, 350.
Sutors of Cromarty, 175.
Swans, 93, 117.
Sweden, 17.
Sweno's Stone, Forres, 184.
Switha, Isle of, 134.
Swona, 156.
Sword, two-handed, 88.
Swordly, 131.
Sybilla, Queen, 236.
Sycamore, 130; large, 292.

Tabor, Mount, 97.
Tain, 129, 169.
—— Firth, 115.
Tantallon Castle, 319, 320.
Tap o' Noth, 201.
Tarbet, 62, 63, 69.
—— House, 175.
Tarbet Ness, 172.
Tarbet, New, 64.
Tarf, river, 20.
Tarradale, 110.
Tay, Firth of, 222.
—— Loch, 233, 235, 236; Priory on island in, 236; river, 233, 254, 255; inscriptions on bridge over, 234, 235, 238.
Taymouth, 64.
—— Castle, 234, 235, 237, 238.
—— Road, 229, 233.
Tea at Hopetoun, 3.
Tellve Castle, 93.
Terry, river, 118.

Teviot, river, 329.
Thatched cabins, 34, 41, 42, 44, 89, 159.
—— church, 131, 144, 349.
Thane of Sutherland, 166.
—— of Cawdor, 181.
Thomas, Bishop, 170.
—— Dr., 5.
Thorns, Captain, 3.
Thornton, 58.
—— Castle, 325.
Thrumster House, 160.
Thunderton House, 190.
Thurso, 124, 132, 133, 134.
Tibbermoor, 249.
Tibbers Castle, 9.
Tigh-na-Craig, 110.
Tigh-na-Stalcaire, 95, 96.
Tilt, river, 229, 230, 233.
Tin ore, 131.
Tinto, 43.
Tiresoor, 91.
Tiree, 78, 82, 87, 88.
—— Bailie of, 88.
Toasted ears, 133.
Tobacco, 8, 30, 51.
Tongue, 124, 129, 130.
—— House of, 131.
Tongue and, 20.
Torbreck Hill, 7.
Torfæus, 137.
Torsk, 145, 153.
Torryburn, 280, 288.
Torrisdale Head, 130, 131.
Travers, Mrs., 5.
Trapaud, Governor, 100, 102, 181.
Treig, Loch, 125.
Troddan Castle, 93.
Trout, 63, 131, 144.
Tub, Marquis of Annandale's, 40.
Tulliallan Church, 288.
Tullibardine Church, 242, 243.
—— Earl of, 242, 258.
Tummel, Loch, 233; river, 229.
Turriff, 195, 196.
Tweed, river, 20, 40, 328, 329, 341.
Tweeddale, Marquis of, 3, 283, 301, 311, 316, 317.
Twizell, 348.
Tyndrum, 64.
Tyne, River, 315, 316, 320.
Tynninghame, 320.
Tyrie, Rev. James, 142.

Uagbeg, 165.
Uagmore, 165.
Ubbanford, 347.
Udny Castle, 199.
Ugie, river, 196.

INDEX.

Uisneach, sons of, 70.
Uist, 91, 92, 93.
Urie, Robert, 4.
Urn, 68, 110, 140, 241.
Urquhart, 192, 193, 199.
—— Castle, 101, 102.
—— Mr., 176.
—— Lord, 284.
Urr, River, 25, 26.
Urus, 72, 91, 138, 241.
Ury, River, 200.
Usan, 214.
Usher, Archbishop, 79.

VANDYCK'S PAINTING, 316.
Vase, Roman, Fortingall, 237.
Venison, 120.
Vitrified forts, 201, 217.

WADE, GENERAL, 100, 101, 103, 234, 235.
Walker, Rev. Patrick, 32.
—— Mrs., Dunfermline, 286.
Wallace, Sir William, 9, 211, 264.
Wallbrook, John, 270.
Walls, Isle of, 134, 140, 152, 153.
Wamphray, 10.
Wardlaw, Bishop, 271.
Wardlaws of Torry, 280, 288.
Wark, 328, 350.
Waterford, Bishop of, xxxiii, 5.
—— Caves, 127.
Water of Ayr hones, 59.
Watten, Loch, 158.
Wemyss Hall, 265.
—— Lord, 249.
Wenlock Abbey, 53.
Wester, 162.
Western Isles, 81, 92, 94.

Westray, 149.
Whales, 90, 120, 155, 274.
Wharton Hall, 36.
Wheat bread, 133.
Whey, 116, 118.
Whisk of horsehair, 116.
Whisky, antidote for, 89.
Whiteford, Bishop, 39.
—— Rachel, 39.
White-lead, 42.
Whithorn, 14.
Wick, 158, 159, 160.
Wigtown, 14, 17, 18.
Wilde, W. R., xlix.
Wilford, Sir George, 318.
Williamson, John Moffat, 39.
Wilson, Wm., 47.
Windmill, large, 224.
Wine, 118, 130.
Wintan, Andrew, 279.
Winter of 1738, 117.
Winton, 36.
Wirren Hill, 217.
Wishart, Bishop, 268, 270, 304.
Woden's Stone, 144.
Wolf of Badenoch, 188.
Wood, Mr., 257.
Workington, 25, 36.
Wymundus, 81.

YARN, 194, 212.
Yarrow, river, 343.
Yern, 27.
Yester Church, 317; House, 316.
Yetholm, 345.
York, Archbishop of, 81.
—— Buildings Company, 184, 264.
—— Mr., 1.
Ythan, river, 199.

THE END.

Printed by T. and A. CONSTABLE, Printers to Her Majesty,
at the Edinburgh University Press.

www.ingramcontent.com/pod-product-compliance
Lightning Source LLC
Chambersburg PA
CBHW022140300426
44115CB00006B/269